Everyday Life
in
Central Asia

Everyday Life
in
Central Asia
Past and Present

EDITED BY

Jeff Sahadeo and Russell Zanca

INDIANA UNIVERSITY PRESS
Bloomington and Indianapolis

This book is a publication of

Indiana University Press
601 North Morton Street
Bloomington, IN 47404-3797 USA

http://iupress.indiana.edu

Telephone orders   800-842-6796
Fax orders   812-855-7931
Orders by e-mail   iuporder@indiana.edu

The paper used in this publication meets the minimum requirements of
American National Standard for Information Sciences—Permanence of Paper
for Printed Library Materials, ANSI Z39.48-1984.

Manufactured in the United States of America

Library of Congress Cataloging-in-Publication Data

Everyday life in Central Asia : past and present / edited by Jeff Sahadeo and
Russell Zanca.
       p.   cm.
Includes bibliographical references and index.
ISBN 978-0-253-34883-8 (cloth : alk. paper) — ISBN 978-0-253-21904-6 (pbk. : alk.
paper) 1. Asia, Central—Social life and customs. 2. Ethnology—Asia, Central.
       I. Sahadeo, Jeff, date II. Zanca, Russell G., date
                    DS328.2.E94 2007
                    958'.04—dc22
                                                          2006037058

       2 3 4 5   12 11 10 09 08

To the countless Central Asians who have opened their doors and hearts to us and with whom we have shared meals and affection, joys and frustrations, and hopes and fears. We hope this book makes some contribution toward a deeper understanding of how much we all deserve a better world, even as we seek different pathways toward that end.

Learn and learn, ask and ask, do not be afraid.

—Theophrastus Philippus Aureolus Bombastus von Hohenheim (Paracelsus—16th century mystical philosopher, physician, and alchemist)

CONTENTS

ACKNOWLEDGMENTS

Above all, we thank our informants, colleagues, and friends in Central Asia, for whom living day to day has become an increasingly challenging task. The warm hospitality and spontaneous joviality they show to us belies their modest means and anxieties over an uncertain future. Their cooperation with our contributors has allowed the publication of some wonderfully innovative pieces. We felt honored to edit the words of writers and scholars of such talent. Other important figures played crucial roles in this volume. Janet Rabinowitch's enthusiasm inspired its creation. Lisa Greenspoon assisted us with the editing process. Dennis Grammenos contributed his time and talent in producing the maps. Miki Bird, Jennifer Maceyko, and others at Indiana University Press provided friendly and helpful guidance. Candace McNulty gave the work a thorough copyedit. Funds from Carleton University supported the creation of the volume. Our own friends and families provided advice and constant encouragement throughout the project.

Everyday Life
in
Central Asia

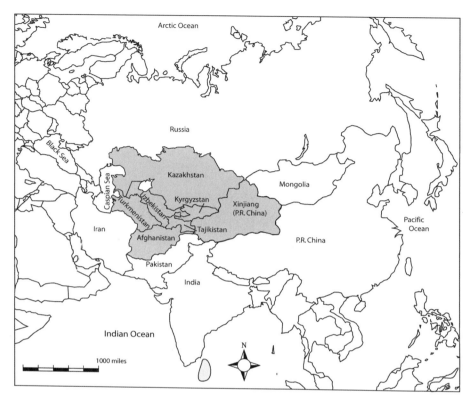

Central Asia

States and Cities of Central Asia

Ferghana Valley

Introduction: Central Asia and Everyday Life

For its citizens, contemporary Central Asia is a land of great promise and peril. Promise, for the end of Soviet rule has allowed new opportunities for social mobility and cultural expression. Peril, for political and economic dynamics have imposed severe restrictions on independent activity and widened the gap between rich and poor. In this volume, we will examine how ordinary residents of Central Asia, past and present, lead their lives and navigate shifting historical and political patterns. Contributors, drawn from a wide range of academic disciplines, will tell provocative stories of Turkmen nomads, Afghan villagers, Kazakh scientists, Kyrgyz border guards, a Tajik "strongman," and guardians of religious shrines in Uzbekistan. These and other narratives of ordinary citizens and their everyday lives will intertwine with important questions and relations of gender, religion, power, culture, and wealth. Moving tales of personal struggle mix with those of success as Central Asians confront, adapt to, and seek to influence global movements and trends as well as increasingly strong and invasive states. We expose a vibrant and dynamic world of everyday life in urban neighborhoods and small villages, at weddings and celebrations, and around classroom tables as well as the dinner tables of the peoples of Central Asia.

Examining Central Asia from the perspective of everyday life offers important new insights on the region. In the past decade-plus almost the only facets of Central Asia exposed to the Western public at large came in terms of building democracy, religious extremism and terrorism, natural resource holdings, and the war in Afghanistan. Occasionally, there has appeared the odd human interest or features story in newspapers or on radio, such as textile-making traditions, bride kidnapping in Kazakhstan, the reinvention of the Silk Road, or the continued semi-nomadic existence of Chinggis Khan's mountainous descendants. While such reporting has served to illuminate certain features of daily life in Central Asia since the collapse of Communism, it rarely provides the contextualization to furnish readers or listeners with a richer historical or social awareness of a particular contemporary situation. We learn that key relationships—between men and women, for example—and key concepts—such as Islam—are in continuous flux, meaning different things at different times to different people. Central cultural events, including feasts and holidays, are at once intensely personal and indicate complicated interactions both within peer communities and with larger outside units, in particular the state. The rich contributions in this volume undermine stereotypes of the region's citizens as beholden to past traditions—be they age-old or Soviet—or as compliant subjects of authoritarian rulers. Yet readers should nonetheless recognize the extraordinary strain placed on these societies. We will read of tragedies in the past, as millions of women and nomads faced punishments, including death, for defying dictates of the Soviet state. We will also read articles that set the stage for tragedies in the present, such as the killings of hundreds of civilians in Andijon, Uzbekistan, in May 2005.

In bringing together twenty-three essays that include topics such as family life, cuisine, gender, state and government, entertainment, religion, and minority populations among Kazakhs, Turkmen, Uzbeks, as well as Russian settlers, we treat the transformations of society and culture with both respect and subtlety where our research has forced us to confront colonialism, violence, and domination. Trenchant critiques of tsarist and Soviet policies are balanced with the understandings of identity and self that we have learned through our work among Central Asians during the past decade or so. Furthermore, part of what will make this volume so appealing to people interested in Central Asia is the gamut of disciplinary expertise, from anthropology, history, political science, and sociology to musicology, rendering our approaches to everyday life diachronic and variegated.

EVERYDAY LIFE

Everyday life offers both new findings and new ways of looking at Central Asia. Until the 1990s Western social scientists and historians knew relatively little about daily life in the region, even during the nineteenth and twentieth centuries, despite the vast pre-Soviet and Soviet literatures extant there and in the West. The simple fact was that we had no formed ideas about the day-to-day—how people shopped, what sorts of vacations they took, what they commonly ate, how they negotiated their own legal systems, what kind of common medical care was available, what entertainment they enjoyed, etc. After the Soviet collapse, as a new generation of mainly Sovietology-trained scholars started on their doctoral research, this territory ceased being *terra incognita,* and we now had somewhat confused but nearly complete access to all sorts of peoples in all sorts of settings as well as to archival collections long off-limits to Westerners. We present a virtual treasure trove of findings from today's leading Central Asianists, who have the extraordinary advantage of being steeped in Soviet history and scholarship as well as Central Asia's indigenous intellectual past and present. Our scholars are keenly aware of the history that has shaped Central Asia and resulted in all sorts of influences from language and politics to ethnicity and religion.

Now, the idea of everyday life does not quite seem to be tinged with excitement to everyone, and possibly because most of us think of it as so mundane, we also do not often choose to step back and examine it. On the other hand, when we have the opportunity to live away from our own society and away from so many of the things that are totally familiar to us, we become very taken with how other people get on in daily life—shopping, entertaining themselves, dressing, worshipping, going to school, and so on. We tend to develop this kind of curiosity not necessarily because life elsewhere in all of its habitual minutiae is so interesting but rather because it is so unfamiliar, frequently seeming not to make very much sense. While we usually think of quotidian existence as routine, habitual, and designed to satisfy our basic biological and psychological needs (as the renowned anthropologist Bronislaw Malinowski may have understood it), we might also take a moment to see how everyday life actually is not so routine, but something that we constantly re-make and reorganize as we go through various phases in our lives, concerning ages, seasons, locations, and interests, among others. Our goal in this book is to give our readers a grounding in how Central Asians live lives both immersed in the events of the day and very much consumed by doing a good job of making it to the next day.

These contributions fit within the ever-expanding scholarly literature on everyday life. Ever since Fernand Braudel's magisterial examination of the quotidian in late medieval and Renaissance Europe, Erving Goffman's study of our habitual conduct in common public settings, and Michel de Certeau's groundbreaking work on the daily experiences of ordinary people resisting and challenging the ruling structures of modern Europe, books dealing with everydayness have exploded in the social sciences and humanities. Today everyday themes encompass such dispersed subjects as Native Americans, contemporary architecture, and Stalinism. While everydayness may seem intellectually fashionable now, the turn toward investigation of commonplace activities and settings allows scholars, readers, and students the chance to understand how people live their lives by taking intense stock of their environments and their involvement within them. The relating of everyday experiences contains the potential to ignite readers' passion and imagination, doing for them what rarely occurs when we trudge through dates, personalities, and structural institutions.

CENTRAL ASIA, PAST AND PRESENT

Central Asia is a notoriously difficult region to define. We follow a general cartography encompassing the lands framed between the Caspian Sea and several mountain ranges. From the Caspian, the region extends northward to the tip of the Urals, east to the middle of the Altai and Tien Shan mountains, and south to the Hindu Kush. Of course, Central Asia is defined as much by politics and demography as by geography. Our borders correspond largely to the lands conquered by the Russian empire as it moved across the steppe in the eighteenth and nineteenth centuries. Later, the Soviet Union divided these territories into union republics: the Kazakh, Kyrgyz, Tajik, Turkmen, and Uzbek Soviet Socialist Republics. The Soviet Union later invaded Afghanistan, also within the geographical boundaries outlined above, and the object of contest with the British Empire since the nineteenth century. The territories we cover—the newly-independent five "'Stans" of Kazakhstan, Kyrgyzstan, Tajikistan, Turkmenistan, and Uzbekistan, as well as Afghanistan—exclude the eastern border region of Xinjiang, China, which shares ethnic as well as historical connections to the former Soviet states. The volume also excludes territories present in broader definitions of Central Asia, which alternately stretch to include the Transcaucasus, Iran, Mongolia, and Pakistan.[1] As Scott Levi's background essay shows, however, migrations, exchanges, and invasions have linked these neighbors to Central Asia in various periods throughout history.

Physical geography varies greatly across the region. Grasslands and plains dominate the northern areas, part of the great Eurasian steppe belt. Quickly, the land to the south becomes semidesert and then desert. The majority of the population in Central Asia clusters along two rivers—the Amu Darya and the Syr Darya—and oasis areas of the desert. Before the Soviet era, settled populations in the central deserts coexisted with pastoralist nomads who traversed the plains, as well as the more arid western reaches near the southern Caspian and the mountains of the Tien Shan. Continental climate provides for great fluctuations in temperature, both between summer and winter and between day and night. Summer temperatures can reach well over forty degrees Celsius in most lowland areas of Central Asia. Arable land and water resources in this mostly desert climate, always at a premium, have sparked multiple conflicts. Water nurtures rich loess soil in oasis areas and sustains animals that were the livelihood of nomadic tribes. The difference between lowlands and high mountain ranges provides another striking contrast. While the Kopet Dagh, Pamir, Tien Shan, and Altai mountain ranges provide natural boundaries for politicians, officers, and cartographers to delineate, they have proven easily passable by various invading forces over the centuries.[2]

Scott Levi's background essay provides a rich introduction to the peoples and the early history of Central Asia. Readers will gain an understanding of important migrations and invasions over the centuries, the arrival of various religious movements, most notably Islam, and the delicate balance between nomadic and settled societies. We will limit our survey here to the periods discussed in subsequent contributions, which unfold as Central Asians live under and react to imperial, Soviet, and post-Soviet rule. Tsarist soldiers swept across the steppe in the eighteenth century and then over oasis areas, largely divided between the khanates of Khiva and Kokand and the emirate of Bukhara. Only British troops in Afghanistan halted the Russian advance, and the two countries delimited borders in the region in 1895. Conquest by outside powers, as Levi describes, was nothing new in Central Asia. Some nomadic tribes sought alliances with the invaders to settle disputes with neighbors, and oasis merchants and leaders profited from access to imperial trade routes. Cities grew as, with the presence of Russian settlers, artisanal products found new internal as well as external markets.

British and tsarist officials did not initially seek to alter patterns of everyday life in Central Asia, not challenging, for example, the role of Islam. Afghanistan and areas of modern-day Uzbekistan retained degrees of political autonomy. Yet the European invaders introduced fundamental administrative and technological innovations. Imperial officials used superior military knowledge and weapons to exercise violence on the local population and extract resources from the land. The region became a producer of raw materials, primarily cotton, for European economies, tying local peasants to global markets. A new generation of modernist Muslim intellectuals, the Jadids, sought to assimilate the educational and technical advances of the colonizer, hoping to use these tools to overcome imperial rule. Jadid influence remained limited, however. Most Central Asians followed social and religious leaders who had accommodated themselves to their imperial overlords and remained largely resistant to social and cultural change at the level of daily life. At the turn of the century, the arrival of hundreds of thousands of Russian settlers on the steppe disrupted nomadic land-use patterns and dispossessed settled farmers of their property. Anger at settlers and other inequalities of Russian rule exploded in a 1916 rebellion that tsarist troops violently suppressed, resulting in unknown thousands of deaths and driving at least 300,000 nomads across the border to China. Afghans also rose against British control in 1919.

Dreams of independence were realized in Afghanistan, but not in Russian-held areas of Central Asia. A local movement that demanded autonomy following the 1917 Russian revolutions was crushed by Russian settlers and soldiers. V. I. Lenin and leading Russian Marxists decried past colonial exploitation but refused to relinquish control of the region and its rich resource base. As articles by Victoria Clement and Shoshana Keller demonstrate, many Central Asian notables and intellectuals, including the Jadids, saw Bolshevism as a modernizing force and joined the new Soviet order. Soviet policies sought to deliver education, medicine, and social services to peoples across Central Asia. Officials believed that such efforts would modernize patterns of everyday life, from farming techniques to Islamic beliefs and gender relations, which they saw as inherently backward. To replace ostensibly outdated affiliations and loyalties to extended families, clans, villages, and Islam, Soviet planners ordered the creation of modern national territories and identities in the 1920s. Scholars and officials partitioned the peoples of the region into Kazakhs, Kyrgyz, Tajiks, Turkmen, and Uzbeks.[3] In a confused process, national labels and borders divided families and villages. The fertile and densely populated Ferghana Valley was carved into Kyrgyz, Tajik, and Uzbek sections based on arbitrary criteria that included language, cultural traditions, and economic activity. Effects of this complicated situation were muted in the Soviet era, when people traversed borders freely and Moscow made major policy decisions. As Morgan Liu and Madeleine Reeves show, however, this experiment in nation making has had profound consequences in the post-Soviet period.

Central Asians felt the profound effects of Soviet modernization in the 1930s, as Doug Northrop and Marianne Kamp illustrate in their contributions. Campaigns, often violent, sought to penetrate all levels of everyday life. Communist leaders forced millions of nomads to settle and millions of peasants to grow grain, cotton, and other commodities for the Soviet state in collective farms. Campaigns against Islam and against gender inequalities, symbolized by the wearing of the veil, also resulted in hostilities. Other initiatives included European-style education and housing, discussed respectively in the Keller and Liu articles. I. V. Stalin distrusted the will and ability of local allies such as former Jadids to effect such radical change. Thousands were purged from the Communist Party; many of these were killed. An estimated two million Russian administrators and skilled workers flooded Soviet Central Asia. Their presence, as well as other aspects of the 1930s Soviet legacy, continue to have a strong impact on everyday life in the region, as several articles in this collection discuss. A new generation of Central Asian leaders, recruited and trained under Stalinist rule, joined these Russians in administering a profoundly altered Central Asia.

Relative stability reigned in the years following the 1930s and World War II. The war itself brought significant changes to Central Asia. The Soviet Union began investment in industrial projects, from tractor and airplane factories to hydroelectric and aluminum plants. Cities and worker settlements grew, even as the majority of the population remained in villages. Universal education was made available, virtually eliminating illiteracy in a region where only the elites could read and write before 1917. Health and social welfare programs, albeit of low quality, also spread throughout the area. At the same time, as Keller argues, more negative aspects of Soviet rule crept into everyday life. Corruption and bribery proliferated, primarily but not exclusively among Soviet officials. Central Asians of the "titular" nationality (Turkmen in the Turkmen SSR, for example) gained leadership posts in republican Communist party and state organs, but were always closely watched by ethnic Russians who maintained control of the economy, military, and security. The absence of Central Asians in leading positions in Moscow helped turn many local elites against the Soviet system; stripping the central state of resources was one response to growing frustration. At the level of everyday life, payoffs for even the most basic state service became common. Only briefly mentioned in our contributions are other consequences that increased elite and popular dissatisfaction with Soviet rule in the 1980s. Development schemes destroyed the environment. The most renowned catastrophe is the dessication of the Aral Sea, formerly the world's fourth largest lake, which lost more than 40% of its area between 1960 and 1987 as Soviet planners diverted inflows for cotton production. The reduced level and poisonous quality of the pesticide-laden water that reaches the sea have resulted in a public health disaster of great proportions, one current leaders have been largely unwilling to address.[4] Soviet investment also proved insufficient to provide opportunities to a rapidly growing population, as rural Central Asians had the highest population growth rate in the USSR. Soviet leaders began to encourage underemployed Central Asian rural youth to move to the more industrialized heartlands of the Soviet Union in the 1980s, but this initiative failed to address structural deficiencies in the regional economy.

The Soviet invasion of Afghanistan in 1979 also catalyzed local frustration against the Soviet regime. The USSR had maintained a deep interest in Afghanistan following the 1919 British withdrawal. The Soviets provided resources, advisors, and technical expertise to Afghan leaders, though the latter also accepted aid from the United States. Unlike the situation in Soviet Central Asia, massive social and economic investments were not realized, and the majority of the largely rural population had little contact with the central state through the 1960s. Apparent Soviet successes in modernization attracted the attention of Afghan military officers and urban youth. Communist power grew in democratic elections, and the party won a violent struggle for power in 1978. Modernization plans met with stiff resistance, as the United States sought allies to combat Communist influence. Afghan leaders seeking to install Islamic law in the country gained strength. Against military advice, Soviet leaders ordered an invasion in December 1979. The first troops into Afghanistan were primarily Central Asian in origin. Although largely staying loyal, these soldiers did not fulfill Soviet hopes of transmitting the greatness of the Soviet Union to their Afghan "brothers." Some, resenting the leadership of Slavic officers, deserted. The USSR sent in 350,000 more, predominantly Slavic, troops from 1979 to 1989. A determined Afghan resistance, funded by anti-Communist states, gained skill in guerilla warfare and fought Soviet forces to a standstill.

Mikhail Gorbachev, acceding to leadership of the Communist Party in 1985, faced a declining economy and social apathy across the USSR, as well as the Afghan imbroglio. In Central Asia, intellectuals and many Communist party members responded to his campaigns of *glasnost* (openness) and *perestroika* (restructuring) by demanding greater rights for local languages and nationalities against the privileges of Russian-speaking minorities. They also sought economic diversification and environmental protection. Islam, which maintained both an official and an unofficial presence in the nominally atheistic Soviet Union, emerged as an attractive social, cultural and, for some, political alternative to the Communist system. Ultimately, however, political maneuvers in Moscow precipitated the collapse of the USSR before these movements gained resilience. As a result, republican communist parties maintained power and steered their Soviet socialist republics toward independence.

The initial leaders of the newly independent states of Kazakhstan, Kyrgyzstan, Tajikistan, Turkmenistan, and Uzbekistan had all served as first secretaries of the republican communist parties. Reinventing themselves as nationalists, these leaders proclaimed democratic, constitutional republics. With the exception of Tajikistan, which, as Greta Uehling discusses, plunged into a violent civil conflict, these leaders held power throughout the transition period. Soviet-style bureaucracies and methods of rule, as a result, still predominate. As several of our contributors discuss, these new regimes, with the exception of Soviet Kyrgyzstan, have not allowed free and fair elections. They have not created independent judiciaries to supervise the constitutions. Opposition has been stifled. At the level of everyday life, our contributors have noted growing frustration and pessimism as early hopes that the end of the USSR might lead to greater freedoms and prosperity for average citizens have evaporated. Instead, Central Asian states have retreated from providing basic services and social welfare programs, all the while continuing to develop their economies to benefit insider elites.

Events in Afghanistan following the late 1980s withdrawal of Soviet troops have had a profound impact on the region. Years of civil war followed as international attention waned, the country having lost its Cold War importance. A movement of religious students, or Taliban, gained strength and attracted large numbers of villagers from southern Pashtun tribes. The Taliban captured the capital, Kabul, in 1996. Taliban leaders oppressed both women and other ethnic groups, including northern Tajiks and Uzbeks and the Shi'a Muslim minority Hazaras of central Afghanistan who are the subject of Robert Canfield's contributions. The Taliban gained international support and funding from Osama bin Laden as well as from Islamist networks in Pakistan. Central Asian leaders opposed the Taliban, fearing a radical Islam would threaten their own secular, Soviet-style rule. But news of continued hostilities in Afghanistan served a useful purpose in turning the great majority of Central Asians away from thoughts of supporting political Islamist movements. The United States, following its invasion of Afghanistan in October 2001, expressed support for the Central Asian leaders who pledged to aid the so-called war on terror. International backing, however, only emboldened leaders to intensify oppression of local opposition movements, secular or Islamist. Anger against ruling regimes across Central Asia has broadened as residents see their everyday life worsening. In 2005 alone, mass demonstrations led to the ouster of Kyrgyz president Askar Akaev, prompted a government massacre of unarmed civilians in Andijon, Uzbekistan, and caused worries in Afghanistan that the US-supported government of Hamid Karzai is far from stable.

PURPOSE AND STRUCTURE

Links between past and present form an important part of this volume. Most importantly, several of our contributors note the significance of the Soviet transformation of Central Asian culture and society. In addition to political leaders and systems, the continuities of the Soviet era are anchored in multiple aspects of everyday life—the way people read, learn, work, and think. Soviet legacies go to the heart of the modern identity of various Central Asian peoples. We focus specifically on what Central Asians themselves have to say about this identity issue, which varies, of course, depending on their level of interest in notions such as cultural dominance and transformation. We aim to impress upon readers the centrality of the intertwined Russian, Soviet, and Marxist transformations among ordinary people from the semi-desert environments of western Uzbekistan to the lush valleys of the Pamir Mountains shared by Tajiks and Kyrgyz, to say nothing of the cosmopolitan settings of Almaty and Tashkent.

Our authors also show that the imperial and Soviet experiences themselves were shaped at the level of everyday life by local customs, behaviors, and traditions. Identification with tribes, extended families, or villages persists alongside loyalties to "new" nations and states. Ideas of local customs, Russian culture, socialism, and Soviet modernity commingle as well as clash in everyday practices of meals and parties, holidays, music, and religion. Ordinary people in Central Asia emerge in our volume as agents in a series of complex transformations. Transformation partly understood as culture change is a natural aspect of the human condition, though it of course varies according to numerous factors, ranging from degrees of cross-cultural interchange to levels of political oppression and economic domination. Although we, and our authors, stress the agency of our subjects in navigating political and economic change, we also are aware that power continues to play a large role in everyday Central Asian life, and political and economic elites exert great pressure upon the less privileged members of society. We also do not ignore the importance of everyday traditions, even as these traditions evolve, as anchors in uncertain and changing worlds.

Another important aim of this book was to cover an exhaustive range of everyday life activities. Readers will learn how Central Asians worship, are educated, eat, treat minority populations, recollect the past, work and earn money, get married, determine proper gender roles, reflect on urban and rural living, celebrate holidays, and conduct all manner of daily business. Our contributors tell stories from viewpoints of individual Central Asians, the state, or even themselves as they come into contact with, or become a part of, the everyday lives of their subjects. Although the authors are overwhelmingly Western, they represent a wide sample of nationalities and disciplines. Historians, anthropologists, political scientists, and sociologists all weave their own personal and disciplinary styles into their telling of stimulating narratives on everyday life in Central Asia. The predominance of pieces on ex-Soviet Central Asia reflects the great difficulties conducting fieldwork in war-torn Afghanistan, and the country's status as a unique field within the history and social sciences of Eurasia. Nonetheless, we have felt it important to discuss Afghanistan, and to include the two pieces by Robert Canfield, given the linguistic and cultural affinities of these peoples, to say nothing of their intertwined histories and contiguous geographies. Canfield's pieces also meet another important goal of this book: exposing curious readers to this part of the world in a way that prioritizes accessibility and investigates realities that readers can relate to their own lives. Although there is a growing scholarly literature on Central Asia, beyond the mass of quasi-scholarly and superficial security and international relations studies, we feel that very little of it speaks to non-specialists. Since we ourselves have written much of this new scholarly literature, we hope our efforts here to describe and explain everyday life in Central Asia, without sacrificing intellectual quality, will appeal to a broad audience in ways that are informative, concise, and, perhaps most importantly, interesting.

As we travel further into this new millennium, many of us in the social sciences tend to evaluate the processes of globalization and transnationalism with a hypercritical eye because of their many destructive results. Be that as it may, the processes have at least a potential positive side, and that is to allow learning a great deal more about people and places from whom we have been long isolated. Central Asia gives us a good opportunity to share with readers how globalization and transnationalism affect and are affected by these peoples. Terrorism, poverty, extremism, dictatorship, ecological disaster, mafia capitalism, cronyism, and corruption in fact characterize a good deal of Central Asia accurately; but much about these conditions is also exaggerated and overemphasized at the expense of all kinds of positive or life-affirming developments, including political activity, the pursuit of intellectual life, the practice of religion to improve one's life, green movements, independent trade and vibrant commercial pursuits, and renewed interest in family planning.

The book is divided into six sections, though readers will find connections that run between articles in different parts of the study. A short introduction precedes each section, in which we provide a brief background and discuss key themes and concepts developed by the authors. In an effort to give readers a sense of what Central Asia is and what makes it unique geographically and historically—that is, what gives it its boundedness or particularity—we asked Scott Levi to write an introductory background essay, dedicated exclusively to past vicissitudes of the cultures and civilizations of Central Asia in such a way that our readers would have a view at once synoptic and detailed, to set the context for the articles dealing with contemporary people and issues. As readers proceed from Levi's essay, they will find the continued importance of customs and practices developed centuries earlier, and also understand how different concepts of everyday life evolved and transformed, from the 1800s to the current day.

NOTES

1. For one such broader view, see, for example, A. H. Dani and V. M. Masson, *History of Civilizations of Central Asia* 6 vols. (Paris: UNESCO Publishing, 1992).

2. On the physical geography of Central Asia, see Peter Sinnott, "The Physical Geography of Soviet Central Asia and the Problem of the Aral Sea" in *Geographic Perspectives on Soviet Central Asia*, ed. Robert A. Lewis (London: Routledge, 1992), 74–97; Ian Murray Matley, "The Population and the Land," in *Central Asia: 130 Years of Russian Dominance, A Historical Overview, 3rd Edition*, ed. Edward Allworth (Durham: Duke University Press, 1994), 92–130.

3. For more details on this process, see Arne Haugen, *The Establishment of National Republics in Soviet Central Asia* (New York: Palgrave Macmillan, 2003).

4. On the Aral Sea, see Erika Weinthal, *State Making and Environmental Cooperation: Linking Domestic and International Politics in Central Asia* (Cambridge, Mass.: MIT Press, 2002).

PART ONE

Background

Events and memories of the distant past continue to weigh heavily on the peoples of Central Asia. Issues of origins, heritage, and lineage pervade everyday life, as several articles in this volume will show. Scott Levi traces key factors that have, over centuries, shaped the region. Nomads and settled populations coexisted in a symbiotic, albeit tenuous, relationship. Invasions, migrations, and resettlements across the steppe and oases continually transformed Central Asia. Levi finds a syncretic process, where new conquerors and arrivals at once altered and adapted to the societies and cultures of previous inhabitants. Ethnic and religious identities underwent continual modifications. Levi describes how Turks became known as Kazakhs, Kyrgyz, Turkmen, and Uzbeks, and how Iranians became Tajiks. The lines between ethnic groups shifted due to socioeconomic, political, and demographic factors. Islam, spreading across Central Asia from the eighth century to the eighteenth, also continually evolved, adopting beliefs and practices from older religious systems and adding those from new arrivals. Empires and invasions wreaked violence and destruction but provided Central Asians with memories of great civilizations that produced global achievements in philosophy and science. Peoples of the region today can recount in detail the accomplishments of the great historical figures such as Chinggis Khan, Amir Timur (Tamerlane), and Babur. Many trace their own lineage back centuries, with relations to past dynasties still a source of prestige. Of all the invaders to Central Asia, Levi finds the Russians most disruptive of patterns of culture and everyday life. New technologies and administrative methods subjected the local populations to a distant ruler, fixed national identities, and isolated the region from the influences elsewhere in Eurasia. Millions of ethnic Russians joined the peoples of the region, further complicating social relations.

Upon independence, Central Asians have revisited various eras in their history. Mosques are being rebuilt and other holy sites restored. Statues of centuries-old local warriors and scholars have replaced those of Karl Marx and V. I. Lenin. Rituals suppressed in the Soviet era are once more being celebrated. Levi's article should remind us that the events of the present, as well as the memories of the past, are always in flux. Central Asia, as a crossroads of Eurasian politics, economics, and culture, will remain subject to outside influence and internal upheavals. Everyday life has shown a remarkable capacity to adapt and synthesize past and present, providing sources of identity and steadiness in a continually shifting region and world.

1. Turks and Tajiks in Central Asian History

Scott Levi

In its modern context, the term *Central Asia* is most commonly used to re-fer to the ex-Soviet states of Kazakhstan, Kyrgyzstan, Tajikistan, Turkmen-istan, and Uzbekistan. Each of these nation-states was established in the early part of the twentieth century, and each was assigned a name based upon the ethnic group that comprises the majority of the state's population. Significant numbers of these groups also live in the territory of northern Afghanistan and the Xinjiang province of eastern China. If there is one primary distinction that can be made among these peoples, it is that the Tajiks alone have an Indo-European heritage and speak a language closely related to the Persian (Farsi) of modern Iran. The four other Central Asian peoples (Kazakhs, Uzbeks, Kyrgyz, and Turkmen) are all Turkic, which is to say that their languages belong to the Uralic-Altaic language family and they are therefore unrelated to the Tajiks. But identifying that simple dis-tinction tells us little about what it means to be a Tajik, or what historically differentiates "Oghuz" Turks, such as the Turkmen, from "Qipchaq" Turks, such as the Kazakhs.

The ethnic identities of the modern Central Asian peoples largely be-came crystallized during the Soviet era, but their respective histories have unfolded over many centuries. Subsequent chapters of this volume will introduce readers to important aspects of everyday life in contemporary Central Asia. The purpose of this essay is to provide a brief survey of the lengthy historical processes that have gradually come together to shape the ethnic landscape of the region. The short discussion here can only intro-duce this complex topic. Readers whose interest in Central Asian history has been piqued are encouraged to refer to the list of references below.

To begin, it is important to recognize one of the defining features of Central Asian history: the relationship between pastoral-nomadic peoples of the steppe and the sedentary farming peoples of the agricultural oases to the south. Nomadic peoples by definition spend their lives migrating from one area to another, always working to ensure that their animals have adequate water and fresh pastures. Generally speaking, this precludes nomads from engaging in agricultural activities and leaves them dependent upon their sedentary neighbors for necessary foods (e.g., wheat for bread). Similarly, sedentary communities engage in farming and look to their nomadic neighbors for supplies of animals and animal products (e.g., wool for clothing). The relationship between these two peoples can therefore, at least to some extent, be characterized as symbiotic: they lived independently but needed each other to survive. Still, this relationship was not without its tensions. Throughout the course of Central Asian history, it is a recurrent theme that wave upon wave of pastoral-nomadic peoples have periodically quit the steppe to take up residence in a neighboring sedentary society. Any of a number of factors in the everyday life of a nomadic people might precipitate these frequently violent migrations. These include: a rise in population pressures in the steppe brought about by naturally increasing populations and demands for grazing territory in times of plenty; shifting climatic patterns that periodically render entire portions of the steppe uninhabitable for years at a time; and, of course, displacement caused by the migrations of other peoples from elsewhere. Additionally, events as unpredictable as a sudden freeze or an epidemic disease can devastate an entire herd, the sum of a tribe's wealth and the basis of their lives. It is not difficult to understand how such circumstances might motivate nomadic peoples to expand their territory elsewhere at the expense of another nomadic group, or to invade a sedentary society and forcibly take what is needed to stay alive.

CENTRAL ASIA'S IRANIAN HERITAGE

The Tajiks are not the earliest "aboriginal" inhabitants of Central Asia, but their ancestors have inhabited Central Asia far longer than any of the other nationalities listed above. Archeological evidence suggests that sometime around the year 2000 BCE, groups of Indo-Iranian tribes moved southward from what is today Russia and gradually emerged as the dominant ethnicity across both sedentary Central Asia and the steppe, either displacing those peoples who preceded them or absorbing them into their own societies. Iranian peoples retained a largely uncontested position in these areas for some 2500 years, giving rise to numerous vast nomadic confederations in the steppe as well as sedentary empires further to the south. These are the ancestors of the modern Tajiks.

Largely because of their persistent conflict with the Greeks and their inclusion in the narrative of the Hebrew bible, the historical record of the ancient Iranian peoples first becomes clear with the Achaemenid "Persian" Empire. In the early sixth century BCE, the Achaemenid dynasty emerged as a powerful state centered in the southern Fars province (Pars in Greek, hence "Persia") of modern Iran. By the middle of the century, the Achaemenid emperor Cyrus II had firmly established the groundwork for his Persian Empire and expanded his control in all directions. Cyrus was followed by Darius I (r. 522–486 BCE), celebrated in history as Darius the Great and credited with promoting the Zoroastrian religion and consolidating Persian authority over the lands of Central Asia.

Zoroastrianism is a dualistic faith that pits good against evil. Followers of the Avesta, the sacred Zoroastrian texts, worship light and fire as symbols of life, wisdom, and the great god of creation, Ahura Mazda. These are held in opposition to the darkness and corrupting evil of Angra Mainu. While it seems certain that the peoples of Central Asia had been exposed to the Zoroastrian faith by the fifth century BCE, the religion did not become formalized in a meaningful way until much later. This can at least partly be attributed to disruptions brought about by the Greek conquest of the Persian Empire under Alexander of Macedon (Alexander the Great, r. 336–323 BCE) and the centuries-long Greco-Persian interlude that followed. In general, Alexander and his Hellenistic successors exhibited a lack of interest in supporting Persian cultural traditions, such as the Zoroastrian religion.

In the third century of the Common Era, another Persian dynasty emerged in the Fars province and rapidly extended its control across the formerly Achaemenid lands, stretching from North Africa to the Indus River in modern Pakistan, and including the ethnically Iranian Soghdian city-states of Central Asia. In many ways, the Sasanian era (224–651 CE) represents a pre-Islamic "Persian Renaissance." The Sasanians portrayed themselves as the heirs of the Achaemenid Persian tradition, and they rallied their Persian subjects to purge the Hellenistic (and other) influences that had been incorporated into Persian culture during the five centuries since Alexander's conquests. Toward this end, the Sasanians sponsored Zoroastrianism as the classical "Persian" religion, and they elevated it to an esteemed position across their empire. During these centuries, Zoroastrian practices were popularized, codified, and made more uniform.

Although some practices in Central Asia differed significantly from those in Iran, the Zoroastrian cultural heritage of Central Asia remains the ancient Persians' most apparent legacy in the region, and it has proven to be extraordinarily persistent among the descendants of the ancient Persians and also the Turkic Muslims of modern Central Asia, comparatively recent migrants into the region. This is most notable in the popular celebration of the ancient Zoroastrian holiday of *Nau Ruz* [*Navruz*] (literally "New Day"), an annual celebration of the vernal (spring) equinox, the day on which the amount of darkness and sunlight are equal as the world emerges from the cold slumber of winter and awakens to the approaching summer. While *Nau Ruz* has no foundation in Islamic theology, its annual occurrence is much anticipated in modern Central Asia and it is arguably the most widely celebrated holiday in the region. Special dishes are carefully prepared (*sumalak* for women and *khalim* for men), and children are entertained with traditional games, competitions, and pageantry.

Appreciating that Zoroastrian traditions have informed aspects of everyday life in Central Asia for well over 1,500 years, we should not overstate the Sasanians' cultural influence and political authority over the Soghdian Central Asian city-states. As a confessional faith, Zoroastrianism proved to have only a weak hold over the peoples of Iran and Central Asia. With the rise of Islam in the early seventh century and the subsequent Arab-Muslim conquests of the Sasanian Empire, Persian state-sponsorship of Zoroastrianism was withdrawn, Zoroastrian institutions fell into decay, and with few exceptions (e.g., the Parsis of India), adherents gradually came to identify themselves as Muslims. In the centuries prior to this, the Soghdians are known to have boasted a largely independent and unique society with a highly active commercial culture. This can be attributed to another defining feature of everyday life in Central Asia: the region's position at the hub of a vast network of trans-Eurasian caravan routes that connected virtually all of the classical civilizations of Europe and Asia.

It was in the early centuries BCE that the east-west "Silk Road" trade in luxury goods from China and India first rose to prominence, and in subsequent centuries the Soghdians developed a vibrant merchant diaspora with communities dispersed across much of Asia. From their central location in the oasis towns of Central Asia, Soghdian merchants mediated the trans-Eurasian trade in all varieties of valuable commodities and bulk goods. These included especially precious stones from the Pamirs and Hindu Kush mountain ranges, Central Asian slaves, horses from their nomadic neighbors in the steppe, Siberian furs, precious metals from the Mediterranean, and fine porcelain and countless bolts of silk from China. Soghdian towns grew as commercial centers large and small, equipped with numerous caravanserais and bazaars where local goods were sold alongside merchandise from across Asia and the Mediterranean. The Soghdian merchant diaspora also participated in the transmission of religious traditions across much of Asia. Soghdian communities in China commonly adopted Buddhism, while Zoroastrianism, Manichaeism, Nestorian Christianity, and Judaism all enjoyed popularity in Central Asia in this period.

As observed above, in the ancient period, the nomadic peoples of the steppe were predominantly Iranian. However, as the Soghdian civilization flourished in sedentary Central Asia, a new group of nomadic peoples emerged in the steppe. In the middle of the fifth century, a confederation of Turkic tribes from around the eastern Altai Mountains moved westward and began to exert pressure on the various Iranian steppe nomadic groups. From the middle of the sixth century, as the Iranian groups migrated in large numbers into India, Turkic tribes replaced them as the dominant population of the pastoral-nomadic steppe. The Turk Qaghanate (also referred to as the Kök Turk Empire, or the First and Second Turk Empires, ruling from 552–659 and 682–744, respectively) exercised control over a vast domain extending from the Black Sea to Mongolia. In the 560s, the Kök Turk Empire—in collaboration with the Sasanians—invaded Central Asia and divided the territory between them. This Turko-Persian alliance was short-lived, however, as lucrative commercial interests in the Mediterranean quickly led the Turks to turn against the Sasanians in favor of Byzantium, the Persians' Greek rivals to the west. Soon thereafter, the Turks moved further south and asserted political authority over the Soghdian city-states. Although this period did not see significant Turkic migration into the sedentary areas of Central Asia and its impact on the everyday lives of Central Asian peoples was limited, it was a momentous event that marks the beginning of the long process of Turkic migration into Central Asia—a process that has gradually led to the emergence of Turkic peoples as the dominant populations in the formerly Iranian stretches of sedentary Central Asia. For the time being, however, Turkic migration southward was stalled: first in the mid-seventh century by the westward expansion of the Chinese T'ang Dynasty (617–906), and more directly in the early eighth century by the arrival in Central Asia of a conquering force of Arab Muslim armies.

Muhammad, the Prophet of Islam, died in Arabia in the year 632, and just two years later the second Caliph ("Successor"), Umar (r. 634–644), led the Arab troops to victory over the Sasanians at the Battle of Qadisiyya. The Persians lost their capital of Ctesiphon, near modern Baghdad, and were forced to retreat from what is now Iraq. By the year 651 the Arab troops had extended their control over virtually all of Persia, reaching even as far as the Amu Darya, and the Sasanian Empire was eliminated. The Arab conquest of the Soghdian principalities began in the year 709, when Qutayba bin Muslim, the governor of Khurasan (northeastern Iran), organized the first Arab raids of Bukhara. In succeeding years the Muslim armies turned their attention to Khwarezm [Khorezm] and then Soghdiana, thereby inserting the emerging Arab power into a tripartite struggle for dominance in Central Asia that involved the Muslim Arabs, the T'ang Chinese, and a number of competing groups of Turkic tribes. The Chinese had just a few years earlier defeated the Second Turk Empire when, in the year 749, a Chinese army crossed the Tien Shan Mountains and asserted authority over the Ferghana Valley (in the southeast corner of modern Uzbekistan). The Arab Muslims had meanwhile extended their influence eastward as far as Tashkent. In 751, the struggle between these two remaining superpowers culminated northeast of Tashkent at the Battle of Talas. As the Arab-backed troops of Tashkent faced off against the Chinese-backed troops of Ferghana, a number of Turkic tribes defected from their Chinese patrons, and the Arab side was victorious. The T'ang were pushed back to the east, and it would be a thousand years before another Chinese dynasty would again exert its influence westward across the Tien Shan. Islam emerged as a dominant force in the new Arab province of Mawarannahr ("that which lies beyond the river," an Arabic version of the earlier Greek "Transoxania").

Mawarannahr was placed under a series of Arab regional governors in the early years of the Abbasid Caliphate (750–1258). Consolidation of caliphal control over the region was difficult at first, but was considerably advanced as the aristocratic Central Asian landlords rapidly embraced Islam and professed their allegiance to the Sunni Muslim caliph in Baghdad. Already in the ninth century, Central Asia produced its first Islamic ruling family, the Samanids (819–1005), an Iranian dynasty from near Termiz that had converted to Islam earlier in the eighth century. The Samanids gradually rose in power, and in the year 875 political expediency led the Abbasids to recognize them as the official rulers of both Mawarannahr and Khurasan. The Samanids earned a reputation as enlightened Muslim rulers, and their era is considered to have been one of prosperity and great support for literature and scholarship. In this period Central Asia produced such illustrious scholars as Jafar Muhammad al-Khwarezmi, author of *al-Jabr* (*The Reduction*), the basis for the mathematical field of algebra (al-Khwarezmi's name has also been memorialized in the English word "algorithm," meaning a decimal calculation); Ibn Sina, known to his contemporaries as the Prince of Physicians and famous in Europe as Avicenna, author of the authoritative encyclopedic medical resource, *The Canon of Medicine*; and the famed astronomer al-Biruni, who in the eleventh century—some 500 years before Galileo—turned his keen mind to the stars and calculated that the Earth did indeed revolve around the Sun.

The Samanids' legacy in the arts and sciences was great, but their greatest achievement was arguably their synthesis of the Islamic faith with Persian language and culture. After two centuries of Arabic dominance, the Samanids rehabilitated the Persian language as an Islamic literary language in Central Asia and Iran. In subsequent centuries, this would greatly facilitate the process of Islamization across the region and lay the foundation for Central Asia—especially the Samanid capital of Bukhara—to emerge as a great center of Islamic civilization. It should be noted that the spread of Islam in this period was not limited to the sedentary areas: through their proselytizing missionary activities, wandering Muslim mystics (*Sufis*) even promoted the expansion of Islam among the nomadic peoples of the steppe.

The Samanids were able to prosper at least partly because of their success at maintaining a well-fortified frontier against their Turkic nomadic neighbors to the north. These fortresses were used as much for defense from nomadic raids as they were for providing the Samanid Muslim

Samanid temple in Bukhara (tenth century).

troops with a staging point for their own raids into the steppe. This afforded the Samanids an unlimited supply of Turkic slaves ("*ghulams*" in Persian, "*mamluks*" in Arabic), a commodity in high demand due to the legendary military skills of the nomadic Turks. As economic crises and internal conflict weakened the Samanid state at the end of the tenth century, its ability to maintain a firm barrier against the rising pressures of the steppe deteriorated. At the turn of the millennium, political control over the agricultural oases of Central Asia shifted from Iranian hands to successive waves of invading Turkic and Mongol nomads, where it remained until Russian colonization in the nineteenth century.

THE TURKS

A confederation of pastoral-nomadic Turkic Muslims commonly referred to as the Qarakhanids had been encroaching on Samanid territory for decades when they entered Bukhara in the year 999 and shortly thereafter extinguished the teetering Samanid dynasty. Turks had long been present in Samanid territories as slaves and soldiers, but it is with the arrival of the Qarakhanids that we can locate the early stages of Turkicization of sedentary Central Asia: the long process by which Turkic-language speakers gradually became the dominant population of the region as they either subsumed the Iranian-speaking Tajiks or relegated them to the mountainous periphery of the upper Oxus Valley, the territory that is today Tajikistan. It should be emphasized that the ethnic transformation of Central Asia from an Iranian region to a Turkic one has been a very gradual process that, even a thousand years later, still continues among the significant, but diminishing, Tajik minority of Uzbekistan. We will return to this subject below.

The Qarakhanid migrations represent a momentous event in Central Asian history. Their control over Mawarannahr was, however, short-lived. Just decades after the Qarakhanids arrived in Bukhara, their authority over Central Asia was successfully challenged by another group of Turkic pastoralists. Ethnically Oghuz Turks had been a dominant population in the western steppe since the T'ang Chinese defeated the Second Turk Qaghanate in the mid-eighth century. In the late tenth century, a number of the Oghuz tribes joined under the leadership of a commander by the name of Seljuk. This Seljuk confederation soon thereafter converted to Sunni Islam and migrated southward, where they served as mercenaries for the Samanids in their struggle with the encroaching Qarakhanids. Pushed to the south, in the year 1055 the Seljuks invaded Baghdad, extinguished the Shi'a Muslim Buyid dynasty, and returned the capital to Sunni authority. This earned the Seljuks the gratitude of the caliph, who bestowed upon their leader the title Sultan and the legitimacy to rule in his name wherever their conquests might take them. Just a few years later, in 1071, the Seljuk Sultan Alp Arslan led his Oghuz followers to victory over the Byzantine Emperor Romanos in eastern Anatolia (Asia Minor, modern Turkey), which was thenceforth opened to Turkish migrations. Many more Oghuz Turks later joined their kinsmen in Anatolia, beginning the gradual transformation of this formerly Greek Christian region into a Turkish Muslim one.

After their victory in Anatolia, the Seljuks turned their attention back to Central Asia and, from their capital at Merv (in modern Turkmenistan), overran the Qarakhanids. By the end of the eleventh century, the Oghuz had emerged as the dominant Turkic population across much of Central Asia and the Middle East. It was in this period that the designation Turkmen (also the antiquated Turcoman or, more correctly, Türkmen) began to be applied to Muslim Oghuz Turks. Although the Turkic populations of Turkey and Azerbaijan are of similar ancestry to the Turkmen in Central Asia, the centuries-old designation "Turkmen" continues to apply only to the descendants of the Central Asian Oghuz tribes, the titular population of Turkmenistan.

The Seljuk ruling family quickly fragmented into a number of smaller sultanates, and they remained dominant in Central Asia only until 1141. Their fall from power came at the hands of the Qarakhitai, a Buddhist Turko-Mongol nomadic confederation pushed westward into Seljuk territory after they themselves had been expelled from northern China (where they ruled as the Khitan from 907 to 1115). Their reign over Mawarannahr did not disrupt everyday life for the Muslim inhabitants of the region as they largely governed through local Muslim authorities. By the beginning of the thirteenth century, a local aristocratic dynasty, the Turkic-Muslim Khwarezmshahs, deposed the Qarakhitai to establish themselves as the independent rulers over all of Central Asia and nearly all of Iran. Ultimately, however, events of subsequent years would unfold in ways quite contrary to the wishes of the Khwarezmshah.

In order to understand why that was the case, we shall first turn our attention to historical developments further to the east. In the mid-sixth century, as the First Turk Empire was extending its control over the Oghuz tribes in the west, they were similarly incorporating the Kyrgyz tribes further to the east. At that time, the Kyrgyz confederation of Turko-Mongol tribes was the dominant power in the upper Yenisei River region of Siberia, located to the north of Mongolia and west of Lake Baikal. After the dissolution of the Turk Qaghanate in 744, the Kyrgyz were subordinated to the Uyghur Qaghanate, which governed a sizeable territory from its capital in western Mongolia. This continued until the year 840, when the Kyrgyz began a rebellion that led to the collapse of the Uyghur Qaghanate. A considerable Uyghur population subsequently relocated southward from Mongolia into the northeastern portion of what is today Xinjiang, China, where they established the Uyghur kingdom of Qocho. The Uyghur governed a remarkably cosmopolitan commercial and agricultural state, which flourished for some four centuries. The Kyrgyz, meanwhile, prospered as the dominant power in the upper Yenisei River valley through much of the ninth and tenth centuries, and they remained important even after their dominance was lost to other rising tribal groups. Late in the twelfth century, a young Mongol warrior named Temujin gradually rose in power and coerced many of the Turkic and Mongol tribes of the region, including the Kyrgyz, to accept his authority. In 1206, Temujin was elevated to the position of Chinggis Khan (or Genghis Khan, "Oceanic Ruler").

It is doubtful that any single event in Central Asian history was more influential in furthering the Turkicization of the region than the resettlement of countless Turks and Mongols from the northern steppe to the south during the Mongol conquests. These migratory groups included the Kyrgyz, who were active participants in the Mongol conquests and many of whom permanently abandoned their Siberian homeland for the Tien Shan Mountains, settling in the area that would become modern Kyrgyzstan. Much later, in the fifteenth and sixteenth centuries, proselytizing Islamic Sufi priests found a receptive audience among these Kyrgyz. The epic poem *Manas* provides remarkable insight into the traditions and culture of the Kyrgyz people from their times in the Siberian steppes. This collection of heroic stories numbers more than a million lines (more than twenty times the combined length of Homer's *Iliad* and *Odyssey*) and, since it was begun more than one thousand years ago, has until recently been passed down through oral tradition by the Manaschi, traditional Kyrgyz bards. The Manas epic is honored today as the greatest cultural monument of the Kyrgyz people.

In 1209, just three years after Temujin was proclaimed Chinggis Khan, the Uyghur rulers of Xinjiang willingly submitted to the emerging Mongol power, and it did not take long for Mongol troops to extend their conquests further to the west. In 1218 they invaded Semirech'e (*Yeti Su* in Turkic: the Seven Rivers region east of Lake Balkash, in modern Kazakhstan), overthrew the Qarakhitai, and became neighbors to the Khwarezmshah Ala al-Din Muhammad (r. 1200–1220), arguably the most powerful Muslim ruler in the world at the time. The Khwarezmshah's harsh treatment—murdering one and sending two home in shame—of envoys dispatched by Chinggis Khan in 1219 to resolve a previous grievance led the latter to disengage his troops from northeastern China and unleash the full force of his Turko-Mongol military against the sedentary population of Central Asia. As the force approached, Ala al-din Muhammad fled to an island off the southern coast of the Caspian Sea, where he died in 1220. The Mongols swept through Central Asia, Afghanistan, and Iran, and they sacked and demolished such great cities as Gurganj, Utrar, Bukhara,

Samarkand, Balkh, Herat, Merv, and Nishapur, to name just a few. The impact of the Mongol conquest was so complete that, for the next six centuries, the Chinggisid royal family would serve as a sort of Central Asian ruling caste. With few exceptions, one's right to rule was derived from the ability to trace one's ancestry back to Chinggis Khan himself.

Following Chinggis Khan's death in 1227, the Mongol Empire was divided among the royal family into four appanages (*ulus*). Chinggis Khan's oldest son, Jöchi, had died before him, and Jöchi's heirs were granted control over his ulus: the northern steppe as far to the west as the Mongol troops could conquer (which ultimately included much of modern Russia west of the Irtysh River). This would become the Qipchaq Khanate, more popularly referred to as the Golden Horde, and we will return to it below as the homeland of the Uzbeks and the Kazakhs. Chaghatai, the second oldest son and most fervent supporter of the Chinggisid law code (the *yasa*), was granted the central steppe area in the Ili River valley, and he eventually enlarged his domain to include both Mawarannahr and Xinjiang. Central Asian Islam continued under Chaghatai rule, although it did so in a considerably less advanced position. The Mongols' destruction of formerly great Islamic centers of learning across the region was compounded by Chaghatai's hostility toward the religion, which left regional governors scrambling to protect the Muslim population rather than working to advance Islamic civilization. This began to change in the year 1326 with the conversion to Islam of the later Chaghatai Khan Ala al-din Tarmashirin, although eight years later he was deposed and killed for having forsaken the yasa of Chinggis Khan. The Mongols of the Chaghatai Khanate were not yet ready to embrace a Muslim ruler, but Islamic law (*sharia*) would soon replace the Chinggisid yasa in Central Asia.

Among the many tribes permanently relocated to Central Asia during the Mongol conquests was the Barlas—a tribe from Mongolia that had gradually become ethnically Turkic and Muslim, and had grown influential in the Chaghatai Khanate. In the mid-fourteenth century, a young Muslim noble of the Barlas tribe named Timur (1336–1405, also Timur the Lame, or Tamerlane) was appointed assistant to the Chaghatai governor of Mawarannahr. The young upstart quickly shook off his overlord and, by 1370, established his own authority over the Chaghatai domains in Mawarannahr. His military campaigns were nearly constant from this period, and he was rarely found in his celebrated capital of Samarkand. Between 1372 and 1388 Timur consolidated his control over Khwarezm, and in later years he continued his conquest and pillaging with numerous expeditions into Iran, India, Anatolia, Transcaucasia, and the territory of the Golden Horde in modern Russia. Timur died in 1405 in Utrar, on his way to campaign against Ming China. It is telling that, despite Timur's unquestionable position of authority, the legitimacy to rule in Central Asia remained entrenched in the Chinggisid

View of Old Bukhara with Timurid architecture and Kalyam Minaret in center.

Frontal view of Gur Emir, Tamerlane's tomb in Samarkand (fifteenth century).

tradition. Thus, for most of his reign Timur governed through a puppet Chinggisid, and he was widely known by the relational title of Son-in-Law (*guregan*), which he acquired by marrying into the Mongol royal family.

Timur's heirs, less destructive than their progenitor, focused their efforts less on conquest and more on consolidating their control over Central Asia and Iran. Their considerable success at revitalizing Islamic civilization and reconstruction, both in architecture and the arts, has commonly led scholars to refer to Central Asia's fifteenth century as the Timurid Renaissance. This was the era of such historical figures as the poets Abd al-Rahman Jami and Mir Ali Shir Navai (Navai is celebrated as the founder of the modern Uzbek literary language), the painter Bihzad, and the austere Sufi Sheikh Khoja Ahrar, under whose leadership the Central Asian Sufi orders—and Sunni Islam in general—was returned to an elevated position in Central Asian society. Cities such as Samarkand and Bukhara were adorned with mosques and madrasas, which were once again vibrant centers of learning where students studied the most advanced texts in astronomy, mathematics, and medicine alongside Islamic theology. Timurid control over Central Asia lasted until the ruling family was unseated at the end of the fifteenth century by yet another wave of Turkic Muslim nomads, this time the Uzbeks, who pushed southward into Mawarannahr and forced Zahir al-Din Muhammad Babur (1483–1530), the last of the Timurid ruling clan in Central Asia (and a Chinggisid on his mother's side), to relinquish control over his ancestral capital of Samarkand and flee his Central Asian homeland.

The invading Uzbeks were a confederation of Qipchaq Turkic tribes of the Golden Horde who, our sources report, had converted to Islam under the leadership of the Chinggisid (more precisely, Jochid) ruler Uzbek Khan (r. 1313–1341). It is likely that the ethnic designation of "Uzbek" is a derivation of his name as it became popularly used in reference to his followers in the Qipchaq Steppe. Prior to their southward migrations, the Uzbek tribes appear in the historical record as the scourge of Amir Timur and the frequent target of his military campaigns. It was observed above that, following Timur's death in 1405, his heirs withdrew from the steppe and focused their efforts on consolidating their control over the sedentary areas of Central Asia and Iran. This left a power vacuum in the southern stretches of the Qipchaq Steppe (in modern Kazakhstan), and as the fifteenth century wore on a segment of the former Golden Horde moved southward into this area under the leadership of Abu al-Khayr Khan (1412–1468). Because Abu al-Khayr Khan's ancestry was traced to Shiban, the fifth son of Jöchi, his descendants are commonly referred to as the Shibanids.

Abu al-Khayr Khan led his Uzbek followers southward toward Mawarannahr and established a capital city at Sighnaq, some 350 kilometers northwest of Tashkent on the banks of the Syr Darya, near the Aral Sea. The Uzbek tribes quickly established themselves as a powerful northern neighbor to the Timurids, and it was not long before they began to run raids into Khwarezm and interfere in Timurid areas further south. This political situation was further complicated in 1456 with the arrival of a new power from the east: the Qalmaqs. This confederation of Buddhist Mongol tribes stormed westward, waged a victorious war against the Uzbeks and put the Uzbek capital under an unsuccessful siege. Abu al-Khayr Khan survived the humiliating defeat, but his position of authority was irreparably damaged as many of his followers began to see him as a weak leader. Two members of the Chinggisid royal family abandoned the Uzbeks and fled back to the steppe, where they were welcomed by the Chaghatai Khans and were later joined by a significant portion of the Uzbek tribes. Those Uzbeks who defected from Abu al-Khayr Khan's leadership became known as Kazakh-Uzbeks or just Kazakhs ("freemen" or "tribeless" in the sense of being unaffiliated). In 1468 Abu al-Khayr Khan died in battle, desperately trying to reassert his control over the recalcitrant Kazakh tribes.

Soon thereafter the weakened Uzbeks became subordinate to the Chaghataids, who had substantially increased their power, encroached on Timurid territory, and in 1487 established a western capital at Tashkent. Timurid authority in Mawarannahr deteriorated even further as the end of the century approached and two Timurid cousins, Ali and Babur, found themselves in a bitter struggle for the throne in Samarkand. Shibani Khan, a grandson of Abu al-Khayr Khan, took advantage of the Timurid conflict and led his Uzbek tribesmen into Mawarannahr, ostensibly in the name of his Chaghatai patrons. The Uzbek troops first conquered Bukhara and then, in the year 1500, took Samarkand. Inflated by his victory over the Timurids, Shibani Khan quickly threw off his patrons and within just a few years extended Uzbek control across virtually all of Mawarannahr and on to Balkh, Herat, and further into Khurasan. Central Asia was once again in Chinggisid hands. All was not lost for the Timurids, however. After many more years of hardship and failures, Babur and his entourage made their way to Kabul and, in 1526, emerged victorious over the Afghan rulers of north India. There Babur established his own Timurid dynasty, the celebrated Mughal Empire (1526–1858).

The early years of the "Uzbek period" in Central Asian history were politically unstable. In 1510 Shibani Khan was killed in battle, and Shibanid rule in Central Asia collapsed before the end of the century. In 1599 a new Chinggisid dynasty, the Astrakhanids (also referred to as the Janids, or the Toqay-Timurids), was elevated in Bukhara. Still, the Uzbek tribes had arrived in Mawarannahr to stay. They were only the most recent of many pastoral nomadic groups to have quit the steppe to take up residence in the southern stretches of Central Asia, but their arrival added a sizeable Turkic population. The Uzbek tribes established an even more dominant presence in subsequent centuries as they were joined by incoming waves of Nogay tribes from the north, another nomadic Turkic group closely akin to the Uzbeks.

THE RISE OF RUSSIA

Russia's emergence as an expansionist empire began in the year 1480 when Tsar Ivan III (the Great) freed his people from the "Mongol Yoke" and ushered in a new era in Russian history, characterized by more than four centuries of territorial expansion. Within just a few decades, Russian conquests became a new factor contributing to the growing pressures in the northern steppe. In the 1550s, Tsar Ivan IV (the Terrible) annexed the Khanates of Kazan and Astrakhan, two Chinggisid successor states of the Golden Horde. A century and a half later the Russian Empire stretched across Siberia to the Pacific Ocean, and Russia was already thirty times larger than France when, in 1730, it turned its attention southward, toward the Qipchaq Steppe. The Kazakh tribes occupying the region were divided into four competing political units: Bukey's Horde, the Little Horde, the Middle Horde, and the Great Horde. Initially these rival Kazakh powers exhibited considerable interest in forming alliances with Russia, and even accepting Russian suzerainty, so that they might benefit from superior tsarist military strength in inter-tribe conflicts. The Russian advance through the steppe would not be so easy, however. The Kazakhs did not hesitate to cast off their alliances with Russia when they were no longer useful. Russia eventually tired of Kazakh duplicity and, from 1822, adopted a more aggressive position. By 1848 the Russians had effectively extinguished the Kazakh Hordes, and by the end of 1864 the Russian Empire included virtually all of the territory of modern Kazakhstan.

The second wave of Russian expansion in Central Asia began in 1865 with the conquest of Tashkent, soon thereafter proclaimed the capital of Russian Turkestan. At that time the sedentary populations of Central Asia were under the authority of three rather compact Uzbek states: the Bukharan emirate governed much of Mawarannahr, up to the nomadic Turkmen tribes that controlled the territory east of the Caspian Sea; the Khanate of Kokand (Qoqand) was centered in the Ferghana Valley but had expanded its territory to such an extent that it rivaled Bukhara in population and exceeded it in size; and the Khanate of Khiva ruled over Khwarezm. Soon after taking Tashkent, tsarist forces seized considerable Bukharan territory, and in 1876 eliminated the Khanate of Kokand and annexed the Ferghana Valley. The conquest of Central Asia was effectively completed in 1884, when the Russian victory at the Battle of Merv ended the determined resistance of the Turkmen. Much of the region was administered directly out of Tashkent, although the Khivan Khanate and Bukharan emirate were permitted to limp on into the twentieth century as shrunken and weakened protectorates.

It is perhaps worth mentioning that, although military conquest is nearly always bloody, and this is perhaps especially true in Central Asia, the bloodshed involved in the Russian conquest of the region was exacerbated by the implementation of revolutionary new military technologies. The most notable of these was an early version of the machine gun—each thunderous repetition from which must have seemed like a brazen announcement to the Central Asian Turks that their once-proud military traditions had no place in the modern world. It should also not be overlooked that the Russian colonial era brought to the region many other new technologies, as well as economic policies, medical capabilities, and educational opportunities. The colonial administrators of Russian Turkestan maintained a general policy of trying not to interfere in the everyday lives of their Central Asian subjects, but their impact was nonetheless overwhelming. Indeed, Russian colonization marks the beginning of what would quickly become the most profound social revolution in the history of Central Asia.

Shortly after the success of the Bolshevik Revolution and the establishment of the Soviet Union in late 1922, Central Asian peoples were divided into new ethnically based political units according to the provisions of the National Delimitation of the States (*natsional'noe razmezhevanie*). In October of 1924, the Uzbek and Turkmen Soviet Socialist Republics (SSR) were established; the Tajiks were granted an Autonomous Region within the Uzbek SSR; the Kyrgyz (at the time officially referred to as the Kara-Kyrgyz) were granted an Autonomous Region that was eventually assigned to Russia; and the Kazakhs (at the time officially referred to as the Kyrgyz) received the Kyrgyz Autonomous Soviet Socialist Republic. Between 1924 and 1936 each of these political units achieved the full status of a Soviet Socialist Republic, and each was assigned a name based upon its dominant ethnic population. In the case of Uzbekistan this involved the imposition of an "Uzbek" national identity over the diverse Turkic peoples who had migrated into that territory over the previous thousand years, some of whom were indeed members of Uzbek tribes but many of whom were not. The new Uzbek literary language was not the language of Shibani Khan's Uzbek conquerors; rather, it was derived from the "Turki" that was spoken in the Chaghatai Khanate and popularized in the fifteenth century by Mir Ali Shir Navai (Navoi). This at least partially explains how it is that, despite the fact that Amir Timur was a member of the Barlas tribe and several times fought against the Uzbeks of the Golden Horde, the peoples of modern Uzbekistan proudly claim him as their own and refer to him as *Buyuk Babamiz:* Our Great Forefather.

During the Soviet era Central Asian peoples were assigned to rigid political boundaries, but the region's ethnic landscape continued to change. Among the most obvious ethnic transformations of the twentieth century are the forced relocation of some peoples to Central Asia (e.g., Chechens and Crimean Tatars) and the rise of considerable Russian populations across the region. The collapse of the Soviet Union in 1991 has led many of these peoples to depart Central Asia for Russia (or elsewhere), but millions of ethnic Russians remain. According to the 1999 Kazakh census report, Russians accounted for roughly 30 percent of the total population of Kazakhstan; Kazakhs themselves comprise barely more than 50 percent. The experience of Uzbekistan is also unique in that, for reasons that are still debated, the borders of that state were drawn to include Bukhara, Samarkand, and several other ethnically Tajik cities. This has given rise to considerable discontent among the Tajiks of Tajikistan, many of whom argue that they have been relegated to Central Asia's mountainous periphery and denied their rightful claim to the great centers of the region's Iranian heritage. Political realities in post-Soviet Uzbekistan have also gone some distance toward further advancing the lengthy process of Turkicization among the Tajik minority. The combination of overwhelming economic difficulties and the privileges bestowed upon the titular population have led many "Uzbekistani Tajiks," or children of mixed Tajik-Uzbek marriages, to reject their Iranian ancestry and adopt, at least at the official level, a new identity as Uzbeks. Despite the rigid codification of Central Asian nationalities in the Soviet era, the ethnic landscape of post-Soviet Central Asia continues to exhibit a remarkable dynamism.

REFERENCES

Bartol'd, V. V. *Turkestan Down to the Mongol Invasion.* 2d edition. Trans. and rev. V. V. Bartol'd and H. A. R. Gibb. London, 1928.
Bregel, Yuri. *An Historical Atlas of Central Asia.* Leiden: Brill, 2003.
Canfield, Robert, ed. *Turko-Persia in Historical Perspective.* Cambridge: Cambridge University Press, 1991.
Christian, David. *A History of Russia, Central Asia and Mongolia, vol. 1.* Oxford: Blackwell, 1998.
Frye, Richard. *The Heritage of Central Asia.* Princeton: Markus Wiener, 1996.
———. *The Heritage of Persia.* London: Wiedenfield and Nicholson, 1962.
Golden, Peter. *An Introduction to the History of the Turkic Peoples.* Wiesbaden: O. Harrassowitz, 1992.
Grousset, René. *The Empire of the Steppes: a History of Central Asia.* Trans. Naomi Walford. New Brunswick, N.J.: Rutgers University Press, 1970.
———. *History of Civilizations of Central Asia,* 6 vols. Paris: UNESCO, 1992–.
Sinor, Denis, ed. *The Cambridge History of Early Inner Asia.* Cambridge: Cambridge University Press, 1990.
Soucek, Svat. *A History of Inner Asia.* Cambridge: Cambridge University Press, 2000.

PART TWO

Communities

Communal units, in the past and present, have been of critical importance across Central Asia. For pastoralist nomads and settled peoples alike, groups linked by kin, territory, religion, or a shared sense of identity have not only offered camaraderie and shared values, but also provided support vital for everyday existence. In a region endowed with a harsh climate and scarce resources, communities secure food and shelter; arrange marriages and distribute labor and supplies; and defend against unwelcome incursions from outsiders. Communities have also acted as anchors in times of transition. Group loyalties today remain multilayered, even as many residents of Central Asia identify themselves as Afghans, Kazakhs, Kyrgyz, Tajiks, Turkmen, or Uzbeks, or, in a larger sense, as Muslims. Extended joint families, tribes, clans, villages, and urban neighborhoods (*mahallas*) are central to individual and group identities and relations, as described in the articles written by Adrienne Edgar, Robert Canfield, and Morgan Liu. Edgar discusses kin-based communities among nineteenth-century Turkmen nomads as vital sources of political and economic solidarity in regions where police or courts were virtually nonexistent. Resource scarcities and power imbalances perpetuate village solidarity in twentieth-century Afghanistan, according to Canfield. Even in contemporary urban Kyrgyzstan, Liu finds a high degree of identification with the centuries-old mahalla, where residents share common courtyards, work, socialize, and pray together. Communal loyalties are less evident, however, in mixed, new districts constructed following the British and Russian conquests.

Mutual accountability and support remain hallmarks of community identity and solidarity in Central Asia. Extended families, clans, villages, and tribes share risks, resources, and rewards. Members support each other in order to uphold the community's power, status, and honor, all vital concepts in the steppe, villages, and cities. Leadership operates on the principle of community consensus. Inequalities and tensions nonetheless exist within communal groups. The patriarchal nature of Central Asian communities has led women to be highly valued but also tightly controlled. As our contributors note, women, despite their important work, from food preparation to animal care to planning of family budgets, have been isolated and subjugated in everyday life. The Soviet era provided multiple opportunities for women to participate in public life, but gender divides persist; across Central Asia, for example, it is very rare to find women driving cars. Other sources of tension exist as well; Liu hears grumblings from the young and the poor, also on the margins of community decision-making. Age and wealth are important markers of status. Gossip, subterfuge, and deception, as Canfield notes, are tools of resistance the less powerful can use without toppling a community that serves so many critical functions.

Communities do not operate in isolation. Interdependencies produce a variety of relationships, some symbiotic and others conflictual. Edgar and Liu present, in past and current times, the importance of the bazaar as a site of exchange that at once exhibits group specializations and facilitates mutual associations. Weddings are another vital part of community life that reveal the balance between isolation and association. Some communities, such as Edgar's Turkmen nomads, seek endogamy. In exogamous communities, the choice of a spouse is a highly charged process. As Canfield demonstrates, tense negotiations revolve around the selection of the bride, who generally must leave her community for her future husband's, and the bride-price (or bride-wealth). Particularly in rural and village communities, a bride's ability to work and bear children makes her an important commodity. High bride-wealth discourages polygyny among all but the affluent in settled areas; both practices are extremely rare in post-Soviet Central Asia. Other valuable, contested resources include food and fuel supplies, territory—either arable, for settled peoples, or suitable as feeding grounds for pastoralists—and animals. Scarce resources and the harshness of the environment lead groups to cooperate as well as clash. Edgar mentions the strict custom of sheltering weary or lost travelers; as pieces in subsequent sections will show, hospitality towards strangers is seen as a vital part of Central Asian culture, as a way to demonstrate goodwill and kindness but also to accumulate favors that hosts expect will be repaid at an opportune time. As we will see, state authority in the twentieth century has gradually, though not completely, replaced inter-group negotiation or violence as a means to settle disputes.

From desert tribes to urban mahallas, communities have experienced complicated relationships with the state. Through the nineteenth century, emirs and khans demanded fealty and taxes but rarely interfered in the everyday functioning of Central Asian communities. States that followed the arrival of European conquerors imposed far more invasive legal, political, and bureaucratic systems. Community leaders in many cases accepted positions as employees of the state and pledged to follow its rules in exchange for retaining a degree of personal power and community autonomy. These leaders also saw the state as a potential ally in struggles with rivals. As Canfield writes, however, state agents proved unpredictable in their judgments of inter-group conflict. A perceived cozy relationship with the state, which often involved tax collection, eroded leaders' status within their community. The Soviet Union, especially in the post–World War II years, provided many of the everyday benefits and securities once offered by autonomous communities; as articles in future sections show, this aspect of the state remains highly valued among Central Asians today. At the same time, as Liu argues, many Central Asians equate the dehumanizing architecture of gray, concrete apartment blocs and the invasive role of government officials, many of whom were ethnic Russians, with a loss of community. Communities also infiltrated the Soviet state, as members used official positions to benefit their extended family, villages, mahallas, or other connections. Recent scholarship has noted the increased importance of now-politicized "clans," groups of functionaries whose primary loyalty is not to the central state, in post-Soviet Central Asia. The extent to which we can tie these clans to past community units is debatable; what is clear, however, is that communities, operating between the state and the individual, provide stability, particularly in periods of stress and transformation. The dynamic and disordered nature of societies and polities over the last two centuries has perpetuated the importance of community life as a central part of everyday existence in Central Asia.

These articles provide valuable insights into everyday life beyond their explorations of communities. Edgar recreates the everyday world of nineteenth-century Turkmen nomads—the way tribe members work, live, migrate, socialize, as well as conceptualize their place in the world—through a depiction of a young Turkmen couple. Both of Robert Canfield's contributions relate stories told to him by Afghan elder Mir Gholam Hasan during fieldwork in the late 1960s. Canfield returns to these tales, unpacking them to discover not only key Afghan village social structures, mechanisms, and beliefs, but also the complicated and multi-layered nature of story-telling and the ways people construct realities and shape the truth to suit their own convictions or experiences or to work to their own benefit. Morgan Liu takes us on a walking tour through Osh, Kyrgyzstan, past the central bazaar and the "old" and "new" cities, which inhabitants perceive as emblematic of two different worlds, one local and traditional, and the other foreign and modern. Liu finds a complicated relationship between tradition and modernity as he shows the way that global shifts and trends, from industrialization to capitalism to Islam, have permeated the everyday life of Osh's residents.

2. Everyday Life among the Turkmen Nomads

Adrienne Edgar

The year is 1862, and the scene is the western Karakum Desert near the Caspian shore. In the distance, tiny figures of humans and animals are visible in the shimmering heat. As they grow closer, the blurred images become a colorful procession. The women, clad in embroidered robes and elaborate headdresses, lead a row of grumbling camels with heavy loads piled high on their backs. A number of small, half-naked children, some wearing embroidered skullcaps festooned with silver coins, trot alongside. A group of older boys herds a large flock of sheep and goats. The men, who wear brightly colored robes and imposing black hats made of sheep's wool, watch over the women and children from a distance on horseback. When the group arrives at its designated camping spot, the site of a subterranean well, there is a flurry of activity. The men unsaddle their horses as the boys prepare the livestock for milking. The women take down the tents from the camels' backs and prepare to assemble them. First, they erect a lightweight wooden framework to form the skeleton of the round tent known as a yurt. Next, they attach felt coverings to the walls and roof and place carpets on the floor. The children rush to hang the woven bags containing the family's other belongings—clothes, food, cooking implements—from the inside walls of the tent. Within a few minutes, a Yomut Turkmen village has appeared amid the barren sands of the desert.[1]

Several hundred years ago, this nomadic way of life was common to most Turkmen. A variety of Turkmen tribes migrated across a nearly 10,000-square-mile expanse of arid Central Asian territory that stretched from the Amu Darya in the east to the Caspian Sea in the west. In the mid-nineteenth century, the largest and strongest tribe was the Teke, which inhabited the southeastern regions of Turkmenistan bordering on Iran and Afghanistan. The second largest tribe was the Yomut, which inhabited two main regions: the Gurgan and Balkhan regions of southwestern Turkmenistan near the

Caspian Sea (this is the region in which the scene described above took place) and the northeastern regions bordering on the Khivan khanate.

Large herds of sheep, goats, and camels provided meat, milk, and wool to Turkmen families, which moved frequently in search of fresh pastures. The Turkmen also bred horses that were famous for their speed and stamina. In the steppe and desert regions of Central Asia, pastoral nomadism was well suited to arid conditions in which the cultivation of crops was difficult or impossible. The nomads traded with neighboring sedentary peoples, exchanging animal products for agricultural and manufactured goods they could not produce on their own.[2] By the end of the nineteenth century, however, only about 20 percent of Turkmen were fully nomadic. The rest had moved into the fertile oases along the edges of the Karakum Desert and begun to cultivate grain, vegetables, fruits, and cotton. Some migrated into the oases along the southern fringe of the Karakum, conquering those lands from their Persian inhabitants and becoming settled or semi-settled. Even for these agricultural Turkmen, however, sheep and goats remained an important part of the economy; most households practiced some combination of farming and livestock herding.[3] Turkmen who led a settled existence were known as *chomur,* while those who migrated with their flocks were known as *charwa.* In practice, the line between nomadic and sedentary Turkmen was blurred. Among the Yomut, for example, it was common for a lineage or family to include both nomadic and settled members, a division of labor that permitted a high degree of economic self-sufficiency.[4]

Though stateless themselves, the Turkmen tribes had had extensive contact with sedentary peoples and states for centuries. They had traded with and preyed upon neighboring settled peoples, acknowledged sedentary rulers as their nominal sovereigns, and been courted as military allies. The Turkmen were key political actors in the Khivan khanate for centuries, and played an important role in the rise to power of the Qajar dynasty in Iran. Beginning in the second half of the eighteenth century, some Turkmen tribes acknowledged themselves as nominal subjects of Khivan khans, and others as subjects of Iran and Bukhara.[5] Until the nineteenth century, however, most Turkmen groups had not come under the effective control of any state; when states tried to impose their will, Turkmen groups were able to retreat to remote desert areas for refuge.[6]

Because the Turkmen nomads themselves were almost universally illiterate and left few records behind, we must rely to a large extent on accounts by outsiders to reconstruct their lives. These accounts, many of them by European travelers and adventurers, tend to stress the exotic and dangerous aspects of nomadic life. They describe the Turkmen as violent and rapacious desert robbers and slave traders. At the same time, they wax lyrical about the freedom and equality the nomads seemed to enjoy. A life spent on horseback in the open desert, unburdened by a home or large number of possessions, had considerable appeal for many Western travelers. Despite the biases and limitations of these accounts, they can teach us a great deal about the everyday life of nomads.[7]

Let us imagine that a young man named Tagan is among the nomadic group that has just set up camp. Tagan is eighteen years old and recently married; he shares a yurt with his wife, parents, two unmarried sisters, and several brothers and their wives and children. (His name, which means "tripod" in the Turkmen language, is commonly given to the third son.) Tagan's family migrates together with a group of other families, all of whom are closely related; the neighboring yurts contain households headed by Tagan's paternal uncles and his eldest brother. Although his nomadic existence may seem harsh and difficult to outsiders, to Tagan it is the most desirable of all possible ways of life. Like his father and grandfather before him, Tagan views the mobility of the nomadic way of life as a guarantee of independence. Tagan and his relatives do not bow to any outside authority; if a neighboring state or tribe becomes too demanding or intrusive, the nomads can simply pack up their tents and move to a more congenial area. Along with this freedom from state authority goes a notable absence of inequality and coercion within Turkmen society. While custom requires Turkmen to respect their elders, there are no hereditary leaders who can force other Turkmen to do their bidding. Leaders are chosen by consensus and can only lead with the agreement of the community.[8]

Because tending livestock is considered a more prestigious occupation than cultivating crops, Turkmen typically settle on the land only if forced to do so by economic misfortune, such as the loss of their flocks to disease. For similar reasons, settled farmers who become wealthy often choose to become migratory pastoralists once again. Because nomadism is so highly valued, even Turkmen farmers lead a semi-nomadic life, living in yurts instead of in permanent structures and migrating occasionally with their herds. As one nineteenth-century observer wrote, "Strictly speaking, even the settled ones don't live all the time in the same place."[9]

Tagan is glad that his family, which belongs to the Yomut tribe, is exclusively nomadic and able to live on its large herds of sheep, goats, and camels. Like other Turkmen nomads, Tagan looks down on peasants as weak and easily victimized. In fact, Turkmen themselves are notorious for victimizing settled villages; some tribes make a practice of kidnapping Persian villagers in areas bordering on Turkmenistan and selling them in the slave markets of Khiva and Bukhara.[10] Like all the young men of his tribe, Tagan can handle himself well on horseback and is an excellent marksman. Such martial qualities are essential in the desert, where each group must be able to protect itself from enemies and would-be plunderers. Tagan's lineage, though not engaged in the slave trade, frequently skirmishes with the Kazakh nomads to the north, who have competed with the Yomuts for centuries over pastureland. Recently, Tagan went on his first *alaman,* or raid, in which a group of Yomut horsemen made off with a large flock of sheep belonging to a group of Kazakhs that had intruded on the Yomuts' territory. For Tagan and his kinsmen, this was not theft but a perfectly legitimate way of defending their tribe's interests and honor.

Tagan takes pride in his ancestry and can recite his genealogy going back at least seven generations. Like most nomads, the Turkmen identify with their tribe or clan rather than with a specific place. Their society is organized according to descent in the male line, with all those who call themselves Turkmen tracing their ancestry back to a single individual, the mythical Turkic warrior Oguz- (Oghuz)-khan The population is divided into a number of large tribes—Tekes, Salïrs, Sarïks, Yomuts, Choudïrs, Göklengs, and Ersarïs—each of which is thought to descend from one of Oguz's sons or grandsons. These tribes, in turn, are divided into sections and subsections, each of which is also presumed to descend from a common ancestor.[11] Yomuts who meet fellow tribesmen in the desert immediately try to place each other by asking who their fathers, grandfathers, and great grandfathers were. The genealogical traditions of the Turkmen are passed down orally. A favorite pastime at weddings and other events bringing together large numbers of Turkmen is to listen to a *bakhshi*, a traditional performer of epic poetry and song, recount the exploits of the tribe's ancestors. Tagan is especially proud that his family claims pure Turkmen ancestry, known as *ig*. While Turkmen sometimes intermarry with slaves or the children of slaves (mostly Persians who had been captured in Turkmen raids), their descendents are forever considered to be of *gul* or slave ancestry and therefore inferior to the "pure" Turkmen.[12]

Kinship and genealogy are not just sources of pride to the Turkmen; they are also vital sources of economic and political solidarity. Members of a large extended family—a group claiming a single ancestor three to five generations in the past—are expected to support and help each other constantly. They jointly pay for weddings and other expensive celebrations. They are collectively responsible for the protection of guests to whom the group grants its hospitality. (Providing hospitality to travelers is a strict obligation in the desert.) And while livestock belongs to individual households, the kin group jointly owns rights to land and water resources.[13] Kin groups also provide protection for individuals in cases of political conflict or violence. If a member of the group is taken captive for ransom by an enemy tribe, his relatives are obligated to help pay the ransom. If a family's livestock is stolen by marauding enemies, the group joins together to replace it. Murders are avenged by means of the blood feud, which requires the victim's relatives through the male line— those who trace their common descent back seven generations or less— to avenge the crime by killing either the murderer or a member of his family.[14] In a society without police or courts, kinship mechanisms help to deter crime and to ensure a rough form of justice; without strong family support, however, an injured individual has no recourse.

Let us go into Tagan's family yurt in order to take a closer look at Turkmen domestic life. Several generations live together in this large round tent: the patriarch of the family, Tagan's father, and his wife, their grown unmarried children, and several of their married sons with their wives and children. The newest member of the family is Tagan's bride, Yazgul, whose name means "spring flower" in Turkmen. Yazgul, who is fifteen years old, sits in a corner of the yurt sewing quietly, with a scarf drawn up over her mouth. According to Turkmen custom, she is not allowed to speak or eat in the presence of her husband's senior relatives—his older brothers and their wives, and his parents. She holds the end of the scarf between her lips as a symbol of this prohibition. Unlike some Central Asian Muslim women, Turkmen women are not veiled, but once married they must follow certain rules of social avoidance designed to show respect for their older in-laws. Yazgul may speak freely to her husbands' younger relatives, both male and female, but she must not speak to her father-in-law and elder brothers-in-law. At first she must also remain silent in the presence of her mother-in-law and older sisters-in-law, but these women may invite her to drop the *yashmak* (meaning both the scarf and the avoidance practices) after she has given birth to several children. Meanwhile, Yazgul must use gestures or communicate through an intermediary (most often one of her husband's younger siblings) if she wants to say something to her senior in-laws.[15] The prohibitions on interaction with senior in-laws also apply to Tagan, who is not permitted to speak to Yazgul's parents. But since Yazgul's parents live far away, the rule does not affect Tagan's daily life to any significant degree.[16]

Yazgul and her husband belong to the same tribe and subtribe. (Turkmen are endogamous, meaning that they prefer to marry within their tribe and even within the extended family; marriages between first cousins are not uncommon.) Although the marriage was arranged by their parents while they were still children, they had never met before the wedding. They were married a year ago, but Yazgul has only recently returned to her husband's home after completing a period of enforced separation known as *gaitarma*. According to this peculiar Turkmen custom, a new bride spends only a few days with her husband after the wedding, then returns to her own parents' home for an extended period (the exact length of the separation varies by tribe). During this period, the new husband and wife are not allowed to see each other at all. While some determined young couples try to sneak out of their tents for a rendezvous, the young man risks a beating from his wife's relatives if he tries this. The reason for the practice of *gaitarma* is unclear. Some Turkmen say that it allows the young bride to finish putting together her trousseau of clothing and household goods, while others say that it is a way of ensuring that the groom's family pays the bride-wealth it owes to the bride's family. (Bride-wealth is the amount the groom's family must pay, usually in livestock and household goods, to obtain the right to marry the girl.) Some point out, with a twinkle in their eye, that mandatory separation increases desire and affection between the spouses.[17]

The qualities that make a young woman sought after as a wife include not just beauty and a virtuous character (the ideal wife is submissive to the authority of her husband and parents), but also talent as a homemaker. For this reason, a young widow with housekeeping experience commands a larger amount of bride-wealth than a virgin bride. Yazgul is very busy in her new home, since it is the young daughters-in-law who keep the household running. They do almost all of the household work—setting up and taking down the yurt, cooking, cleaning, making the family's clothes, milking the animals, and bearing and caring for the children. Their mother-in-law supervises the work. In what little spare time remains after completing all these tasks, Yazgul helps the other women to weave the beautiful, hand-dyed wool carpets for which Turkmen nomads are famous. The Yomut women spin the wool from their own sheep and produce the dyes for the carpets from natural pigments found in their environment. These carpets are ideally suited to serve as the nomads' primary household furnishings and decorations, since they are lightweight and can easily be carried from place to place. A source of beauty and color in a harsh desert environment, they can also be sold in the urban markets of Central Asia to earn cash income for the family.[18]

As Yazgul becomes older and has children of her own, her life will improve. Giving birth to sons will dramatically increase her status. In Turkmen society, the well-being of each family and lineage depends on having a large number of healthy young men. A son belongs to his birth family for life; he helps tend the livestock, brings wives and future children into the family, cares for his parents in their old age, and protects his family in conflicts with outsiders. A daughter, by contrast, is a "guest" who moves away and is no longer considered a member of her birth family and lineage when she marries. Her children belong to her husband's lineage.[19] For these reasons, the birth of a son is greeted with ecstatic and noisy celebration, while the birth of a daughter is a more subdued occasion. A family with several daughters might even express its dissatisfaction by naming one of the girls *Ogulgerek*, which means "we need a boy." If Yazgul has a number of sons and presides over a large and growing family, she will eventually become a proud and respected matriarch who enjoys far more freedom and authority than she does now as a young bride.

Nomadic groups like Tagan's and Yazgul's no longer migrate through the desert regions of Turkmenistan. In the Soviet era that began in 1917, the remaining Turkmen nomads were forced to settle; many were forced to join collective farms during the Soviet collectivization campaign of the

1930s. In a particularly ill-conceived policy, Turkmen living in desert regions unsuited for agriculture were required to give up their nomadic way of life and become cotton farmers. The result for many was impoverishment and starvation. There was strong resistance to Soviet state coercion in the nomadic regions of Turkmenistan, and thousands of nomads fled with their families and flocks across the southern Soviet border into Afghanistan and Iran in the 1920s and 1930s.

For those who stayed in Soviet Turkmenistan, the twentieth century brought huge changes. The former nomads learned to live in permanent structures and to send their children to Soviet schools; many of them joined the Communist Party and served in the Red Army. For women, the changes were particularly dramatic. Unlike their mothers and grandmothers, young Turkmen women under Soviet rule could pursue higher education and careers as teachers, doctors, and government officials. They were encouraged to join the Communist Party and participate in public life. Even women who lived in remote villages attended years of school and had literacy rates vastly higher than in the pre-Soviet era. At the same time, Soviet authorities sought to ban customs and traditions that they deemed "backward," such as polygyny, the exchange of bride-wealth, and the blood feud. Yet Turkmen villagers continued to follow many of the customs that began under nomadic conditions of life, particularly those that had to do with marriage and the family. To this day, young women still avoid speaking to their elder in-laws, young men pay bride-wealth when they marry, and brides return to their parents' home for a period of *gaitarma* after the wedding.[20]

NOTES

1. This description is partly based on an account by the Hungarian traveler and adventurer Arminius Vambery. See Vambery, *Sketches of Central Asia* (Philadelphia: J. B. Lippincott, 1868), 76–77; see also Charles Marvin, *Merv, the Queen of the World, and the Scourge of the Man-Stealing Turcomans* (London: W. H. Allen, 1881), 98–102.
2. Mehmet Saray, *The Turkmens in the Age of Imperialism* (Ankara: Turkish Historical Society Publishing House, 1989), 26–28, 30–31; see also William Irons, *The Yomut Turkmen: A Study of Social Organization among a Central Asian Turkic-Speaking Population* (Ann Arbor: University of Michigan, 1975), 25–26.
3. Yuri Bregel, "Nomadic and Sedentary Elements among the Turkmens," *Central Asiatic Journal* 25, no. 1–2 (1981): 5–37; Wolfgang König, *Die Achal-Teke: Zur Wirtschaft und Gesellschaft einer Turkmenengruppe im XIX Jahrhundert* (Berlin: Akademieverlag, 1962), 41–43. See also "Turkmeny iomudskogo plemeni," *Voennyi Sbornik* no. 1 (January 1872): 65–66; K. Bode, "O turkmenskikh pokoleniakh iamudakh i goklanakh," *Zapiski russkogo geofraficheskogo obschestva*, kn. 2 (1847), 218–220.
4. "Turkmeny iomudskogo plemeni": 65–66; K. Bode, "O turkmenskikh pokoleniiakh," 218–220; Saray, *The Turkmens*, 23–24, 26; Irons, *The Yomut Turkmen*, 21–27; on the transition to sedentary agriculture among the Ahal-Tekes, see König, *Die Achal-Teke*, 30–43.

5. Karpov, *Ocherki po istorii Turkmenii*, 14–15; Irons, *The Yomut Turkmen*, 5–7.

6. See Saray, *The Turkmens*, especially chapter 4; Irons, *The Yomut Turkmen*, 7; A. Kuropatkin, *Turkmeniia i Turkmeny*, (St. Petersburg: n.p., 1879); 31.

7. For examples of such accounts by Europeans, see the Vambery and Marvin books cited above, as well as *The Country of the Turcomans: An Anthology of Exploration from the Royal Geographic Society* (London: Oguz Press and the Royal Geographical Society, 1977); Kuropatkin, *Turkmeniia i Turkmeny*; Edmund O'Donovan, *The Merv Oasis: Travels and Adventures East of the Caspian During the Years 1879–80–81* (London: Smith, Elder, and Co., 1882).

8. Y. E. Bregel, *Khorezmskie turkmeny v XIX veke* (Moscow: Izdatel'stvo vostochnoi literatury, 1961), 122–44.

9. Irons, *The Yomut Turkmen*, 26–27, 69–71; Bregel, "Nomadic and Sedentary Elements," 36–37; "Turkmeny iomudskogo plemeni," 65–66; Kuropatkin, *Turkmeniia i Turkmeny*, 34.

10. For an account of Turkmen slave-raiding, see Vambery, *Sketches of Central Asia*, 209–229.

11. A. M. Khazanov, *Nomads and the Outside World* (Cambridge: Cambridge University Press, 1984), 138–139; Irons, *The Yomut Turkmen*, 40–44; König, *Die Achal-Teke*, 81. On the origins and early history of groups calling themselves Turkmen, see Peter Golden, *An Introduction to the History of the Turkic Peoples: Ethnogenesis and State-Formation in Medieval and Early Modern Eurasia and the Middle East* (Wiesbaden: Otto Harrassowitz, 1992), 207–219, 221–225, 307.

12. On *ig* and *gul*, see Bode, "O turkmenskikh pokoleniiakh," 224; A. Lomakin, *Obychnoe pravo Turkmen* (Ashgabat: n.p., 1897), 33–34; König, *Die Achal-Teke*, 79.

13. König, *Die Achal-Teke*, 72–73, 80–81; M. A. Nemchenko, *Dinamika turkmenskogo krest'ianskogo khoziaistva* (Ashgabat: Turkmengosizdat, 1926), 5; Irons, *The Yomut Turkmen*, 47–48.

14. Lomakin, *Obychnoe pravo Turkmen*, 52; Irons, *The Yomut Turkmen*, 61, 114.

15. P. S. Vasiliev, *Akhal-tekinskii oazis. Ego proshloe i nastoiashchee* (St. Petersburg, 1888), 17; Irons, *The Yomut Turkmen*, 104–107; D. G. Yomudskaia-Burunova, *Zhenshchina v staroi Turkmenii: bytovoi ocherk* (Moscow/Tashkent, 1931), 30–33; Sharon Bastug and Nuran Hortacsu, "The Price of Value: Kinship, Marriage, and Meta-narratives of Gender in Turkmenistan," in Feride Acar and Ayse Gunes-Ayata, eds., *Gender and Identity Construction: Women of Central Asia, the Caucasus, and Turkey* (Leiden: Brill, 2000), 133–135.

16. Irons, *The Yomut Turkmen*, 109–111.

17. Irons, *The Yomut Turkmen*, 136–141. Yomudskaia-Burunova, *Zhenshchina v staroi Turkmenii*, 29; Carole Blackwell, *Tradition and Society in Turkmenistan: Gender, Oral Culture, and Song* (Richmond, Surrey: Curzon, 2001), 76–77.

18. B. Belova, "Zhenotdely v Turkmenii," *Turkmenovedenie*, no. 12 (December 1928): 36; Blackwell, *Tradition and Society in Turkmenistan*, 44–49.

19. Bastug and Hortacsu, "The Price of Value," 118–121; Irons, *The Yomut Turkmen*, 163–164.

20. On marriage and family customs in contemporary Turkmenistan, see Bastug and Hortacsu, "The Price of Value," 128; Blackwell, *Tradition and Society in Turkmenistan*, chapters 5 and 6.

3. Recollections of a Hazara Wedding in the 1930s

Robert L. Canfield

From late fall 1966 to summer 1968 I was doing field work in the Bamian valley and its environs in Afghanistan.[1] As part of that research I collected a number of statements by people in the region that provide clues to the nature of social life and affairs in previous decades as well as during the period of field work.

Of course statements like these have a number of problems: people have evident limitations in their knowledge; they indeed convey misinformation, often unintentionally, because they are biased by their vantage points and interests and, with respect to their recollections of the past, they are selective in memory. Just as people create a sense of place and significance in their stories about present situations, they create a sense of the past through their own accounts of it, and in any case the telling itself is typically influenced by issues vital to the narrators at the time of telling. Narratives create reality as much as they reflect it. So we cannot take what people tell us at face value, as if it were a precisely accurate representation of the situations described.

But what people say about their past experience does reveal useful information about them and their social worlds. Their narratives give cognitive and emotional coherence to people's experience, enabling them to identify with a past and to define and negotiate their current experience. They enable people to conceive of what to expect and what to take as the operating conditions of their experience. They contain "schemas" that typify situations, display prototypes of events and roles, showing ideal forms of behavior and their consequences. They thus reveal the beliefs, attitudes, ideologies, visions, and dreams that inform people's imaginative worlds. Stories illuminate what is "real" and important to people. As idealized portrayals of lived experience they reveal the status quo, the grounds of authority that are taken for granted—and so invest the experiential landscape with moral significance. Oral statements can thus be useful historical texts even if they are not to be taken at face value.[2]

BAMIAN IN THE EARLY 1930S

I here recount a statement about an event that took place in eastern Bamian in what I presume to be the early 1930s. Actually what we know about the region at that time is rather feeble. We know that well into the nineteenth century the Hazaras had been highly stratified, dominated by powerful chiefs known as *mirs* who were supported by cadres of close kinsmen and dependents. But as a result of a widespread rebellion against the Amir of Kabul in 1891–1893, Hazara society was thoroughly crushed. Their leaders—not only the mirs but also virtually all other notable figures— were either executed or imprisoned, and hundreds, possibly thousands, of ordinary people were carried off into slavery.[3] The structure of social affairs in the Hazarajat in subsequent decades is relatively poorly known.

This is one reason that a statement about affairs in the 1930s is of interest; it gives us a glimpse into what was going on in the Hazarajat in the 1930s, a glimpse from which we may make some surmises about the structure of social relations in that period. We presume that the Kabul regime was gaining administrative strength in its provinces (*wulāyats*, governorships) throughout this period. Governors were receiving better military support and larger administrative staffs, and they stayed in the area for longer periods even if they circulated back to the capital periodically. Government controlled courts were being established. In fact, provinces were getting smaller; the country was being carved up into smaller and smaller provincial administrative units. The four great provinces of the country that had been maintained in the previous century—Kabul (which included Bamian), Kandahar, Herat, and Mazar-i Sharif—were in the twentieth century divided and subdivided. There were seventeen provinces in the 1950s (based on a map produced in the 1950s in my possession) and as many as twenty-eight in the 1960s. This was taking place as the country was being more effectively brought under the direct control of the state. More governmental institutions became accessible to local populations. More government officials came to know the local goings-on in the provinces (Canfield 1971). Despite a general preference among the local populations for resolving disputes through the mediation and adjudication of their own notables, more disputes were being brought to state officials for resolution.

According to local sources, early in the twentieth century government institutions were fairly limited. In the nineteenth century a governor had been established in the markaz of Bamian supported by a few gendarmes.

Presumably his main role was to ensure the peace, but he would surely have been commissioned to keep abreast of affairs in the region and to enforce government policy. He exerted much of his influence through the representatives of the local populations, locally called mirs (or by the state *maliks*), who were required to collect taxes for the government, conscript troops, and levy workers for government projects as needed. Such was the status of the mirship by this time; the great mirs of the previous century were long gone, and the local representatives were now, in the early part of the twentieth century, as much agents of the state as they were of the local citizenry they were supposed to represent. They held their office essentially by the sufferance of the provincial governor, who was gradually able to enforce state policies with greater effectiveness. By the 1930s the state loomed in local affairs. Thus, local mechanisms of social control—whatever they were—were giving way to the advancing presence of government.

But what were those local mechanisms? How were the various populations of the rural areas managing their local affairs? This is the value of the oral statements I collected in the 1960s, as they describe events and situations that took place in the speakers' own experience or were described to them by parents or grandparents. Such statements provide clues as to how the society was structured and social affairs managed.

A WEDDING STORY

A statement about an event that took place in eastern Bamian in the 1930s gives us some clues. The statement was made by a local notable in Shibar, Mir Gholam Hasan, from the Darghān (Darghū, in local speech) clan of Hazaras, about problems he had in obtaining a wife from Sheikh Ali, a region northeast of Shibar.[4] The narrative was part of a much longer rehearsal of his life. The event he described took place when he was a young man. As he was in his 60s when I knew him, I surmise that it occurred in about the time of Nadir Shah (1929–1933).

When I knew him Mir Gholam Hasan was the mir for the Ismailis in Shibar. He could read and write and also had some land and a brother living next door who was also fairly well off. That is, he had some skills for dealing with the government and a bit of leverage in his community. In fact, this was not enough to hold onto his position, as within a few years a rival would bring him down and take his place. His duties brought him into contact with government officials at the *alaqadārī* (a subgovernorship) in Shibar near his home and at the governor's offices situated at the markaz of Bamian. Because he had served as mir for some time, he was fairly well known in the wider community. He personally knew the *pir*, the sacred leader, of the Ismailis, Sayyed-i Kayan, and the pir's several sons as well as most other mirs and *arbābs* of the province. In his long life he had had sev-

eral wives, four of whom had died, but he had no male issue. Two daughters had been born to one of his wives some years earlier and they had
grown up, married, and now had children of their own. When I knew Mir
Gholam Hasan he had two wives, one about thirty years old and the other
about twenty. The younger one had in fact been selected with the help of
the older wife, as she had borne him only one child, a daughter who was
still small. The younger woman, it was hoped, would bear him a son. But
as it turned out she had tuberculosis and would pass away in 1968. The
story that follows (minimally polished) is about how he obtained one of
his earlier wives, actually the mother of the two married daughters; it was
intended to show that families did not like to give up their daughters to
suitors from far away.

Before I got this wife there was a man named Gholam Reza from
Sheikh Ali who was her father [of the girl], but he died. A man named
Mirza Osayn married the widow, who already had four daughters by
Gholam Reza. This Mirza Osayn said to me that he would give one of
them to me, but he said, "Give me 1,000 *afghanis* [Afghan unit of cur-
rency]." He promised his first daughter, whom I had already seen. When
I brought the 1,000 afghanis, I asked for her according to our agreement,
but he didn't agree to give her right then . . . Then twenty days later, when
I went again to ask about the marriage, the man asked for 10,000 afghanis
for the bride-price. So in ten or twelve days I obtained the money, and took
it to him. Then the man made a promise that on a certain day I and my
people should come. "Send your gifts and we will have the marriage."
The gifts and food were to be sent a few days in advance of the wedding feast. So I put 10 ser[5] of flour on a donkey, and 10 ser of rice on another donkey, along with two ser of *rowghān* [clarified butter] and 5 sheep
and 40 meters of cloth and sent them to him. Then we went a few days
later to the agreed-upon marriage feast. The distance was great, so I didn't
take a lot of men, only forty. Along the way Mirza Osayn came with all
the mirs of Sheikh Ali on horses. We were on horses too, and they came to
a place and stopped us on the road. Then Mirza Osayn asked us, "Where
are you going?" And he said, "Go back to your house, there will be no
marriage now." Then I said, "I can't go back now, I have brought my *qawm*
[clan, lineage] and my people. If I go back now, I will be embarrassed." I
had with me Mir Awdur and Sayyed Tabar, and they took the biggest man
of Sheikh Ali aside and sat with him—this man was Firqa Isā Khān. Then
they offered him a turban and a cloak [*chapan*] to persuade Mirza Osayn
to go on with the marriage. Then this man went with them to the house of
Mirza Osayn and all went there with them. This was the month of Ramazan [the month of fast], and on the way these men with me had not eaten at
all. When we got there Mirza Osayn told us that there was no food there; it
had all been eaten. Then I bought two sheep from someone else in Sheikh
Ali, and I bought roghān and rice and flour, etc., and then we took this to
him but he still didn't give this to our people. They were left hungry all

night. Then Mirza Osayn brought a mulla, Mulla Faqir, to do the *nekā* [wedding ceremony] and he sealed the marriage. During the night Mirza Osayn fed ten of the elders from his own community [*deh:* village, hamlet] in two separate rooms, but the others of us were left hungry. That night we gave this rich man the turban and chapan and to three other elders we gave three turbans. Then at two in the morning he told me and our people that we must leave now. And he said, "If the people of Sheikh Ali know that you take the girl you will not be able to have her"—that is, we should take her secretly. So we took her that night, and went home. Our men had been away for two days and nights without eating any food. They arrived about two or three in the afternoon.

The next day early in the morning the people of Sheikh Ali came to Mirza Osayn, maybe a hundred men, and said they would not allow him to give this girl to the people of Darghān [Mir Gholam Hasan's clan]. When he told them that the girl had already been taken away they were much distressed, but they went away to their own homes. At my house I held a big party for two or three nights, had musicians and lots of food, and a hundred fifty or two hundred people came. . . .

The idea of these people was that a woman should not go out of their valley. They were angry at me because I wanted to take away that girl. They said, "Are there no men in Sheikh Ali that we should give the girl to him? We are people of Sheikh Ali and he is from the people of Darghān. She should stay here among us, she should not go out. We have plenty of men for our women." . . . They thought, "It is not good that our qawm should not build a household while another qawm does so with one of our women."

The only point of Mirza Osayn was that he should take the money and lie his way out of it. He is now in Kabul. . . .

After four or five years these two daughters were born [to this wife]. The she died. One year after her death, this Mirza Osayn came and said he thought I had killed her. He said, "If I had had time I would have taken blood from you because of this."

This Mirza Gholam Hosayn . . . caused a lot of trouble for his own people in Sheikh Ali. He went to the alaqadār and claimed that someone had stolen this or that, then took money from this man [the one he had accused] to leave him alone. He did this several times, and then finally the people of Sheikh Ali complained that "this man has given us enough trouble." He was put in jail. He was there in Charikar for one year. Then somehow he got out, although he was supposed to come to Kabul for two more years. Now he is secretly living in Kabul, and has paid a man to try to spring him out of his jail sentence.

COMMENTARY

Some clues as to the social conventions of the time can be gleaned from this narrative, although it also leaves us with a number of questions. For one thing, there is no evidence of a formal adoption procedure. It was presumed that Mirza Osayn had the right to give the daughters of his new wife in marriage however he wished. There is nothing notable here—but this fact accrues more significance as we reflect on the following issues.

First, the prices in this story are difficult to compare with prices at other times because the value of the afghani varied. The price Mir Gholam Hasan paid may have been somewhat larger than what was being paid later. In about 1948 a relatively wealthy Hazara man paid 3 bulls, 3 large copper cooking pots, 1 muzzle loading rifle, and 3000 afghanis in silver coin. In the 1960s a bride among the Tajiks at the Bamian markaz (where things were more expensive than Shibar or Sheikh Ali) went for 10,000 cash, plus 1,000 pounds of rice, 150 pounds of roghān, 8 lambs or kids, 10 donkey-loads of wood, 4 loads of brush fuel, 150 pounds of wheat, 8 pounds of kerosene, 30 pounds of salt, 4 pounds of tea, 35 pounds of sugar, 150 pounds of potatoes, 30 pounds of onions, the non-cash goods being valued at 3,000 afghanis in all (Canfield 1973: 125). This may have been an unusually high price; obviously the reputation of the girl and her family has much to do with the price.

Moreover, cash was not easy to come by in this economy, and the amount of it involved here seems substantial. By the 1960s cash was in broad use in the markaz of Bamian and along the roads where there was considerable traffic, but in the villages of Shibar people didn't have much cash. The amounts of money demanded for this transaction in the 1930s seem much higher (in real terms) than were required in the 1960s. Most curious to me is how quickly the mir obtained so much of it. This was a lot of money. He would have had to borrow at least some of it, perhaps most of it, and from several sources. He might have obtained some by selling some sheep or goats but he would not have sold land, which normally changes hands only *in extremis*.

We might also note that it was not uncommon for the family of the bride to prolong the solicitation process, so Mir Gholam Hasan no doubt expected to have to come up with more money. There is no hint here that he objected to the price. Suitors often had to make several contacts with the family before the final deal could be struck.

It is notable that Mir Gholam Hasan considered a group of forty men from his community a small number at the time. In the 1960s that number would have been substantial. The same holds true for the number of horses. Forty from Shibar, a hundred from Sheikh Ali—in the 1960s nothing like so many horses were in evidence. In place of the horse, of course, had come the automobile. Indeed, the few families who had been able to afford a truck were the only ones that seemed to be doing better in Shibar. Most people's fortunes were declining. In the two-year period I was in Bamian a few people I knew in Shibar rented out their land and moved to the city for work. The decline in the number of horses was merely one indicator of the economic decline of the area.

Another piece of evidence rests on the reality that food constituted a critical kind of currency sealing the bonds among these people. In this society, where storage of food could be a problem, raw food would have been especially appreciated, as it could be disposed of in different ways: given as gifts to pay off debts or cooked for guests.[6] Twice Mir Gholam Hasan provided raw food, and both times it was given to other guests while he and his wedding party remained hungry. In this community, where there must have been few public sources of sustenance, there would have been no other source of food than that provided by one's hosts. That nothing was given was an outrage. Such behavior would have seriously damaged anyone's reputation. In a society where food is perishable and protection requires loyal friends, a reputation for trustworthiness, reliability, and consistency was a kind of currency, the basis for obtaining help and credit when needed. Such qualities were prominently displayed in the way one treated guests.[7] Hospitality was the supreme demonstration of character. A person with a reputation for niggardliness, conniving, or exploiting of friends and neighbors was vulnerable, because fortunes could turn abruptly. The behavior of Mirza Osayn was scandalous.

In the same vein, the feast that never took place was presumably supposed to be a public means of sealing the marriage—not only between husband and wife but also between two communities. But the elders of Sheikh Ali were balking. We are not told what was going on at the feast for the Sheikh Ali elders, but presumably it was given to accomplish something of interest to Mirza Osayn. Was this supposed to be a pay-off for help and loans already given? It seems evident that one reason for the feast was so that Mirza Osayn could persuade them to accept the marriage.

The intensity of the opposition to the marriage, revealed as the point the speaker made of the story, opens a further question. The narrator intended to show how resistant a community can be to the marriage of their girls to someone outside. The stated reason was Mir Gholam Hasan's clan identity as a Darghān Hazara. Was there or had there been animosity between the people of Darghān and Sheikh Ali? Was this the only reason? We do not know if there was anything about Mir Gholam Hasan himself that detracted from his candidacy.

There were several clues as to the way public affairs were being managed. First, the notables of the two communities were managing affairs, and they did this by giving favors to each other. The elders of Shibar took aside the "biggest" man in Sheikh Ali and persuaded him and two other men, by means of gifts, to help move the wedding proceedings along. Turbans and chapans, nice ones, were valued and accepted as substantial gifts.

The number of people involved on either side of this transaction—for the marriage was of course a social transaction—marked the importance of the wedding. Here we see more suggestive possibilities. Forty men from Shibar, a hundred from Sheikh Ali—a feast of the elders of these two communities, along with the mulla's nekā—this would have legitimated the marriage. But government officials are conspicuous by their absence. As large a gathering as this was, it included no official. Presumably none had been invited. In fact, we might presume that no alaqadār had been posted in Shibar yet, in which case there would have been no official to invite. I have been told that when the alaqadār first arrived he had no place to live; he rented a room in Bulola until facilities were built for him and his gendarmes. That the alaqadār was later used by Mirza Osayn to exploit his neighbors and that his neighbors complained to the government about him suggests that officials were soon to appear in the region and that state institutions were gaining a larger influence on local affairs.

And then, the "biggest man in Sheikh Ali" was Firqa Isā Khān—a reference to the officer's rank, Firqa Misr (roughly equivalent to a captain). But Hazaras did not normally hold officer's ranks in the army. Could the term have been mere respectful hyperbole for someone who had achieved a non-commissioned rank? Or had he in fact been an officer in the army? His eminence in the community would have come in part from wealth: could his wealth have brought him status in the military? Or did it work the other way around? In any case, he was home, and no longer in military service. And he was influential.

Whatever the mechanisms of social control, by appearances Mirza Osayn was in trouble. In fact, as in many such cases, the way he exploits the situation, that is, the liberties he takes with the conventions of courtesy, reveals something about how the society was constituted; we often learn about how things should be when they are violated. Mirza Osayn's attempts to exploit his guests and his neighbors through the giving of cooked food reveals that in this society this was one way to keep neighbors and kinsmen under control. Eventually, as the narrator tells us, Mirza Osayn pays a price for what was obvious manipulation and exploitation of the people around him. The first batch of raw food sent to him disappeared—according to him, eaten. Perhaps he doesn't dare reveal what he did with it. What were the circumstances? Was he already in debt and obliged to use the food to pay off? His marriage to the widow of Gholam Reza would have been less costly than to a virgin. Perhaps his choice of this wife was a means of gain, as the daughters could be married out for a good bride-price.

The second batch of food, given to him raw, was served to his own neighbors, the elders in his own qawm. Why to them and not his wedding guests? Apparently the feast was an attempt to win their consent for the marriage. Obviously he wanted the bride-price money, but the community was opposed to the transaction. His insistence on pushing the transaction through in any case was revealed in his suggestion to the mir that the girl must be taken by stealth. Mirza Osayn had failed to win the consent of his community. This is evident, if not by his suggestion, by the arrival of the elders the next morning; a lot of them came to stop the transaction. It looks like he deceived them, agreeing to their demands during the evening feast but allowing the men from Shibar to take her secretly in the night. Mirza Osayn is portrayed here as manipulative and contentious in other contexts. After this affair he made accusations against his neighbors in order to extort money. Eventually the community, the elders, would in disgust bring charges against him, an extreme measure. The main moral message here is that Mirza Osayn was irresponsible, but there is another subtext, that the people of Sheikh Ali were conservative, even backward. In fact, Mir Gholam Hasan may have elided over a historic tension between his clan and Mirza Osayn's.[8]

The absence of any reference to the women may not be surprising—after all, this is a man's story—but like the dog that didn't bark, the absence of the role of women in it is a powerful statement nonetheless.[9] In fact, of course, the women were not marginal to these affairs. They would have prepared the food that was served. And of course the girl was the prize. In this polygynous society, where several women could be matched to one man, marriageable girls were always in short supply. The story reveals the limitations on the rights of the women. Their life and their world were confined to the household. In whatever sense the women exerted influence, it was limited to the household sphere. And control of the women by the men was considered only natural.[10]

The limited power of women was implied in Mirza Osayn's accusation of murder. That Mir Gholam Hasan's new wife had died was apparent, but no one could know for sure precisely what caused her death, as social life took place within the walls of the household (the *awlī*). The women's world was inside the awlī; no one outside the family could know for sure all that took place there. No one could be sure in the case of her death that she was not killed, so there was room for suspicion. That she died could be taken as a sign of abuse. And it could be used against the male of the household.

In fact, in this society rumors abound, and the rumor that the mir's wife had been killed was in the air. I was told more than once that Mir Gholam Hasan had killed several wives. I asked one person how he knew this: "They are all dead, aren't they?" he said. No one outside the household could know for sure the cause of the woman's death. Purdah, the seclusion of women, provided privileged seclusion as well for men. As the men of the family—a father or older brother in a woman's natal household or a husband or husband's brother in her married household—had responsibility for household affairs, the practice of seclusion provided opportunities for them to do things that were quite inaccessible to outsiders and invited insinuation. In a society in which gossip was powerful because reputation, a "name," was the main ground on which one developed alliances, acquired credit, and obtained help, Mirza Osayn's accusation was a serious threat.

Two nuances can be derived from the accusation of murder. From one point of view women's rights were assumed to be in the hands of the men—fathers, brothers, husbands. From another viewpoint it was morally wrong for a man to kill his wife, even if the act could not be discovered. The uncertainty entailed in the seclusion of women—a broadly accepted social practice—allowed the insinuation of murder—a broadly proscribed social action—to be used as a device for character assassination. No one will ever know whether any of Mir Gholam Hasan's wives was murdered, and that ambiguity allowed gossip to besmirch his reputation. But it is worth noting that by the 1960s state institutions were being used by women as well as men, perhaps in greater numbers than before. I came to know of several suits by women against the men of their household, most of them over rights to land. The status of women was no doubt changing.

REFLECTIONS ON THE CONCEPTUAL SIGNIFICANCE
OF THIS TEXT

Such are the images that can be conjured on the basis of this text. But Mir Gholam Hasan's tale raises some conceptual issues for the comparative study of the human condition. My colleague John W. Bennett has often remarked that what is enduring of ethnographic writing is the details, not the theory that is proposed to inform it. This is because theory is subject to fads, and each particular fad of the time fades—whereas ethnographic descriptions often have elements that continue to hold interest. True, the professional social scientist does gravitate to the ideas in an article or book; we only glance over the details in order to get to the point and the conceptual issues it is supposed to reveal. But the non-professional, easily bored with the abstract, responds to narratives. What most people respond to is the human interest. Pierre Bourdieu has noted that the theoretical formulations of some social scientists can be likened to a map, "an analogy that occurs to an outsider who has to find his way around a foreign landscape," whereas for an insider—a native of the terrain—a place, a custom, a social practice, is discovered experientially, sequentially; one comes to know one's own terrain through "practical space of journeys actually made" (1977:2). It's the difference between learning how to live in a society through direct encounters with people and places rather than learning a set of rules that govern behavior. Bled out of our theoretical formulations, says Bourdieu, is the uncertainty entailed in human affairs. What animated Mir Gholam Hasan about this affair was the outrage, the offense of people who failed to follow ordinary courtesies. He thought he had paid the price for a bride, but it turned out his payment disappeared and he had to pay again. Even then he had to carry off the girl in the dead of night in order to have her. In this affair there were surprises at many points: a band of horsemen on the road to block his way, a prospective father-in-law reluctant to hand over the girl that had been paid for, an evening in an inhospitable community, extra costs for the food that wasn't served, and the near failure to obtain the bride who was the object of the whole expedition. A social world devoid of those surprises, of the ambiguities and uncertainties entailed in the course of affairs, as Radcliffe-Brown or Levi-Strauss would have it, might have seemed systematic and orderly but would have lacked the critical elements of his experience. No wonder the non-professional considers "theory" boring.

Mir Gholam Hasan's tale of interruptions, extortions, misrepresentations, threats, and demeaning behavior reveals another dimension of human experience that is poorly captured in social theory: namely, that the human imagination is animated by struggles over what is right or wrong, what ought to be and isn't. It is through the recounting of an experience that one grasps its moral import. The moral assumptions that go without saying are internalized through such recounting (White 1992; Brison 1992). This, in the end, is the broader or deeper significance of Mir Gholam Hasan's account of his attempt to get a wife; it was a story about a world that human beings long for and yet never quite discover. What he learned—about what not to expect, what not to do the next time—is implied in this account. Unfortunately, we do not know how it affected his next attempt to get a wife, nor how his richer understanding was rewarded.

The more we know about the ambiguities and contradictions, the disappointments, deceptions, and uncertainties of people like Mir Gholam Hasan, the more reason there is to disavow the common supposition that the lives of people in other societies are simpler, more predictable. It is not that old certainties are now disappearing in the modern world, leaving our societies with multiple solutions, multiple attempts to characterize the human condition, but that there never are and never were many certainties in practice. Uncertainty has always been the human condition. It is only from a distance, as we look with nostalgia on other peoples and societies, that we can regard their life as ordered, regular, and systematic. In fact, the better we understand the words of other peoples, the more clearly we understand that their life is anything but. What we discover in the lives of human beings—in other societies, in other times, as well as our own—is conflict and ambiguity, anxiety, frustration, disappointment. And that draws us back to our starting point, the quest to understand through narrative.

NOTES

1. Bamian town, locally known as "markaz," the center, is the provincial capital of Bamian province. The affair described here took place in the eastern extremity of the province, Shibar.

2. Oral History Research Office©, Columbia University Libraries 5/09/01 "Philosophy behind the Collection," (http://www.columbia.edu/cu/lweb/indiv/oral/philosophy.html). For a fuller discussion of these issues as well an extensive list of sources, see Brison (1992).

3. Kakar 1971:159 ff.; Mousavi 1998:120 ff.

4. Writings on marriage practices in Afghanistan are considerable. Most ethnographic reports on this region have something to say about marriage practices and weddings. Tapper (1991) has an extensive discussion of marriage as a custom and practice, mainly among Afghan Pushtun. Grima (1992) provides a rich sense of the women's attitudes and experience among Pakistani tribal Pushtun. Emadi's critique of the treatment of women in Afghanistan (2002) is a recent discussion of marriage practices. See also Centlivres-Demont 1981; Shalinsky 1989.

5. A *ser* is 16 *paw*, which technically is 15 pounds, a *paw* being slightly lighter than a pound.

6. This is a familiar topic in anthropological literature. The most famous work on the subject was Mauss (1954) but many others have commented on the importance of food in solidifying social relations: Bourdieu (1977); Firth (1929); Levi-Strauss (1990).

7. Edwards (1996:67 ff.) discusses hospitality as a Pushtun custom, but it is no less mandatory among the Hazaras.

8. See my article on Birgilich for a suggestion that there may have long been tension between these two clans on the basis of the importance of a Sayyed family situated at the frontier between their respective territories.

9. See Canfield (2004).

10. This control extended to brothers as well as fathers and husbands. In *Behind the Burqa* Salima, a progressive Afghan woman, says (according to Yasgur, 2002:55–56), "It was not uncommon for a brother to kill a sister if he believed she was being rebellious, promiscuous, or disobedient. It was considered an honor killing." After their father died, her brother refused to allow her to attend medical school. "Why would you do this to me?" she asks. His answer: "Because I can."

REFERENCES

Bourdieu, Pierre. 1977 [1972]. *Outline of a Theory of Practice.* Cambridge: Cambridge University.
Brison, Karen J. 1992. *Just Talk: Gossip, Meetings, and Power in a Papua New Guinea Village.* Berkeley: University of California.
Canfield, Robert L. 1971. *Hazara Integration in the Afghan Nation.* Occasional Paper Number 3. New York: The Afghanistan Committee of the Asia Society.
———. 1973. *Faction and Conversion in a Plural Society: Religious Alignments in the Hindu Kush.* Anthropological Paper Number 50. Ann Arbor: Museum of Anthropology, University of Michigan.
———. 2004. Review article: *Searching for Saleem* by Farooka Gauhari, *Zoya's Story* by Zoya, *Veiled Courage* by Cheryl Benard, and *The Sewing Circles of Heart* by Christina Lamb, with an Appendix on other works on women in Afghanistan. *Iranian Studies* 37(2): 323–333.
Centlivres-Demont, Micheline. 1981. Rites de mariage en Afghanistan: le dit and le vécu. In *Naître, vivre et mourir: actualité de Van Gennep.* Neuchâtel: Musée d'ethnogrphie. [on marriage rites].
Edwards, David. 1996. *Heroes of the Age: Moral Fault Lines on the Afghan Frontier.* Berkeley: University of California.

Emadi, Hafizullah. 2002. *Repression, Resistance, and Women in Afghanistan*. New York: Praeger.

Firth, Raymond W. 1929. *Primitive Economics of the New Zealand Maori*. London: Routledge.

Grima, Benedicte. 1992. *The Performance of Emotion among Paxtun Women: "The Misfortunes Which Have Befallen Me."* Karachi: Oxford University.

Kakar, M. Hasan. 1971. *Afghanistan: A Study of Internal Political Developments, 1880–1896*. Kabul: privately published.

Lévi-Strauss, Claude. 1990. *The Raw and the Cooked*. Translated from the French by John and Doreen Weightman. Chicago: University of Chicago.

Mauss, Marcel. 1954. *The Gift: Forms and Functions of Exchange in Archaic Societies*. Glencoe, Ill.: Free Press.

Mousavi, S. A. 1998. *The Hazaras of Afghanistan: An Historical, Cultural, Economic and Political Study*. Surrey, UK: Curzon.

Shalinsky, Audrey C. 1989. Talking about Marriage: Fate and Choice in the Social Discourse of Traditional Northern Afghanistan. *Anthropos* 84: 133–140.

Tapper, Nancy. 1991. *Bartered Brides: Politics, Gender and Marriage in an Afghan Tribal Society*. Cambridge, UK: Cambridge University.

White, Hayden. 1992. Historical Emplotment and the Problem of Truth. In Saul Friedländer, ed., *Probing the Limits of Representation: Nazism and the Final Solution*. Cambridge, Mass.: Harvard University.

Yasgur, Batya. 2002. *Behind the Burqa: Our Life in Afghanistan and How We Escaped to Freedom*. Hoboken, N.J.: John Wiley & Sons.

4. Trouble in Birgilich

Robert L. Canfield

Anthropologists today see "culture" as reproduced, constructed in social interaction. It is not so much received ready-made from the past as it is a fund of meaningful forms—words, images, gestures, monuments, etc.— that actors may deploy or invoke (or ignore) according to their interests in defining situations. "Reality" in this sense is constructed, piecemeal, as people engage socially (Barth 1993). In this interactive process people may even deliberately, consciously, construct a "reality" that no one believes in—what Fredrick G. Bailey calls a "collusive lie" (1991:34, 35). Collusive lies are the public conventions that groups agree to live with, for whatever reason, whether or not everyone agrees with them or is wholly committed to them. In such cases, individuals have particular reasons for joining in the collusion; collusive lies are merely negotiated agreements for practical purposes. Underneath the conventions that collectivities agree to comply with are individual understandings and private motives. This situation allows individuals to have agendas that are concealed in public interaction. In this article I examine an affair in which a contested issue is resolved by an agreement that no one believed in and in which, it turns out, some people had intentions that were concealed from the rest. Subterfuge infected the whole business.

A DISPUTE IN SHIBAR

The affair took place in the 1960s in east-central Afghanistan, well before the several wars that disrupted the region in subsequent years. This article can be regarded as a mere memoir of a society now long passed. I describe the affair in three parts: first, a few notes on the social context; then, a summary of the events as told to me; then, some interpretive comments on the story. I conclude by returning to the topic of how social realities are constructed, and in particular of how social affairs in the course of daily events are fraught with ambiguity and sometimes subterfuge.[1]

THE CONTEXT

The story was told to me in 1967 by Mir Gholam Hasan, a man who served as *mir* on behalf of several households in the region to the government. A mir was a representative of a group of communities to the local government. They were usually chosen by consent of both sides, but because the mir himself could read and had special access to officials and other notables, he had certain advantages over his client communities. Sometimes a mir could become so dominant that he could make excessive demands on his clients.

The critical event was a fight over bushes. In the Hazarajat the scattered clumps of thorn bushes growing in the mountains are vital fuel. In many communities one of the important tasks is to stockpile bushes for winter, when cold temperatures are severe and can last for weeks. Because some communities have less thorn bush in their neighboring highlands, men and boys may range far and wide in the search for bushes; at the same time the owners of well-stocked mountains can be protective of what they have.

The fight took place in the highlands above the valley of Birgilich, which lies just north of the road between Shibar and Bamian in east-central Afghanistan. In this valley and its environs Ismailis and "Twelver" (Ithnā Ashariya) Shi'a populations were interspersed, usually in separate communities. The fight occurred between a group of Ismailis from a tributary valley known as Jawzar and the Shi'a Sayyeds who presided over affairs in Birgilich.

The Ismailis complained of abuses by the Sayyeds, who in any case had substantial leverage over their Hazara neighbors because of their special status as a sacred lineage within the Shi'a community. Also, many of them studied Islamic subjects and, as religious specialists, led in collective prayers and preached and taught among the Shi'a; some of them, in response to popular demand, wrote charms that putatively protected from harm or healed from illness. Also, Sayyeds were thought by some of the common people to have the power to divine. (Once I met a man who was searching for a Sayyed who might divine for him whether his sick wife would live or die; if she was going to die anyway he didn't want to bother taking her all the way to town to see a doctor.) As a result of these special services Sayyeds enjoyed respect and often received gifts from the common people. Some Sayyeds were, in fact, venerated as *pirs*—that is, as having special powers because of their putative access to God. Also, most Sayyed families were well connected in the wider social world, as they often intermarried with other notable families. Such connections—laterally to other eminent figures and vertically to dependent populations—enabled the more powerful Sayyeds to acquire wealth as well as exert influence on public affairs.[2] A Birgilich Sayyed had for many years been the mir of the people of the valley, including the Ismaili communities of the tributary valley of

Jawzar. At the time of the fight that person was named Shah Osayn. As it would turn out, the whole matter was in a sense about him.[3]

MIR GHOLAM HASAN'S STORY

Three men from Jawzar went up into the mountains to collect bushes above Birgilich [whose vegetation was claimed by the Sayyeds]. These men had often gone into these hills to collect bushes surreptitiously at night, but in this instance they went up during the day, and they were caught up there by some of the leaders of the Sayyed community. There was a fight and the leader of the Jawzaris, Ali Jam, was seriously injured in the head.

The men from Jawzar went to the *alaqadārī* [the local government office] of Shibar, and complained against the Sayyeds of Birgilich, claiming that the Sayyeds had attacked them and seriously injured Ali Jam. The alaqadār sent the police out to look into the situation and examine Ali Jam's condition. When they returned they brought some of the Sayyeds back and imprisoned them at the alaqadārī.

The alaqadār in Shibar tried to settle the dispute, but without success. The wrangling went on for a year. We [the mirs of the region] did everything possible to settle this dispute. The several mirs representing other communities in Shibar also joined in the fracas until virtually all the mirs of the region were somehow involved in the negotiations.

One factor that made the dispute more intense and drew wider circles of people into it was the sectarian enmity between the two sides. The people from Jawzar were Ismaili, while the Sayyeds were Shi'a [i.e., Twelvers]. The dispute attracted support from Ismailis and Shi'as from all over Shibar. As funds flowed in from the surrounding populations, the Ismailis had the advantage. The Jawzari Ismailis themselves numbered about 150 households whereas the Sayyeds of Birgilich had about 20 households, and in Shibar generally there were more than 1,000 Ismaili households versus only 700 Shi'a households.

Eventually, the dispute was formally passed on by the alaqadār to the governor's offices in Bamian. Even then, however, there was no progress. The struggle continued for about two years. Every week we went day after day to Bamian. Then we would come back to the alaqadārī. Then we would go to the governorship in Bamian. I was on the side of the people of Jawzar, whereas Shah Osayn [although mir of the Jawzaris] was on the side of the Birgilichi Sayyeds. Several of us, including Mir Ahmad Jan and some others, went to Bamian and made a petition. We paid maybe 60,000 *afghanis* [Afghan unit of currency] in bribes—at first. This was important for all of us, because if these Sayyeds could get away with this they would have extended their power over everyone here. So we helped the Jawzaris. We paid out a lot of money in bribes, and so did the Sayyeds. They assessed their households for money. In the end they were impoverished.

Many times we came and went over this argument. Then after some time the Sayyeds took some sheep, and a *chapan* [cloak], and several of their elders went to the house of Ali Jam, and they proposed to settle the argument. Still, Ali Jam refused to settle.

After all this money was spent a new *hakem* [subgovernor], Jan Muhammad Khan, came to Bamian, and he was assigned to settle it; he was the brother of the king's chief clerk. Then several elders from the Sayyeds changed their story. They went to the new hakem and said, "These people, Ali Jam and the others, actually stole our cow." It was a lie.

Jan Muhammad wanted to settle this dispute, and he proposed a compromise. "Why don't you write that you looked all over and you couldn't find your cow? You can say 'Our cow just disappeared.' Maybe a wolf has eaten it or something. You could bring a horn or a bone and show that it disappeared. If you do this, I will let you go. Do this so I can get this case over with. I want to close this dossier." So everyone went back to the alaqadārī and there they had to answer more questions. They wrote, "This cow was not stolen by these people," and they took some bones to the government. The owner of the cow said that it hadn't disappeared but was eaten by wolves. And he said, "These men are not thieves. They didn't steal my cow." In fact, there was no stolen cow—the whole thing was a farce. Now everyone was lying. The point was to get free of the government. When the matter went back to Bamian the Sayyeds said, "Yes, a wolf ate our cow." So the whole thing was finished. The Jawzaris and the Sayyeds were both let go.

It took more than two years and it cost a lot of money, but Jan Muhammad Khan settled it. Now, thank God, people are free from this trouble. But it cost a lot. Both sides spent a lot. There was no punishment for either side in this final argument. The bribes from the two sides came to 80,000 afghanis. The Sayyeds lost a great deal because some of them had been thrown in jail, and they turned out to be liars.

Actually Ali Jam and the others did this intentionally. They intended to have an argument so they could get free of the Sayyeds. The Sayyeds were very cruel and oppressed them. They would make them work on their land if they owed them money, and they would use their cows to plow. Even though the Jawzaris had previously taken bushes at night, this time they went up there openly in broad daylight. . . . They wanted to be free from these Sayyeds. Previously these people were very *ājez* [poor, weak]. Later, when they had become knowledgeable and wise, and knew that other people would come to their side, like the people of Shibar and others, then they knew these people were for them, so they went and took the bushes so that they could be free of the Sayyeds.

Also, they thought I would help them. They wanted me to serve as their mir, not the Sayyeds [i.e., Shah Osayn]. But before they went up the hill to take the bushes they didn't let me know about it. They had decided it among themselves. These hundred houses had decided to do this, "so that we can be free of these Sayyeds."

INTERPRETIVE COMMENTS

Note that the mirs in this story—the official intermediaries between local communities and the government—tried at first to resolve the dispute informally. This was because the costs in bribes rose as more officials became involved. In fact, I was told by government officials as well as the local people that bribes were considered necessary by the local people in order to ensure that they would get a fair hearing. Several officials explained to me that their refusal of a bribe (a "gift") would have been taken as a sign of bias against the giver, implying that they had already decided against the giver. No one believed he could get a fair hearing without paying out substantial amounts to the (poorly paid) officials who handled their case.

In this dispute the Sayyeds seemed to be weakening as the acrimonious proceedings dragged on. This was evident, first, in their attempt to persuade Ali Jam to give up on his claims against them, and later in their attempt to change the story from a fight about bushes to a quarrel over a stolen cow. They were trying to direct the problem back upon Ali Jam and his friends. Could they have thought that the new hakem might not understand the reasons for the fight over bushes? Perhaps they supposed that an urban bureaucrat would regard a fight over a stolen cow as more authentic.

But the new hakem, in seeking a compromise, created yet another story: he proposed that the problem be stated as the disappearance of a cow rather than its theft. In such a case no one would be at fault. Whatever the reason for the fight, the hakem's proposal took the case a long way from the original issue of rights to bushes or a fractured head. We do not know why the hakem was so eager to get the matter over with. Was he under pressure from higher authorities? Why did he feel it necessary to change the story? Whatever his situation, by that time everyone—maybe even Ali Jam—was ready to find a way out. The lost cow story worked, even if it was a complete fabrication, because no one could bear to carry on—and perhaps because all sides were broke. And now—at least, as the hakem proposed it—no one was at fault.

Even so, it turns out that falsification was already intrinsic to the affair from the beginning. What originally seemed accidental, the Sayyeds catching the Jawzaris in the midst of a theft of their bushes, was actually a deliberate provocation. The Ismailis of Jawzar were actually the ones picking the fight. The bush collecting was itself a kind of subterfuge aimed at prompting the Sayyeds to pick a fight that would occasion a furor, which would engage the rest of the community in Shibar, thus enabling the Jawzari Ismailis to extricate themselves from the control of their Shi'a mir, Shah Osayn. It was a roundabout way to break the bonds of dependency. So there were several narratives of "reality" in this affair. There was the story told by Ali Jam's friends when they went to the alaqadārī; there was the story the Sayyeds told in rebuttal. There was the story about the stolen cow invented by the Sayyeds when they went to the hakem; there was the story of the lost cow (possibly, the hakem said, eaten by wolves—very unlikely in summer), the report placed in the official record. And there was the story about the secret plan of the Jawzaris to extricate themselves from Shah Osayn.

A subterfuge theft that prompted a fight that was supposed to create a regional donnybrook and humiliate the Sayyeds in order to break their control over their Ismaili clients was, therefore, as Mir Gholam Hasan said, a farce all around. Whatever really happened, what is accessible to us now, is a series of fabrications.

ON THE SOCIAL CONSTRUCTION OF REALITY

As Fredrik Barth puts it, when people "work" to construct their realities they create situations that have multiple and contrary realities (1993:4). Societies are disordered systems, "where . . . such relatively determined connections as there are will generate processes and angles at odds with each other, producing innumerable large and small incoherencies in culture and in the body politic" (1993:5).[4] Mir Gholam Hasan's tale focuses on an obvious instance of reality construction, that is, the fictitious story created by the hakem. But there was another instance of reality construction here, one working at odds to and hidden within the public rigmarole. When the Jawzaris secretly hatched a plan to create a situation that would prompt a fight, they were conceiving of a new reality: that conditions were right to wrest themselves free of Shah Osayn. As Mir Gholam Hasan put it, "Previously these people were very *ājez* (poor, weak). Later, when they had become knowledgeable and wise, and knew that other people would come to their side, . . . then they knew these people were for them, so they went and took the bushes. . . ." The Jawzari plan was another construction of the situation in Shibar. Narratives like the Jawzari's scheme to start a fight over bushes and the hakem's fabricated story about a lost cow make situations understandable; they help people organize social life—even, sometimes, the official record.

NOTES

1. This report is part of a larger project to make available to other scholars my interviews in Bamian during the period of my field work in 1966–1968 and in subsequent interviews with Hazaras elsewhere.

2. Like eminent religious families elsewhere, a member of the Birgilich Sayyeds sometimes served as mediator between feuding tribes. In the 1830s, when Charles Masson (1842:437 ff., especially 448) passed through, an eminent Sayyed in Birgilich was trying to arrange safe passage for a group of Pushtuns through Sheykh Ali Hazara territories.

3. Hazara Sayyeds are mentioned frequently in the literature: Bacon 1958:25, 32; Ferdinand 1959:16, 17; Harpviken 1996; Monsutti 2004; Mousavi 1998:26; Poladi 1989; Schurmann 1962:104.

4. This analysis has been enabled by Barth's distinction between the way meanings are deployed by actors and the way they are deployed by observers. Those who act invest their behavior with meaning through intentions that are culturally informed, whereas those who observe must impute to the behaviors of others their own culturally informed presumptions. As Barth puts it, "To the actor, the event of own behavior is an act by virtue of the intent that shapes it. . . . To other parties, . . . event becomes act through interpretation, through the way its purposes and entailments are understood at the time of its manifestation" (Barth 1993:158–159). This difficult but original and creative work has been strangely ignored. Steedly's review of anthropological writings on Southeast Asia (1999) omits any reference to it, even though she mentions the companion piece by Unni Wikan (1993); Clifford Geertz (2000), who cites many other works on Southeast Asia, makes no mention of it.

REFERENCES

Bacon, Elizabeth E. 1958. *Obok: A Study of Social Structure in Eurasia.* New York: Wenner-Grenn.
Bailey, F. G. 1991. *The Prevalence of Deceit.* Ithaca, N.Y.: Cornell University Press.
Barth, Fredrik. 1993. *Balinese Worlds.* Chicago: University of Chicago Press.
Canfield, Robert L. 2007. "Recollections of a Hazara wedding in the 1930s." In Jeff Sahadeo and Russell Zanca, eds., *Everyday Life in Central Asia.* Bloomington: Indiana University Press.
Ferdinand, Klaus. 1959. *Preliminary Notes on Hazara Culture.* Historisk-filosofiske Meddelelser udgivet af Det Kongelige Danske Videnskabernes Selskab Bind 37 (5).
Geertz, Clifford. 2000. *Available Light.* Princeton, N.J.: Princeton University Press.
Grevemeyer, Jan-Heeren. 1988. "Ethnicity and National Liberation: The Afghan Hazara between Resistance and Civil War." In Jean-Paul Digard, ed., *Identité et Expérience Ethniques en Iran et en Afghanistan.* Paris: Centre National de la Recherche Scientifique, pp. 211–218.
Harpviken, Kristian Berg. 1996. *Political Mobilization among the Hazara of Afghanistan: 1978–1992.* Oslo: Institutt for Sosiologi, Universistetet i Oslo (M.A. Thesis), Oslo, 1986.
Masson, Charles. 1842. *Narrative of Various Journeys in Beloochistan, Afghanistan,*

and the Panjab, Including a Resident in Those Countries from 1826 to 1836. 3 vols. London: Richard Bentley.

Monsutti, Alessandro. 2004. *Guerres et Migrations: Réseaux Sociaux et Stratégies économiques des Hazaras d'Afghanistan*. Paris: Editions de l'Institut d'ethnologie, Neuchâtel.

Mousavi, S. A. 1998. *The Hazaras of Afghanistan: An Historical, Cultural, Economic and Political Study*. Surrey, UK: Curzon Press.

Noelle, Christine. 1997. *State and Tribe in Nineteenth-Century Afghanistan: The Reign of Amir Dost Mohammed Khan (1826–1863)*. Richmond: Curzon Press.

Poladi, Hassan. 1989. *The Hazaras*. Stockton, Calif.: Mughal.

Schurmann, H. F. 1962. *The Mongols of Afghanistan: An Ethnography of the Moghols and Related Peoples of Afghanistan*. The Hague: Mouton.

Steedly, M. M. 1999. "The State of Culture Theory in the Anthropology of Southeast Asia." *Annual Review of Anthropology* 28: 431–454.

Wikan, Unni. 1993. *Managing Turbulent Hearts: A Balinese Formula for Living*. Chicago: University of Chicago Press.

Wood, John. 1841. *A Personal Narrative of a Journey to the Source of the River Oxus by the Route of the Indus, Kabul and Badakhshan: Performed under the Sanction of the Supreme Government of India in the Years 1836, 1837, 1838*. London: John Murray.

5. A Central Asian Tale of Two Cities: Locating Lives and Aspirations in a Shifting Post-Soviet Cityscape

Morgan Y. Liu

This is a tale about an old Silk Road city called Osh, the second largest city in the Kyrgyz Republic with a quarter million people today.[1] This tale is recounted as a virtual walking tour through the urban landscape that will divulge the city's remarkable ethnic mix, colonial past, and rapidly shifting present. Within its crowded limits, Osh harbors contrasting life worlds: different districts, livelihoods, lifestyles, and aspirations that appear to diverge even more since the dissolution of the Soviet Union and independence of the Kyrgyz Republic in 1991. Osh is a tale of two cities because, like many other ex-Soviet Central Asian cities, it developed during the twentieth century divided between a traditional Central Asian sector and a modern Soviet sector. The bifurcated image of Osh captures the coexisting presence of divergent orientations and aspirations within the city. For the city's residents, the Soviet sector carries associations of what is considered modern urban life, European civilization, ethnic pluralism, Russian domination (during the Soviet period), and Kyrgyz rule (since independence, for ethnic Kyrgyz have inherited the dominant governing authority). The rest of the city, composed of residential neighborhoods called *mahallas* and populated mostly by ethnic Uzbeks, is associated variously with Central Asian traditionalism, Islamic mores, patriarchy, close community, and Uzbek territoriality. Although everyone, regardless of ethnicity or position, tends to see this stark contrast between Osh's "two cities," realities on the ground are not so simple. The characterization of an entire city sector or ethnic group can at best identify tendencies, not unchanging essences, and the correspondence between places and attitudes is never one-to-one.[2] The purpose for our walking tour is to consider—literally from the ground—the often hybrid and ambiguous nature of lived experiences.

Mother and daughter in Osh, Kyrgyzstan.

But even though no one acts or thinks completely according to stereotypes of being "modern," "traditional," Kyrgyz, Uzbek, or Russian in everyday life, Osh's residents usually conceive of the differences in livelihoods and lifestyles as being absolute and unbridgeable. This is in part because the Soviet state had promoted an ideology that held that each ethnic group (what was called "nationality") had its own determinate set of characteristics—traditions, material culture, foods, dress, music, language, etc.—that were essential to the identity of each group. In Osh, these essentialized differences become problematic in light of the city's severe shortage of land, which heightens the sense of competition between groups and their differing ways of life. Because Osh is squeezed between mountains to its immediate south and the border with Uzbekistan to its immediate north, land use for agriculture, industry, mahalla neighborhoods (mostly Uzbek), and apartment complexes (Kyrgyz, Russian, Uzbek, and others) have been in a perpetual zero-sum deadlock. Competition for land came to a terribly violent head with a case of conflict over territory between ethnic Kyrgyz and Uzbeks in 1990. This brings us to the first stop in our walking tour.

We begin at a small, unobtrusive stone monument located at a critical junction point in the city. The stone sits at the intersection of a vast field to the north, an Uzbek mahalla neighborhood to the south, and the Oshskiy Region apartment complex to the east. At this junction, Soviet city, Uzbek mahalla, and collective farm converge. Here is also where Kyrgyz and Uzbeks clashed violently on June 4, 1990 (exactly one year after the Tiananmen Square massacre in China, coincidentally), over whether that agricultural field (from an Uzbek-majority collective farm) should be converted to housing land for Kyrgyz families who are rural migrants to the city. This started the so-called Osh Riots, which led to days of chaos and mass inter-ethnic killings on both sides. The inscription on the stone monument reads "To the Victims of June 4, 1990," in Russian, English, and Arabic script. Other than a much smaller incident a year later, no such event has erupted since in the region, and everyday tensions between Kyrgyz and Uzbeks have greatly subsided in the city. The basic problem of chronic land shortage and contrasting life worlds, however, remains unabated. Our walking tour of Osh is thus no idle tourist excursion. It provides a street-level view of a complex sociopolitical reality and shows that issues of wide import, such as the development of post-socialist economies and governments, and of inter-ethnic relations, need to be examined through the details of everyday lives.[3]

BAZAAR NEXUS

The walking tour continues in Osh's main bazaar (open-air market), the boisterously vibrant economic nexus of the city, where all sorts of people converge, converse, and conduct business. The carnivalesque character of the bazaar confirms Osh's centuries-old reputation as a center of regional and long distance trade: between the sedentary urban dwellers and the nomadic herders of the vast Ferghana Valley in which Osh is situated; and as a stop before Kashgar (in China) across the mountain range along one route of the Silk Road. While Central Asian bazaars tend to be squarish in layout, Osh's bazaar is elongated because it is located on the Akbura, the central river that bisects the city. The entire city, in fact, lies nestled along the Akbura's steep river valley, its neighborhoods and zones defined by the river's straight axis and the rising topography on both flanks. Osh's main bazaar, like any other sizable Central Asian market, is divided into areas differentiated by product and specialty. Strolling down the bazaar's parallel aisles of open-air stalls and rows of enclosed shops on the sides, one is met with a great variety of sundry personal items—soap, cosmetics, pens, notebooks, batteries, small toys, calculators, watches, etc. The products offered from one stall to the next do not vary significantly: if one seller carries Colgate toothpaste or Comet cleanser, so do all her neighbors, given that they often use the same supplier. The bazaar being a place to haggle, there may be small differences in opening price and willingness to come down. A few book tables dot the scene, including one that sells only Islamic books teaching ex-Soviet Central Asian Muslims such foundations of the faith as conducting prayers, pronouncing Arabic, and understanding basic doctrine.[4] Off the bazaar's main axis, several large outdoor areas with concrete tables and permanent overhead roofing are divided into sections selling fruits and vegetables, meat, and raisins and nuts. Moneychangers operate from a row of enclosed shops, their windows opening to the vendors of flat bread (*nan* in Kyrgyz, *non* in Uzbek) in covered wheelbarrows.[5]

In contrast to the relatively mono-ethnic character of many Central Asian settlements outside of the capitals, such as Andijon, 40 km away, and other nearby cities of comparable size in Uzbekistan, Osh is awash in evident diversity.[6] Besides Kyrgyz, Uzbeks, and Russians, Osh is home to smaller populations of Ukrainians, Germans, Tatars, Uyghurs, Tajiks, Koreans, Roma (commonly called Gypsies), and others.[7] Until as late as the 1960s, there were relatively few ethnic Kyrgyz living within Osh. Kyrgyz, who led a nomadic pastoral life in the mountainous areas before the Soviets, were forced into permanent settlements and collectivized by the state during the 1930s, and Kyrgyz villages dominate the rural areas of the Kyrgyz Republic to this day. But because, in 1924, Osh was placed into a newly created Kyrgyz territorial unit, which became a Soviet Socialist Republic (a full Union member) in 1936, Soviet nationalities policy pushed for ethnic Kyrgyz, the "titular nationality," to be actively promoted to serve alongside Europeans in leadership positions. The demographic majority of the city itself, however, has been Uzbek.[8] As an ancient city along one branch of the Silk Road trade route, Osh has harbored a sedentary population engaged in trade and craft production for centuries—a population that came to be

Members of a women's mosque in Batken (Osh Province), Kyrgyzstan.

known as Uzbek with the Soviet creation of national identities. Uzbek residents of the city tend to see it as properly belonging to them, and resent being called an ethnic minority, because the city's population is majority Uzbek (although the province as a whole has a Kyrgyz majority).[9]

It is in public spaces such as the bazaar that Osh's ethnic diversity is evident in the languages spoken. When a Kyrgyz and an Uzbek converse, the Kyrgyz speaks in Kyrgyz and the Uzbek speaks in Uzbek, and they understand each other well. This is not only because the two Turkic languages are related, but also because Osh residents of either ethnicity grow up hearing both. Kyrgyz and Uzbeks from rural monolingual backgrounds could not talk nearly as well to each other, because the two languages do have important differences.[10] Russian, still the regional *lingua franca*, is spoken between Russians, other non-natives, and Central Asians, the latter speaking Russian with their own accent, even those educated in Russian language schools. Most non-natives do not speak Central Asian languages, although a few do if they grew up living and playing in Uzbek and Kyrgyz neighborhoods, and since independence, Kyrgyz language classes are compulsory for all school children regardless of ethnicity. Osh's independent television station, OshTV, established after independence, broadcasts its news trilingually. In one segment, the news anchor can be reading in Kyrgyz, in the next, a correspondent reports in Uzbek, and then an interview proceeds in Russian. Meanwhile, in the already noisy bazaar, announcers incessantly broadcast personal advertisements (usually apartments or cars for sale) over loudspeakers in those three languages.

Uzbeks conduct the largest (though an increasingly smaller) proportion of the total market selling, almost all the service labor (haircutting, restaurant cooking, key making, audio/video cassette duplicating, money changing, automobile repair), and much of the craft labor (blacksmithing, furniture making, metal gate welding, small-scale construction and house repair, etc.). In other words, Uzbeks run most of the small-scale, day-by-day economic activities of the city, which are associated with their history as sedentary farmers, craftsmen, and traders. Kyrgyz sell commodities associated with their pastoral past: milk products (including *kymyz* or fermented mare's milk in the spring—sour and smelling like strong cheese and quite refreshing), wool, and felt rugs and hats; but since independence they increasingly sell agricultural and manufactured products as well. Russians have tended to sell items or services of more specialized taste, such as European furniture, lighting fixtures, pets, Russian books, stamp collecting, or computer repair; although other groups are moving into these markets. There is always the pitiful sight of Russian *babushki* (elderly women) sitting by bed sheets strewn with family possessions for sale (dishes, samovars, old books, etc.) to supplement their meager, if not unpaid, pensions. Many Russian families left for Russia in the early 1990s, but these remaining elderly tended to be too old or poor to leave.[11] One seeks out the few local Korean sellers for pickled delicacies whose flavor contrasts with the unspicy Central Asian foods. With the city's factories closing or slowing down significantly, great numbers of the unemployed have moved into selling and shuttle trade, among them more and more Kyrgyz. And so, since the Kyrgyz Republic's independence, ethnic specializations in selling have begun to blur, although Uzbeks will continue to dominate the skilled craft market for some time.

During the Soviet period, Osh's bazaar operated only a couple of days a week, selling mostly the produce of farmers from surrounding areas. People bought manufactured goods mostly from the state-run stores throughout the city, at fixed, stable prices set by the state, and the products were made elsewhere in the Soviet Union, or occasionally in Eastern Europe (East German goods being particularly prized). Throughout the former Soviet bloc during the 1990s, many wistfully remembered the predictability and security of life under state socialism, even if the availability and quality of goods had often fallen short. People had the sense that the state was fulfilling its "paternal" role in caring for its citizens through its central control of the economy.[12] Older Uzbeks in Osh talked to me about the sense of public morality in early Soviet times, where bazaar sellers could leave their goods unattended overnight without fear of theft. This moral sensibility was eroded by Soviet rule, they say, and has worsened since in the cut-throat profiteering at the bazaar today. After independence in 1991, the bazaar exploded in size and volume of business, now operating from dawn to evening every day of the week. The state stores closed down or were converted to private shops, whose numbers steadily increased through the 1990s. Goods started appearing from Turkey, Iran, Pakistan, the UAE, Western Europe, and the United States, but most overwhelmingly from China. These included not only practical items like shampoo or pasta, but icons of global popular culture, such as posters of Arnold Schwarzenegger and Jackie Chan, or stickers of Indian film stars. Uzbek stars like Yulduz Usmanova and Sherali Juraev as well as Russian and European artists dominate the cassette music sold, and American artists are also found. The Beatles are a perennial favorite. This is the recent globalization of Central Asia as seen from the bazaar.

But besides being a site where the global comfortably sits with the local, the bazaar has become a place where growing inequalities of opportunity and contrasts in aspiration sit uncomfortably with each other. For the many Osh residents who lost jobs or pensions after 1991 and had to become sellers to make ends meet, unemployed manual laborers and academic scholars alike, the bazaar represents shattered lives and despair. For entrepreneurs able to capitalize on new opportunities in the literal market economy, the bazaar is the source of wealth and great expectations. For some, the wild fluctuations in price reveal a lapse in the state's maintenance of economic order and a rise of exploitative criminality. For others, the post-Soviet market rewards hard work and business acumen, and provides in-demand consumer commodities previously unavailable.

SOVIET CITY

Osh's Soviet sector is confined along either bank of the Akbura, defined by several straight avenues parallel to the river. Walking away from the bazaar along the avenues, one sees buildings with prim, sometimes grandly official architecture, most under five or six stories tall, since Osh lies in an earthquake zone. These were the key institutions of Soviet rule and life, as Osh, the second largest city in Soviet Kyrgyzstan and today's Kyrgyz Republic, has been a provincial capital and economic anchor of the republic's south. Soviet rule generally held the agenda of bringing a progressive socialist civilization to what was seen by Russians as a backward, tradition-bound population. Not only was the Soviet city to provide the infrastructure enabling the material conditions of modern life, it was also to "raise" the cultural and intellectual level of the populace. The appearance and functions of this urban sector reveal even today how the Soviet state sought to transform and administer Central Asian society. Cars and busses pass by provincial and city administration buildings, performance centers, the city hospital, newspaper offices, post office, wedding registry, schools, the university, archaeological museums, the public library, the TsUM (central department store), the *Dom Byta* (building housing various services like barber, laundry, etc.), a movie theater, restaurants, small shops, hotels, apartment buildings, public parks, swimming pool, stadium, and the Lenin statuary. Each institution represents a piece of what was an elaborately theorized and centrally planned urban design whose goal was to regulate and channel the everyday lives of the Soviet citizenry. The state thought about and laid out where people were to live, to work, to be educated, to shop, to obtain services, to deal with government agencies, and even where they were to have fun. In theory, they did so for molding the Soviet person (progressive, hard-working, selfless, and healthy) as much as for efficiency. In practice, the social engineers were mostly unable to attain their ideals for city and citizen. Moreover, even though Osh's Soviet sector may seem modern when juxtaposed to the rest of the city, those from the Kyrgyzstani capital, Bishkek, or from large cities elsewhere remark how "Central Asian" Osh appears overall. Everywhere in the Soviet city are reminders of the distinctive locality: from the robes of elderly men, headscarves of married women, and colorful *atlas* dresses of younger women, to the local appropriations of officially designed spaces (such as small-time street sellers, yurts displayed for holidays, etc.). Near the center of the city stands Sulaiman (Solomon) Mountain, a site of pilgrimage and folk religious practices particularly engaged in by women. The distinction between Osh's old and new cities is actually not clear-cut, as we will also see when we visit the mahallas later.

The keystone of the Soviet state's agenda for governing a city like Osh was, however, the development of industry. Industry figured centrally overall in state planning for the Union, not only to fulfill goals for material, technological, and military advancement, but also to demonstrate to the world that Soviet socialism was the superior system, particularly in its ability to improve "backward" regions such as Central Asia. This grand scheme had a profound impact on the city's life. Along the Akbura River away from the urban center lie the industrial zones that house Osh's textile plant, silk plant, construction materials plant, bus servicing depots, and factories for milk, meat, and vodka (which some residents see as a deliberate Russian affront to their Islamic sensibilities). It was Osh's industry that employed most of its residents and fueled its tremendous growth in the twentieth century. The textile plant, located on the northern end of the city, operated as Osh's single most important economic locomotive, once employing well over ten thousand people. When it was completed in 1975, this factory complex had already spawned a flurry of urban development, including a sprawling apartment neighborhood to house the newly arrived

labor force (including Kyrgyz from the nearby mountainous regions, Uzbeks from Uzbekistan, and many others), and a vast regional transit network to bus workers in daily. Entire agricultural villages on the outskirts
of Osh were absorbed into its urban grid as new neighborhoods, their
winding dirt streets made into straight paved ones and then connected by
regular bus service to the central bazaar. Many of the older lifelong Osh
residents that I got to know (all Uzbek) worked in some activity related
to the postwar industrial boom: as drivers, mechanics, cooks, construction workers, factory managers, etc. Even though Kyrgyz were promoted
to some high posts as the republic's titular nationality under Soviet nationalities policy, it was mostly the Russians, Ukrainians, Germans, and
other non-natives who served as the directors, rectors, editors, doctors,
and engineers of these state-run political, economic, cultural, and educational institutions during the Soviet period.[13] Kyrgyz have replaced them
in these posts steadily since independence, except for some new institutions such as the Kyrgyz-Uzbek University, where most of the top people
are Uzbek.

All of the people who worked in these industries had to live somewhere in this crowded city. Soviet planners after World War II envisioned
a kind of apartment block community called the *mikrorayon* as the best
solution to the housing stock shortage throughout the Union at the time,
because it provided residential space and utilities on a large, economical
scale.[14] The mikrorayon (meaning micro-region) was a planned pedes-
trian-oriented zone of multi-story residential buildings integrated with a
variety of services and retail outlets within a short walking distance. Services were distributed spatially so as to minimize the time that a resident
needed to spend outside the region except for work, making it in theory
almost self-contained. Starting in 1955, mahallas near Osh's main bazaar
at the city center were razed to create the Oshskiy Region across from
the Textile Industrial Complex, and starting in 1961, more were cleared
to make the Zainabetdinova neighborhood. Recall that our walking tour
began at the stone monument that sits at a junction between the Oshskiy Region and the edge of a mahalla that was spared demolition. Located next to the main bazaar, these two microrayons now form the most
densely populated, ethnically diverse, and active parts of the city. Children play in the inter-building spaces, where women also conduct some
of their housework, such as carpet-beating, and groups of people meet
and chat in the warm months. At some pedestrian intersections, sellers
of candy, cigarettes, and sunflower seeds sit on small, improvised tables.
Music is often heard blaring into the evenings, especially when there is
a Kyrgyz wedding, which takes over the courtyard in front of an apartment building: rented yurts are raised, food is cooked, and sometimes
a horse is slaughtered. Even if most neighbors of the host family are not
invited (and other parts of the wedding happen in a restaurant for in-

vited guests only), these festivities have a communal aspect because they take place literally at the center of the community. While residents do not know most of their neighbors well in these apartment complexes, especially with the greater residential mobility since the 1990s compared with the Soviet era, people are quite aware of each others' personal situations. Gossip does travel pervasively in these neighborhoods, much more than in typical apartment buildings in the West, although not as quickly as in Osh's mahalla neighborhoods.

Since 1991, market forces have been reworking some of these spaces and progressively eroding evidence of the Soviet hand that authored this part of the cityscape. State-run stores selling things no one wants have given way to private ones selling in-demand consumer items (clothes, shoes, baby strollers, imported foods, etc.), some with glassy Western-style storefronts juxtaposed jarringly against the gray concrete backdrop. Osh used to have, for example, quite a few bookstores, named only by their municipal number, that still sold arid tomes until the early 1990s. One of them was remodeled into an Italian pharmacy with a contoured exterior suggesting a Frank Gehry look. Restaurants have mushroomed during the 1990s, including those with ethnic cuisine (Uyghur, Russian, Chinese, or American). Since 2000, internet salons have spread throughout the city, frequented mostly by male youth obsessed with action gaming or with getting English-language exposure via web and email, and competing with the billiard rooms that blossomed in the 1990s. A few discos and casinos have opened, and near a wide bridge spanning the Akbura, concentrations of young women driven to prostitution await their clientele in the late evenings. Narcotics are quite available for those who seek them because now Osh acts as a drug hub for trafficking from Afghanistan via Tajikistan to Russia and Europe—the dark side of its legacy as trade city extraordinaire.[15] If the heavy hand of the Soviet state had intended to mold its citizens and cityscapes, the "invisible hand" of the market is now rapidly redefining both.

How are the lives and aspirations of residents of Osh's apartment neighborhoods being shaped? The majority simply try to survive the intense economic hardships of the city's massive unemployment and unpredictable inflation. Those old enough to remember wax nostalgic about Soviet life, and not only about its economic stability. Educated Osh residents, particularly among Russians and others, mention that they miss the cultural life available then in the form of the Russian theater, art, novels, and literary newspapers. "All people think about today is money," they say, and society has lost its civilized sensibilities, becoming as crass as the bazaar itself. These kinds of comments reveal a continuing affinity for the Russian-European intellectual life sustained by institutions of the Soviet Union, and a sense of aloofness from both the traditionalism of Central Asian cultures and the philistinism of Western consumer capitalism. But on another front, an increasing number of Osh's young from all ethnicities are turning to learn English, computers, and business skills. Usually from a Russian-language school background and speaking Russian as their best language, they seek to master English and other so-called world languages at university or independent tuition schools. These progressive urban youth see themselves as cosmopolitan and value the multi-ethnic character of the city and republic, reflecting former President Akaev's slogan, "Kyrgyzstan is Our Common Home." The more successful ones land jobs in the many foreign NGOs or United Nations agencies that are present in Osh. Despite personal hardships, these youth tend to be quite optimistic about the future prospects of a Kyrgyz Republic pursuing a course of liberalization: free markets, convertible currency, membership in the WTO, open media, civic organizations, and democratic process.[16] They are aware that the landlocked and resource-poor republic struggles economically and will always be to some extent beholden to the big powers out there, namely Russia, China, and the United States. Nonetheless, they believe that openness to global markets and models of governance will eventually bring a better future for all. Very few of these youth are turning to Islam as the key to making sense of present hardship or to effecting desired outcomes. If they turn to religion, they mostly look to evangelical Christianity or Bahaism, which they regard as connected to the outside "modern world," in contrast to either Islam or Russian Orthodoxy, which the Central Asian states officially recognize as the indigenous faiths of the region. Although small in numbers, evangelical groups in the city increasingly come under the leadership of local believers rather than foreign missionaries, and their activities have attracted mostly residents of the Soviet sector. In all, the aspirations of those residents gravitate toward a combination of Russian-Soviet life and Western forms, and tend to avoid delving into Central Asian heritages, even though every place in Osh is to some extent layered with all of these influences.

ENTERING THE MAHALLA

Most Uzbeks in Osh do not live in the post–World War II multi-story apartment complexes or low-rise neighborhoods that house the predominantly Kyrgyz and Russian labor force and administration.[17] They live instead in the distinctive neighborhoods called mahallas, which occupy just over half the city's land area. One does not have to walk far at all from a main thoroughfare in Osh to enter a mahalla. Turning into a mahalla's narrow street, perhaps just off a main thoroughfare or behind a public building, one has the sense of entering a microcosm, as the visual, audio, tactile, and olfactory cues of the built environment suddenly shift. Unlike the rational, deliberate look of the rectilinear Soviet sector streets, a mahalla's narrow, and sometimes unpaved, winding streets have an improvised, lived-in look.[18] Uzbek houses (*uy*) show little of themselves to the street; windows are kept barred and draped, if they are present at all on the plain exterior walls of mud or factory brick. Metal gates of various designs and colors along the street front the passage into each house, which is actually an integrated ensemble of separate structures arranged around an outdoor central courtyard—the *hovli*. Each house is inhabited by one multigenerational household, different generations living in different structures that all open to the courtyard, which acts as a common area for domestic activities. This socio-spatial arrangement contrasts with the apartment building, where there is less flexibility in how one uses space and less social contact with neighbors. One schoolteacher described his courtyard as a sort of "inside outside"—an outdoor space where you can dress and behave at ease, because you are within your house: "So you're stepping out with a T-shirt? [That's OK.] It's your own hovli. You're watching the kids? Yelling at the kids? It's your own hovli. Now, in the apartment building, two apartments may be next to each other, but you live by yourself. . . . On your own land, you live under your own conditions, in your own hovli—a free life." Paradoxically, so goes the claim, apartment life is crowded yet alienating at the same time, while hovli life is neighborly yet private at the same time. The co-presence of community and freedom in the mahalla is enabled by the way space is partitioned into hierarchies of intimacy: from room to hovli to the mahalla's narrow streets to its larger thoroughfares. These spatial hierarchies organize everyday activities and socialization into graded domains of intimacy or formality. It is interesting that Soviet urban planners (and now their Kyrgyz successors) found the mahalla a space-inefficient form of housing. Although a mahalla cannot achieve the residential densities of a mikrorayon, the mahalla embodies a rather ingenious scheme of spatial partitioning that enables the co-presence of wide-ranging activities within a small neighborhood scale. It is the kind of social life that mahalla spaces enable that sheds light on why Uzbeks have overwhelmingly preferred living in courtyard houses over apartment buildings. When old mahallas in Osh's city center were demolished in the 1960s to make room for the city's postwar industrial boom, most of the displaced Uzbeks preferred to move to inhospitably hilly lands outside the city and create new mahallas from scratch than to take apartments in the new mikrorayons built there. Not all Uzbeks value mahalla in this way. Some see its community as forced and oppressive, and the young women, in particular, dread the endless work needed to maintain a house. Moreover, the apartment complex harbors its own forms of close community, as we saw above.

Much of the mahalla's social life takes place on the street. The mahalla street acts not so much as an interstice between places but as a socially significant place in itself. Osh's mahalla streets are densely social places, some of them teeming with activity in the mornings, and from late afternoon to after dark in the warmer months. A group of young men squat

over a card game at an intersection. Young women with infants chat by
an open house gate. Pre-teen girls chat as they line up at the street fau-
cet to fetch water for cooking. A young married woman throws bucket-
fuls of water from the narrow canal that runs along many streets onto
the dusty street near her gate, and bends over sweeping the area clean.
Mostly older men gather outside their mahalla mosque even before the
call to prayer is issued from its loudspeakers, and they stroll home in
various groups afterward. A pre-teen girl sits behind a table at an intersection selling candies and cigarettes, eating her own inventory of sunflower seeds. A street-facing house window converted into mini-shop displays detergent and sour yogurt balls. The smell of baking *non* (flat bread)
is wafted from a clay oven in someone's courtyard. An open doorway reveals weighing scales on a blue table and a sign saying, "Halva, 23 *som*
a kilo."[19] Being an intensely social place, the mahalla harbors dense cir-
culations of people, things, money, and above all, talk. News and gossip
flow quickly in mahallas, where most families know each other, possibly
(in older neighborhoods) for generations. People know who is getting
married, who passed away, who just came back from the hajj, who is ap-
plying to study in America. The children who fill the streets with their
noisy play during after-school hours always seem to know the current
whereabouts of everyone in the neighborhood. Face-to-face social contact
within and across mahallas also happens at communal events such as
weddings, circumcisions, funerals, Hajj return celebrations, and *Navruz*
(Central Asian/Iranian New Year). These events are held in a host family's courtyard, were crowds of people sit, stand, or work in groups according to gender and age cohort, but the activities spill out into the street, so
the entire neighborhood is drawn into the event.

In many mahallas, peer groups of about fifteen members hold regular
gatherings called *ziyofat* (an Uzbek word meaning feast).[20] Meeting weekly
or monthly and hosted successively by each member on a rotating basis,
ziyofats are occasions of eating, money exchange, chatting, and group
discussion. Since Soviet glasnost of the late 1980s (but especially since independence in 1991), some of these groups in Osh have become focused
on the study of Islamic practice, doctrine, and Arabic recitation. During a young men's ziyofat that I attended in 1998, for example, the local
mosque's imam was teaching the motions and words of *namaz*, the prayer
recited and enacted five times a day. I also attended an elder women's ziyofat, which was memorizing Arabic letters and the ninety-nine Quranic
names of God, and an elder men's group studying from a pre-Soviet Turkic text explaining doctrine. Young women do not have such venues, as
they are burdened with housework from dawn to after dusk every day
in the courtyard and kitchen. These ziyofat are not run or monitored by
the city's official clerical administration, which is aware of and condones
these self-initiated, self-run groups. Although a local imam may run one,

most are taught by non-clerics with greater knowledge through previous study with recognized masters since glasnost (and a few surreptitiously throughout the Soviet period).

The grassroots efforts in Osh's Uzbek mahallas to increase Islamic knowledge and practice since the early 1990s has various motivations: a communal desire to reinstate a tradition persecuted by Soviet rule, a personal desire to live in obedience to God, and/or a way of increasing social prestige. I asked one man why there seemed to be so much interest in Islam among the young men of this mahalla. He replied, "You are asking the wrong question. It is not a matter of interest. We must practice Islam, or else there will be shame to our families. It is a matter of shame, not interest." Some of these youth, even though appearing more "conservative" than those living in the apartments, are also interested in computers, cell phones, English, and travel to foreign cities for trade and employment (quite a few do so in China and South Korea). This man had spoken out during a ziyofat, urging his peers to rise early every day to recite prayers because they must set a positive example for their children in the future. Indeed, among particularly older Uzbeks in Osh (men and women over forty), there is a deeply-held conviction that Islam has beneficial effects on society that are crucial to their success as a community and republic. For these people, Islam is necessary for the proper moral formation of persons (a notion they call *tarbiya*, the discipline of Islam) that would produce a peaceful and hard-working populace necessary for political and economic development. It acts as an antidote against rampant post-Soviet ills such as idleness, disrespect for authority, sexual immorality, alcohol or drug use, criminal activities, official corruption, ethnic violence, etc. The discipline is intimately connected with the mahalla: it is in its spaces of dense sociality and mutual accountability that individuals can be effectively trained through informal policing of behavior and fear of social sanction.[21] Not all mahalla residents, to be sure, share in this view of Islam and mahalla life. Many Uzbeks, particularly among the young, the poor, the Russian-educated, or women, see the mahalla as oppressive and Islam as the provenance of the elderly or wealthy, who have time on their hands to be involved in religion. Nonetheless, everyone recognizes that this vision for Islam on communities exerts a palpable influence, for good or ill, on everyday life in the Uzbek community.

Whatever the images of mahalla as representing "authentic, traditional" Uzbek life, especially in contrast to life in the Soviet sector, the reality is again not so clear-cut.[22] Mahallas today have changed much in both physical and social makeup since the pre-Soviet era. The Soviet state's administration of the population has reconfigured many mahalla layouts, named streets and numbered houses (not to mention assigned people last names—all such designations never existed before); provided new building materials; put in municipal electricity, gas, and phone lines; created mahalla committees with official functions and, in the early Soviet period, propagandistic agendas; and appointed mahalla heads who report to the city administration. These are all a part of the state's so-called techniques of rule, intended to make the population amenable to visibility and control.[23] Residents have also remarked to me that social relations in the mahalla today lack the sense of respect for elders, concern for community, honesty, industriousness, and propriety of women's behavior compared to what they understand mahalla life to have been like before the Soviets. These "Soviet erosions" are what they hope Islam will mend in the coming years. The post-Soviet surge of Islamic activity in Osh is at its core an effort to cultivate a desired vision of communal life: peace and prosperity through religious discipline.

It is significant to note that such aspirations are not seen to be in conflict with the desire for the country's economic or political liberalization. Most mahalla residents affirm a desire that the Kyrgyz Republic move toward capitalism and democracy, even though their thoughts about what those would mean in practice for their context are always vague. They have strongly disagreed with the rapid pace of reforms in the Kyrgyz Republic during the 1990s and the massive unemployment and inflation that it brought. They tended to prefer instead the gradualist, state-managed approach exemplified next door in Uzbekistan and its president, Islam Karimov. Yet after a decade of post-socialist development, many Uzbeks in Osh are beginning to see that their lives are faring better, in some cases much better, than their co-ethnics in Uzbekistan, a country suffering from a stagnant economy still controlled to a large extent by state hands. Interestingly, the Uzbek new rich are among those who are turning most fervently to Islam.[24] As their poorer neighbors have cynically remarked, they do have the time and resources to participate in ziyofat, Islamic study, and the expensive pilgrimage to Mecca. They too have an optimistic outlook on their futures, but it is one that they see Islam as playing a crucial role in effecting. But what links Islamic knowledge and economic empowerment, and is the convergence of the two coalescing into particular political interests? Are the ziyofats becoming social and intellectual bases of a future political mobilization, even while Kyrgyzstan's existing opposition parties deteriorate in influence? In fact, the emergence of *nouveaux riches* among both Kyrgyz and Uzbeks (along with poverty for the majorities of all ethnicities) shows signs of developing common interests in maintaining the local status quo that cross-cut ethnicity. This is beginning to blunt the sharp division between Kyrgyz and Uzbeks in the city as emergent class distinctions become increasingly important in the Kyrgyz Republic's second decade of post-socialism. These suggestive trends take us beyond this walking tour and require further research. This leaves us perhaps at an optimistic place regarding the city's future, which is moving progressively away from the stone monument marking the 1990 riots, where we began.

CONCLUSION: TWO CITIES, TWO VISIONS

Our tour of Osh is a tale of two cities because its urban form integrates both a Soviet colonial city and a so-called traditional city of the mahallas (with the bazaar sitting at their interface). The distinction in space marks a distinction in livelihood, lifestyle, and aspiration, even though these divisions reveal surprising blurring and hybridity when seen from the ground. What makes this Central Asian city interesting is that its apparent split personality points to a fundamental dilemma for Central Asia today: how it should orient itself with respect to competing visions of good society that traffic globally with increased vitality since the end of the Cold War. Post-Soviet Central Asia has become a nexus where the grand projects of liberal democracy and capitalism are intersecting with Islamic efforts to remake society. While liberalism promises prosperity and security through free markets, democracy, and "civil society," the Islam of Osh's ziyofats strives to build prosperous and just societies through the moral cultivation of persons and communities. Changes in Osh since 1991 reflect this convergence of agendas, which works itself out not so much as a "clash," but often as mutual coexistence or accommodation. And so, Osh makes for a rather revealing walking tour, divulging the idealized contrast of modernism and traditionalism as well as points of their integration in the everyday lives and spaces of its residents.

NOTES

1. Since 1995, the country has been officially called the Kyrgyz Republic (*Kyrgyz Respublikasy*), although "Kyrgyzstan" is widely used. The adjectival form "Kyrgyzstani" refers to the state (as in citizenship), while "Kyrgyz" refers to the ethnic group or language.

2. For example, new neighborhoods of single houses for mostly Kyrgyz are neither mahallas nor Soviet-planned. Even the built environment of two sectors themselves does not represent pure type, as design, construction materials, use, and social life cross-cut the ideal categories, as we will see.

3. This account is based on over two and half years of residence and fieldwork in Osh, over the period from 1994 to 2003.

4. Legally available since independence, Islamic books are all in Uzbek language, revealing that most of the popular interest in Islam lies with the city's Uzbeks. These books are published in places like Tashkent, Istanbul, Moscow, and Kazan (Tatarstan, in the Russian Federation).

5. Operating only since independence, money changers hang signs displaying current exchange rates for the rather stable Kyrgyzstani som against the US dollar, euro, yen, Uzbekistani so'm, Kazakh tenga, and Chinese yuan, indicating the most relevant foreign contacts for Osh residents.

6. This is not to say that Central Asian ethnic groups only live in concentrations outside of the capitals, but for a middle-sized city, ethnic diversity is particu-

larly evident in Osh's public spaces. There are certainly villages with a mixed Kyrgyz and Uzbek population in both the Kyrgyz Republic and Uzbekistan, but the scale is much smaller than Osh. Kyrgyz are quite dominant, however, in numerous Kyrgyz villages toward the mountainous areas, as Uzbeks (and Tajiks) are in villages of the Ferghana Valley's heartland.

7. Germans and Koreans were moved to Central Asia *en masse* by the Soviet government before and during World War II. Roma in Osh speak Uzbek and are in many ways indistinguishable from Uzbeks, as noted by ethnographer and Osh native Shavkat Atakhanov, who has done fieldwork in a Rom (locally called Luli) mahalla in Osh; see Asankanov and Atakhanov 2002.

8. Actual percentage figures are in great dispute, some claiming that Uzbeks are no longer the majority, because it depends on what areas are formally considered part of the city proper. Uzbeks accuse the Kyrgyz government of gerrymandering Osh's boundaries during the 1990s to include Kyrgyz-majority areas "outside" the city and excluding mahallas that are "clearly inside" the city.

9. When the Soviet republics were delineated, Osh was made a part of Soviet Kyrgyzstan in order that the latter, a mountainous rural republic, could have a major urban center to administer and anchor the centrally planned economic zone of southern Kyrgyzstan.

10. Besides phonetic and grammatical divergences, Uzbek has many Persian and Arabic words, while Kyrgyz has affinities with Mongolian.

11. Russian out-migration diminished by the late 1990s. There are reports of some returning to Central Asia, having found life in Russia more difficult and unwelcoming than they had imagined. These Russians have lived all their lives in Central Asia, and are seen as partial foreigners by those living in Russia.

12. Anthropologist Katherine Verdery calls this notion "socialist paternalism," where the state "acted like a father who gives handouts to the children as he sees fit," Verdery 1996:25. For ethnographic studies of people struggling with disruptive post-socialist change throughout the former Soviet Union and Eastern Europe, see Berdahl, Bunzl, and Lampland 2000; Burawoy and Verdery 1999; Humphrey 2002.

13. Uzbeks did run some institutions in Soviet Osh, especially cultural ones like the Uzbek language newspaper (state run) and the Uzbek Drama Theater.

14. See Andrusz 1984.

15. See Specter 1995.

16. Initially, the Kyrgyz Republic steered decisively toward rapid political and economic liberalization, prompting some observers to call it Central Asia's "island of democracy." But in the mid-1990s, it became increasingly clear that President Akaev's practice was not matching his rhetoric (Anderson 1999:55–62; International Crisis Group 2004), leading ultimately to his surprisingly quick and bloodless ouster in the March 2005 "Tulip Revolution."

17. Since the 1990s, more and more Kyrgyz are buying or building houses in certain new neighborhoods like Aktilek (opened in response to needs expressed in the Osh Riots) and in more central parts of the city.

18. Newer mahallas established in the postwar expansion of the city tended to have roughly rectilinear layouts and a major internal street, which was wider, paved, and straight.

19. The *som* is the Kyrgyz Republic's national currency introduced in 1993. This country is the first Central Asian republic to leave the Russian ruble zone.

20. Very similar mahalla-based meetings of peer groups are found in Uzbekistan, called *gap* ("talk") and in northwest China among Uyghurs, called *oturash* ("sitting").

21. Their association of mahalla to national renewal is also probably influenced by post-Soviet Uzbekistan's nationalist ideology and campaign to use the mahalla in that effort. The year 2003 was proclaimed to be mahalla *yili* (Year of the Mahalla) in Uzbekistan. Osh Uzbeks watch much state-controlled television from Uzbekistan and are influenced by the nationalist propaganda from this neighboring state.

22. Representations of mahallas as sites of a timeless Uzbek traditionalism are perpetuated in many scholarly works, such as Poliakov and Olcott 1992; Shalinsky 1993.

23. For theories and case studies of state techniques of rule, see Hansen and Stepputat 2001; Scott 1998.

24. Their motivations differ from the marginalized poor who turn to Islamist movements that seek to overthrow existing governments or at least implement Islamic law at the state level. The Islam of Osh's ziyofats—what they call "the true Islam of our fathers" rather than the foreign "Wahabbi" movements—advocate no such political revolution, but emphasize personal piety for communal renewal within the existing state.

REFERENCES

Anderson, John. 1999. *Kyrgyzstan, Central Asia's Island of Democracy?* Amsterdam: Harwood Academic Publishers.
Andrusz, Gregory D. 1984. *Housing and Urban Development in the U.S.S.R.* London: MacMillan.
Asankanov, Ablaibek, and Shavkat Atakhanov. 2002. "The Gypsies of Central Asia." *Anthropology and Archeology of Eurasia* 41:9–15.
Berdahl, Daphne, Matti Bunzl, and Martha Lampland (eds.). 2000. *Altering States: Ethnographies of Transition in Eastern Europe and the Former Soviet Union.* Ann Arbor: The University of Michigan Press.
Burawoy, Michael, and Katherine Verdery (eds.). 1999. *Uncertain Transition: Ethnographies of Change in the Postsocialist World.* Lanham, Md.: Rowman & Littlefield.
Hansen, Thomas Blom, and Finn Stepputat (eds.). 2001. *States of Imagination: Ethnographic Explorations of the Postcolonial State.* Durham, N.C.: Duke University Press.
Humphrey, Caroline. 2002. *The Unmaking of Soviet Life: Everyday Economies after Socialism.* Ithaca, N.Y.: Cornell University Press.
International Crisis Group. 2001. "Kyrgyzstan at Ten: Trouble in the 'Island of Democracy.'" Osh, Kyrgyzstan/Brussels: International Crisis Group.
———. 2004. "Political Transition in Kyrgyzstan: Problems and Prospects." Osh, Kyrgyzstan/Brussels: International Crisis Group.
Poliakov, Sergei Petrovich, and Martha Brill Olcott. 1992. *Everyday Islam: Religion and Tradition in Rural Central Asia.* Armonk, N.Y.: M. E. Sharpe.
Scott, James C. 1998. *Seeing Like a State: How Certain Schemes to Improve the Human Condition Have Failed.* New Haven, Conn.: Yale University Press.
Shalinsky, Audrey. 1993. *Long Years of Exile: Central Asian Refugees in Afghanistan and Pakistan.* Lanham, Md.: University Press of America.
Specter, Michael. 1995. "Opium Finding Its Silk Road in the Chaos of Central Asia." *New York Times*, A1, May 2, 1995. New York.
Verdery, Katherine. 1996. *What Was Socialism, and What Comes Next?* Princeton, N.J.: Princeton University Press.

PART THREE

Gender

Gender and studies interested in gender concentrate on the roles played by both sexes in society, as well as what members of both sexes feel are appropriate and desirable roles for each throughout various phases of an individual's life. Generally speaking, twentieth-century gender studies have focused on the positions of girls and women in culture and society rather than boys and men or more complicated issues of homosexuality and transgender identities. A new generation of scholars in gender studies is now broadening the approach of the field.

Gender has occupied an important place in the historical and social science literature of the lands of the former Soviet Union. This stands to reason because a major part of the Bolshevik Revolution of 1917 dedicated itself to the liberation of all women throughout the former tsarist empire. If women's liberation were to play a key role in the radical restructuring of society and the types of functions that people play within it, revolutionary changes that would transform gender relations had to begin in early childhood. Both within home life and in the Soviet educational system, girls had to be taught what their possibilities could be, and whether or not they would have to clash with patriarchal figures and values or the religions to which they belonged if they were to achieve new social statuses, from major cities and provincial towns to collective farms. As the articles by Douglas Northrop and Marianne Kamp display, the Soviet establishment sought to transform gender roles through a restructuring of many of the most mundane features of everyday life in Soviet Central Asia, seen as potentially the most resistant region to women's "liberation."

Soviet politicians and scholars continually furnished voluminous literature and statistics to provide evidence for increasing gender equality in Soviet social and economic life, making pointed comparisons to the tsarist past as well as contemporary Western Europe and North America. Many of these claims were exaggerated, but the Soviet system created all kinds of educational, professional, and political possibilities for women that simply did not exist prior to the Bolshevik Revolution. In Central Asia, however, the facts of social and cultural life, particularly as reflected in everyday attitudes toward girls and women's public and private roles as well as toward the proper division of labor in society, did not so readily change. In essence, while Soviet leaders found it relatively easy to legislate and effect institutional transformations, it was not nearly so easy to overturn patriarchal norms, expectations, and entrenched patterns of daily life behavior. Determined Communists of the Soviet era, regardless of ethnic or national origins, nonetheless did not tread lightly on local notions of gender decorum. Recent scholarship has shown that Soviet initiatives did eventually serve to undermine traditional gender roles as well as local forms of Islamic faith. Yet oppressive and patriarchal though many practices of early twentieth century Central Asian culture may have been, the greatest controversies over cultural life between the sexes have revolved around the perception that changes have been driven by foreigners with alien values and ideas. Such local reactions have forced many in the Western world to question the inherent sense of righteousness that would seem to make the practical and intellectual support of women's liberation anywhere axiomatic. Perhaps unfortunately, the less one's depth of knowledge about someone else's culture is, the more likely one is inclined to support some act or movement that is seen to confer universal benefits.

Having said that, we and our contributors have witnessed what appears to be a steady sociocultural erosion of women's rights since the fall of the U.S.S.R., despite the official commitment of Central Asian governments to the Soviet-era laws and principles that regulated and promoted equality between the sexes. While some may point to the increase in devout Islamic dress codes, including veiling, among urban and rural women, we think that this is of less concern than the way in which sexist and chauvinist ideologies have crept back into vogue, very often indeed with a specious appeal to Islam. Uehling's article personally captures how Tajik women and men now try to "naturalize" men's and women's roles—basically by cutting women out of most responsible and profitable spheres of the economy, not to mention discouraging them from pursuing professional careers. But lest the reader think that this retrogressive tendency only really matters in terms of education and jobs, as vital as these two realms of human development are, we should point out that girls and women face newer restrictions and demands in relation to their socializing, potential marriage partners, reproductive choices, household work burdens—including childcare, cooking, cleaning, and shopping—and even to whom and how they shall be married.

Our contributors to this section are among the first generation of Western scholars to have access to in-depth studies of, and interactions with, Central Asian societies. Previously unavailable textual and human sources have enabled them to expose how daily life has been played out and mediated between the sexes during the nineteenth, twentieth, and early twenty-first centuries. Marianne Kamp and Douglas Northrop take us into the earlier half of the twentieth century to explore the planning and execution of women's liberation campaigns that affected the minutiae of daily life. Situating her article, derived largely from a then contemporary Uzbek women's journal, Kamp discusses the concept of modernism pervading Uzbek life in the 1930s. She does this by profiling the new stresses and strains in the life of a young Uzbek woman who is becoming a Soviet person, too. Her explanation illustrates just how a young woman had to negotiate the path to a new life given local outlooks and attitudes. Moreover, she points to the changing nature of basic customs, such as a wedding, and how life-cycle events reflected aspects of cultural transformation. Northrop delves into the 1920s–1930s Soviet policy of liberating girls and women by having them cast off the veil, a violence-promoting effort that struck simultaneous blows at traditional society and Islam. His article demonstrates the reach, and the limits, of the new state's power into all kinds of domains of everyday life, and how state representatives and ordinary citizens accommodated and/or resisted such encroachments.

Elizabeth Constantine and Greta Uehling present two deeply personal accounts of the place of gender in rapidly reconfiguring contemporary Central Asian societies, including rural and urban Uzbekistan and Tajikistan. Constantine provides a unique perspective from her fieldwork in Uzbekistan's Ferghana Valley as she describes how younger and older women relate to their own roles and status in their culture. She proves yet again how cautious we must be whenever we generalize about any group or class of persons, even in a setting as small and seemingly undifferentiated as a "typical" Uzbek village. Uehling provides a sometimes harrowing account of changing perceptions of gender in post-Soviet and rather disordered Tajikistan. She speaks to how recent socioeconomic changes coupled with an upswelling of religious feeling have forced gains made by women quite a few steps back. She relates her thinking via personal experiences with a Tajik family as well as a local "strongman" with whom she shares a very interesting evening. Their conversations, as Uehling records them, make for unique and fascinating reading in the new scholarship on gender relations in contemporary Central Asia.

6. The Limits of Liberation: Gender, Revolution, and the Veil in Everyday Life in Soviet Uzbekistan

Douglas Northrop

Banners waved, music played, and local newspapers reported an "unceasing hubbub of girls' voices, happy songs, [and] infectious dancing" among the crowds in early October 1935, when the First All-Uzbek Congress of Laboring Female Youth opened in Tashkent.[1] Amid triumphal Stalinist pageantry, several hundred young women arrived in the Uzbek capital city to discuss the issues and problems faced by indigenous women in Soviet Central Asia. The delegates came from throughout Uzbekistan and across the region, and a few hailed from farther away, from Moscow and other Muslim areas such as Azerbaijan. Most were young, married Uzbek peasant women who had joined the Young Communist League (*Komsomol*) after completing rudimentary schooling.[2] They embodied the promise of Soviet liberation after nearly twenty years of Bolshevik power, as Soviet press coverage related in glowing terms how far Uzbek women had come since 1917—and especially since 1927, when the Communist Party had with great fanfare launched a major ongoing campaign to improve the social status of women in Central Asia. The 650 young women at the congress—politically active, economically independent, and apparently eager to fight local patriarchy—were taken as living evidence of this campaign's success. Soviet newspapers proudly noted that some delegates had even trained as parachutists: a far cry from the strict practices of female seclusion and heavy horsehair veils that were said to have shaped their everyday lives before the arrival of Soviet emancipation.[3]

Amid the pomp and circumstance, however, dissonant notes could be heard. Even as they tried to leave listeners with an upbeat, inspirational message, many speakers pointed to continuing failures of the party's concerted effort to "liberate" the Muslim women of Uzbekistan. In one of the

An Uzbek woman with her children. She wears a head-to-toe robe of heavy cotton, known as a *paranji,* which holds in place over her face a *chachvon,* or mesh screen of woven horsehair
Rossisskii gosudarstvennyi arkhiv kinofotodokumentov.

main speeches at the congress, I. Artykov, a top leader of the Uzbek Komsomol, tried to outline the profound yet contradictory meanings of Soviet power in the ten-year-old Uzbek Soviet Socialist Republic. By 1935, Bolshevik efforts in Central Asia had focused on women's liberation for almost a decade, and Soviet authorities and women's activists had mobilized the full force and considerable authority of the Stalinist state to make this vision a reality. What had their efforts meant in practice? One of Artykov's examples, which recounted the life story of Ashur-Bibi Tashmatova, a young Uzbek girl orphaned early in life who now worked productively for the Soviet state, provided an unexpectedly revealing answer. Despite her ostensible status as a liberated Soviet woman, Tashmatova's biography actually served more to show that everyday life in Uzbekistan had changed only in some ways, and not always in the direction the party had intended. More than anything else, her story illustrated the severe constraints that existed on Soviet power in Muslim Central Asia during the 1930s.

Artykov started by describing Ashur-Bibi Tashmatova's difficult childhood. After being orphaned at a young age, he said, Tashmatova had been raised by two older sisters. Unfortunately, one sister died when she was just nine years old and the other when she was thirteen. Her only brother was then working in a distant province, so Tashmatova was left alone and soon found herself forced to marry her elder deceased sister's forty-five-year-old husband. This man already had seven wives, Artykov noted, not to mention business connections in Afghanistan (where he had lived for several years) and personal links to prominent anti-Soviet figures. Tashmatova's life became still more difficult when her new husband returned from Afghanistan and started working as a Soviet official (of all things) in the town of Denau. Several times she ran away from him, but on each occasion he used his new government connections to have her caught and forcibly returned to him. Fortunately, Artykov said, at this point the Soviet police discovered his association with anti-Soviet "bandits," and he was condemned to death and shot.

To the assembled delegates, many Young Communists and all Stalinist heroes, this story of revolutionary justice must have struck an inspirational note. The Soviet courts had ferreted out a traitor and thus struck a blow simultaneously against the forces of political counterrevolution and cultural patriarchy. At last, they might have expected to hear, Soviet power had enabled Tashmatova to achieve economic independence, political liberation, and personal fulfillment. It was an article of faith to many party activists that women in Soviet Uzbekistan could achieve full equality with men, and that they had the opportunity to attain levels of political consciousness that were impossible before 1917. Artykov's story, though, took a different turn. "After her husband had been shot," he continued,

> other men courted and wooed her, and in the end she was again given forcibly into marriage, to one Jumamir Nasarov, the head of a local village soviet and before that a wealthy *boi* [landlord]. She was his second wife, and afterward he took a third. To prevent anyone holding him to account for his polygyny, he went to ZAGS [*Zapis' aktov grazhdanskogo sostoianiia*, the local Soviet civil registry office] and divorced both of his first two wives—but told them that according to the [Islamic law] code of *shariat* they [still] had to live [with him].

Fearing that Tashmatova's brother might return and see him mistreating his sister—and that he might then be denounced to Soviet authorities "as a former kulak and polygynist," Nasarov hired assassins to have the brother killed.

At this point Tashmatova surely could be forgiven some disillusionment with the Soviet cause. Yet she remained loyal, Artykov proudly declared, as she continued to plead for help from the authorities:

> Ashur-Bibi went several times to the village soviet for help, asking for a divorce, but every time she was told that no divorce could be granted without her husband's permission.[4] Finally she turned to a local agrono-

mist, who wrote to the district [capital], whence came a committee of inquiry that arrested Ashur-Bibi's husband. From there he managed to escape from custody, and—knowing that she had been the main reason for his arrest—he tried repeatedly, over several days, to kill her. Afterward he was again arrested and deported outside Uzbekistan.

At this point—at last—Ashur-Bibi Tashmatova seemed to be free. In 1931, Artykov said, she finally threw off her heavy black veil, joined the Young Communist League, and became a full-fledged Soviet worker, accepting a job as director of a nursery.

This was the moment of transfiguration required in any heroic Stalinist narrative. But what was her new, unveiled life like? How did it compare with the dark past? Artykov concluded his tale by describing Tashmatova's current home life—and made it clear that much still remained to be done:

> Now she has a third husband. He, Babahanov, is a Soviet worker, a Komsomol member, the assistant director and secretary of the village soviet. She also was married to him against her will. For five or six months they lived together well, but afterward he started to demand that she abandon her social work, started to beat her and, finally, making use of his position in the village soviet, wrote an attestation of divorce, put it in her coat pocket, gathered up all of his things, and left. When he was called before the district executive committee and asked on what basis he had written this attestation, he declared that it had been a joke.

By 1935, Artykov noted, she had lived with Babahanov for two years, but had experienced only insults and mockery, even occasional threats on her life. Shortly before the congress convened, moreover, she had come to Tashkent for training—and he mailed her a divorce. One more time she sought official help, turning to her local Komsomol and her district party leader for assistance—but, Artykov concluded ruefully, "they did nothing."[5]

Fluid social structures, population mobility across supposedly inviolable international borders, and the stark weakness of government and party organizations—indeed, local officials' active opposition to party policy: these are only some of the themes that emerge through this story of an orphaned Uzbek girl shuttled from one abusive husband to another. Apparent, too, is the Soviet emphasis on measuring the political and cultural level of Central Asian Muslims through the character of their intimate and family lives. This equation made it very difficult for even loyal women like Tashmatova to negotiate the conflicting demands that they faced. The complexities turned up by the tale of Ashur-Bibi Tashmatova—and, no less important, the way Artykov chose to tell her story—captures the unsettled flavor of this encounter between Soviet power and Muslim Central Asian society.

A QUOTIDIAN REVOLUTION: VEILS AND FAMILY LIFE IN THE SOVIET EMPIRE

Why did this encounter develop into a confrontation over the Uzbek family? What was at stake in the telling of Tashmatova's story? How did such apparently mundane details of everyday life take on broader political significance? How did women like Tashmatova maneuver between the demands of the Soviet state, on the one hand, and the requirements of religious devotion and perceived national customs, on the other? By 1935, when Artykov addressed the congress in Tashkent, the wider Stalin Revolution had been underway for seven years. This was an era of massive state and party campaigns that sought nothing less than to build a new kind of civilization in the USSR. While the capitalist West languished amid the Great Depression, these all-encompassing Stalinist campaigns aimed to restructure Soviet society completely, most obviously through rapid industrialization and the forced collectivization of peasant agriculture. They also aimed to create a new kind of Soviet citizen, through a "cultural revolution" that intended to produce a New Soviet Man (and, albeit usually less prominently, Woman). These were also the years of vast party purges and ultimately the nightmarish Great Terror of 1937–1938.

All of these campaigns had an impact on Soviet Central Asia: millions of Muslim nomads and peasants were settled on collective farms and put to work in new factories. In the later 1930s, top party officials were shot or sent to Siberia, while the landscape itself was reworked in huge projects such as the Ferghana Canal, which aimed to boost cotton production by making the desert fertile. Indigenous populations were simultaneously being recast, taught the various components of "cultured" behavior: to read Marx and Lenin; to visit a doctor when ill; to appreciate modern science, engineering, and art; and to wash one's body with soap. And as the unhappy tale of Ashur-Bibi Tashmatova makes plain, in southern Central Asia the turmoil of building a new world was also expressed in other realms of everyday life. New identities—local, regional, and national—emerged especially from bitter struggles over gender roles and intimate family relationships. Why?

By this point Bolshevik leaders had struggled for almost two decades to apply a Marxist framework to Central Asia. In 1917 the area had still been very rural, and the few urban workers who did exist tended to be Russians. Most lived separately from the local population in Europeanized "New Cities" that were built after the tsarist conquest. The lack of an indigenous proletariat complicated efforts to find allies in the region and led Bolsheviks to seek other ways to translate the party's program for building socialism into the largely Muslim cultural world of Turkistan. At first they had tried to transform Central Asia by repeating campaigns that had been employed in Russia. Antireligious campaigns criticized Muslim clerics as "class oppressors," and a large-scale land and water reform in 1925–1926 aimed to redistribute these key resources to poor and landless peasants. By 1926, though, attacks on wealthy landlords and Islam had proved for the most part unsuccessful at creating either visible class identities or widespread pro-Bolshevik sympathies. The local Communist party was still tiny, isolated, and largely alien. It numbered only a few tens of thousands of members, concentrated almost entirely in the cities and drawn disproportionately from the ranks of recent immigrants to Central Asia.[6]

In response, in late 1926 the party's top regional leaders in Tashkent, acting through the supervisory body of the Central Asian Bureau (*Sredaz-biuro*), decided, at the urging of enthusiastic activists in the party's Women's Department (*Zhenotdel*), to try a new approach.[7] Local society was patriarchal, they reasoned, and many Muslim women, forced to stay hidden in public and secluded at home, saw themselves as victims of indigenous men, as much as of previous Russian imperialist oppressors. Party and Zhenotdel leaders thus developed an interpretation of Central Asian society in which all Muslim women were deemed victims of patriarchal oppression—in Marxist terms, they functioned as a "surrogate proletariat."[8] In this view, women represented a massive, latent group of potential allies that the party could mobilize by publicizing a message of gender equality and liberation. If the Revolution was to succeed in Central Asia, in other words, it had to be translated into everyday life. To most Soviet women's activists—many of whom had little experience in the Islamic world—it seemed self-evident that such a message would be welcomed by their Muslim sisters.

Party activists in Tashkent launched their campaign on the socialist holiday of International Women's Day (March 8) 1927, calling it a *hujum*, or assault, against the "moldy old ways" of female seclusion and inequality. This campaign's goal was nothing less than the complete and immediate transformation of everyday life, or *byt* (in Uzbek, *turmush*), as measured especially in the realms of gender relations and family life. The hujum took different forms in different places, but in Uzbekistan, as well as Tajikistan and Azerbaijan, it aimed above all at the eradication of the head-to-toe veils that many urban Muslim women, and girls over the age of nine or ten, wore in the presence of unrelated men.* Despite the almost complete absence from party ranks of Uzbek women to help lead this effort, the mostly Russian activists of the Zhenotdel aimed to complete the heroic liberation of Central Asian women in less than six months—a schedule that would enable them to celebrate success by October 1927, the tenth anniversary of the Bolshevik Revolution.[9]

---

*These veils consisted of a heavy cotton robe (*paranji*) worn over a face screen of woven horsehair (*chachvon*).

It was at this point that Ashur-Bibi Tashmatova's struggle became a state priority, as a bitter and often violent confrontation ensued in the lives of thousands of local women like her. The campaign against the veil was complicated, contested, and contradictory; over the next fifteen years, it transformed all sides. Soviet reformers and their Muslim opponents alike came to define their cultural practices and social values through the everyday customs of millions of individual women. On the one hand, state action thus created unexpected possibilities for women: intensive efforts to transform and liberate Muslim women remained among the highest state and party priorities in Central Asia, even as women's issues fell from prominence elsewhere in the USSR during the 1930s. On the other hand, this common ground of debate ultimately helped define a specific, local, and deeply gendered vocabulary for both Central Asian Bolshevism and Uzbek national identity, and it left these women personally in a very difficult position, facing strong pressure from all sides.

How did they respond? This is a difficult question, because few of these women left written records to explain their opinions or motivations. But there are ways to use the sources that have survived to identify a broad spectrum of female (as well as male) views. For many local women, gender concerns were fully as important as party activists had hoped—and for these women, the hujum was a welcome portent of greater equality in male-female relations. Hundreds, even thousands of such women threw off their veils and kept them off. A handful went so far as to join the Zhenotdel, working assiduously to unveil others and to eliminate all forms of indigenous patriarchy. A few, such as the prominent women's activist Tojikhon Shadieva, became personal icons of liberation, with their life stories recounted in popular books, newspapers, museum exhibits, and inspirational films.[10]

Who were these women that responded to the Soviet call? Some were the wives and relatives of Communist Party members, especially high-ranking ones, who faced strong pressure to liberate their families at the outset of the unveiling campaign. Desperately poor female beggars and especially prostitutes—few of whom in any case had worn veils before—also sought Zhenotdel aid and support. Other Uzbek women unveiled for just the reasons party activists expected: they resented the restrictions placed on local women. For these women, the Soviet campaign brought new possibilities, even a real liberation. Although some unveilings were coerced by over-eager Bolshevik activists, the positive appeal of the campaign was also evident in the social locations of women who flocked to the cause. Shadieva, for example, came from a poor family: at age eleven, she had been married against her will to a middle-aged folk-healer, becoming his eighth wife.[11] Local women who unveiled during and after 1927 hailed disproportionately from such marginal social positions: orphans, widows, and runaway girls, for example, sought refuge in Soviet institutions and women's clubs far out of proportion to their overall numbers.[12] This may have been due to their socialization in (and financial, physical, even emotional dependence on) state institutions. Equally plausible, though, is the possibility that they were enabled to unveil by their position outside local kin networks. They were thus less constrained by male relatives or social pressure, and perhaps more able to act as they wished.

But for the most part, Uzbek women who considered unveiling (or otherwise cooperated with Soviet activists) faced enormous pressure from their families and neighbors. While at home, husbands could prevent them from attending Soviet meetings or parades, and threatened divorce if they unveiled.[13] Outside the home, any unveiled woman was assumed to be the equivalent of a prostitute, and frequently was treated as such. Fights broke out when schoolchildren taunted classmates about their newly unveiled mothers—who had, they shouted, taken up prostitution.[14] Unveiled women bolstered themselves for harsh criticism every time they stepped outside. Raised in a culture that stressed honor as a paramount female virtue, they faced mockery and ridicule at every turn. The continual mutterings of "prostitute" from passersby had an effect, sometimes reducing the demoralized women to tears; they pleaded for help from Soviet authorities, saying that soon they would be driven to re-veil.

Consider the primary document included in the appendix below. This petition, written in 1928 by twenty schoolteachers in Samarkand, shows these women willing to speak up, to criticize and challenge the Soviet government for its lack of support, and to demand more help. It also gives a taste of the everyday danger these women faced: violence, either real or threatened, fundamentally shaped their daily lives. As this document reveals, participating in the hujum meant taking serious risks: in the late 1920s thousands of Muslim women in Central Asia were attacked, and frequently raped, for taking part. Hundreds were killed; some of the corpses were mutilated in grisly fashion. Often investigations concluded that male relatives of the victim—husbands, fathers, brothers—had carried out these murders to remove a perceived smirch on the family's honor.[15]

Yet men and women alike played a complicated role in this story. Some indigenous men in the party, after all, were among those trying to persuade (or force) local women to unveil. And for their part, only a relative handful of Uzbek women actually joined the Communist Party, or participated actively and consistently in the hujum.[16] Many others tried to ignore the campaign, refusing to attend parades or official meetings, avoiding Soviet officials, and staying away from the Europeanized New Cities. Most indigenous women probably went about their daily lives as they always had done. Since few explained themselves in writing, historians now can only guess at their innermost views and beliefs. Yet the surviving sources do make plain the creativity of the ostensibly silent Uzbek woman in adapting the conflicting demands of the hujum to her world. Some women, for instance, removed their paranji and chachvon, as called for by official campaign slogans ("Down with the paranji!")—but then covered themselves just as completely with a shawl or other type of cloak, or in some cases a tablecloth. Others unveiled at demonstrations, only to re-veil before reaching home.[17] When forced by party or Soviet officials to participate, many women showed themselves masters of *seeming* to cooperate, only as long and as far as was necessary. As the Andijon Zhenotdel put it in an unusually perceptive and discerning report in early 1928,

> In the beginning [we] tried to prepare an accounting of the veiled and the re-veiled, but afterward became convinced that it was impossible to take such an inventory. After March 8, the paranjis that had been cast off and burned stuck tenaciously to the women's faces. Under the various influences of cultural traditions, the stagnation and ignorance of the local men, and the agitation of socially alien elements, women re-veiled themselves again with paranjis, with the sleeves of their cloaks [*khalats*], or with shawls. This category of "temporarily unveiled" is difficult to count as either "unveiled" or "veiled." Many women go unveiled at meetings, at family circles, and also in the New City, but in their own *mahalla* (neighborhood) walk about veiled. It is the same in the villages.[18]

The same report went on to note that when jobs were available at the local cotton processing and dairy factories, only unveiled women had been considered eligible. Hence, many women left their veils at home to apply— but put them on again as soon as they left. The report concluded,

> The Uzbek woman is very cautious. She boldly and confidently walks to women's meetings—unveiled. And to [Soviet] family circles; she goes [unveiled] wherever she knows that she will not run into insults, ridicule, and mockery. [But] it is hard to find unveiled women at the bazaars, or on the lively streets of the Old Cities. Here [the Uzbek woman] tries to cover herself, that is, [she veils] in those places where insults can most often be heard directed at the unveiled.[19]

Perhaps most surprising to Soviet activists at the time (and to many Western readers today), a few women even led the charge on the other side, bitterly denouncing the hujum, flatly refusing even to discuss the possibility of unveiling, and harshly criticizing women who did take part. Party activists were befuddled to find veiled women as well as men behind the street harassment and insults. In a handful of explosive cases, indeed—discussed only in whispers, and recorded in top-secret party dossiers—Uzbek women even organized violent resistance to their own "liberation." In May 1929, for example, the secret police reported on one such anti-Soviet gathering of two hundred women in rural Andijon province. The women complained that their veils had been forcibly confiscated on March 8, and they decided to hold a protest march on May Day—but events soon spiraled out of control. Led by Ugul Bi Rajababaeva, the wife of a former Soviet official, they marched to the local Soviet office building and demanded the return of their veils. When they were rebuffed, Rajababaeva pulled a knife on a senior police officer, who quickly fled the room. The women regrouped and about a dozen of them decided to try again— two days later, they showed up at the police officer's home, armed with knives and stones. Neither the officer nor his wife were at home, though, so the battalion of angry women then roamed the town, confronting and "savagely beating" unveiled women they found on the street.[20]

The story of how Uzbek society responded to the unveiling campaign is obviously complicated. Given the various and conflicting meanings applied to the veil, though, the tenacity with which it was both attacked and defended becomes more understandable. In the longer term, the Soviet decision in 1927 to focus on dramatic public unveilings proved mostly counterproductive; by hardening Muslim hostility toward Bolshevik agitators perceived as foreign urban atheists, it made cultural change more rather than less difficult. And by deeming the veil a preeminent symbol of Muslim Uzbek culture, the Bolsheviks only gave it new strength. Conflict over women's lives—as seen in the congress of 1935 and in the ongoing street confrontations—thus represents a story of resistance and power, but one far more complex than it first appears. Bolshevik leaders inadvertently reinforced the seclusion of Uzbek women in the short term, effectively creating powerful resistance to their own women's liberation policies. Despite stated goals to the contrary, that is, Soviet efforts played a large role in creating the veil as a national symbol and an emblem of a "tradition" that was in fact quite new.[21]

Although the campaign of 1927 aimed to eliminate the veil within six months, it actually took far longer—perhaps thirty years or so—until the paranji and chachvon did fade from everyday use. The reasons for this shift in the 1950s and 1960s fall outside the scope of this essay, but they arose in a fundamentally different historical context—one shaped especially by the massive, social, cultural, and demographic changes during and after World War II. That war played a key role in remaking Central Asia. It was a hugely destructive conflict—roughly 27 million Soviet citizens and soldiers died overall—and Central Asians participated fully. Millions of Slavic citizens were evacuated to the East, to the Urals and Central Asia; many Russian orphans were settled with poor Uzbek families, as local Muslim men marched away to fight Hitler. Everyday life in Central Asia—not to mention the attitude of Central Asians toward the Soviet state, which so many died to defend—changed fundamentally in the 1940s. The veil's slow decline fits into this broader postwar Sovietization of everyday life and culture in Uzbekistan.[22]

Yet the hujum's other, sometimes unintended, legacies did not disappear. At a minimum, the importance of the unveiling campaign and the fierceness of the conflict that ensued showed how intricately gender relations came to be interwoven with relations of social and political power in Central Asia, and how women became central to and emblematic of an emerging Uzbek national identity. Indeed, women in some places (especially the Ferghana Valley) started wearing veils once again following Uzbekistan's independence in 1991, as a way of expressing their national as well as religio-cultural identity.[23] It was no accident, then, that in 1935 Artykov had chosen to deliver his political message by retelling several individual women's life stories, among them that of Ashur-Bibi Tashmatova. To many Bolsheviks, the veiled woman was self-evidently an oppressed creature, symbolizing all that was most backward and primitive in the tsarist (capitalist) empire. She showed, they thought, the undeniable need for immediate Soviet uplift and emancipation. To the party's opponents, though, the unveiled woman, equally obviously, meant something else altogether: foreign, colonial control, along with sexual license, poor character, uncertainty over children's patrimony, the explicit denial of God and his law, and ultimately nothing less than the end of the world. Women such as Tashmatova were the ground for this struggle, and women's own agency thus remained a troublesome and difficult issue. Women's status as conscious actors, as people continually making decisions and individual choices to respond to the world around them, greatly complicated these countervailing narratives of liberation and resistance.

APPENDIX

Petition signed by twenty female schoolteachers and submitted to the Samarkand City Soviet, 1928. (RGASPI, f. 62, op. 2, d. 1692, ll. 51–52.)

If your fine statements about the liberation of women were sincere, then we ask you to consider this petition at the next meeting of the city soviet and to finally resolve, once and for all, the question of unveiling before March 8 [International Women's Day].

In the past, when we languished [at home, surrounded by] four walls, we endured the outrages of our husbands; now we, liberated women, appear as prostitutes in the imaginations of women who still wear the paranji.

Is this the reward of a proletarian government to us?

Having started [to pursue] the issue, you did not drive it to a conclusion, and then [you] declared that unveiling is a matter of the free will of women themselves. Based on this declaration, nearly all of the women who still wear the paranji are denouncing us for having sold out our faith, calling us shameless [women] and dogs of the street. . . .

At the time of our liberation, you told us that with regards to people who responded badly [both] to liberation and liberated women, you would take the very strictest measures. In this we still are not satisfied. On the streets, at weddings, in other gatherings, everywhere and all around, we see and hear [nothing but] scornful attitudes and bad opinions, both from men and from women who are not unveiled.

[The petitioners admit that reporting such episodes to the *Zhenotdel*, the city soviet, or the district party committee (*raikom*) has sometimes secured results: arrests and some convictions have followed.]

But this has not at all given us any guarantee against cases of murder during our trips out of town or, just as much, the fermentation induced on secluded, out-of-the-way streets by the appearance of [our unveiled] faces. Against whom, then, can our lifeless body be avenged?

If even we working women, the loyal followers of Lenin, are [treated like this, facing insults and humiliation with every step], then nothing will be left for us but to shout '*Voidod!*' ['Help!']* and to shout it not once, but thousands of times.

If you are not able to bring about the liberation of women, then we cannot go any further. [But] if a tree's roots remain [strong], then it will not wither away when attacks come on the surface.

If you really intend decisively to attack the paranji, then we request of you the following:

1. If a woman in a paranji brings wares to the market, let no one buy from her.
2. Cooperatives are not to sell goods to women in paranjis.
3. The judicial organs are not to hear the requests of women in paranjis.
4. Women in paranjis are not to be given medicines by clinics and drugstores.
5. Members of the party and Komsomol, if their wives wear the paranji, are to be removed from their positions.
6. The daughters and sons of merchants are not to be accepted in Soviet schools.

If you do not implement these requests of ours before March 8, then do not blame your Red Teachers if they once again begin to wear the paranji.

[signed]

NOTES

This essay is revised and expanded from Douglas Northrop, *Veiled Empire: Gender and Power in Stalinist Central Asia* (Ithaca: Cornell University Press, 2004).
    1. M. P., "Chudesnyi splav," *Pravda Vostoka* (hereafter *PV*), 3 October 1935.
    2. According to statistics compiled at the Congress, of the 650 women in atten-

---

*"*Voidod!*" literally means "Help!," but is uttered only at moments of extreme distress, sorrow, and despair.

dance, 576 were younger than age 24; 495 were ethnically "Uzbek"; 424 had joined the Komsomol; 451 were married; 502 were peasants; and only 90 had more than an elementary education. See Özbekiston respublikasi markaziy davlat arkhivi (hereafter ÖzRMDA), f. 86, op. 10, d. 634, ll. 346–350, or the published records at *Pervyi s"ezd trudiashcheisia zhenskoi molodezhi Uzbekistana* (hereafter *PSTZhMUz*) (Tashkent, 1936), 123–125.

3. M. P., "Chudesnyi splav."

4. She must have wished the village soviet to force her husband to grant her a religious (shariat) divorce, since he already had obtained a civil divorce at ZAGS.

5. She may have been seeking help to secure alimony, not necessarily trying to prevent the divorce. This story is taken from ÖzRMDA, f. 86, op. 10, d. 634, ll. 243–245. An edited version—omitting some of the most revealing information, such as the back-and-forth movement into Afghanistan—was published at *PSTZhMUz*, 63–64. Some stylistic editing in the published version is reflected in the story as quoted here.

6. In early 1926 the Uzbek SSR's Communist Party organization, the KP(b)Uz, reported a total of 18,351 members and candidate members, or less than 0.5 percent of the republic's overall population. Within this group, Europeans outnumbered Uzbeks, 9,043 to 7,736; men outnumbered women fifteen to one; and almost a third were completely illiterate, with only 2.2 percent boasting a higher education. (Z. Simanovich, "Itogi partiinoi perepisi v Uzbekistane," *Izvestiia TsK KP(b)Uz*, no. 1 [1926], 9–10.)

7. It had been two centuries since Peter the Great ended the seclusion of elite Muscovite women.

8. An American political scientist formulated the phrase. See Gregory J. Massell, *The Surrogate Proletariat: Moslem Women and Revolutionary Strategies in Soviet Central Asia, 1919–1929* (Princeton: Princeton University Press, 1974).

9. A reckoning in July 1927 found only 457 Uzbek women in the KP(b)Uz. (ÖzRMDA, f. 86, op. 2, d. 27, l. 37.) This figure represents less than 2 percent of the Uzbek Communist Party's membership rolls; it also means that an essentially invisible proportion (roughly 0.03 percent) of the overall Uzbek female population had been enrolled in the party. On the expected rapid speed of the campaign, see ÖzRMDA, f. 86, op. 1, d. 5134, l. 25; Rossiisskii gosudarstvennyi arkhiv sotsial'no-politicheskoi istorii (hereafter RGASPI), f. 62, op. 2, d. 1205, l. 4ob, and d. 1242, ll. 31 and 140ob; and Prezident devoni arkhivi, f. 58, op. 3, d. 1560, l. 57. Also Serafima Liubimova, "Oktiabr' i truzhenitsa zarubezhnogo Vostoka," *Za partiiu*, no. 3 (1927): 77–80. On these activists, see *Khudzhum: Znachit nastuplenie* (Tashkent, 1987) and *Probuzhdennye velikim Oktiabrem: Sbornik ocherkov i vospominanii* (Tashkent, 1961).

10. See, for instance, S. Normatov, *Tadzhikhon* (Tashkent, 1966).

11. Her husband, who was in his forties, reportedly had eight wives already, but one had died. Some sources, such as Normatov, list Tojikhon's age at marriage as fourteen rather than eleven.

12. Such women are discussed at *PSTZhMUZ*, 63–66.

13. RGASPI, f. 62, op. 2, d. 1214, ll. 28, 38, 115, 146–147, and 154.

14. Ibid., l. 56.

15. Ibid., l. 75.

16. By 1933, the number of Uzbek women in the party reached approximately 3,500, or perhaps 0.2 percent of the indigenous female population. See Northrop, *Veiled Empire*, 227.

17. RGASPI, f. 62, op. 2, d. 2056, l. 56, and ÖzRMDA, f. 86, op. 1, d. 5719, l. 16, and f. 736, op. 1, d. 933, l. 64ob.

18. RGASPI, f. 62, op. 2, d. 1690, l. 11.

19. Ibid, l. 13.

20. RGASPI, f. 62, op. 2, d. 2064, ll. 51–51ob.

21. Before the mid–nineteenth-century tsarist conquest of Central Asia, urban women had worn a different sort of head covering, the *mursak*, which did not cover the face. The paranji and chachvon only started to emerge after the 1860s and 1870s—and at least a few mursaks were still in use as late as 1910. (See M. A. Bik-zhanova, "Mursak—starinnaia verkhniaia odezhda uzbechek g. Tashkenta," *Trudy AN Tadzhikskoi SSR* 120 (1960): 47–53.) In 1917, moreover, most of the Muslim women who wore veils in Turkistan came from relatively affluent urban families. The full horsehair-and-cotton ensemble discussed here became a national emblem of the Uz-bek people only later, *after* 1927. It appears to have spread into rural areas, and into lower-class families, largely as a response to the hujum and its explicit assault on local cultural practices.

22. For more details, see Northrop, *Veiled Empire*, 347–52.

23. Shodier Mutahharkhonughlu, "Chodradagi aellar," *Movarounakhr musul-monlari*, no. 1 (1992): 9–13. For a Western account, see Carol J. Williams, "Taking an Eager Step Back to Islam," *Los Angeles Times*, 3 June 1995.

7. *The Wedding Feast:* Living the New Uzbek Life in the 1930s

Marianne Kamp

Rural Uzbeks began to experience rapid change in the 1930s, when the Soviet Union initiated collectivization of agriculture. Collectivization ended private ownership of land, and it destroyed much of the traditional village hierarchy as the state arrested and exiled many wealthy landowners and members of the Muslim clergy. More broadly, farmers became farm-laborers, while collective farms began investing in institutions such as schools and clinics to benefit their members. Modern, Soviet education started to become widely available, and it spread new ideas and new life goals among rural Uzbek youth. Girls in Xorazm [Khorezm] province (in Uzbekistan's northwest), who ten years earlier would have been veiled in a *paranji* and *chachvon*,[1] and who would have been illiterate, now not only could attend primary school (if their parents permitted them), but might even aspire to a career outside the village.

The writers for *Bright Life*, a magazine for Uzbek women and girls, wanted to inspire their readers to seek education and become employed outside their homes, both goals that the Soviet state and the Communist Party promoted. But *Bright Life*'s authors were also trying to negotiate the complexities of combining modern, working life for women with Uzbek values. How could a young Uzbek woman fulfill the Soviet goals of education and socially useful labor while also fulfilling Uzbek expectations that she would respect elders, marry according to her parents' wishes, and be loyal to parents and to her community?

In "The Wedding Feast," published in 1937, the heroine, Gulshad, is a young woman from a small village in Xorazm, whose story is designed to model for readers how to balance modern Soviet values with Uzbek family and community expectations. Gulshad's story also encompasses the political struggles of the time, echoing the Communist Party's interpretation of class conflict, and demonstrating to readers the average person's need to be vigilant against enemies of the Soviet state. The year 1937 was dominated by the arrest and trial of hundreds of thousands of Communist Party members. In Uzbekistan the people who were swept away were often associated with Jadidism, a prerevolutionary movement that had argued for the reform of Islam through modern education. Those arrested in 1937 were also often accused of nationalism (promoting Uzbek interests ahead of Soviet interests) and of association with the Basmachis, Central Asian rebels who had fought against the establishment of Soviet power. In this story, Gulshad's nemesis represents the dangerous Uzbeks who need to be removed from society, while she and Sobir, the young man she loves, represent the ideal type of Communist youth (members of the Communist Youth League (*Komsomol*)). While loyal to the goals of the Soviet state and the Party, Gulshad and Sobir also continue to practice respect to elders and social hierarchies, and show the generosity and hospitality that Uzbeks hold in high regard.

TOI (THE WEDDING FEAST), FROM *BRIGHT LIFE*, BY M. ABDULLA[2]

Gulshad turned eighteen years of age, having finished the regional Women and Girls Educational Technical School and returned home. Her mother, Nurjon-xola,[3] was heartened and reassured by her daughter's return to the village immediately after graduation. She hugged and kissed her, and then invited her girlfriends to visit. The girls from Gulshad's village circle, who had not seen her for a year, were invited in. They surrounded her with questions, and she, answering very precisely, uplifted the village girls and gave them wings.

After the girls had expressed their thanks to Auntie Nurjon for her hospitality and were leaving, a young man appeared at the door dressed in a Komsomol uniform. He looked the girl up and down, and finally he quietly moved his lips. "So, girl," the young man said, smiling, "You're here too?"

"Come in, comrade teacher," said the girl, royally, "It looks like your mother-in-law doesn't love you."[4] The girls laughed and began to leave. After making their greetings, Gulshad invited the young man in.

"Come, my son," said the old woman, meeting him in the entry, "You've been good from the start, always bringing news every day. Now since Gulshad has returned, you yourself have disappeared." The young man, uncomfortable and embarrassed, said, "Nurjon-xola, work has increased."

They entered the courtyard porch. The young man was invited to sit on a quilt on the platform. Nurjon-xola lit up the samovar. Gulshad put layered *patir* (an oily bread), sugar, and candy on the tablecloth in the middle of the platform, and sat at the young man's right side. The girl had changed. A year ago she was not so filled out. Her body was fuller. Her shyness had also disappeared. Her conversation was meaningful.

The young man, after drinking a bowl of tea, raised his head and looked at the girl with distinct pleasure. The girl, whether from shyness, or because she wanted to, stared at the floor. The young man's eyes began to pass over the girl from head to toe. The girl was dressed well. The young man started to think, "But if she is a widow's daughter and isn't working anywhere, where did she get these clothes? Is she about to be promised to some young man?"

The young man poured more tea for himself, and asked, "Gulshad-xon, have some tea. Are you uncertain? I mean to say, after finishing school, you're not still shy, are you? How many people have graduated? What grades did you get? Won't you tell me a bit about it?"

The girl started talking. "Sobir-aka, shyness comes and goes. I just do not know where to start talking in your presence. But you found some good topics."[5]

She talked for a long time, about school, the place of her school, public service, the wall newspaper, the theater circle, how many people graduated from the school, and that she had received a prize of some clothing and books for graduating with excellent marks. The old woman smiled at her daughter, who was so engrossed in her conversation that she piled word on word, and said to Sobir, as if to brag, "Do you see, no other old woman in the world has a daughter like this one!"

The young man left, promising to return another day. Nurjon told her daughter that there was no one else like Sobir, and wished her good fortune with him. She said Sobir would not take the money she had borrowed from him, though she tried to return it. Gulshad wondered why. Nurjon answered that he would say, "But your daughter is in school." Nurjon told Gulshad she thought Sobir was in love with her. Gulshad paused. She said that she thought very highly of Sobir, but that she did not want to marry yet. She still planned to study more: "Let me finish the institute, and then, if it is still right, you tell him yes. May god make your life long."

Nurjon changed so fast that no blood was left in her face. Tears began to flow. It was as if a blackness swept over her eyes. She shouted with a strained voice, "What? You will study more?" But no matter how angry her mother became, Gulshad just smiled, and smiling continued her path . . .

Gulshad was in the village three months. During the day she carried out educational work among the women of the collective farm, helped with farm work, and in the evening taught literacy classes. During this short time, she made twenty-two women and girls and seventeen men literate, and twenty-two people semi-literate.[6] The local government rewarded her for her work. She also worked heart-and-soul with the village activists. She took up two projects with local youth. One of those was to teach women and girls revolutionary law. The second was a wall newspaper. The newspaper was very interesting, and most of the writers came from among collective farm women and girls.

Nurjon-xola was boundlessly happy. Her love could not be contained in her heart. Her daughter was earning the healthy sum of 300–400 *som* per month, and besides that receiving prizes. And she was on the collective farm. They were working for a high harvest of cotton. Many advances in pay were being made to the collective farmers, including Nurjon. The days passed this way. One evening, at six-thirty, the postman came and called Nurjon-xola to the door. Because the old woman was illiterate, she could not sign for and take the letter that arrived. So she called to her daughter. The letter was a commission for acceptance to the teacher training institute in Tashkent.

Gulshad put the letter in her pocket, turning away from her mother, who stood looking, and set off for the village school. Built by the volunteer labor of the workers in the village, the school was European in style and was large, made up of twelve rooms. Hurrying, she went into the first-, second-, and third-grade rooms, without finding the person she sought, and then went in and out of several more rooms. After searching the last rooms, she went to the director's office and waited, talking with a fat person in the entry.

"Excuse me, uncle," said Gulshad, wrinkling her brow, "Is Sobir in the office?"

"Daughter, what is the matter?"

"It is a very essential matter that I have," she said, opening the office door.

The fat man was surprised, as Gulshad looked past him and then went in. This person was Imam Xo'jaev.

In the office, Sobir and the October collective farm boss, Eshimqo'l-aka, were sitting. They were also surprised, but stood up for Gulshad's entrance. "Sobir-aka," said the girl, "I got an answer." She showed the letter from Tashkent. "My commission was accepted, and I have to be there on August 10."

Eshimqo'l stroked his mustache and said, with an open face, "Oh! And because of this such happiness?"

Sobir remained quiet, not saying a word against, and not congratulating. Eshimqo'l told Gulshad she needed to stay in the village and teach for a year before they would send her for more education, but she took Sobir's hand and ran home with him, inviting him for *plov* (pilaf) to celebrate. Nurjon first thought that her prediction of their engagement had taken place, but then became angry when she learned that Gulshad was intending to go away again for more education. Nurjon complained that she was old and widowed, and needed Gulshad's help. Then she told a story about Gulshad's father.

Her father was a Bolshevik, who wound up in the fight against Junaid

Khan and his Basmachis. A number of Bolsheviks were killed. Gulshad's father was taken prisoner and tortured before he was killed, when Gulshad was seven years old. "The one who killed your father was an Ishon[7] named Islam Xo'ja. His children are now working in Soviet jobs."

This was the first time Sobir had heard this story, and he listened carefully, his anger against these bloodsuckers rising. The earlier mood had completely gone, and they talked for an hour and a half about this offense. Then Nurjon brought the food in. They returned to the subject of education. Nurjon showed she did not want Gulshad to go, but Sobir, whether he wanted to or not, said, "Nurjon-xola, let Gulshad-xon go to Tashkent to study. I will get news about how she is. We made an agreement, your daughter and I; first she will go to study, and then I will. So you should give your consent to this. All right, auntie?" She agreed, and they celebrated.

When Gulshad went to study, in her first letter to her mother she described airplane flight, and all her new impressions—the trams, the school, the social order, the amazing streets of Tashkent, the weaving factory, the giant enterprises. Sobir read the letters to Nurjon, who kept them. She replied, and the letters went back and forth.

One day, when Nurjon was tired after working in the cotton fields, a repeated knock at her gate woke her from her nap. She called to the knocker to come in, and when she got up, she found a very distressed Sobir. He showed her the letter in his pocket, but it was not a tragedy. Gulshad had finished her studies with the degree "excellent," and now, rather than sending her back to Xorazm for a year's break, the directorship of the school assigned her to teach in short courses at the institute in Tashkent. No matter how Sobir tried to calm her, Nurjon's panic soared.

They talked and decided they would both go to Tashkent to see Gulshad. But the collective farm boss forbade it. Naturally they could not send Nurjon to Tashkent at the height of the cotton season. And Sobir had sent a request to enter the regional teacher's course to raise his qualifications. He had received an appointment to take a three-month summer course. So they gave up that idea.

September came, and the cotton harvest began. Nurjon picked as much as anyone. Eshimqo'l went to the fields to check up on the harvest. The picking was frenzied, and some of the girls were not separating prime cotton from lesser cotton. He told Nurjon, "If you don't make the quality of picking improve, I won't give you what I received from Tashkent." Nurjon asked what came, and the other pickers also asked. He told them that Nurjon's daughter had sent five hundred *som*. Everyone's mouths dropped open in disbelief. The others started saying, "Maybe I should educate my daughter. I should go to Tashkent and study."

Two years passed. Gulshad finished the institute, and she was made director of a ten-class Uzbek school in the city. She went home for a month to rest, and then returned to take up her duties. When she went to work, she again encountered a man named Imam Xo'jaev. He had been made a teacher at her new school. Whenever she ran into him, she grew unhappy inside, thinking of her father.

Preparations were going on for the 1937–1938 school year, and the Komsomol held organizational meetings. The teacher Turdiev said that last year there were shortcomings, and that Imam Xo'jaev was a nationalist, as he had said that the Jadid Cholpan should become part of the "Soviet platform," and he had tried poisoning the youth with his thoughts. As the conversation continued, others said that these were not mere accidental utterances from Imam Xo'jaev. "Comrades," said Gulshad, "Few people who do not know Islam Xo'ja the Ishon." She explained that Xo'jaev was from an alien class, that in 1924 his father (Islam Xo'ja) had fought against Soviet power, and had murdered her father Avaz the Bolshevik. The gathering expelled Imam Xo'jaev.

When the cotton season was over and Nurjon-xola had met her quotas, she received permission for a three day leave to visit her daughter. First she had to get to the city, thirty kilometers away. When she had made this journey five years earlier, she went by donkey cart, and it took five hours. Now the road had been graveled and made appropriate for motorized vehicles. She rode in a truck to town, and let the driver know how amazed she was at the speed, "This truck really flies well, Shermat! This gives me great pleasure, my child!" Shermat explained that the collective farm head had written to Kalinin (President of the USSR) to request more trucks, so that they could raise their cotton output by 100 percent. "And then you can ride along with me to the city every day, all right, auntie?"

When Nurjon-xola arrived at the house where her daughter lived in the city, she ran into a fat man, dressed in a long, embroidered shirt, waiting at the door. She recognized him; it was Imam Xo'jaev! He told her that he was very angry at her daughter, who had thoroughly shamed him, accusing his father of murder. Because of this he had lost his job as a teacher. But Gulshad would not let him enter. Nurjon had no sympathy: "Son of a dog! It wasn't a lie!" And Nurjon went inside to see her daughter.

Inside, Gulshad was talking to a young man who plainly admired her. She introduced him to her mother as a former classmate who had come all the way from Ferghana to see her. He told her that he would go wherever the government sent him to work, and noted that Gulshad shared his attitude. "I'm asking your daughter whether this coming year we can both go and work in Ferghana. We would need your agreement, mother." Nurjon was silent, not knowing what to say, and Gulshad changed the subject. After they talked for a while, the young man had to leave.

Nurjon drew a letter out of her handbag and gave it to her daughter. Gulshad smiled; it was from Sobir. Nurjon said that Sobir wanted to make a firm promise with Gulshad. Gulshad looked up with tears. All through her studies and this year of teaching, she and Sobir had kept the promise to write to each other. In this letter, Sobir greeted her, and then asked her to marry him. He noted that the twentieth anniversary of the revolution was coming, and that "we are both born in the year of October. On that great day, I'm asking that we could celebrate our wedding. What do you say, my beloved?"

All sorts of things went through Gulshad's head, from her studies, to gentle Sobir, to the young man who had just come to see her. Nurjon asked, "Will you marry him, since you are not yet married? Or someone else?" Gulshad answered, "I've always intended to marry the man I choose." Nurjon asked, "Who is it you want?" But Gulshad did not answer immediately. Finally she said that the one she wanted is "Sobir-aka. You knew that he is the young man I love." Nurjon was happy, and they began making wedding plans.

Nurjon mentioned that she had seen Imam Xo'jaev that morning. Gulshad said that she would go report on him today, so that the matter could be finished. Nurjon told her to be careful. Three days passed. Nurjon returned home to tell Sobir of Gulshad's agreement.

Gulshad helped with Komsomol planning for the October holiday at her school, and then asked permission to go home for her wedding. On November 5 she set out for her village (the holiday was November 7). Nurjon had carried out all the preparations for the wedding. After making quilts and bedding and clothing for the bride and groom, she discussed all the expenses with Eshimqo'l and Sobir, and they decided on which day to hold the feast for the kolkhoz members. She thought the feast should last three evenings, and demand 12 *puds* of rice, 15 *puds* of *non*, and the butchering of three sheep.

Eshimqo'l listened to Nurjon's thoughts, but would not give permission for such a great expenditure. And Sobir as well rejected the idea of having such a large, old style wedding feast. Nurjon argued, "But Eshimqo'l, is it such a shameful thing to give the people a feast? If we were not well off, it would be different, but our storehouses are full. May our collective farm thrive! And besides, both my daughter and son-in-law are earning a lot of money. It would be in our power to give the village a ten- or fifteen-day feast!"

They decided to hold the feast for the village for one day and one evening. The wedding began after the November 7 public holiday meeting. They invited the collective farm members and the teachers and brought in singers and dancers. The role of hosting the feast was entrusted to Eshimqo'l, as a Party member and collective farm boss, and to the secretary of the Komsomol, Siddiqov.

The feast had an abundance of food, and everyone was completely stuffed. The stews and pilaf, prepared full of fatty meat, kept flowing. The *patir non*, made with layers of fat and cream, went in want of eaters.

It was an amazing situation. Even though there were so many little children at the feast, the candies spread all around the tablecloths did not all disappear. In the evening, carpets were put in the middle of the square, and brilliant electric lights strung around the edges, so that the middle of the night was bright as day.

The entertainment began with young men wrestling, followed by dancers and singers performing. Then it was the old people's turn to dance. Nurjon went out, and before she danced, she told the crowd that her happiness was overflowing. "God grant long life to Stalin, the student of Lenin who set us free!" Everyone echoed her sentiment in shouts and clapping.

The plov was served, and afterwards came folk dancing. Finally, there were European dances, the foxtrot and rumba. Gulshad and Sobir danced. And thus they went on with the process, studying, becoming educated, working, and thus establishing the new life.

ANALYSIS

Uzbeks, especially rural Uzbeks, in the 1930s usually arranged marriages for their sons and daughters (and still do today). Soviet law declared that the bride and groom in a marriage should themselves freely and personally consent to their union. In the 1920s, the Communist Party in Uzbekistan tried to spread awareness among women that they could not be forced into marriages against their will. While some radical authors argued that young people should freely choose their own partners, many Uzbek reformers instead tried to modify, but not entirely reject, Uzbek practice by encouraging youth to seek parental advice and permission in marriage while at the same time taking an active role in choosing the right sort of mates for themselves. Jadids, the reformers of the early twentieth century, had stressed the importance of marrying appropriately, not for love, but rather with concern for shared values, compatibility, and mutual support. In Soviet Uzbek tales of young marriage, love plays a role, but alone, love can lead youth to ruin, while shared Soviet values are the basis for happy marriage.

Gulshad has freedoms and experiences far beyond those of her village girlfriends, through leaving the village for higher education. Her relationship with Sobir, a young village teacher, is founded first on her respect for him as an educator, and as a member of the Communist Youth who shares her interest in fulfilling the Soviet dream of improving life through education. Her encounters with him are daring, by village standards. Where seven years earlier village women would have worn full veils and maintained almost total social separation from non-family men, Gulshad runs to the school, finds Sobir, pulls him from a meeting, and leads him by hand to her house in order to share news of her educational opportunity with him.

However, all of Gulshad's meetings with Sobir take place at her home, with her mother present. While many Uzbek families might have found even this to be permissive behavior, the author's version of proper modern relationships for Uzbek youth, while recognizing Sobir and Gulshad's own interests and choice, is nonetheless oriented toward serious planning for marriage. Although Gulshad puts marriage off for two years, adhering to a Soviet ideal that women should gain education first before starting family life, only once—when her classmate visited her in the city and tried to convince her to marry him and move to Ferghana—does she show any indication of wavering in the decision that she and Sobir had made to improve their education, and then to marry.

Sobir, in this story, is the ideal new Soviet Uzbek man. He shows Uzbek virtues in his concern for an illiterate widow, writing letters for her and reading her daughter's letters, and in his generosity, loaning her money and refusing to take repayment. He shows Soviet virtues in his commitment to education and to the improvement of his village and himself. And he demonstrates the new life in his relationship with Gulshad, showing more concern for her goal of becoming a highly trained teacher than for his own immediate happiness and desire to marry. At the same time, his interactions with Gulshad have details that Uzbek readers would see as appropriate: he admires her beauty, her figure, and her new dresses, while she modestly looks at the floor. She offers him a bowl of tea, and respectfully calls him "aka." After he drinks, he invites her to drink tea as well, so that social forms and hierarchies are respected, even as Sobir shows Gulshad the respect that is part of Soviet equality. Gulshad, although educated, is silenced by the shyness appropriate to unmarried Uzbek girls, and Sobir kindly prompts her to talk by asking her about her own experiences in school.

While Gulshad and Sobir represent new Soviet life, Gulshad's mother, the widow Nurjon-xola, experiences some difficulty with the new ways. She assumes that Sobir's interest in her daughter is about marriage, not about Soviet personal improvement, and she believes that Gulshad's one year away from home for teacher training is far beyond what any girl should expect. She wants her daughter to marry and stay in the village, and is emotionally distraught that Gulshad wants to continue her education, leaving her mother alone. She tries to convince Gulshad that she needs her help, and yet throughout the story, Nurjon proves to be an energetic and successful worker on the collective farm. The author's greatest difficulty is to enable Gulshad to defy her mother's wishes, by continuing her education, without portraying Gulshad as rebellious or allowing her to undermine the Uzbek value of respect for elders. Gulshad responds to her mother's histrionics with patience and smiles, and she fulfills her duty in other ways, by writing constant letters to her mother and turning over a large part of her earnings to her. While Nurjon is unhappy about her separation from her daughter, her pride in Gulshad's success, her own rising standard of living, and her ability to present her daughter as an example to the whole collective farm of Soviet success and Uzbek filial respect overcome her early anger and distress. Sobir assists greatly in this negotiation of Uzbek values, by taking Gulshad's side and letting Nurjon know that as Gulshad's future husband, he wants Gulshad to study, and by taking Gulshad's place in Nurjon's life, looking after her and caring for her in her daughter's absence.

The politics of the late 1930s enter this story both through a conscious presentation of Soviet values and through the plot twist involving Gulshad's antagonist. Gulshad's father, an early Uzbek Communist, had been murdered by Basmachis during the guerrilla campaign of the early 1920s. Nurjon knew the identity of at least one of the killers, Islam Xo'ja. His name, and Nurjon's story, indicated that he was a member of the Islamic religious establishment, as well as an enemy of Soviet power. Imam Xo'jaev, the fat man whom Gulshad first encounters at Sobir's school and whom she later meets again when he is appointed to teach in the city, is Islam Xo'ja's son. When Gulshad is directing a school in the city, other Komsomol members attack their fellow teacher, Imam Xo'jaev, as a Jadid sympathizer and a nationalist. Gulshad, in a demonstration of loyalty both to the Party and to her widowed mother, denounces Imam Xo'jaev for his relationship to her father's killer. He is dismissed from his job, as an "enemy of the people." While a reader from a later time period might understand this episode as Gulshad's using her own political standing to bully and take revenge, readers of the time were likely to be convinced by arguments that Basmachis, Jadids, and nationalists posed a genuine threat to the Soviet state, and hence to their own livelihoods, and they needed to be found and denounced.

The story culminates with Gulshad and Sobir's wedding, which once again draws together Soviet and Uzbek ideals. Sobir writes to Gulshad to make his marriage proposal, and asks that they be married on the most important Soviet holiday, the anniversary of the 1917 revolution. Traditionally, Uzbeks considered the best time for weddings to be between the two major Islamic holidays, Ramadan and the Feast of the Sacrifice, or near Navruz, the Central Asian New Year (March 21). Now the most festive time of the year, and hence the proper time for a wedding, would be the Communist holiday commemorating the revolution. When Sobir and Nurjon were planning the wedding, with the help of Eshimqo'l, there were numerous traditional obligations. Nurjon prepared a dowry for her daughter of clothing and house furnishings, and also presented *sarpo* (traditionally, clothing from head to toe) to her son-in-law. Bolshevik reformers had attacked only one of the gifts the Uzbeks traditionally gave at marriage—*qalin*. This was a payment of money or goods given by the groom to the bride's parents, and it was understood as a payment for the bride, a bride-price or bride-wealth. There is no mention of *qalin* in this story, but the dowry and *sarpo* provided by the bride's mother appear unquestioned, as a normal, acceptable, and honorable outlay.

Then there was the wedding feast. Throughout the early twentieth century there were cultural struggles over wedding feasts, which were demonstrations of hospitality and generosity. Families would go into debt in order to put on the requisite bride's party, groom's party, and then the wedding feast for the whole community. Jadid reformers of the early twentieth century argued that this was a waste of money, and that weddings should not be occasions for conspicuous consumption. Central Asian Bolsheviks made the same arguments to the public in the 1920s and 1930s, and in the early 1930s Party officials often tried to preclude opportunities for big wedding feasts. Nurjon, in 1937, has to discuss the smallest details of her feast plans with Eshimqo'l, the Party secretary and head of her collective farm. While he and Sobir disagree with Nurjon over a three-day feast, echoing Communist concerns, Nurjon, in fact, captures the political mood of the moment. In 1936, after years of severe hunger and hardship, Stalin declared, "Life has become more joyous, comrades!" and thus suggested an end to the ascetic side of Communism. Life on collective farms in Uzbekistan was better in 1936 than it had been in 1933, and Nurjon argues that when they are well off, giving the people a big feast, a joyous occasion, is the right thing to do.

The wedding, though only one day long, satisfies Nurjon's desires to match the expectations of her Uzbek community by demonstrating overwhelming hospitality. With the whole village present, she still provides so much rich food—richness signified in mentions of fat—that her guests stuff themselves and there is food left over. While the wedding is "Red"—i.e., Soviet, in that men and women are both present in the same place, rather than "Old Style," in which men and women celebrated separately—the sequence of entertainments follows Xorazm Uzbek ideals: wrestling, followed by professional singers and dancers, and then by the elderly dancing. After the guests eat the final course, always pilaf, there is folk dancing, in which all participate. Finally, to show that Gulshad and Sobir are not only fully Uzbek, but also sophisticated and favorable to Soviet internationalism, they also dance a foxtrot and a rumba.

In this story of Soviet modernization and Uzbek tradition, the pervasive effects of Soviet government and Party control appear in small details. Gulshad is impressed by all of the technology and infrastructure in Tashkent, but even the village leaves its isolation: graveled roads and automotive transport make the village more connected to the city. Gulshad's wedding feast is illuminated with electric lights, another rare wonder of modernization for rural people. At the same time, Soviet modernization also meant massive government control and intervention in everyday life. Nurjon, Gulshad, and Sobir had to ask permission from Eshimqo'l to take time off, to pursue education, to visit, to set a wedding date, and to plan a wedding feast. Gulshad was assigned to a workplace after finishing the institute. Her teacher-friend articulated the proper Soviet attitude toward all of this control: he would go wherever he was sent.

Gulshad's story depicts the everyday life of a certain group in Central Asia in the 1930s, those who were fortunate enough to benefit from Soviet modernization, and who happened to be favored, rather than harmed, by Soviet politics. Unmentioned are the massive upheavals of collectivization that resulted in dislocation and thousands of deaths in rural Uzbekistan.

NOTES

1. The head-and-body covering robe, and the horsehair face veil.

2. "Toi," *Jarqin Turmuş*, 1937:10–11, pp. 16–20. The story is rather long, so some sections of it are direct translation, and others a condensed version. Translation by Marianne Kamp.

3. In Uzbek, honorific kinship terms are added to names. Nurjon-xola means Aunt Nurjon.

4. A teasing comment that can be leveled even at an unmarried person, like Sobir, suggesting that the one does not look well fed or taken care of, or perhaps faced a quarrel at home.

5. Sobir-aka means elder brother Sobir, indicating that Gulshad regards Sobir with respect. Sobir refers to Gulshad as Gulshad-xon; this suffix is usually attached to women's names, and indicates equality or affection and respect to a person who is younger than or the same age as the speaker.

6. Literate meant students learned to read and write. Semi-literate meant they learned only to read.

7. Ishon is one of many Muslim religious titles in Central Asia. Ishon was most frequently used as the title for the leader of a Sufi organization.

8. Practical Consequences of Soviet Policy and Ideology for Gender in Central Asia and Contemporary Reversal

Elizabeth A. Constantine

Whether the Soviets succeeded or failed in their efforts to transform Central Asian societies is one of the central questions that continue to preoccupy scholars of the region. The Soviets manipulated the position and status of women to meet their ideological and economic goals, sought to undermine traditional Islamic patterns of life, and attempted to create new, Soviet patterns instead. Western social scientists, journalists, and developers have devoted great attention to the transformation of Central Asian societies. However, in most of these evaluations of the cause, course, and outcome of social change, gender has been neglected.

Contrary to general belief, I suggest that the Soviets enjoyed considerable success in their efforts to transform traditional gender roles and attitudes among Uzbek women. I do this first by comparing prerevolutionary gender roles to present day ones, then by focusing on domestic organization and the minutiae of everyday life as the place where Soviet government legislation, the pronouncements of policy-makers, and media representations of the Soviet ideal of womanhood took their effect. I suggest that Soviet policy and ideology on women (which produced and sustained a national persona in the form of a new Soviet woman that shaped the concept of "womanhood" in Soviet Uzbekistan) resulted in new gender role definitions and expectations for Uzbek women. Since independence in 1991, however, the Uzbek government under President Islam Karimov has abandoned the socialist program with regard to women. The ideal Soviet woman drove a tractor or got a Ph.D.—the new Uzbek woman is a young bride surrounded by relatives running the household. Karimov's government has posted significant gains in its campaign to roll back the Sovietization of Uzbek women by promoting ideals of womanhood that are either prerevolutionary or touted as such. This new old model of womanhood is a major factor in the growing marginalization of women in Uzbek society today. The emphasis on state-sponsored ideology should in no way be understood to undervalue the importance of economic factors in the decline of women's overall status in Uzbek society. Economic pressures and ideological responses to the entire process of transition are working together to bring women down from the relatively higher profile they occupied during Soviet times.

Western scholarship on the Soviet experience in Central Asia contains some useful work, but too many scholars rely exclusively on Soviet data and accept Soviet assumptions along with that data. Generally speaking Western scholars analyze the impact of Soviet rule in terms of theories of colonialism or modernization. The former acknowledges the occurrence of considerable structural and institutional changes but exaggerates the extent of cultural and attitudinal resistance to change among Central Asians. Those who favor modernization theory judge the outcome a total success[1] or a complete failure.[2] The results of Soviet policies are assessed by social scientists "in terms of their deviance from the presumed trajectory of Western 'developed' societies, or the degree of conformance to imagined Soviet ones."[3] In regard to women, these same scholars suggest that less educated, overly fertile rural women (abundant in Uzbekistan) represent "traditional," with better educated, working, urban women representing "modern." The few studies of Uzbek women under Soviet rule assume women's roles have been based primarily on Central Asian and Muslim cultural expectations, and that Soviet rule had limited influence if any on their creation. Depending on the scholar and his or her approach to the topic, Islam and/or the failure of Soviet rule are blamed for gender inequality in Central Asia. Central Asian women are portrayed as the embodiment of Islam—helpless victims of a religion that oppresses women; or as victims of a failed Soviet system—a system unable to emancipate them or dramatically change (read: "fix") their lives. That women are social actors and not just passive receptors of party policy (or Islam) has never been considered. Nowhere in this literature are we exposed to the desires and actions of Uzbek women themselves, who were faced with the daily choice of implementing party policy, adapting it to their own purposes, or resisting it.

While one cannot deny the persistence of pre-Communist patterns of values and behavior patterns in Uzbekistan today, neither can one ignore the continuing importance of Soviet rule on the lives of ordinary women— by which I mean those women who were not directly engaged in the ongoing ideological and power struggles of the regime. During the Soviet period, Soviet policy catapulted Uzbek women into spheres traditionally occupied by men, and women were encouraged to take on qualities that were traditionally regarded as male. Additionally, the Soviets unleashed ideological campaigns in the form of printed discourse designed to manufacture an acceptable social identity and change the attitudes of Uzbek women. Women, unlike men, had special books and women's magazines instructing them how to be women by inscribing acceptable "Soviet" social practice. Soviet books, magazines, and newspapers not only promulgated values and attitudes, they also offered women ways to understand the Soviet world. How women reconciled these conflicting expectations has yet to be examined. Instead, it is assumed that, in spite of new roles and expectations for women, gender values and behavior patterns remained unchanged due to the failure of Soviet rule in Central Asia.

One way to resolve some of the problems inherent in the existing literature on Central Asian women is to recognize that gender is a profoundly important analytical concept in assessing social change in the region. What gender is or means in any particular culture at a specific historical moment should be explored and not presumed. By examining changes in gender roles, and Uzbek women's own perceptions of their gender roles, we may discover that the Soviets experienced success, not failure, in their attempt to engineer social change.

In the fall of 1994 I checked out a book called *Paranci va cacvan azadlik dusmani* (*The Veil: Enemy of Liberation*) from the Alisher Navoi Library in Tashkent. This book, published by the Central Committee of the Uzbek Communist Party in 1940, is a collection of essays and testimonials by prominent Uzbek women exhorting their "sisters" to cast off the veil and other outworn, prerevolutionary traditions. Like many publications of its kind, *The Veil* is highly political and devotes more space to Stalin and his good works than to the need for women to change their lives. It seemed unlikely to me that anyone other than a student of the "woman question" (*zhenskii vopros*) would be interested in it.

As I waited for my coat, the book sat on the counter. When it was finally my turn, the coat-check woman, an Uzbek woman in her late sixties, grabbed the book and asked me if I was reading it. I told her that I was and asked her if she had read it. She told me that it was one of the first books she had ever read, and that it had meant a great deal to her because it portrayed the progress made and respect gained by Uzbek women since the Revolution. She especially admired the women who related their personal stories of unveiling and told me how her mother had spent her whole life covered and for the most part housebound. I was somewhat taken aback by this, as I had assumed that no one ever got anything out of books like these. I asked her if she'd read other, similar texts. She said yes, that years ago there were many such books about women and that she had read them all, and that they had changed her life. She was proud that, unlike her mother, she could read and write. She was even prouder of the fact that, aged nearly seventy, she was still working and contributing to society.

This was the first of many encounters that would strengthen my conviction that Soviet rule had had a much more profound impact on the daily lives of ordinary Uzbek women than has been generally supposed.

Before looking at the present situation of women in Uzbekistan, it is helpful to understand their past. What little we know about women's lives in prerevolutionary Central Asia comes from Russian ethnographic accounts or traveler's accounts.[4] The picture provided by these suggests a system that falls into the pattern of what anthropologists describe as the classic patriarchy of the extended patrilocal household: that is to say, a system characterized by the early marriage of girls, who upon marriage live with their husband's family, under the domination of the oldest male, which is usually her father-in-law. Moreover, a new bride was subordinated not only to the males of the family but also to the senior women.

What little status women acquired was done through marriage. Generally, a young girl had no say in the selection of her mate. Rather marriage was considered a contract between the families of the bride and groom. Women were married young—usually between the ages of nine and fifteen. Both *kalym* (*khalim,* or bride-wealth) and dowry varied from one region to another, but everywhere *kalym* depended on the wealth and status of the groom, whereas dowry depends on the economic standing of the bride's family.

Polygyny and divorce were both practiced; polygyny was expensive and divorce generally left women destitute, so that both were relatively rare. One account by Paul Nazaroff does contradict this. Nazaroff hid from the Red Army in a Central Asian household for many months in 1919, and he wrote that divorce was very common and that Central Asian men had an "easy come, easy go" attitude toward wives in general.[5]

Prior to the Revolution, Islam in Central Asia was a highly formalized religion ruled over by a strong clergy. Religion dominated all aspects of life. Urban women, especially those of Bukhara, Samarkand, and Khiva, were veiled and secluded. Rural women generally did not veil, and, since most rural women were involved in some aspect of agriculture, they were often seen publicly working in the fields.

The education of youth was associated with religion, and both boys and girls could attend school. Girls were generally educated at special single-sex *maktabs* or at home by women teachers (*atun-bibi*). Girls received similar educations to boys, but it was probably only in a few upper class families that truly educated women were to be found. The extant descriptions of prerevolutionary life in Central Asia suffer from a lack of completeness, but the interviews that I conducted with elderly women pretty much concur with the general picture. In the interviews with women in their sixties and seventies, most described their mothers as having married young, illiterate, and without any work outside the home. About half of my respondents in the village where I worked said their mothers were veiled, while the other half said their mothers had covered their heads but not their faces.

When the Soviets came to power they utilized legal and educational institutions as well as the media to undermine traditional patterns of life and change the status and position of women. Women's equal rights and responsibilities were enshrined in the constitution of the USSR and in various laws. Immediately after the Revolution the government proclaimed that men and women were equal in all aspects of social, economic, and political life. The basic education law in 1918 introduced the legal right to education at public expense; thus began Central Asian society's introduction to the diffusion of secular value, scientific-technological knowledge, socialistic-communistic principles, and materialism.[6] The family code adopted in 1919 guaranteed women's legal rights; a decree issued in 1921 set the minimum marriage age for women at sixteen, banned polygamy and *kalym*, and stipulated that marriage be contracted only by mutual consent. Registration of marriages was required of all citizens at the Soviet civil registry office. Between 1924 and 1926 a slew of new laws guaranteed women's equality in divorce proceedings, property matters, and electoral participation.

Soviet policies toward women in the late 1920s and early 1930s were determined less by any rhetorical commitment to equality than by the economic needs of the state. Women were needed in production, and to encourage their entry into the labor force legal actions were supported by administrative agencies such as the *Zhenotdel*,[7] which played an important role in the politicization of Central Asian women. Throughout the 1920s the Zhenotdel tried to establish an institutional framework for drawing women into the building of a new society by establishing daycare centers and other services. Additionally, the Zhenotdel created clubs and networks for women, and its activists led campaigns to initiate divorce and mass public unveilings and played an important role in *hujum*—the campaign organized to rid Central Asia of veiling and seclusion. The Soviet leadership considered veiling and seclusion symbols of the backwardness of women. The abolition of both was deemed a necessary step for women to achieve equality in their political, economic, and social lives. The Zhenotdel was abolished in 1930 and replaced with women's sections (*Zhensektorz*) in urban areas to ensure women's participation in production. By 1934 these were dissolved in the USSR as a whole, but they were maintained in the Muslim republics because of the perceived continued opposition to women's participation in the workforce.

During the 1930s women disappeared from the Soviet agenda; the official word from above was that Soviet women had achieved emancipation and therefore there was no woman question. Industrialization and collectivization were the main goals of Stalin's regime. As Soviet society developed, women's freedom to participate in the workforce was transformed into a duty. World War II and the resulting acute need for labor gave Uzbek women the opportunity to "stand cheek by jowl with her husband, father, or brother in the struggle for new life." During the 1940s and 1950s Soviet women were routinely portrayed in various media as the "great strength" of socialism and "the pride of the Soviet people."

Uzbek women were no exceptions. In the 1960s the woman question was reopened when the Soviet leadership became concerned about the growing demographic contrast between Muslim Central Asia and the European republics. Birthrates were falling and women's participation in the work force was high in the latter, while in the former birthrates remained high and women were still underrepresented in the work force. Islam and conservative patriarchal attitudes were blamed for what appeared to be persistent backwardness.

The woman question surfaced again during *perestroika.* This time the focus was on the "double burden" of housework and paid labor. In Central Asia traditional Islamic culture was blamed for the double burden. Western social scientists concede that Soviet rule improved some things for women, namely education and access to health care and to the labor force. The most commonly cited detriment of Soviet rule is the double burden. Scholars of Central Asia also note the discrepancy between the ideal of Soviet womanhood (portrayed usually as an efficient woman happily driving her tractor to overfulfilled quotas and glory; a socially open person, easily collectivized and able to quickly and deeply transform her behavior) and what women see on the ground. Unfortunately, the gap is mostly assumed and rarely studied. The fact that many Uzbek women wear headscarves and *ishton* (trousers worn under dresses) allows for the assumption that little has changed for Uzbek women.

Anyone who spends time in Uzbekistan will learn that Uzbek women are acutely aware of these competing ideologies, Soviet and traditional. Women do not take these ideologies lightly, and the longer I lived in Uzbekistan the more I realized that women negotiate them. One of my village informants, a thirty-eight-year-old woman and economist, told me, "When we made the transition from feudalism to socialism we somehow failed to lose the scarf and ishton. We lost our religion, we forgot our traditions, but we still have to cover up." She discussed the many contradictions inherent in her life—pleased to have been educated, pleased to work, but saddened that something in her mind so superficial as dress was all that remained from the past. In the post-Soviet era many women are striving to hang on to the Soviet roles ascribed to women and reluctant to take steps back into the past, even when such regression is advertised as "reclaiming Uzbek cultural traditions."

One of the questions I asked my respondents was what had changed for their generation with respect to their mothers' and grandmothers'. All were quick to point out that their mothers had been oppressed while they had choices, choices that they intend to pass on to their daughters. Young women were incredulous when discussing the marriage age of their mothers: they couldn't believe how young their mothers had married, and that their mothers had blindly accepted their marriage partners. Even though many of my respondents had married younger than the legal age set by the Soviets (and from my point of view incredibly young) and were in marriages arranged either by their parents or by some outsider, they had the perception that later marriage is good, and that women should have some choice in the matter. They hoped that their daughters would marry even later than they had, and only after the acquisition of an education. In the village where my husband and I lived, dating *a la Uzbek* (for lack of a better phrase) was becoming fashionable. Young girls were encouraged to meet with young men (properly chaperoned, of course) and to indicate their likes and dislikes to their parents. While parents still exert a great deal of influence in this matter, girls are not blindly led into marriage. In the words of our host family, "This is healthier." This, however, appears to be changing. According to statistics published in 1998 by the Ministry of Heath in Uzbekistan, the average age of marriage for men and women is going down. In 1990 men on average married at the age of twenty-four; in 1997 this figure dropped to twenty-three. Women in 1990 married on average at age twenty-two; by 1997 this dropped to age twenty.[8]

Education is another area in which Soviet rule exerted a positive influence. Since independence, this too is changing. An ongoing debate in our household centered on the education of our host family's two young daughters. The mother, a young woman named Feruza, is the village piano teacher at school. She wanted to enroll her daughters in the Russian school, believing it to be the better school. She herself had been educated in the Russian school and in a Russian conservatory in the provincial capital. Her husband had been educated in Uzbek schools. Feruza never failed to take the opportunity to point out that her husband was educationally inferior to her and that she didn't want her daughters to receive the same inferior schooling. She also hoped that a good education would assure them places in an institution of higher learning. Her husband argued that since Uzbekistan was now independent his daughters no longer needed an education. He also noted the cost of education. In the area of education in post-Soviet Uzbekistan one finds the troubling emergence of hidden discrimination against women. During the Soviet period higher education was more or less free. Today it is common practice to pay for education, and many parents prefer not to pay to educate daughters. As late as 1988, the gender ratio at Uzbek universities was roughly equal, with 46% of students female and 54% male. A report by the Asian Development Bank in 2001 noted that young men now constitute the main student body in higher education institutions and that women's enrollment is declining.[9]

Most of my respondents think smaller families are better. Our host family has two daughters, and they were stopping with that. The biggest complaint that women made was about the difficulty in acquiring birth control. Intra uterine devices (IUDs) continue to be used,[10] but many women have them removed rather than deal with the uncomfortable side effects, which include bleeding and pain. Abortion as a form of birth control is not uncommon. While conducting my interviews, I was questioned by almost all of my respondents about my own birth control practices. I was a novelty to both the urban and rural women I worked with (to be my age, married, and childless took real doing). In gatherings of all women, my "success" was frequently discussed in far greater detail. It was of course assumed that at some point I would have children. The prevailing attitude was that smaller families were better (at most four children, and even that seemed too many; 30 percent of my respondents answered that for them two children were enough) and that greater access to birth control was necessary.

Soviet policy-makers considered Central Asian cultural values and traditions incompatible with the ideological goals of the state. The Soviet state launched attacks against old cultural identities in an effort to replace them with new Soviet ones. The attack against Islam was especially harsh. Scholars of Central Asia emphasize the survival of Islam when arguing that Soviet rule failed in Central Asia. Most argue that it is especially in the rural areas that Islam survives. Based on my research and experience, I have to argue the opposite. Religion is making its comeback not predominantly or exclusively in the rural areas, as is often reported. Rather religion is making a stronger comeback in urban areas. In the fall and spring of 1991 and 1992, and in 1996, I had the opportunity to study with an *atunchi*, Nodira, in Tashkent. Nodira was training young girls in the way of Islam and preparing them for marriage and, later, motherhood. She did not have any difficulty finding students. Most were from conservative families in Tashkent who were not pleased with the Soviet (read: Russian) values that pervaded Uzbek society. These girls studied Arabic and Chaghatay in addition to studying proper behavior. All of them veiled. When I met her again in 1996 she told me she had to turn students away.

Such teachers are easy to find in Tashkent but I was unable to find such a teacher in our village. In my rural experience I saw little outward manifestation of religious behavior. In our host family none of the men prayed at home or in the mosque. Furthermore, alcohol was a steady part of our diet, especially my husband's. The women we lived with rarely drank (they had the occasional symbolic swig), but did not cite religious reasons for their abstinence; they simply stated that it was not something women do. Men tended to argue that drinking and Islam were *not* incompatible. There was also no effort to pass on religious teachings and traditions to children in our family or in the village. However, all of my respondents, without exception, identified themselves as Muslims, and the cultural context of lifestyles include many things that we in the West perceive as Islamic norms (e.g., the subordinated status of women).

When I expressed my desire to participate in religious activities with women (e.g., *bibi seshanb* or *myshkylshod*[11]—women's social gathering) my host laughed and asked me why I wanted to hang around with old ladies. She respected these women but, for her and for her husband, religion was something that was embraced down the road and not at present. I did participate in a few ceremonies and all of the participants were over forty.

The examples I give are only meant to illustrate that Uzbek women internalized much of Soviet ideology. Uzbek women value education for daughters and sons, they value work, they desire smaller families, and they believe in state-supported child care and other services. The children in our village family attended daycare even though their mother had the summer off from work—she believed that her children should socialize with others and she liked having the time to visit friends and work around the house. Her biggest concern was that the daycare would close (as many in the area were) and that she would have to find some way of taking care of them as well as spending additional money to feed them.

Following the dissolution of the Soviet Union, the Uzbek leadership abandoned the socialist program—though not with regard to every sphere of national life. With regard to the dismantling of the socialist command economy, for example, Karimov's government's initiatives have been slow and halting at best. Many more vigorous steps have been taken in other areas. One of the more fully elaborated and vigorously promulgated components of this ideology is an imagined prerevolutionary past in which the restriction of women to the private sphere supposedly enriched the lives of women and the entire nation.

While we must take care not to ennoble Soviet rule in Uzbekistan—a system founded, after all, on physical terror and ideological monopolization—we must also take care not to ignore how Soviet rule changed the lives of Uzbek women, and how the lives of Uzbek women under Soviet rule compare with the lives of Uzbek women in the present, post-Soviet period. For one thing, a substantial majority of Uzbek women believe that the Bolshevik Revolution brought in conditions for women that were vastly better than they had enjoyed under the emirates.

Contrary to what we would expect to find, this belief becomes stronger as one moves from the cities into the countryside, where the majority of Uzbeks still live. But more importantly, what we know about Uzbek women's lives today suggests that their perception of their Soviet experiences is quite closely grounded in reality. Female literacy, which reached levels approaching 100 percent under Communist rule, is now slowly falling as a result of increased political emphasis on traditional roles for women and a reduction in the minimum age for marriage. Female unemployment is believed to be as much as 50 percent higher than male, and even that figure masks the increased number of women working in dangerous jobs, or in the informal economy, or in conventional jobs but stuck underneath a glass ceiling that, while by no means unknown in Soviet times, has become considerably less porous since independence. Domestic violence, also not unknown before 1991, has become a more serious problem, while new threats, like sex slavery, have appeared alongside it. The question today is whether the present period will take its place in a trajectory of constant improvement in which Soviet rule represents a way-station between the emirates and independent modern Uzbekistan, or whether it will come to be seen as a golden age for women, a chance that the country's post-Soviet rules allowed to slip away. What is needed is a commitment by the Uzbek government to release money and other forms of real political support for services that women need, and not just pious paeans to women as idealized national hearth-keepers.

NOTES

1. Rakhima Kh. Aminova, 1985; D. H. Alimova, 1987; Bibi Pal'vanova, 1961.
2. William Fierman, 1991; Sergei Poliakov, 1992; Boris Rumer, 1989.
3. Nazif Shahrani, 1993:123–135.
4. Summaries of late nineteenth- and early twentieth-century ethnography in Central Asia can be found in N. A. Kisliakov, 1962. Other useful sources for information on nineteenth- and early-twentieth-century life can be found in A. N. Zhilina, 1982; K. Shaniazov and Kh. Ismailov, 1981; and O. A. Sukhareva, 1966.
5. Paul Nazaroff, *Hunted through Central Asia* (Oxford: Oxford University Press, 1932).
6. William K. Medlin, William M. Cave, and Finley Carpenter, 1971: 66.
7. In 1919, the resolution "Work among Women Proletariat" passed and led to the establishment of *Zhenotdels* (women's sections) throughout the Soviet Union. The role of the Zhenotdel was threefold: 1) expand the influence of the Party over women by enlightening them about politics and life; 2) draw women into party activities, trade unions, and cooperatives; and 3) promote the construction of public daycare and dining facilities to ease the burden on women. To achieve these broad goals the administrative work of the Zhentodels was broken down into three subdivisions and one sector each with specific goals: 1) organizational and instructional work, 2) agitation and propaganda, and 3) the press. The sector work among women of the East was to supervise the liberation of Muslim women. For elaboration, see Mary Buckley, 66–67.
8. *Status of Women in Uzbekistan*. According to government statistics, 10,847 Uzbek women below the age of eighteen married in 1998. In the same period, only 183 men under the age of eighteen married. *Women of Uzbekistan*, 1999.
9. *Women in the Republic of Uzbekistan: Country Briefing Paper*. The ADB notes, "Where poverty and gender do result in unequal opportunity for men and women is in higher education. Women's participation rate is falling here, particularly at the more prestigious institutions. For example, women's enrollment at the Tashkent Institute of Finance declined from 65 percent in 1991 to 25 percent in 1997. In 1993, 18 percent fewer girls graduated from vocational schools than did boys, and 22 percent fewer from undergraduate and graduate programs in institutes of higher learning." Likewise, the education of girls increasingly has a geographical and class component. As education costs rise, rural families are choosing not to educate their daugh-

ters. Some NGOs in Uzbekistan working on women's issues suggest that women's declining participation in education can be linked to the influence of traditional factors.

10. In 2003, contraceptive use remained heavily biased toward the IUD (intrauterine device) in part because the IUD is the method favored by the state health care system and the only method provided free of charge. Other methods of contraception are expensive and not easily accessible. See: International Planned Parenthood Federation at http://www.ippf.org/imspublic/IPPF_CountryProfile/IPPF_CountryProfile.aspx?ISOCode=UZ.

11. Many Uzbek women participate in women-only rituals derived from practices associated with pre-Islamic female divinities. These ceremonies were conducted by *otins* or *mamo-mullas.* At a *bibi seshanba,* for example, women asked for protection for their families. It was practiced on Tuesdays. Participants gathered at the hostess's house where they were read *suras* (chapters or sections of the Quran) and *hadiths* (sayings and practices of Muhammad) and heard stories from the life and times of Fatima, Muhammad's daughter, by an *otin.* Special foods were prepared for the gathering. Another ceremony, *bibi mushkulkushod,* or Lady Solver of Difficulties, was held on Thursdays with the objective of chasing away ill luck already at hand. A woman suffering some misfortune went to her neighborhood *otin* with two loaves of hot bread, two handfuls of black raisins, two lamps with cotton wicks, and a small sum of money. The *otin* then gathered and led a group of women in asking *Bibi Mushkulkushod* to intercede. Maxmud Sattor, 1993, 188–190.

REFERENCES

Alimova, Diloram. *Reshenie zhenskogo voprosa v uzbekistane* [Solutions to the woman's problem in Uzbekistan, 1917–1941]. Tashkent: Fan, 1987.
———. *Zhenskii vopros v srednii Asii: istoriia izucheniia i sovremennyeproblemy* [The woman question in Central Asia: a history of its study and contemporary problems]. Tashkent: Fan, 1991.
Aminova, Rakhima Khadievana. *The October Revolution and Women's Liberation in Uzbekistan.* Moscow: Nauka, 1985.
Bacon, Elizabeth. *Central Asians Under Russian Rule: A Study in Culture Change.* Ithaca, N.Y.: Cornell University Press, 1974.
Bikzhanova, M. A., Zadykhina, K. L., and Sukhareva, O. A. "Social Life and Family Life of the Uzbeks." In S. Dunn & P. Dunn., eds., *Introduction to Soviet Ethnography,* v. II. Berkeley, Calif.: Highgate Road Social Science Research Station, 1974: 239–271.
Buckley, Mary. *Women and Ideology in the Soviet Union.* HemelHempstead: Harvester/Wheat-sheaf; Ann Arbor: University of Michigan Press, 1989.
Center for Economic Research, Report 9704 (1999) available at http://www.undp.uz/cer/Reports/9704/Eng/par1.htm.
Fierman, William, ed. *Soviet Central Asia: the Failed Transformation.* Boulder, Colo.: Westview Press, 1991.
International Planned Parenthood Federation. http://www.ippf.org/imspublic/IPPF_CountryProfile/IPPF_CountryProfile.aspx?ISOCode=UZ.
Isamiddinova, D., N. Sirojiddinov, M. Tokhtakhodjaeva, G. Tansykbaeva, M. Khakimova, B. Alimukhamedov, A. Novotny, R. Zabikhodjaev, N. Kasymova. *Report on the Status of Women in Uzbekistan.* Tashkent: Center for Economic Research (CER), 1999.

126 / *Elizabeth A. Constantine*

Kisliakov, N. A. *Patriarkhal'no-feodalnye otnosheniia sredi osedlogo sel'skogo naseleniia bukharskogo khanstva v kontse XIX–nachale XX veka. Trudy Instituta Etnografii, novaia seriia, tom LXXIV* [Patriarchal and feudal relations among the sedentary rural population of the Bukharan Khanate in the end of the nineteenth and beginning of the twentieth century. Works of the Institute of Ethnography, new series, vol. 74]. Moscow: Nauka, 1962.

Medlin, William K., William M. Cave, and Finley Carpenter. *Education and Development in Central Asia: A Case Study on Social Change in Uzbekistan.* Leiden: E. J. Brill, 1971.

Nazaroff, Paul. *Hunted through Central Asia.* Oxford: Oxford University Press, 1932.

Northrop, Douglas. "Hujum: Unveiling and the Religious Response, Uzbekistan, 1927." Paper presented at the Middle East Study Association (MESA) 30th Annual Meeting, 21–24 November 1996.

———. "Subaltern Dialogues: Subversion and Resistance in Soviet Uzbek Family Law." *Slavic Review,* Spring (2001): 115–139.

———. Uzbek Women and the Veil: Gender and Power in Stalinist Central Asia. Ph.D. dissertation, Stanford: Stanford University, 1999.

Olcott, Martha. "Women and Society in Central Asia," in William Fierman, ed. *Soviet Central Asia: The Failed Transformation.* Boulder, Colo.: Westview Press, 1991.

Pal'vanova, Bibi. *Docheri sovetskogo vostoka* [Daughters of the Soviet East]. Moscow: Gospolitizdat, 1961.

———. *Emancipatsiia Musul'manki: opyt raskreposhcheniia zhenshchiny sovetskogo vostoka* [Emancipation of the Muslim Woman: the experience of the liberation of women of the Soviet East]. Moscow: Nauka, 1982.

Pierce, Richard. *Russian Central Asia: A Study in Colonial Rule 1867–1917.* Berkeley: University of California Press, 1960.

Poliakov, Sergei. *Everyday Islam: Religion and Tradition in Rural Central Asia.* Armonk, N.Y.: M. E. Sharpe, 1992.

Rumer, Boris. *Soviet Central Asia: "A Tragic Experiment."* Boston: Unwin Hyman, 1989.

Sattor, Maxmud. *O'zbek udumlari* [Uzbek traditions]. Tashkent: Fan, 1993.

Shahrani, Nazif. "Central Asia and the Challenge of the Soviet Legacy." *Central Asia Survey,* 12(2): 123–135.

Shaniazov, K., and Kh. Ismailov. *Etnograficheskie ocherki material'noi kultury Uzbekov konets XIX–nachalo XX v.* [Ethnographic remarks on the material culture of Uzbeks at the end of the nineteenth and beginning of the twentieth centuries]. Tashkent: Fan, 1981.

Sukhareva, O. A. *Bukhara XIX–nachalo XX v (pozdnefeodal'niy gorod i ego naselenie)* [Bukhara in the late nineteenth and early twentieth centuries (late feudal city and its population)]. Moscow: Nauka, 1966.

Women in the Republic of Uzbekistan: Country Briefing Paper. Asia Development Bank, (2001) available at: http://www.adb.org/Documents/Books/Country_Briefing_Papers/Women_in_Uzbekistan/Chap_2.pdf)

Women of Uzbekistan, Statistical collection of the State Department of Statistics under the Ministry of Macroeconomics and Statistics of the Republic of Uzbekistan, 1999.

Zhilina, A. N. *Zhilishche narodov Srednei Azii i Kazakhstana* [Dwellings of the peoples of Central Asia and Kazakhstan], Moscow: Nauka, 1982.

9. Dinner with Akhmet

Greta Uehling

This article explores post-Soviet gender ideologies in Tajikistan by un-packing a series of encounters, especially my dinner with "Akhmet," in northern Tajikistan. I traveled to Tajikistan from my home in Tashkent, Uzbekistan, where I was conducting anthropological fieldwork. A Tajik family I met through mutual friends in Uzbekistan had invited me to visit, and it seemed like an ideal opportunity to expand my knowledge of the region. The husband of the family, "Enver," had invited me to stay and offered to introduce me to a number of informants for the project I was completing. The trip would draw me into by far the most dangerous of my ethnographic encounters in the former Soviet Union.

I met Akhmet because Enver asked him to accompany us across the border. Enver's wife and children had been away on vacation, and Enver decided to bring us all across the border at the same time. The plan was for me to stay for a week, interview a number of consultants, and then re-turn to Uzbekistan. In late 1998, the Uzbek-Tajik border was an extremely tense one. In some locations, there were as many a seven checkpoints with armed guards within one border crossing. Thus getting across the border was no simple task. In fact, the first border checkpoint we approached re-fused to let us pass. We returned along the road we had come, then ap-proached a different border crossing, stopping along the way at a café where Enver's wife Jamila and his daughter Alima drank orange sodas and Akhmet changed the plates on his car. My first inkling that Akhmet had unusual connections was that he had managed to obtain both Tajik and Uzbek license plates. On our second try with the Tajik plates at an-other border crossing, the guards were more receptive. Akhmet's casual self-introduction, including his position as head of tax inspection, led the guard to back away from the car, bow slightly, and wave us through.

Akhmet dropped us off, exhausted and dehydrated, at Enver and Jamila's home. As he unloaded our bags and closed the trunk he sug-gested that he come back the next night so we could go out to dinner.

While I assumed, based on their smiles and nods of approval, that Akhmet was inviting the whole family, I learned as I was getting ready that he (and the family) envisioned the dinner as something more like a "date"— I would be alone with him for the evening. The toasts Akhmet offered that night are mined for what they can reveal about gender and power in post-Soviet Central Asian life. They index a post-Soviet gender ideology profoundly stressed by the transition. Building on the idea that conversational discourse is an important site in which cultural meanings are negotiated and challenged (Austin 1962; Hanks 1996; Ries 1997), I explore toasts as a social and linguistic ritual. They yield insight not only into the encounter between an anthropologist and consultant, but the wider social context in which Soviet gender norms were being critiqued and Tajik gender regimes were being negotiated.

More specifically, the toasts I explore index a gender ideology that reflected the Soviet legacy *and* a reaffirmation of "traditional" male and female roles. For example, marital infidelity was reframed as a Muslim tradition called "polygyny," lending it an aura of respectability. The naturalization of difference led to a concept of "women's happiness" that was developed as a unique category of experience. In other words, the maternal role was affirmed, the domestic was idealized, and women's "inherent" differences from men were to be developed and accentuated.

Gender organizes social differences that help reinforce other hierarchies. I therefore also consider the ways in which my consultant's position as a tax inspector involved him in networks of taxation and tribute, privilege and profit that facilitated his construction of himself as male. For example, the family I stayed with described him as a "big" or "important" man, and his possession of multiple weapons had earned him deference from other interlocutors. In a place where the government and criminal networks overlap, Akhmet was able to "sell" not only his ability to inspect, negotiate, and insure compliance, but to charm, entertain, and seduce. What follows builds on Humphrey's (2002) argument that post-Soviet "Mafias" have come to stand for a way of life. I further suggest that his quasi-legal activities were fundamentally gendered, having as much to do with reinforcing constructions of masculinity as filling a vacuum left by the collapse of state structures. Conveying aspects of everyday life at the top of the Tajik social structure, this brief exploration will add a personal and ethnographic dimension to knowledge of Central Asia gleaned from sociology, political science, and history.

LATE TWENTIETH-CENTURY TAJIKISTAN

Tajikistan is a landlocked and mountainous country located in the heart of Central Asia, north of Afghanistan, south of the Kyrgyz Republic, and east of Uzbekistan. High mountains and arid plateaus characterize much of the country, but Tajikistan also has some of the most densely populated arable land in the world and a predominantly agrarian population. The physical geography of Tajikistan, with mountain passes that are closed by snow at certain times of year, has supported the development of culturally distinctive groups. Most of them are part of the Iranian cultural world, and Muslim. Typically, a distinction is made between the peoples of the plains in the north, where I visited, and the people of the mountains in the center, east and southwest, who were somewhat more isolated and developed stronger regional and local identities. Tajikistan is by no means exclusively Tajik: there are large Uzbek communities, as well as communities of Arabs, Jews, Kyrgyz, and since the Soviet period, Russians, other Slavic people, Armenians, Germans, and Crimean Tatars.

Following Tajik independence from the Soviet Union in September 1991, the country was torn by strife. The initial struggle for post-Soviet power was carried out peacefully in the context of a democratic election, but after a former leader of the Communist Party was elected president, the legitimacy of the presidency was widely contested. Tension between the president's supporters and opposition groups escalated to civil war. Between 20,000 and 60,000 were killed in the first year of fighting, and most commentators estimate that some 50,000 lives were lost between May and December 1992. According to UNHCR, 600,000 people, or one tenth of the population, were internally displaced, and at least 80,000 sought refuge outside the country, in Afghanistan. In the context of fighting, many unarmed civilians were murdered. A peace process initiated by the UN eventually resulted in a political and military settlement that was based on a power-sharing formula. After the June 1997 General Agreement on the Establishment of Peace and National Accord, there were numerous skirmishes between government forces and militia groups, as well as attempted and successful assassinations of political opponents, and the kidnapping, ransoming, and murder of Westerners that seems to accompany many modern wars.

While some of the tensions had been expressed in ethnic terms, the conflict in Tajikistan was primarily a civil one in which different interest groups mobilized to wrest control of the state and its resources, and gain an influence over the ideas and principles on which the newly independent country would be based. At issue was whether Tajikistan would be secular or Islamic, democratic or authoritarian. The conflict was in part a product of the Soviet era, when Soviet authorities forcibly transferred people from one region to the next to provide labor for new industries and intensive agricultural projects. The inter-regional exchanges led to greater integration, but also created conflict by sparking competition and greater consciousness of differences. I visited Tajikistan in this period after the civil war, as the skirmishes were winding down. I went in spite of the security risks because I knew that, traveling with locals in a private car, I would not attract a great deal of attention. Having lived in the region for over a year, my clothes and demeanor were by then less American, and my facility in Russian led many to assume I was from one of the Baltic states.

Since the end of the war, the Tajik government has sought to rebuild Tajikistan's destroyed economy, especially with Russian aid. It has also sought international investment, primarily in mining. But the country is still marked by the wars. One of the poorest of the former Soviet republics, Tajikistan presents social and economic indicators suggesting there was a decline until after the General Agreement was signed. Tajikistan has typically had the lowest rating of the USSR successor states on the UN human development index. Illegal trafficking in the main exports (aluminum, cotton, gold, and narcotics) is believed by many to be the most dynamic sector of the economy. Strengthened criminal networks left over from war and Soviet collapse bring politicians, bureaucrats, border guards, and militia leaders into a web of patron-client–type relationships that permeate the social landscape, creating an atmosphere of fear and mistrust. These relationships are of course not neutral but permeated (and strengthened) by the prevailing gender norms and ideologies. Hence even the mundane, everyday aspects of gender belong not to "human nature," but to an ever-changing social landscape formed out of cultural meanings and social practices.

EVERYDAY LIFE AFTER CIVIL WAR

The "everyday" has to do with "those most repeated actions, those most traveled journeys, those most inhabited spaces that make up, literally, the day to day" (Highmore 2002: 1). But the everyday also pertains to a quality that infuses the least examined aspects of life, emerging from background practices that are so taken for granted that, most often, they go unnoticed. While we often think of the everyday as that which is most familiar, as Highmore points out (2002), in modernity conditions disrupt our ways of being in the world, and the everyday becomes a process of making the unfamiliar familiar, incorporating the new, and folding traditions back into forms of adaptation and change. The everyday is therefore an ideal site for exploring gender and gender relations, which to my view are at once the core of our most habituated ways of being in the world and the locus of our most intense struggles for change.

In the Tajikistan of 1998, the everyday had been radically circumscribed, and seemed almost flattened by the prospect of violence. Most of the families I visited lived very constrained lives, confined by apprehension to their homes. The monotony of the long, hot days was broken only by the clink of tea cups, the crunch of another melon being opened and sliced, and once in a while the sound of distant gunfire. On my first day at their house, Enver left early to go to work. I stayed and chatted with Jamila, who, having been gone for over a month, moved from washing to cooking and back again, pausing only to pull her long hair back and tell me stories from their lives.

Enver came home for lunch and in richly praising his wife's cooking, lamented that while women used to be known for their ability to make everything from scratch, this is no longer the case. Jamila added that a friend's daughter had commented that she does not consider housework to be her work, and that she did not go to school so that she could stand in the kitchen. Enver and Jamila disagreed with this view, and exchanged a knowing look. They explained their relationship in terms of mutual dependency: Enver's devotion to Jamila emerging from his reliance on her, and a metaphysical connection—she hands him a *piala* (cup) of water, he drinks it and it "turns into" him, a sort of relational metaphysics linking them in their dependency. When she hears him coming in the door after work, she comes to greet him bringing a bowl of warm water and a towel so that he may wash. Then she points his slippers in the right direction so that he slides into them easily on his way to the couch.

Enver supported the idea that men should be able to have multiple wives. This was one point on which Enver and his wife disagreed. Central Asian women seemed to be pulled in competing ways: some wanted to celebrate the traditional power balance within the family, while other were drawn to working along Russian and Soviet lines that would enable them to develop as women. So in some families, *adat* or customary law was followed by women of their own volition and in others the tendency was for men to impose Islamic norms. Enver embedded his explanation of the social usefulness of polygyny (which enables women who would otherwise remain single in a male-dominated society to be married) in a discussion of how women are paradoxically the "stronger" sex— they can endure more, hold back their emotions longer, and assess their world more strategically. He argued that a Muslim woman should know how to present herself as a "dummy" to make her husband feel strong at the same time that she leads him from behind. This view resonated with an analogy I often heard that a husband is the "head" and the wife is the "neck." The idea is that while he might possess the brains, he relies on her to turn him in the right direction and he can do nothing without her.

Everyday life is infused with and structured by gender norms. Enver and Jamila's routine was habitual and in many ways familiar, resembling closely the lives of other families I visited across the region. But this is not to say that it was unquestioned, because their roles, responsibilities, and relationship were the subjects of intense reflection. In fact "everyday" gender relations became a site where it was possible to see radical transformation in the mundane. Prior to the Soviet collapse, both Enver and Jamila had worked—he was in construction, she was a teacher in a local school. During Enver's prison term (for political activity), Jamila had supported their two children until his release. Since the collapse of the Soviet Union however, everything had changed: Jamila's teaching job paid so little that there was little point to keeping it. In order to make a living, Enver had been pushed from construction into the rapidly privatized and criminalized world of mining and business—a transition that brought him directly into contact with Akhmet, who had inspected his business.

As the head of tax inspection, Akhmet had found Enver in violation of certain tax codes and had frozen his assets. They eventually talked, ate, and drank their way through their positioning on opposite "sides" to build a friendship. With the passage of time and an exchange of bottles they had made friends and grown to respect one another. This happened along the lines that Pesman has described, when drinking involves a "theft of time," something that creates a world of "us," where one can open oneself and discuss anything (2000: 172). Drinking creates a realm of sociality that holds the "real" world at bay, and creates new "worlds." Frequently, the worlds that are created in drinking involve an impression of you and me against the world (Pesman 2000). One of the things that makes Soviet drinking a ritual is that, unlike in the West, Soviets drink together. This means that the sip of wine or the shot of vodka is taken in unison, after being consecrated by toasts. The liturgy of toasts is well enough established that there are manuals and guidebooks filled with instructions and suggestions.

Following Tajik independence and all the changes that it brought to their everyday lives, Enver and Jamila ascribed to a masculinism in which Enver was the unquestioned head of the household—a role that sanctioned him to bark commands and verbally abuse his loved ones. Whitehead defines masculinism as a point at which the dominant forms of masculinity and heterosexuality meet ideological dynamics, and are thereby legitimized as privileged and unquestionable (Whitehead 2002: 97). At a broader level, the masculinism is manifested in myriad ways, from a reliance on violence to solve disputes to the sexual division of labor. The politically and socially dominant role of men, however, stands in a complex relationship to Soviet gender norms. While Soviet laws and practices were initially predicated on female emancipation, ambivalence and lack of implementation meant that women had a "double burden" under the Soviet system. Enver and Jamila used their understanding of Islamic customary law to justify the balance of power and responsibilities they found most comfortable, and took for granted that there are fundamental differences between men and women.

DINNER WITH AKHMET

The journey from Uzbekistan into Tajikistan, which had in more peaceful times taken two hours, had taken us close to six hours. Worn out by the road, we retreated to the cramped apartment shared by Enver, Jamila, and their two children. As the time to go to dinner grew close, the family sat down in front of the TV and I realized that they were not preparing to leave. Enver asked me if I had brought any evening clothes, adding, "He is a very big man, you know." Fortunately, I had a black and peach-colored suit folded neatly into the small tote bag I had brought with me. Putting it on, and realizing this was not going to be a "family style" dinner, I began to feel nervous. Given the kind of difficulty Akhmet would experience within his community if anything happened to me, I rationalized that it was safe enough to go. I was also propelled to go by the sense of lethargy and entrapment I felt after a long day in Jamila and Enver's living room with little prospect of interviewing the next day.

We climbed into Akhmet's pale green Mercedes and began chatting about the evening news. They had just broadcast a story about the mayor of a small town nearby who had been shot to death earlier that day along with some of his staff. Having expected Akhmet to shake is head in disapproval, I grew even tenser as he chuckled and smiled, another clue to proceed with caution. Akhmet took me to a local resort or tour base, which had a small restaurant surrounded by a terrace on the shores of a large, calm lake. There were also sports facilities, a hotel, and a swimming pool. As we strolled down a winding path toward the restaurant, the people that we passed greeted Akhmet with respect, bowing, with hand on heart, and then backing away. Many came up to him, kissed his hand, and placed it on their forehead. After being treated like a local dignitary, Akhmet explained that he came here often, to collect table scraps and meat for the bear he kept in a pen in his back yard. In fact, he had sometimes brought the bear here, on a leash. But this did not explain the fearful looks that he received, or just how his position had earned him such deference.

The restaurant itself was a relatively simple affair: white plastic tables and chairs on a terrace covered by a large, gazebo-like structure over a dance floor. We sat down at a table overlooking the lake, and Akhmet looked at one of the waiters and delicately raised a finger. The response was immediate. The waiter put down his tray and, hurdling over the plastic lawn chair in his way, ran to our table. Akhmet ordered a bottle of Tajik wine, "Black Eyes," to celebrate, saying "Don't worry [about drinking too much]. You will sleep here tonight." When he waved away my polite refusal, I sank deeper into my chair—Akhmet's way of operating in the world was disturbingly autocratic, and how I could extricate myself was particularly unclear.

The first toast, as we raised our glasses, was "To chance," because it was by chance that we met. This toast, along with the second one, "To relaxing," set the stage, framing our encounter as a coincidental one that had a potentially deep future: Akhmet said that next time, I would come not to work, but to simply enjoy the beauty of the region; that would be what I would remember when I returned to the United States. The reference to relaxing is an important one, for it points to the way in which drinking is sometimes celebrated as a time outside of the routine and the structure of daily life. In this way, the toast positioned us on the same "side" as fugitives from the world of work and economically determined relations. But the point about relaxing was also inherently gendered. It was repeated at numerous times during my research in Central Asia that work was unhealthy for me as a woman. It would spoil me and render me unfit for marriage, the goal, as far as Akhmet was concerned, for every woman. Akhmet therefore saw my research as irrelevant in the larger scheme of life. "Science, after all, is men's work," he insisted.

Given his general lack of respect for my project, our conversations about my work were somewhat abbreviated. I mentioned, vaguely, that I planned to meet with some local elders. His reply, with a scornful look, was "Do you *need* that? Personally, I think that is the last thing that you need." That meant we had more time to talk about his work, as the head of the tax inspection department. Akhmet framed himself as different from his predecessors, but I suspect the department had been operating in a similar way for some time. Akhmet said he wanted to be known, liked, and respected, "as a person" outside his role. He said that he felt that if he were not on good terms with the people he had to relate with, then they would begin to say bad things about him, and this would make his work harder. He therefore cultivated collegial relations with his counterparts. This was evident when the head of the Tajik security services (formerly the KGB) came and greeted us at our table, grinning at Akhmet with his full set of gold teeth like a Cheshire cat. Akhmet clarified that his ability to make sure he is liked does not mean he is "soft." His allusions to having killed were only thinly veiled by euphemisms.

The third toast he raised was to eyes. This was in part by virtue of the fact that we were drinking "Black Eyes" wine. But it had also to do with eyes being the proverbial windows on the soul, and Akhmet's hope that the drinking encounter would bring about a level of intimacy. Akhmet had begun his efforts to meet my gaze in the car the day before, staring intently at me through the rear view mirror as the others dozed in the heat.

The fourth toast was "To purely women's happiness." By purely women's happiness, he meant the kind of happiness a woman experiences when she bows to her "true" nature as a feminine creature, concerned principally with the welfare of her family and children. Akhmet was incredulous that I had undertaken a project on the scope of an advanced degree, saying, "Honestly, with your hand on your heart, tell me you don't want women's happiness?"

The very notion of something that could be called women's happiness reveals an essentialized view of gender identity as something "natural" and "in the blood." The idea that I was going against nature in following a path of scholarship reflected a gender ideology in which there are clear-cut spheres of men's and women's work and pleasure. The category of women's happiness was formed out of experiences common to women (being courted, becoming a wife, bearing children, etc.). But these activities are not only biological in nature, they are cultural. How one sees and responds to age-mates, who one marries, and when (and if) one gives birth, are all products of cultural and religious traditions.

As for Akhmet, he described himself as something of a playboy (his term) until his mother arranged a marriage for him. The woman she chose was a former student she knew well. Akhmet said that he had never left his wife's trust, but I soon learned that this was only by virtue of never telling her where he was going. The idea was that if she did not know about it, it was not infidelity. It could only be construed as infidelity if she consciously knew she was being betrayed. His mother reinforced this system of trust and fidelity. When he wanted to see his girlfriend, who he kept in an apartment across town, he simply phoned his mother. She phoned his wife and explained that he had arrived, been given dinner, and was sleeping, exhausted, at her home. The belief in men's supposedly uncontrollable sexual appetites was funneled through his family's norms and Central Asian conventions in such a way that his infidelity was treated as "healthy" and "normal." While the practice of real polygyny is still technically illegal, there is considerable evidence that it is nevertheless widespread.

The fifth toast was "To parents, who bring us into the world." This was part of a standard cultural script that prescribes honoring parents and ancestors. Toasts to parents, mothers, and fathers are a ubiquitous element of drinking rituals across the former Soviet Union. In this respect, our drinking and toasts were very Soviet. What gave them a Central Asian spin was the specific relations between children and parents, husbands and wives. The Central Asian dimension for my dinner companion was his very close relationship with his mother. In addition to being linked by her support of his sexual escapades, they were tied by religious norms and conventions. According to Islamic belief, the son must bury his parents. This belief kept Akhmet and his mother very close. Akhmet said his mother begins to worry if he does not visit her for a couple of days because, according to the Quran, one must bury the deceased "before the lips dry out," within about twenty-four hours. Although they lived separately, he said that he saw her as often as his wife and children.

The sixth toast was "To love." This was Akhmet's opening to solicit information: had I been in love? Was I currently in love? With whom? It was also a way of spinning a world around us, ready for habitation. Would he win me over? Would I fall in love with him? Throughout Central Asia, the knowledge that I had reached my mid-thirties and was not only unmarried but without children made me an anomaly, a person whose life begged for an explanation. My strange status was sometimes waved away with projections that these things were yet to come. At other times there were inflated assurances that they could, with a few conversations, "fix" me and provide a spouse. The idea that love often follows (rather than preceding) marriage seemed widespread. Once, when a man I barely knew proposed to me in Uzbekistan, I pointed out, "You don't know me and you can't possibly love me." His reply was, "Ah, but I will." I became fascinated with the calculations that went into marriage proposals. For example, a Tajik friend felt torn in choosing a bride. He was attracted to a girl from the country, who had a deformed foot, because he knew she would be loyal, subservient, and obedient. He also felt drawn to a woman who could provide better intellectual companionship, but he feared she would not stay with him for long.

The seventh toast was "To your (meaning my) health." On one level, this is a generic Soviet toast that shows concern for one's interlocutor. Toasts carrying hopes for health are ubiquitous across the region. But at another level this toast was embedded in the gendered ideology that so dominated the milieu. I was frequently confronted by people who were concerned that if I remained childless, it could have serious health repercussions. In fact, I was often cautioned that if I failed to produce children, I should expect to get cancer and even die. So this toast also carried a question about my health and the extent to which I, as a single and childless person, was a "normal" and "healthy" woman.

The eighth toast was "To friendship," again, planting the seeds of an idea. And the ninth (and last) was "To meeting in the United States." Here, in the final toast of the evening, is revealed one of Akhmet's underlying goals and the overriding subtext of the conversation, which was to expand his personal ties. While he was in a position to simply purchase a ticket, his view of the way the world works was that it turns on personal ties. As such, there would inevitably be a way in which having me as a contact in the United States could advance his goals. As Pesman has argued (2000: 170) the idea of putting a bottle in front of someone to gain access to goods, services, or a promotion is a well-established aspect of Soviet life. But treating this as a bribe, or boiling it down to purely instrumental, economic terms is an oversimplification: drinking and the sharing of bottles is connected to the sense of exchange, of value, culture, and what it means to be a person in Soviet and post-Soviet life. As Pesman puts it, sharing a drink typically involves hours of sitting together. Deals are not only made, but transformed and coupled with a kind of intimacy that emerges from communication. Those who sit together can articulate their common interests.

As we sat and drank and talked, we looked out over the lake, which turned pale violet as the sun began to set. Across the lake, the lights of a small city began to twinkle, and we got up to walk down to the waves that were rippling against the shore. I reached down to feel the warm water. The proprietors of the restaurant turned on music and lights, and Akhmet asked not *will* you dance, but *when* are we going to dance? We *did* dance and finish the bottle of "Black Eyes" before I told him it was time to take me back to Enver and Jamila's house. While there was a great deal of discussion about women's equality within the Soviet system, pronounced power differences between men and women persisted. This was reflected in our encounter when Akhmet chose not to take my refusal of his advances seriously, never asking, "Will you spend the night?" but simply informing me again, "You will spend the night." Suspecting tact and diplomacy were my only recourse (given his gun), I told him I simply refused to even consider staying in the room he had reserved for me at the tour base. To my distress, Akhmet lifted me up off the ground, swung me around and then carried me, with ease, up several flights of stairs towards the lobby of the tour base hotel. Fortunately, when I again protested, Akhmet took "no" as "no," and folded this acceptance into an image of him as a gentleman.

GENDER AND POWER IN CENTRAL ASIA

How does this encounter fit into a history of gender relations in Tajikistan? Central Asia began experiencing increased pressure to modernize with the inauguration of the Soviet regime in the twentieth century. Universal compulsory education was introduced, there were efforts to establish medical and social service networks, and there was a push to secularize society. Part of this process was the campaign for female emancipation. The goal, on the part of the Soviets, was gender equality reflected in the law, in the home, in education, and at work. Although women's choices were expanded, and there came to be more public roles for women, Soviet-style modernity was accepted at the same time that it was also transformed to accommodate traditional concepts (Akiner 1997: 262).

As part of the reaction *against* the Soviet legacy, traditional cultural values are now being reinforced and Islam, in particular, is being called back in. This process is too complex and too contradictory to be understood as retrenchment. Central Asian men and women experience pulls in various directions. Some women have rejected the Soviet model of female emancipation in favor of what could be construed as traditional gender roles. There is also a tendency for Islamic norms of female modesty in dress and behavior to be reintroduced. But, as Akiner has argued (1997), women are in many ways more vulnerable than ever before: state protections are weak, posing a problem for those women without strong family connections. Also, many do not know their rights in Islamic law and are therefore not well equipped to negotiate either within or outside the family. While Soviet policies aimed to institute gender equality, post-independence Tajikistan presents a complicated picture: the rejection of older Soviet norms becomes an important component of cultural nationalism and the reassertion of local traditions.

Akhmet was perhaps the most dangerous person I interacted with in five years of visits to the former Soviet Union. With one gun under the passenger seat of his car, and several more in his office, he was ready to take on virtually anyone. My glimpse of his life revealed a highly gendered world in which "science is men's work" and the good, healthy women stayed home. The rhetoric of violence that underwrote his position was only too clear. He spoke of having "taken people out" and underlined his ability to stay in charge. His cruelty and desire to dominate were perhaps most evident in his relationship with his dog, a large German shepherd, whom he often kept locked up in the trunk of his car. The dog was deeply attached to him, and Akhmet played with this by forcing the dog to run in front of his car until his paws began to bleed from the pavement. Akhmet laughed with pleasure at the dog's pain, and his ability to control the extent to which he was wounded. It was clear from other conversations that he would treat opponents in the same way. Men like Akhmet did not *have* power as much as they *exercised* it, enabled not only by a gender order that validated forms of oppression but also by the socioeconomic collapse that necessitated extralegal forms of income generation and the concomitant use of violence and means of control.

Akhmet's construction of himself as male was built on forms of power he gathered as part of his position within the government. Men as soldiers, generals, and politicians were of course the major players in the Tajik civil war. But a form of violence that also supported the construction of masculinity and power in post-Soviet central Asia was the violence associated with Mafia or organized crime. In Tajikistan, there was importance placed on being a big or important man because, in the absence of the rule of law, it was only in wielding influence through personal connections that a great deal could be accomplished. According to several informants, one of the ways that the tax department routinely collected "revenue" was to go to the market, ask if the vendor had any harder currency, and when rubles or dollars turned up, confiscate them to line one's own pockets. The money was believed to pass up the chain of command and compensate for low state salaries.

In the car on the way back to Enver's house, I looked out over the mountains, which were glowing amber and pink against a violet sky. When I turned back, he was staring at me again from the driver's seat and asked, "When are you going to become a woman?" "In what sense?" I replied. "In the sense that you don't need all this (and here he fell back on the speech fad of rhyming nonsense terms) science-schmience, history-schmistory." For him, "becoming a woman" was more than sexual, having to do with abandoning my project, surrendering to an ostensibly pure and biologically based femaleness. Akhmet's proposal was that I become his third "wife." Like Enver, he framed this within an Islamic teaching that allows men (who can afford to keep them) to have multiple wives. He assured me that I would be very comfortable there and might even consider becoming a businesswoman. Here we see a hybrid or mixing of traditional custom with modern realities and practices that is typical in Tajikistan today. Akhmet affirmed an unapologetic gender asymmetry, in terms of power and status, in the name of "natural" difference at the same time that he recognized women had important abilities to channel toward the building of a new Tajik society.

CONCLUSION

The practices and ways of being in the world that serve to reinforce men and women's sense of them selves *as* men and women are shifting. In Tajikistan, masculinity in particular seems to be produced and maintained in a political context that assumes a "natural" gender order to things. Gender norms and gender ideologies overlap with, and reinforce, other hierarchies of power and privilege. This being true, gender in Central Asia is not reducible to ideas and practices that are either modern or traditional. There is a complex and even contradictory consciousness involved. For example, realizing that he had drunk too much wine, Akhmet decided would be inadvisable for him to drive any further. Invoking self-sufficient American women's nearly universal ability to drive, Akhmet handed me the keys. It was only at this moment, seated firmly behind the wheel, that I knew with any certainty that I would make it back to my friend's house safely. After a few cups of coffee, Akhmet departed for his home on his own. Attitudes with respect to gender and power do not spring into being, fully formed, but emerge slowly out of the values, attitudes, and material realities coalescing out of the present and the past. Everyday life in Central Asia reveals a shift in which the post-Soviet transition has given new acceptability to the gendered attitudes and practices that were considered outmoded and suppressed. What balance will be struck between tradition and modernity is still unclear.

REFERENCES

Akiner, Shirin. 1997. "Between tradition and modernity: the dilemma facing contemporary Central Asian Women," in Mary Buckley, ed. *Post-Soviet Women: from the Baltic to Central Asia*. Cambridge: Cambridge University Press.
Austin, J. L. 1962. *How to Do Things with Words*. Oxford: Oxford University Press.
Hanks, William. 1996. *Language and Communicative Practices*. Boulder, Colo.: Westview Press.

Highmore, Ben. 2002. *Everyday Life and Cultural Theory: An Introduction.* London and New York: Routledge.

Humphrey, Caroline. 2002. *The Unmaking of Soviet Life.* Ithaca, N.Y.: Cornell University Press.

Pesman, Dale. 2000. *Russia and Soul.* Ithaca and London: Cornell University Press.

Ries, Nancy. 1997. *Russian Talk.* Ithaca and London: Cornell University Press.

Whitehead, Stephen. 2002. *Men and Masculinities.* Cambridge, UK: Polity Press.

PART FOUR

Performance and Encounters

As enduring or timeless as a local musical performance, the delicacies of a meal, or the domestic division of labor may seem from an outsider's perspective, these aspects of cultural life are usually just as constructed, contested, and changeable as all others. Timelessness and the oft-vague notion of tradition often come apart not just through a careful examination of works of history, but also via consultations with people of different generations in a single household. Consultations among people of different generations are yet another benefit of careful ethnography, of scholars always reminding themselves not to take things for granted.

Because so many of us began our research after the disintegration of the Soviet Union, we witnessed how Central Asians assessed many of the shifts taking place around them even as they themselves became willing or unwilling agents of change in terms of artistic expression, feasting, hospitality, and housework. Soviet ideology permeated or at least impinged upon virtually every aspect of social life, from child rearing and housework to wedding feasts and choral spectacles, no matter how "traditional" or "hybridized" these practices appeared. Now, as Central Asian states chart their courses as sovereign countries, citizens from all walks of life are caught up in competing ideologies, across broad spectrums, from individualistic to communitarian, from secular to religious. In this regard, both national fortunes and individuals' socio-economic status and gender affect the degree to which continuity or changes are welcome or grudgingly accepted.

In this section, chapters concentrate on the relationship between everyday life and, for example, public spectacular performances in Uzbekistan, Kazakh music and hospitality, the proper conduct of family affairs in Uzbek and Kazakh villages, and the ways in which rural and urban Uzbeks conceive of food as the embodiment of the "good life." In all cases, the authors find that these seemingly mundane matters hold great importance for Central Asians in terms of status and identity. In the cases of Sancak and Finke and Michaels, they become simultaneously educated and implicated in the complex performance of everyday tasks.

Michael Rouland uses a 2005 performance of Kazakh musicians in Washington, D.C., where a panoply of styles and traditions were performed, to set up a panoramic account of Kazakh music over time, and its relationship to everyday life. The Washington performance displays the impact of cultural changes forced from outside on Kazakh musicians; at the same time, Rouland emphasizes that music has served, and continues to serve, as a central marker of local and national identities across this formerly pastoral region. In doing so he discusses how musical performance, instruments, musicians, and their audiences relate to overarching themes that embody Kazakh religious beliefs as well as a pronounced sense of nationhood. Such an argument certainly could be made for many other peoples, but Rouland displays how historical, religious, geographical, and socioeconomic factors led music to play a particularly dominant role in the lived culture of Kazakh peoples. He richly instantiates this particular case via his own ethnomusicological experiences, giving the reader a picture of musical life and its traditions at once succinct and widely informative.

Laura Adams, working with artists and entertainers, discusses performances as spectacles, especially those designed to impart national unity and pride during newer state-sponsored holidays, such as Independence Day and *Navruz* (*Nau Ruz*, the Turko-Persian celebration of the vernal equinox). State officials and cultural producers alike realize the power of holidays as times to celebrate key events in a given people's history while showing off the most entertaining aspects of national expression. At the same time, the author shows the diverse and important meanings these events hold for ordinary Uzbeks, richly describing recipes and rituals as windows to the relationship between holidays and everyday life. Their importance leads to multiple challenges, direct and indirect, of state efforts to shape holidays as spectacle, even as many support recent top-down initiatives in nation building. Adams also uses the changing nature of holidays in independent Uzbekistan, including International Women's Day, to reveal how these events are intertwined with socioeconomic and gender hierarchies, as well as tinted with pre-Islamic, Islamic and, especially, Soviet markers, tying together past and present.

Food, like holidays, emerges as a key site of cultural performance in Uzbekistan. Zanca discusses the Uzbeks' pursuit of culinary practices and habits of gustatory bravado. He highlights the subject of fat in the diet and fatty foods in general to consider how flavors and the sense of fullness continue to shape a "good life" ideal for both rural and urban citizens. Zanca's reading of cuisine as hospitality shows that many Uzbeks engage in a competitive approach toward feasting, especially as they seek to quantify the types and amounts of food they serve vis-à-vis what they would expect to find in cultural settings elsewhere. In addition, readers learn of the kinds of food people most prize, where they enjoy eating favorite foods, and where they go shopping for them.

Sancak and Finke's and Michaels' chapters constitute ethnographies of encounters that expose performance aspects of Central Asian culture. Working in rural Uzbekistan and Kazakhstan in the case of the former and in Almaty, Kazakhstan's largest city, in the latter, these scholars discuss their encounters as guests in people's homes, learning about how Central Asians essentialize their own notions of hospitality—a key element of culture about which they show pride—to outsiders. Learning to live with Central Asians, the authors work, through their own Western lens, to understand how members of different generations define values relating to gender, morality, and attitudes that contribute to notions of living a worthwhile life. Sancak and Finke and Michaels also reveal their informants' difficulties in the perilous and uncertain post-Soviet era as they attempt to conduct themselves so as to lead a goal-fulfilling and success-oriented life. For example, just as some young people pursue newer opportunities to study in Europe or the United States, some parents and men now try to restrict girls' and women's abilities to do what they wish to in life under the pretense of cultural traditions or their own ideas of religious dogma.

In examining detailed encounters from common perspectives that include cooking for guests or discussing how their children should conduct themselves at home, Michaels and Sancak and Finke bring out the frequent comparisons between the Soviet and post-Soviet eras. Comparative discussions of past and present implicate informants and scholars alike in a kind of ideological back-and-forth, now to socialism, now to neoliberalism. While we naturally all have our political biases, often lost in less personal studies than these is the simple fact of ordinary people assessing the material bases of their lives away from oil booms and multi-party systems. Larger political events may be the stuff of headlines, but they are often removed from the simple and direct struggles people deal with each day as they buy school supplies for their children and head to the local marketplaces to find suitable foods to host a dinner party. As scholars living in contemporary Central Asian societies and chatting about the usual minutiae of life with friends and acquaintances, we reflect ubiquitous comparisons between the Soviet and post-Soviet eras on a personal level even as we are aware of larger political implications.

10. An Ethnohistorical Journey through Kazakh Hospitality

Paula A. Michaels

The apartment was located in one of Almaty's hastily built, pre-fab *khrush-cheby*, or "Khrushchev slums," thrown up in the late 1950s and early 1960s to alleviate the USSR's dire housing shortage. Not much to look at, it was clean, comfortable, and a short walk to Almaty's main shopping drag, such as it was. A half-mile long pedestrian mall that connected the bazaar with the central department store, the street had been recently renamed Silk Road (*zhibek zholi*) to underscore its commercial orientation. In the spring of 1992, I had been studying in Almaty, then capital of the newly independent republic of Kazakhstan, for eight months. Initially I had lived in a half-completed university dorm, but a lack of amenities and opportunities to practice my budding Kazakh language skills drove me to rent a room from a Kazakh family. The long bus ride from the apartment to campus was worth it for the experience of seeing Kazakh family life up close.

My host family defied tradition in a number of ways, but, in doing so, was fairly representative of contemporary, urban, educated Kazakhs. The mother, Saule, was divorced and lived alone with her nine-year-old son, Temirbek.[1] Raised in an old-fashioned, rural family, Saule felt stigmatized by her identity as a divorcee. In her own eyes and perhaps in those of others, the failure of her marriage branded her as inadequate as a woman, though she never articulated this sentiment so clearly and directly. Shy and nervous, Saule seemed always on her guard and was difficult to get to know. Perhaps I, the rare, exotic American, exacerbated that aspect of her personality, but even in her dealings with others I observed an inordinate level of anxiety and jitteriness.

It was while living under one roof with Saule and Temirbek that spring that I turned twenty-six, officially passing from marriageable age to old maid by Kazakh standards. Despite the sad and sympathetic looks I garnered from my Kazakh friends, I decided to celebrate the occasion nonetheless. In the fall of 1991, it had been difficult to secure a variety of foodstuffs, but with the price liberalization that came on January 1, 1992, and with the widening of commerce that accompanied the USSR's demise, an unprecedented range of imported products became available to anyone who had money. The opportunity to procure prepared foods, such as jarred spaghetti sauce, was a great relief to me given my limited culinary skills at the time. Kazakh women learn how to cook from scratch at a young age. Their mothers train them to be inventive cooks, making do with whatever they can get their hands on. But I did not grow up at the knee of a Kazakh mother. TV dinners were a staple in our household and, other than meatballs and tuna salad, there was not much depth to my kitchen repertoire. Spoiled by fully stocked supermarkets, I certainly had no idea what it meant to make do with what was available.

With a few store-bought basics, however, I felt confident about my ability to be innovative and adapt to my surroundings. My plan for the party was to buy a few jars of Prego, several *non* or *lipeshki* (round, flat bread), a mild domestic cheese to substitute for mozzarella, some sausage, and *voila*! It might not be the pizza of my Brooklyn childhood, but it would be an approximation that I thought my Kazakh friends would find novel and my American friends would enjoy as at least a faint reminder of home. In anticipation of my birthday party, I had brought back from Moscow a box of cake mix and instant pudding (to be used in lieu of frosting), taking the easy way out despite the widespread availability of flour, sugar, chocolate, and other baking essentials. I believed that, notwithstanding my lack of experience in the kitchen and the foreign environment, I had done pretty well, showing a certain amount of culinary creativity. It was with a mixture of pride and expectation that I awaited the arrival of my three Kazakh and three American guests the Saturday afternoon that had been appointed for the celebration of my birthday. What I had not anticipated was that Saule would greet my menu with horror.

Whereas I saw pizza and cake as perfectly adequate, even classic birthday party fare, Saule believed my menu to be an insult to my guests and a poor reflection on her as the lady-of-the-house. Her neurotic personality only compounded her strict views on how to treat one's guests, notions rooted in the traditional Kazakh values with which she was raised. With Saule underfoot, meddling in my preparations, watering down my pudding mix, and scurrying about to supplement what she deemed my meager offerings, I first encountered what I came to call the "salad-to-guest ratio." One will not find this formula in any Kazakh cookbook, but it is widely held in the minds of hosts and guests alike.[2] While Saule was the first Kazakh to share the formula with me, she was not the last. Saule argued that not just the quantity, but the variety of salads, appetizers, and side dishes had to be proportionate to the number of guests. While it was not necessarily anything more than an approximation, one needed at least three different salads and side dishes for two or three guests, with the number of dishes increasing with the number of guests. Ten guests demanded the variety expand to four or five dishes. Pizza and cake just would not suffice, no matter how much ingenuity or daring it demonstrated for me. American or not, I was a woman being judged by the standards of Kazakh women and, of course, more than my reputation, Saule feared for how my womanly inadequacies in the kitchen reflected on her. It was her house and it would be on her doorstep, so to speak, that the final praise or shame would be laid.

What I had intended to be a fun yet low-key adventure for me in kitchen experimentation turned into a stressful struggle between adherents to clashing perspectives on hospitality. With our potlucks and BYOBs, one can certainly argue that Americans have lost appreciation for, and the art of, hospitality. On the other end of the spectrum, Kazakhs take tremendous pride in the warmth and openness with which they welcome relatives, friends, and strangers alike. Hospitality is deeply entwined with the Kazakh sense of identity. Kazakhs are quick to observe that their hospitality exceeds that of their historically sedentary neighbors and rivals, the Uzbeks. Whether Kazakhs are more hospitable than Uzbeks is not a debate that I have the courage or stamina to enter into, but I can say that Central Asians generally see one's ability to serve as an excellent host or hostess as one of the most important criteria by which a person can be judged.

Tied up with these judgments are questions of gender and economics. As the ones who bear primary responsibility for food procurement and preparation, Kazakh women are evaluated not only on their culinary skills, but on the ambiance they create for their guests through the steady flow of food, drink, and entertaining conversation.[3] The graciousness and poise with which they, for example, serve tea at the meal's end is a source of pride for not only the hostess herself, but for the male head of household, if there is one. A woman's performance in the kitchen and at the table reflect back on her husband, who officially oversees the entire operation. But not only do Kazakh women prepare the food, they also must shop for it, and that in and of itself can be a laborious task. With the collapse of the Soviet Union in 1991 came an economic decline of catastrophic proportion. The relatively lavish entertaining of the Brezhnev era (1964–1982) had begun to erode by the end of the Gorbachev years (1985–1991), but nothing had prepared citizens of the former Soviet Union for the economic crisis that befell them. Women had to put food on tables with drastically diminished financial resources. As difficult as this was day in and day out, holidays, family celebrations, and other occasions for entertaining were even more of a challenge, straining financial resources to their limits and beyond.

This chapter examines how Kazakh hospitality, so central to Kazakh notions of what it means to be a good exemplar of the nation and of humanity, has been understood by Kazakhs and outside observers alike. In order to gain a clearer picture of this facet of Kazakh culture, I will explore three distinct kinds of sources, each of which reflects a different vantage point, period in time, and methodological approach to the study of everyday life. I begin with an examination of Kazakh proverbs about hospitality in an effort to view this issue from its deepest historical roots and from within the culture itself. I then turn to the ethnographic observations made by nineteenth- and early twentieth-century Western travelers to Kazakhstan. The third section of the article draws on my own observations and interviews made between 1991 and 2003. By looking at sources generated at different times and in a variety of ways, I will construct a multifaceted picture of Kazakh hospitality and the role it plays in everyday Kazakh life.

KAZAKH PROVERBS ON HOSPITALITY

In my confrontation with Saule, I would have been well served to remember the expression "When in Rome, do as the Romans do." Its Central Asian corollary, "Even a foolish guest will respect his host," points to the depth of my offense toward Saule in not deferring to her judgment. Sayings like this one are not just good advice, but also suggest the ways in which language can be a source of information about traditional attitudes toward hospitality. The Kazakh language, and its premodern Turkic antecedents, are rich in sayings about hospitality. Traveling across the Central Asian steppes in the eleventh century, the scholar Qashqari gathered folk sayings about a great many aspects of nomadic life, including the relationship between hosts and guests. These sayings served to set a tone for interactions between and to regulate the behavior of guests and hosts. The expression "It is good when there are a lot of guests" suggests the pleasure nomads took a millennium ago when welcoming visitors into their homes. They envisioned a home full of guests as a blessed and happy one. But the joyful relationship between host and guest could be maintained only when each performed his or her role properly. Proverbs offered guidance about behavior, as evidenced by the saying "If a guest is full, then he's ready to think about the road." However grateful and glad Central Asia's nomads a thousand years ago felt for the appearance of a guest, there was a limit to their hospitality. By being generous hosts, they could be assured that their guests would not tarry unnecessarily. Taken together, these expressions suggests something of the boundaries within which hospitality on the Silk Road was both given and received.[4]

Expressions used by contemporary Kazakh speakers show a continuity with these proverbs by similarly offering instruction. Kazakhs today refer to the unexpected guest as *qudai qonaq*, a gift from God.[5] Echoing Qashqari's observations that guests were warmly welcomed, the one who drops in without warning is seen as a divine blessing, rather than a burden or a boor. Kazakhs widely hold the belief that this warm-hearted attitude toward guests and the lavish reception considered appropriate are holdovers from the nomadic pastoral days of yore. In the vast, open steppe, such hospitality toward outsiders could very well be a matter of life and death for the wayfarer who sought refuge in a stranger's yurt, the felt hut in which nomads dwelled. For the host, of course, the favor would no doubt be returned directly or indirectly some day when the host himself was traversing long distances and needed a place to rest. Thus Kazakhs engaged in a kind of economy of hospitality, where food, shelter, and entertainment could be offered with the expectation that it would be repaid, if not by the recipient, then by another household somewhere in the steppe.

The pastoral legacy makes its way into contemporary sayings through the presence of animal imagery. Kazakhs say "Guests will sit like lambs" and "If good guests come, the sheep will have twins." Like Westerners, Kazakhs conjure an image of sheep as passive, content, and relaxed. That guests should sit like lambs suggests that the good host puts his or her guests at ease, and creates an environment for them that is comfortable and inviting. The picture of a sheep bearing twins is one of abundance, wealth, and joyfulness. This expression echoes the notion of the guest being a gift from God, who bestows good fortune and riches on the host who welcomes the guest appropriately. These two phrases, however, also suggest how guests should behave under their hosts' roof. A good guest should evince contentment and ease, and not make demands on the host. The guest who burdens his host will not be a blessing on the house that has opened its doors to him or her. Host and guest are in essence held to a contract that requires them to exchange an open-hearted and generous offering of hospitality for its grateful, undemanding acceptance.

The encounter between hosts and guests does not always transpire according to these ideals, and several Kazakh saying suggest the ways in which hospitality can go awry. Both "A guest sits briefly, but notices a lot" and "If it's a bad house, the guest will know" point to the ways in which the exhibition of hospitality can shed light on deeper, underlying familial dysfunction. The strong and harmonious family can withstand the pressure and scrutiny of hosting a celebration. Tensions will be readily apparent to guests of those families in which there is conflict. Familial discord will spoil the gathering and make it impossible for guests fully to relax and enjoy themselves. Host and hostess will have failed their guests by letting their own troubles intrude on others. The implication of "If it's a bad house, the guests will know" is that the guests themselves will behave poorly, in imitation of what they are witnessing in the household. The host family must work well together in order to fulfill its proper role and support the guest's appropriate performance. A consequence of rupturing this dynamic is illustrated by the saying "If you don't meet your guest, you won't get your desire." Failure to properly and enthusiastically greet one's guests with suitable hospitality can stand in the way of one's own happiness, presumably when God withholds his favor.

WESTERN ETHNOGRAPHY AND KAZAKH HOSPITALITY

Proverbs from ancient Central Asian nomads and modern Kazakhs alike sketch out some of the norms and expectations for hospitality, as well as the consequences for transgressing these parameters. A look at these sources offers an internal perspective, generated by the Kazakhs themselves. But the view from outside is also valuable, providing a complementary vantage point that can flesh out our understanding of traditional Kazakh hospitality. What appeared exotic and unusual to the European or American eye speaks as much or more to the world of the observers rather than the observed, but given the silence of Kazakhs themselves in the written record, we have little else to go on to reconstruct the customs and practices of a bygone era.[6]

After over a century of Russian expansion, by the 1860s the area currently known as Kazakhstan was entirely under St. Petersburg's domination. By comparison to Soviet rule, the Romanovs had relatively little impact on everyday life among the Kazakhs. Russian imperialism arrived, however, coterminous with an explosion of scientific inquiry into places that from the European perspective were remote and unknown. European and, occasionally, American geographers, geologists, and ethnographers, as well as missionaries, military men, and diplomats made their way to the steppes of Central Asia. Hundreds recorded their observations of indigenous life in articles and books that demonstrate varying degrees of insight and depth. Many authors comment on hospitality in the region. In part, of course, that is because these outsiders were in a perpetual state of being guests wherever they went. They continually found themselves facing rituals and customs associated with hosting. Western observers also noted these practices frequently because the scale of hospitality and the beliefs that underpinned them were alien and curious. While the assumptions they made about Kazakhs as a people varied from author to author, there is remarkable consonance on the ways in which nomads in the late nineteenth and early twentieth centuries demonstrated hospitality to their guests.

European observers unanimously declared Kazakhs to be exceptionally generous with their hospitality, confirming the Kazakhs' own assessment of what they see as a national characteristic. In 1873, the United States' Consul General to St. Petersburg made an expedition to Central Asia. Though Eugene Schuyler described Kazakh men as leading "a lazy, shiftless life" and foisting all their work onto their women, he sang the praises of Kazakh hospitality.

They are hospitable, often to a fault, to one of their own race or to a fellow [Muslim], nor do I believe that a Christian would fare worse among them. I certainly, whenever I happened to meet them on the Steppe, was well received, and everything which the family possessed was offered to me. They were sociable, and always eager for fresh news; even the telling or repeating it has a great charm for them; and as soon as a man arrives among them with a piece of news one of the family will immediately start off on a fresh horse and convey the intelligence to some distant acquaintance. In this way news travels through the Steppe almost as if by telegraph. . . . A circumcision, a marriage, or a funeral feast among the [Kazakh] is the signal for a large festival, accompanied by games and horse-races. To these [festivals] men will sometimes ride one or two hundred miles for the mere chance of regaling themselves for two or three days at another's expense and take their share of gorging on the whole-roasted sheep and horses.[7]

Schuyler's description points not only to the warm reception guests of all variety received from their Kazakh hosts, but to the diverse functions of hospitality in Kazakh society. Amid the oral culture of the Kazakhs, in an era before widespread literacy and access to the postal service, telephones, radios, newspapers, and televisions, guests provided valuable assistance as bearers of news. The population of the Central Asian steppe might have been spread thinly across a vast area, but that did not translate into total isolation, either from one another or from the outside world. Schuyler's observations remind us to stretch our perception of what constitutes a neighbor in the context of the nineteenth-century Kazakh way of life. Traveling a few hundred miles for good entertainment and company seems less extraordinary when viewed from this broader vantage point.

Just as the absence of modern technology meant reliance on alternative means of communication, so too steppe life sustained more traditional diversions for Kazakhs. In addition to the horse races and games described by Schuyler, hosts entertained guests with songs and stories.[8] The feasting itself can be viewed as a diversion, something to break the monotony of everyday life. The arrival of a guest at a Kazakh village usually occasioned the slaughter of a sheep and a feast of mutton, the quality of which Western observers praised highly. Writing in the 1880s, one British missionary noted that "some of the extravagant Russian officers, who go to Central Asia to repair their fortunes, and are supposed to have been accustomed to the best cuisines in Petersburg, declare that nothing can excel the [Kazakh] cooking of mutton, which I can so far confirm that, when we entered a second tent in the *aul* [nomadic encampment], and they brought us a dish of this meat boiled, we found it very good."[9] Certain parts of the sheep were considered delicacies and offered as a sign of respect to the most revered guests. To this day, whereas ears are often given to children so that they will learn to listen better to their elders, an honored guest receives the head. In 1914, a Russian woman witnessed this custom when she traveled to Kazakhstan with her two children and husband, an engineer in the city of Lepsinsk, located between Semipalatinsk and Verny [present-day Almaty]. The couple received an invitation from some Kazakh underlings. They sat at the *dastarkhan* [feast table] when

> Suddenly a [Kazakh] appeared with a roast sheep's head, and carried it to the Russian, saying
> "Please, eat!"
> "What's this?" asked the engineer. "The head for me; that won't do at all. I don't want the sheep's head; you must cut me something more tasty."
> "No, please," said the [Kazakh]. "You are the head man, and you must eat the head."
> "That will never do," said the Russian. But they besought him to honor their custom and permit the rest to eat, for until he had started on the head nobody else might begin.[10]

As British journalist Stephen Graham retells the story, it is unclear whether the Russian engineer tried eating the head or not. One suspects that it would have been difficult indeed to reject that which was quite obviously offered as a sign of respect and honor, no matter how shocking it was to the European palate. Not only does this scene record customs still practiced today—offering the head to the most honored guest and waiting for that guest to start before distributing meat to the others—but it highlights the cultural specificity of notions of hospitality and offers one scenario for how cross-cultural communication can go wrong.

While rituals surrounding food, such as the slaughter of a sheep or the serving of a head, were important ways to honor one's guests, a variety of other factors played roles as well. The most venerated guest was, and still is, seated in a position of honor, known as the *tur*, opposite the door to the yurt.[11] Kazakhs today assert that this custom has its origins in the belief that the most secure place in the yurt was facing the door. Fearing being stabbed or otherwise attacked from behind, guests could not relax properly if their back faced the door. By being seated opposite the door they were assured of their security, particularly with the host taking his seat directly in front of them, that is with his own back to the door.

Age, gender, and distance traveled factored into determining the rank of honor among guests. Rules for establishing who was most honored, second most honored, and so on were important because such ratings determined, albeit with a certain flexibility, the order in which guests were to say words of greetings and thanks to their hosts and the other guests. Even more importantly, identifying the most honored guest enabled the host to figure out who sat in the tur and who received the sheep head when the meal was served. The eldest male or the male who had traveled farthest was considered the most honored guest. Nowadays, being a foreigner trumps other factors and can even overcome one's status as a woman, allowing foreign women to occupy the tur seemingly as honorary men for the night. If a foreign male is present, however, no matter how aged or honored the foreign woman may be, it is likely the man will be placed at the tur. In the early twentieth century, before Soviet power had an impact on the status of Central Asian women, the place of honor was the exclusive province of men. Having first traveled to Russia as a Quaker relief worker during the Civil War (1918–1921), Anna Strong ventured across Central Asia in the early 1920s. She was accompanied for part of her journey by a Soviet official, Mamashef, of either Kyrgyz or Kazakh origin. The two arrived at a nomadic encampment, where the residents prepared a feast for them. After two hours of roasting, the head was finally ready to be served, and "it was handed with deference to Mamashef; I rejoiced that he, and not I, was guest of honor to whom such delicacies fell. Mamashef, an important official, was a regular collector of heads."[12] Strong demonstrates relief that she was denied the honor of the sheep head, but more significantly her remarks shed light on a subtle way in which Soviet power had an effect in years to come. Decades of Soviet agitation for women's rights, the dramatic expansion of educational opportunities for women, and perhaps even some knowledge of the women's liberation movement in the West conspire nowadays to guarantee that as a foreign woman traveling in Central Asia seventy or eighty years later, Strong would surely have been deemed the most honored guest. It is unlikely that that status would be afforded to an indigenous woman regardless of her accomplishment, but it is certainly no longer inconceivable.

HOSPITALITY IN CONTEMPORARY KAZAKHSTAN

Soviet power brought countless changes to everyday life in Kazakhstan. Without question the most dramatic and deadly was the forced settlement of the nomadic population during the 1930s. As part of the Soviet effort to reorganize agriculture along socialist lines through the establishment of collective and state farms, Moscow coerced the nomads to take up a sedentary life, cultivate the land, and engage in intensive, rather than extensive, animal husbandry. Kazakhs paid a heavy price for the state's sedentarization project, as approximately 1.5 million people, nearly half of all Kazakhs, perished from famine or fled abroad.[13] The demographic and psychological effects of this tragedy continue to be felt today, from the status of Kazakhs as but a plurality in their own republic to tensions between Kazakhs and Russians, whom Kazakhs hold primarily responsible for the devastation wreaked by Soviet power on their way of life.

Settlement of the nomads restructured economic and social life for

Kazakhs in a fundamental way and touched every aspect of daily life. So-viet authorities used sedentarization as an opportunity to reach out to Ka-zakhs through educational, medical, and other institutions designed to breed a shared Soviet loyalty and identity. Medical workers tried to stamp out the influence of shamans, folk doctors, and mullas. Schools cultivated linguistic Russification, indoctrinated students in Soviet patriotism, and presented Russian literary and scientific achievements as the inheritance of all Soviet peoples.[14] In the face of a connection between Russian lan-guage skills and upward mobility, of an influx of Russian-speaking mi-grants, and of the regime's limited support of Kazakh-language schools, written and spoken Kazakh teetered on the brink of extinction by the 1980s. As a percentage of their population, Kazakhs took greater advan-tage of Soviet higher educational opportunities than did their fellow Cen-tral Asians and thus found themselves more Europeanized than their southern neighbors. With respect to women these educational, profes-sional, and cultural patterns were especially dramatic as compared to other Central Asians.[15] Taken together, these changes meant that Kazakhs were at the close of Soviet power living lives that bore little resemblance to the traditional ways.

The impact of these changes for Kazakh hospitality was no less dra-matic than for other arenas of life. Without question, the infusion of al-cohol into the Kazakh diet constituted the most noticeable shift. With Russification and the greater presence of Slavs came the increasing, even ubiquitous, appearance of vodka and other hard drinks at the Kazakh table. Despite Muslim prohibitions against alcohol consumption, no wed-ding celebration, birthday party, or other important occasion was com-plete without it. With vodka came the practice of toasting, to which no ethnographic accounts that I have encountered from the late nineteenth and early twentieth century make reference. Urbanization also rendered traditional beverages such as *kumyz* [fermented mare's milk] and *shubat* [fermented camel's milk] a rarity at the tables of city dwellers. Even in the countryside these drinks, which had once been part of the daily diet, made their appearance less frequently and were replaced increasingly by vodka and the ill health effects that came with it.

Vodka impinged on health and on the atmosphere around the table, but even in the face of this important change, Kazakhs kept up many of the traditions associated with hospitality. First and foremost, the value placed on the lavish entertainment of guests survived Sovietization. Even after the nomadic life became for most relegated to the past, the pride Kazakhs took in opening their homes to guests persisted. As a collective, conscious sense of Kazakh identity deepened, hospitality turned into a hallmark of "Kazakhness." To identify as a Kazakh meant to value hos-pitality, including the perpetuation of traditional attitudes. Kazakhs, for example, no longer lived in yurts or feared being stabbed in the back, but the place of honor opposite the door made the transition from the felt hut to the Soviet apartment. Sparing no expense and doing whatever was necessary to give the appearance of abundance at the table persisted into the late twentieth century. For urbanites, mutton was still the meat of choice on a special occasion, even if for practical reasons it was only in the countryside that the slaughter of a sheep continued to be the norm for an honored guest.

The economic and political disruption of the Gorbachev era and the post-Soviet period brought a wave of transformation to the exhibition of hospitality among Kazakhs. Most importantly, as the per capita income plummeted, the ability to entertain and celebrate in the lavish ways to which Kazakhs were accustomed became untenable for many. Putting food on the table on an ordinary day became difficult, while hosting a wedding turned into a financial trauma. In the Soviet era, certain goods were not necessarily expensive, but they were hard to find. In the mid- and late 1990s, everything imaginable was readily available, but much was unattainable for the average Kazakhstani. Even in the countryside, by the mid-1990s it was a rarity for a sheep to be slaughtered for a guest, as it was simply too expensive.[16]

How Kazakhs have coped with changing economic conditions obviously breaks down along class lines, but generational rifts are salient as well. According to one informant, "The older generation still does things the old-fashioned way, as in Soviet times." By contrast, young people do not celebrate special occasions as often at home, as was de rigueur before. "Their parents give them money and they go to a café."[17] As for their middle-aged parents, they seem caught in between. They appear to be more reluctant both to entertain at home and to host parties out at restaurants and cafes. Under tremendous financial and temporal pressures, they have little left for the demonstration of hospitality. Parties for this cohort tend to continue to be at home, but are of a more modest scale in terms of both the number of guests and the amount of fare. A greater reliance on high-quality prepared food, which is now readily available in Kazakhstan's cities, may not save the host money, but certainly frees up valuable time for career women.[18]

One way that Kazakhs have found to save both money and time when entertaining is to cut down on alcohol consumption. While I would emphasize that my evidence is sparse, anecdotal, and taken exclusively from an urbanized, elite strata of Kazakh society, both from my conversations with people and from my first hand observations, it seems apparent to me that alcohol consumption serves a far less central function in entertaining than it did even in the early and mid-1990s. With its lower proof, beer is an increasingly popular alternative to vodka at the dastarkhan. In the countryside, hosts offer their guests kumyz instead of hard liquor with greater frequency.[19] One informant described to me her nephew's recent wedding in rural Kazakhstan. Prompted by a reverence for tradition and a newfound religiosity, her brother served no alcohol at his son's wedding. The absence of alcohol was "nothing to be ashamed of" and the celebration "was very peaceful," in contrast to the occasionally embarrassing and riotous displays from inebriated partygoers.[20]

Another informant put a philosophical twist on this pattern, saying "People started drinking less because it doesn't change anything," but I would venture that the reason has more pragmatic origins.[21] Certainly increased religious observance among Kazakhs, especially in the countryside, plays a role. Anti-alcohol public health campaigns and a growing effort among parents to model responsible drinking behavior to their children may be at work as well.[22] The economic explanation, however, must not be overlooked. At a friend's 2003 birthday party, I was surprised by the moderate alcohol consumption and early departure of one guest, who gave the excuse that he had to rise early for work. While such temperance and industriousness would appear normal enough in the West, in Kazakhstan such behavior merits closer examination. In Soviet times, one not infrequently heard the expression "We pretend to work and they pretend to pay us." Those days are long over, and the demands of the market economy mean that jobs are maintained on a competitive basis and wages bear some resemblance to skills and effort. This vastly transformed economic landscape pushes those who want to get ahead and stay there to make choices about how to spend their time both on and off the job. Further, when faced with the limitless variety and possibilities of goods and services that capitalism has to offer, some choose to allocate time and money to pursuits that were unthinkable in the Brezhnev era, when drinking was one of few forms of diversion.

CONCLUSION

Raised in a traditional, rural family and well educated under the Soviet system, Guldarkhan Smagulova has spent her career studying the Kazakh language. Since I met her in 1991, I have called her Guldarkhan-*apai*, or "respected elder," as she taught me to in keeping with Kazakh tradition. Her knowledge of Kazakh customs and beliefs is deep, intimate, and reverent. A sophisticated thinker, she exudes national pride without the kind of mindless nationalism that has done so much damage the world over, including in the former Soviet Union. Her family has fared relatively well in post-Soviet Kazakhstan. With excellent English-language skills, solid work ethics, and capable minds, her two children have achieved success in the banking industry that would make any parent proud. But, despite the way in which her own family has flourished in the face of the economic and political vicissitudes of recent years, it is with a hint of nostalgia that Guldarkhan-apai reflects on the impact of these changes for

Kazakh hospitality. As she put it, "If you can't make a big party to celebrate your son's engagement, then why live on this earth?"[23]

Guldarkhan-apai's words speak to the centrality of hospitality in the Kazakh world view. Evidence in the form of ancient and contemporary sayings demonstrates the value placed on the performances of guests and hosts alike. Foreigners who traveled to Kazakhstan under both Romanov and Soviet domination noted with remarkable uniformity the generous and welcoming receptions that they received from the indigenous population. Soviet power left its mark on virtually every aspect of Kazakh life, from economic organization to language to gender roles. But even as Kazakhs adapted to the transformations that Soviet power wrought in daily life, traditional values, including the emphasis placed on hospitality, shaped their modern expression of customs and practices. Harsh, yet full of possibility, post-Soviet reality has reconfigured the financial and temporal resources available to Kazakhs, who again must find a balance between immediate exigencies and time-honored ways. How the rise of a capitalist economy in post-Soviet Kazakhstan reshapes the expression of hospitality is a transition still in the making, but its impact is already being felt in terms of when, where, and how people entertain.

That Kazakhs love to have guests and celebrate is by no means unique. Hospitality is part of everyday life the world over. But as a Western outsider looking in, one can not help but notice the priority placed by not just Kazakhs, but all Central Asians on what looks to us like quite grandiose displays of hospitality. To understand this emphasis on generous hospitality, one must recognize the meaning it holds for Kazakhs. Poor hospitality besmirches the reputation of both the host and the nation. My desire to serve pizza and cake at my Almaty birthday party in 1992 scandalized my hostess because it fed her anxieties about how others viewed her womanly qualities, and because she feared the judgment my American guests would make about the Kazakh people based on their reception in her home. My efforts to persuade her that to American eyes the offerings were perfectly adequate fell on ears deafened by values that had been drummed into Saule since she was a small child. As seen in the tension between us over that day's preparations, lavish hospitality can be a pleasure to experience, but it is a challenge to present. The pressure to perform can be tremendous, especially on women. Creating a strain that is both financial and psychological, the judgmental eyes of one's guests are always open, watching and evaluating.

My point is not that Kazakh hospitality outshines our potlucks, or that our lowered expectations for hospitality in the West create a more convivial atmosphere. Rather, the Kazakh example conveys how notions of hospitality are culturally specific and how the differences go beyond merely whether or not sheep head is on the menu. Through this examination of hospitality, we gain insight not only into a society's values, but also into its economic structure and its gender relations. The code that regulates Kazakh hospitality has had to change with the times. At present it suggests ways in which the rise of capitalism affects more than just the costs of putting food on the table. Capitalism has begun to shape when and how people interact around the dastarkhan. Long hours at work impinge on how much a hostess can prepare for her guests. She may put on a less lavish party, or rely on store-bought, prepared foods. Fear of being sacked for chronic lateness may curb drinking. The old ways of receiving a guest are not dead yet, but neither are they untouched by the recent upheavals. Like everything else in the post-Soviet world, these customs too have had to adapt to Kazakhstan's integration into a global market economy; and in doing so they seem to be bridging a gap that in the early 1990s seemed so great between one Kazakh landlady and her American tenant.

NOTES

1. For the sake of privacy I provide pseudonyms for my host family, but the remainder of my informants are referred to by their real names.
2. Years after I first observed this salad-to-guest ratio in action in Kazakhstan, I encountered it actually written as a formula in an American cookbook. Apparently the cultural divide is not a wide as I initially believed. See *Gourmet's Casual Entertaining: Easy Year-Round Menus for Family and Friends* (New York: Random House, 2001), 21.
3. For a brief survey of Kazakh women's history, see Paula A. Michaels, "Kazak Women: Living the Heritage of a Unique Past," in *Women in Muslim Societies: Diversity within Unity,* Herbert L. Bodman and Nayereh Tohidi, eds. (Boulder, Colo.: Lynne Rienner, 1998), 187–202.
4. *Soz atasy: Makal-matelder men qanatty sozder. V–XVII ghasyrlardaghy zhazba eskertkishkerdin materialdary zhinaq* [*Father's word: Proverbs and words of wisdom. A collection of memorable materials recorded in the 5th–17th centuries.*] (Almaty: Zhazushy, 1987), 59. I am grateful to Guldarkhan Smagulova for bringing this book to my attention.
5. This expression and the ones in the following two paragraphs are drawn from a discussion with Guldarkhan Smagulova, a Kazakh philologist. Interview by the author, 7 August 2003, Almaty, Kazakhstan.
6. My approach to these ethnographies is informed by Edward Said's benchmark *Orientalism* (New York, 1978), which analyzed the way in which this genre worked to reinforce Europe's imperial agenda.
7. Eugene Schuyler, *Turkistan: Notes of a Journey in Russian Turkistan, Kokand, Bukhara and Kuldja,* edited and with an introduction by Geoffrey Wheeler, abridged by K. E. West. (New York: Scribner, Armstrong and Co., 1876; Reprinted London: Routledge and Kegan Paul, 1966), 22–23.
8. See, for example, Henry Lansdell, *Through Central Asia: Diplomacy and Delimitation of the Russo-Afghan Frontier* (London: Sampson Low, Marston, Searle and Rivington, 1887. Reprinted Nendeln, Liechtenstein: Kraus, 1978), 151; Paul Nazaroff, *Kapchigai Defile: The Journal of Paul Nazaroff,* edited by E. M. Tuner (London: Athenaeum with Frederick Muller, 1980), 55.

9. Lansdell, *Through Central Asia*, 148.

10. Stephen Graham, *Through Russian Central Asia* (New York: MacMillan Company, 1916), 209.

11. See, for example, Landsdell, *Through Central Asia*, 148; Schuyler, *Turkistan*, 30.

12. Anna Louise Strong, *The Road to the Grey Pamir* (New York: Robert M. McBride & Co., 1930), 232. Quite possibly this incident occurred among Kyrgyz, not Kazakhs, but the text is unclear. The consonance of Kyrgyz and Kazakh customs offsets this murkiness and renders the question relatively inconsequential.

13. See Martha Brill Olcott, "The Collectivization Drive in Kazakhstan," *Russian Review* 40 no. 2 (1981): 122–142.

14. See Paula A. Michaels, *Curative Powers: Medicine and Empire in Stalin's Central Asia* (Pittsburgh, Penn.: University of Pittsburgh Press, 2003).

15. Women constituted 45 percent of all Kazakh students enrolled in Soviet higher educational institutions in 1970. By contrast, of Uzbek students only 33 percent were women, and among Tajik students a mere 24 percent were female. Gail Warshofsky Lapidus, *Women in Soviet Society: Equality, Development, and Social Change* (Berkeley: University of California Press, 1978), 153.

16. Interview by author with Guldarkhan Smagulova, 7 August 2003, Almaty, Kazakhstan.

17. Interview by author with Asiya Khairullina, 5 August 2003, Almaty, Kazakhstan.

18. One party I attended in 2003 even included sushi. While this is no doubt a fairly unusual example, it demonstrates not only the hostess's willingness to serve prepared food, which previously would have been considered scandalous, but the increasingly cosmopolitan palate of at least some Kazakhs.

19. Interview by author with Saule Moldabekova, 6 August 2003, Almaty, Kazakhstan.

20. Interview by author with Guldarkhan Smagulova, 7 August 2003, Almaty, Kazakhstan.

21. Interview by author with Asiya Khairullina, 5 August 2003, Almaty, Kazakhstan.

22. Interview by author with Guldarkhan Smagulova, 7 August 2003, Almaty, Kazakhstan.

23. Interview by author with Guldarkhan Smagulova, 7 August 2003, Almaty, Kazakhstan.

11. *Konstitutsiya buzildi!*
Gender Relations in Kazakhstan and Uzbekistan

Meltem Sancak and Peter Finke

It had been one of those hot spring days that make living in Bukhara a challenge for people unaccustomed to the climate. Meltem had been washing clothes and Peter, who was visiting her, had helped to hang them on the line. In less than an hour all would be dry; the hot temperatures are accompanied by great aridity. As there was neither washing machine nor running water in the village, laundering required getting water from the *ariq*, the irrigation channel, heating it on the oven, and then mixing in cold water until it had the right temperature.

A few days later we were chatting with Bahodir, a schoolteacher and the second son of the extended household. He told us that his two sons had been puzzled by what they had seen the other day, because in an Uzbek family, the father would never participate in any activity like our laundering. For them this was very strange.

> I told them, "You know, these people [Peter and Meltem] work differently from us. They work not so much with their hands but with their brains. They do not divide work as we do. That's why Peter is helping Meltem when they do something physically. This is different for me because I work more physically. Among the Uzbeks men do the hard work and women care for the house." [Comment: Like every other teacher in rural Uzbekistan, Bahodir spends much of his free time growing vegetables and potatoes.]

A few days later the topic again turned to our washing clothes together. This time Bahodir was softly complaining about the consequences of our behavior.

> Since that day things have changed. Now Yulduz [his wife] keeps telling me: "Why don't you help me as Peter does Meltem? I also have to

work very hard." Now she keeps attacking me this way. Our constitution has fallen apart [*konstitutsiya buzildi*]!

Bahodir is an open-minded person and was so amused by the incident that he loved to tell it again and again. But this points to a number of issues that many anthropologists experience when they take part in other people's everyday lives. Many everyday practices appear so natural that we hardly realize them when we do them. And even if we are aware of them, it may be difficult to change, because this might have unintended consequences (in this case, spousal relations regarding the division of labor between Meltem and Peter). The presence of anthropologists will have an impact on the studied society whether we like it or not. Finally, anthropology is not a one-way street. The anthropological observer at the same time becomes the observed: in this case by the kids who tried to make sense of seemingly inappropriate behavior.

In this chapter, we will describe everyday life patterns and gender relations in two Central Asian states, Kazakhstan and Uzbekistan, and indicate some differences between these societies. In both settings we lived with rural families for extensive periods.[1] Both hosts were teacher families of the local middle class. This was not so much a matter of choice but of assignment by the local authorities, who tend to think that "average" households are the best fit for anthropologists. Teachers are particularly popular in this respect because they are thought to know local culture and history best. For this reason, not all of the following may be representative for Kazakh or Uzbek society in general or even for the respective villages. The following description then, to some extent, concerns two families, one in southern Kazakhstan and one in central Uzbekistan. We believe that the depiction we present nevertheless provides insight into more general patterns of everyday life in Central Asia as well as differences between the two settings.

We carried out much of this research jointly or in close collaboration as we visited each other or stayed for some time with the same families. This is obviously an advantage in any anthropological setting, because so many encounters make it alternatively easy or difficult to access information, depending upon whether the anthropologist is a man or a woman. In Uzbekistan this was particularly helpful, because segregation greatly characterizes gender relations such that any individual anthropologist has limited access to one half of the social world. At private as well as public parties (*toi*) we would usually not see each other for several hours, after which we would report what had happened on the other side of the curtain.

Both Uzbeks and Kazakhs are Turkic-speaking Muslims. In the West we tend to think of Muslim women as being oppressed and excluded from public life. Travelogues often portrayed women as "chattel," being bought, sold, or returned at the disposal of fathers, brothers, and husbands. Bride-wealth paid by the groom's family to the bride's is cited as proof of this. On the other hand, female status in Kazakh or Kyrgyz society, predominantly nomadic livestock breeders, has frequently been positively contrasted to that of women among the agrarian Uzbeks or Tajiks. This distinction is often explained by the stronger roots of Islam among the latter. A sedentary lifestyle was believed to correlate with a more pious life and thus with a lower status for women (Krader 1963; Bacon 1966).

A similar image dominates contemporary literature on this topic. It is generally assumed that the impact of Soviet education and social transformation on gender relations was more profound among Kazakhs and Kyrgyz than among Uzbeks or Tajiks. Prime indicators for this were lower birth rates and a higher percentage of women in secondary education and in the labor market. Post-Soviet independence, according to a common view, has resulted in a re-traditionalization of society, again more pronounced among the long-since settled people. A fear concerning this effect has sprung up owing to reports on growing Islamic fundamentalism and economic impoverishment, particularly in Uzbekistan, where a rigid Soviet-style government quashes any kind of political dissent (Fierman 1997).

Studies on everyday life often operate within a framework of habitus and practices, grounded in the work of Bourdieu (1977). Precisely because many patterns seem so commonplace and sometimes trivial, we hardly think about them while doing them, rather seeing them as natural and self-evident. Within this framework, however, patterns of social interaction appear to be rather static and overdetermined—so deeply embedded in our conceptions of what is normal that we tend not to question them. Instead, we argue that most everyday life situations are still subject to interpretation and intended or unintended misconduct. Rather than as practices it may be more helpful to see them as institutions, as established rules that grow out of repeated interaction among individual actors and that people follow always to some degree, but never totally (North 1990; Knight 1992; Ensminger 1992). As such they provide guidelines for behavior but are constantly subject to change, because individual actors try to design them according to their own needs and interests. In our view, the concept of institutions better allows us to capture the importance of decision-making processes and negotiations even in the most common patterns in everyday life.

In the case of Central Asia, what to observers resemble age-old cultural patterns that survived the Soviet period are often merely adaptive strategies to cope with a new situation—namely, the decay of infrastructural facilities. This changed everyday life drastically. While modernity is often associated with alienation of people from everyday life and a profaneness of the latter (Highmore 2002), the vast majority of people in Central Asia surely would not regret to see those infrastructural achievements come back. For them, many things that had become part of their lifestyle have disappeared overnight, thus increasing their daily burdens.

GENDER RELATIONS IN SOUTHEASTERN KAZAKHSTAN:
THE VILLAGE OF AQ ZHOL

The village of Aq Zhol, where we conducted fieldwork, lies in the heart
of the Zheti-Su Region, some seventy miles east of Almaty. The village is
unique for a number of reasons. It was founded only in the 1980s as a model
village to demonstrate that in a developed socialist society there would be
no difference between urban and rural lifestyles. The village was designed
as a small town with two-story buildings, broad avenues, and a big department store—for a population of barely four hundred families. Infrastructural facilities like electricity, telephone connections, running hot water, and others were superior to any other Kazakh village we have seen.
Participating in a grand modernization project—socialism—fundamentally
changed the everyday lives of people. At the same time, Aq Zhol was to
represent the multi-national character of the Soviet state. Therefore, the authorities recruited families from all over the Soviet Union to settle in this
village (Sancak and Finke 2005).

This region is primarily one of intensive agriculture. Livestock rearing
has some importance in the surrounding foothills, and in socialist times
the herds were driven in summer to mountain pastures further south. Yet
animal husbandry is clearly secondary to cultivation. The main products
are grain, tobacco, and fruits. Tobacco is the major cash crop, especially
since Phillip Morris set up an agency in the region. Grain is also mostly
raised for sale, as is the case with the produce of the orchards. Vegetables
such as tomatoes, peppers, onions, and cabbage are grown primarily for
home consumption. People rarely sell any surpluses. Wheat production oc-
cupies only some in the village, because it needs more time and care than
most can afford. This is even truer for tobacco growing, which is very labor intensive.

The state farm (sovkhoz) in Aq Zhol had always been privileged with
modern machinery. During the 1980s it regularly won prizes for outstanding
performance. The state farm was dissolved in the mid-1990s and land was
equally divided among all inhabitants. According to national law, people
received not formal ownership but long-term lease contracts. Many of them,
however, did not make much use of their land because they could not afford the necessary inputs (seeds, fuel, and machinery) and because taxation politics seemed predatory. Several cooperatives that should have been
run as private enterprises replaced the sovkhoz as an organization. Most of
them, however, were disbanded within a year as members could not agree
on proper usage of the machinery and the distribution of work hours.

With the demise of the socialist system most people left the village, as
few had put down roots. Before leaving, people tried to sell their houses;
as this proved to be very difficult, they began to destroy them, to sell the

Kazakh village home.

materials at least. In 1997 the village looked like a ghost town, with only one-third of the Soviet-era population. Since then, Aq Zhol has become a prime settlement of *oralman,* or repatriated Kazakhs—those who lived outside Kazakhstan and moved here since 1991. They did so following an appeal by President Nazarbayev, who invited these groups to increase the percentage of ethnic Kazakhs in the country. Most came from Mongolia and Uzbekistan. Those currently living in Aq Zhol mostly came from China, with a few families returning from Turkey. When we visited the village for the first time in 1999, they had arrived only a few years before and still faced difficulties adapting within the new setting. Suspicion and mutual prejudices characterized relations with local Kazakhs (Sancak and Finke 2005).

Domestic Affairs and Economic Relations

In Kazakhstan we lived with the family of Beysen and his wife Nurgül. They had both been schoolteachers in Soviet times and now tried to adapt their life to the new market economy. Beysen and Nurgül have three daughters and two sons. During Soviet times all Central Asian groups had the reputation of exceptionally high birth rates. State policies that provided financial and ideological rewards for many children, such as earlier retirement and honors for mothers, strongly encouraged large families. However, Kazakhs on average had fewer children than other Central Asians. Part of the reason for the number of five in the case of Beysen and Nurgül was the fact that the first three had been girls. The four elder siblings all study or have studied at a university. Only the youngest will stay at home and help his father in the fields.[2] The eldest daughter has a degree from a Turkish university and worked for some years for a Turkish company in Almaty. With this salary she was able to support both her parents as well as her siblings. She was let go, however, and now struggles to find another lucrative job.

Like most of the locals in Aq Zhol, Beysen and Nurgül would consider themselves a modern family, open to new political, social, and cultural developments. Both spouses addressed each other on equal terms, and each openly criticized the other. They would often make fun of each other. The kids were equally open-minded and were not shy in front of their father or mother. Their case was not atypical. In many families in Aq Zhol, gender relations tended to be of a rather egalitarian nature. Kazakh women certainly have more domestic work to do than their husbands, but they take part in all family decisions. Within the household, the hierarchy between husband and wife is often a formal one, more a matter of ideology than of practice, with fewer practical implications. Much of the female work burden is usually transferred first to daughters and later to daughters-in-law. As both sons of Nurgül were not yet married, this was not the case. There is, however, a lot of variance within society regarding gender and intergenerational relations depending on individual characters and their contribution to the household economy.

Beysen and Nurgül moved to Aq Zhol in the 1980s because of the higher salaries paid in this model village. After the dissolution of the local state farm, Beysen decided to quit his job at the local school and acquire a larger piece of land to start an agricultural business. So far he has met with little success, partly owing to the difficult political and macroeconomic conditions. He engages in various ad hoc activities, while his wife is the one who supports the household with the only regular income. In addition, they grow vegetables in the small garden by their house. For a woman to become the main breadwinner, as in the case of Nurgül, is quite common. One reason for this is that, during Soviet times, females constituted a majority among teachers and other employees in the educational and health sectors, and these jobs had a better chance of surviving the transformation. Their husbands had more often been working as mechanics, drivers, or agricultural technicians. As a consequence, they were the first to become unemployed. This may be not only an economic loss but also a psychological hardship, as men are expected to be able to provide their families with what they need. The failure of Beysen to achieve success with his economic adventures was a source of constant dissent between the two. The children earned money irregularly by giving private music lessons or taking part-time jobs at the local school.

The economic situation of Beysen and Nurgül was typical for the locals in Aq Zhol. For many the only steady income is the pensions of the elderly. A few, like Beysen, have tried to build up an agricultural enterprise instead of engaging in subsistence production. Many others hardly use their land at all. Nurgül, as a schoolteacher, had the most regular schedule and left home usually shortly before eight A.M. Others were often still sleeping at this time. Beysen was highly erratic in his daily business as he often had to go away, sometimes for several days, to find spare parts or prepare some transactions. The youngest, the only one consistently around, got up late before starting to work on the fields or to help his father with other activities. His elder siblings considered their home a place for recreation when they were visiting and usually got up late as well. Much of the traditionally female tasks were still with Nurgül, although she was also the main breadwinner. She was responsible for washing, cleaning, and most of the cooking, and she often complained about Beysen, who was seldom at home and too little supportive.

A common argument holds that the Soviet period, rather than liberating women, increased their burden, because they became engaged in wage labor as they continued to be saddled with most of the domestic work (Pine 2002). Indeed, men rarely participate around the house. They are expected to work in the "real world" as well as do domestic heavy labor, including repairing and maintaining the house, the agricultural tools, and the machinery. In everyday life, however, these divisions are much more complex. As the new breadwinner, Nurgül made most household decisions, and she did not ask permission when going to the market or visiting her newly married daughter (whom she had to assist financially). Generally, both sexes engage in farming. Nurgül's main job gave her little time to support Beysen. She did, however, provide most of the labor for the small garden in front of the house.

The division of labor in any given family is a result both of common patterns and of highly specific circumstances like age structure, income, and skills. Among the migrant families, the division follows generally more traditional lines, although women have an important say in decision making as well. The degree of involvement in agricultural activities is another major variable. During sowing and harvesting all members of the household, and sometimes neighbors and kin, work together. The more physically exhausting work—digging, for example—is done by males, while females partake in time-consuming and monotonous work like picking and processing tobacco leaves.

Social Networks and Community Life

All families are part of larger networks combining individuals both within and outside the village. Social relations in Aq Zhol, however, are generally distanced and superficial. In fact, the village can hardly be called a community. There is some vague identity of being someone from Aq Zhol, but this is more defined by being different from any other village in the region (and mainly by such negative criteria as the desperate aspect of the place). With the arrival of the migrants the village became even more divided.

Both groups avoid each other, and most public and private ceremonies are conducted separately. Much of the dispute is about the proper conduct of everyday practices. Attitudes are characterized by a great deal of prejudice, each side claiming to be the "real Kazakh" (Sancak and Finke 2005).

What is striking in Aq Zhol—indeed in many Kazakh villages in the region—is that it has no central place. In many parts of the Middle East such a space would be marked by either a mosque or a local marketplace surrounded by teahouses. Mosques had either been shut down during Soviet times or never existed, as most Kazakh villages are relatively new. The same is true for bazaars, which were equally despised in socialist times. Recently some small commercial stands have appeared, but they do not serve as meeting places yet. The village thus has no institutionalized space for socializing. In contrast to the architecture described below for Bukhara, houses usually stand in the center of a courtyard that has no walls closing it off from the outside. They are surrounded by small plots where people grow potatoes, vegetables, and some fruits.

According to tradition, men should be the public face for their families. Yet both sexes can be seen freely walking the streets, sometimes in mixed groups. Men and women freely talk to each other and visit other families at home without discovering in advance if one might encounter a female alone there. The oralman in particular tend to stroll the streets in groups, although in their case it is mostly elderly men. It is more common, however, to visit each other at home. Appearances in public and private show marked distinctions. Women wear European clothing at work but more traditional outfits at home or when going out in the neighborhood, sometimes including a headscarf. Among the migrants, the situation is somewhat different. Both sexes wear more traditional clothing and women are less visible on the street. They are never veiled, however.

Neither neighborhood nor kinship has much meaning for cooperation within the village. Like most local families, Beysen and Nurgül have no relatives in Aq Zhol. Since all had come here only recently, this is hardly surprising. It is not necessarily a typical feature of Kazakh villages in general.* The absence of affines, however, indicates a lack of interest in strengthening mutual relations within the village. This has partly to do with the relative independence of children in finding marriage partners. Maintaining kin networks, which usually are spread over larger territories, has become increasingly difficult with the decay of public transport. Therefore, individual networks build on a variety of social relations. Non-relatives, named as friends or colleagues, are often of equal importance. This is particularly the case for former schoolmates.

---

*Traditional Kazakh social organization is patrilineal, what anthropologists used to call a lineage system. Every individual is integrated into a hierarchical order of named groups, each of which consists of the descendants of one (real or mythical) ancestor. Only the relatives via the paternal line are recognized within this scheme. That is not to say that non-patrineal kin have no relevance; but they do not form named groups.

When neighbors or relatives visit each other there is usually no segregation by sex. At private as well as well public parties there exists a relatively vague separation, depending on the size of the event. If the number of visitors is small, they may still all sit together in one room; otherwise they will be seated in separate rooms according to sex. Separation is more pronounced among the migrants; in no case, however, were females out of sight when we as foreigners visited their homes, as will be described below for Uzbekistan. Drinking is very common at parties—but far less among the migrants—and also on less formal occasions. As in all parts of the Soviet Union, alcohol has become a central part of everyday life, and Kazakhs are well-known for their drinking habits. The region around Aq Zhol seems relatively modest in this respect. We saw few people drunk on the streets and the parties we went to all kept within limits. Women drink alcohol as well, although less than males.

While much of this seems to resemble traditional village life, the situation has changed dramatically in recent years. One particular issue that has strongly influenced gender relations and everyday practices is the decay of infrastructure and technology. In socialist times every household had electricity and running water. Electricity is still provided, but water has to be taken from a supply line in the garden. Few families have telephones and the post office has been closed. Bus services to the neighboring town have been reduced severely. Social relations within larger kin networks have thus been effectively limited. Women are particularly affected by this decay of infrastructure, because most of the changes concern everyday activities that are most strongly related to cooking and washing. Buying foodstuffs or clothing has become a major chore. There is no village shop anymore, only small kiosks where people sell basic necessities like soap, noodles, cigarettes, and sweets. For all other purchases one has to go to the nearest market in the regional town, which is fifteen miles away. In the first years after independence, many people still lived with the idea in the back of their mind that one day soon the old way would return. Now it became increasingly clear that it will probably be a long time until previous standards are reached again, although with the economic recovery since 2000 things have improved. This has focused everyday life even more on the village. For almost everyone the workplace is in the village, if not around their own house. Also, most leisure time is spent at home or by visiting others within the community.

GENDER RELATIONS IN THE OASIS OF BUKHARA, UZBEKISTAN: GÜLISTON VILLAGE

Uzbekistan is not an easy place for anthropologists. Having worked in Kazakhstan earlier, we were often frustrated. Communication came mainly in the form of small talk and avoided topics anthropologists are typically interested in. This was particularly the case for anything that had to do with politics, religion, and agricultural reforms, but it also extended to conversations about kinship or daily practices. The reasons for this may be manifold. Part of the reticence may spring from dealing with a repressive regime that continues to follow Soviet practices, and has even expanded them. On the other hand, much of this is valid for other Central Asian Republics as well, without the same consequences. Our assumption is that this communication style also has roots in traditional Uzbek patterns of mutual interaction both with strangers and with insiders. The fear of political repression, however, is a very real one and was confirmed to us several times. People reported that after meeting us they were asked by the local KGB what we had been asking (and what they had been telling us).

Our field site in Uzbekistan was very different from the one in Kazakhstan. It is located in the northwestern part of the oasis of Bukhara, one of the oldest permanently settled sites in the world. The oasis presents a prime example of the region's sophisticated irrigation systems, its melding of cultures, religions, and languages, and its architectural beauties. The oasis is situated in the center of a large desert area. This natural boundary is also a social one as it marks the line between sedentary and nomadic ways of life, a boundary that is not so well defined in southeastern Kazakhstan.

The contrast in rural life between Uzbekistan and Kazakhstan becomes apparent immediately when one travels. Uzbekistan's rural landscape is shaped and defined by numerous irrigation channels. Villages form dense clusters of populations with narrow and winding paths. People stroll along the streets in traditional clothing and work the fields in seemingly age-old ways. Only a few roads have been paved, and those are often in bad shape, as there has been very little maintenance work since the 1980s. Village streets are dusty and narrow. Occasionally donkeys are still used as beasts of burden. Most villages have access to gas these days, but the open lines sometimes lead to explosions and casualties. The village of Güliston, where we conducted fieldwork, is quite typical for the region. The population is mixed Uzbek-Tajik, although everyone tends to be bilingual and usually has mixed ancestry. Like most other villages in the oasis, Güliston is rather old. In recent decades neighboring villages, despite growing ever closer, remain different social units with distinct identities.

Living conditions in Güliston constitute a major difference from Aq Zhol. While the infrastructure in Aq Zhol has crumbled in recent years, it is still a place with access to clean water and other features of modern life. Villages in Bukhara often give an impression of having changed little in the last two hundred years. Agriculture is still the backbone of the Uzbek economy but is in dire straits due to state politics. One problem dating back to Soviet times results from the massive development of new cotton fields via the construction of large irrigation channels. Thus less and less

Uzbek village home.

water reaches the downstream oases such as Bukhara or Khorezm, which also resulted in growing levels of salinization. Cotton is still the major product all over the country, although its dominance has decreased since independence from some 90 percent of all state-used land to around 50–60 percent today.

Domestic Affairs and Economic Relations

Our host family in Uzbekistan was comparable, in terms of economic and social standing, with Beysen's. The head of the household, Bahodir's father, had been a school director in Soviet times; his wife had been a teacher too, as are both of their sons. One of the daughters-in-law is a nurse, the other one is also a teacher. The two daughters of the family have married out, one within the village, the other one some fifteen miles away. All four children have two or three children each. In the mid-1990s the grandfather went to Mecca, one of the first in the region to do so. Today he functions as the village *molla*,* which provides the family with some additional income as he is remunerated for various religious services like funerals, marriages or private prayers. Like most Uzbek families, the household consists of three generations. The younger son, Bahodir, as Uzbek tradition demands, lives within his parents' household; the elder one lives

*This transliteration reflects the Uzbek pronunciation of *mulla*.

right next door. As in Kazakhstan, the youngest son inherits the house of his father. At the time of our stay, the household consisted of seven persons. In past decades this number often was significantly higher, as Uzbeks had one of the highest birth rates in the Soviet Union.

A clear gender differentiation exists in Uzbek society, according to which men should be household heads and represent the family in public. Fathers should explicitly exercise dominance over their wives as well as their children, and they often do. Much more than in Kazakh society, gender as well as age relations are characterized by a pronounced hierarchical structure and clearly demarcated roles and obligations. Like most other Uzbek husbands, Bahodir often addressed Yulduz in the imperative form, something that would never occur the other way around. He left no doubt that he had the final say in all domestic affairs as well as in decisions concerning the children. In fact, he rarely consulted his wife for any advice. This dynamic also depends, however, on individual differences and skills within the family. A more self-confident woman can have a far greater standing vis à vis her husband, as well as her mother-in-law. The situation of Gülbahor, the wife of Bahodir's elder brother, was somewhat better in this respect. As she and her husband had a household of their own, the influence of her mother- and father-in-law was less. In terms of age hierarchy, the younger should not address an elder but should wait until approached; children must obey their fathers' orders, and will serve them on occasion. This second hierarchy cross-cuts the first. Women's influence increases with age. Yulduz had a hard time in this respect partly because of her personality. A woman's influence increases with age and after giving birth, especially to sons.

Most rural households subsist primarily on their private plots. This is true even for families like Bahodir's, where several members receive regular salaries or pensions, but these barely suffice to supply flour for a month. People raise potatoes, vegetables, and fruit trees on their plots. They can sell a modest surplus in local marketplaces to buy ordinary necessities. In recent years more and more villagers have began to grow their own wheat primarily for subsistence purposes. Additional sources of income are petty trade, livestock rearing, or driving a taxi. Livestock rearing is a very important source of income because it is for many the only way to put aside larger sums of money, for major expenditures such wedding parties or the building of a house for their son. The life of the former kolkhoz workers is even worse today; generally they no longer receive salaries. For them, the prime way to make ends meet is getting permission to use the land, which still belongs to the state, for themselves after the official harvest is brought in (primarily by planting potatoes and vegetables in late summer). This is, however, only a semi-legal arrangement and thus always risks appropriation.

Gender relations are closely related to the division of labor. Female contribution to income is less than in Kazakhstan. Most of the jobs left remain male-dominated. This is true, for example, for all technical jobs. Since the collectives and state farms have not been dismantled as in Kazakhstan, all machinery input is still in state control and the employees in this sector have a better chance of receiving salaries. In addition, these jobs provide ample opportunity for side incomes. Men hold the ultimate control over incomes and expenditures within the household.

Division of labor reflects a traditional pattern, with females taking care of most domestic affairs and males responsible for outside work. This is not a strict boundary but depends on many variables, including the age structure of the household, the presence of sufficient labor force for the different tasks, and the individual character and situation of its members. For example, Yulduz's long and serious illness meant that her daughter as well as her mother-in-law had to work more and that her boys took over some of her duties. In fact, both spheres, domestic and outside, overlap at various points where both sexes can be responsible or recruited for tasks. In the fields it is primarily the boys who help Bahodir. The boys typically were doing much the same work as their father (i.e., sowing, clearing, and harvesting). Watering, however, would ultimately rest with Bahodir, since this is too crucial an issue to risk any mistake and requires experience that the boys did not yet have. During this period he would sometimes stay overnight to safeguard his right to get water in time. Women usually do the most exhausting and harmful work, such as weeding and picking. Women thus still have the Soviet-style "double burden," even without the previous benefit of monetary income.

During the day women spend most time in the house and yard, while men tend to be away in the fields or doing other jobs. As both Bahodir and Yulduz were still employed, they left home early in the morning and came back sometime in the afternoon. She was expected to be at home when she had no other obligations, while he could visit friends or go to town if he wanted. This would be different for peasant households, although such people also have to work for either the kolkhoz or a private farmer. Depending on the season, their work schedule can be more flexible. Bahodir's father and mother, as pensioners, were actually more typical. She stayed at home for most of the day organizing and supervising work to be done by her daughter-in-law or her granddaughter, whoever happened to be around. Sometimes she left to meet a neighbor or relative in the village for tea. The grandfather was away most of the time. In his case it was not the fields but his job as a molla that forced him to work outside the home.

It would be a mistake, however, to think that these everyday activities are conducted in a quasi-automatic way. While almost all families made use of their plots already in socialist times, these have acquired a very new meaning, becoming fundamental for survival. For this reason the less experienced, like Bahodir, try to find advice from professionals who have spent their lives in the fields. People discuss together the best strategies for planting and irrigation, depending on the specific situation and annual climatic conditions. As was also described for Kazakhstan, there is always a certain amount of bargaining and negotiation in gender relations, as well as in other everyday patterns.

Social Networks and Community Life

One major difference in gender relations and everyday life between the two settings is the embeddedness of the individual in the larger community. The village of Güliston is much more cohesive than Aq Zhol. This is partly due to the latter's artificial character, but it also relates to differences between the two countries. Uzbek villages usually look back on a long history. Internal social stratification is less pronounced and not openly expressed. Conflicts in society are downplayed and not publicly displayed. Moreover, different ethnicities seem to be compatible: in Güliston and surrounding villages Uzbeks and Tajiks intermarry and celebrate most ceremonies jointly.

Just as in Kazakhstan, most villages have no central places where people gather. Few villages have a mosque. Teahouses, very common in other parts of Uzbekistan as a meeting place for men, are also very rare in the Bukhara region. Groups of men strolling the streets as described for Aq Zhol are rare. Men and women stop when meeting each other on their way, but they hardly use streets as public space. Most houses are built of earth and separated by huge walls without windows toward the outside, thus often giving an impenetrable impression. In the courtyards, every family usually has a separate house plus a small garden to grow vegetables, potatoes, and the like. Surrounding houses may face each other without separating walls, especially if they are inhabited by close kin. Everyday life thus takes place behind closed doors. Next to the entrance to the courtyard is the *mekhmonkhona*, the guest room. This is the place where male visitors are seated. It is the most decorated room. As it is close to the main entrance, visitors do not pass by the other rooms where women sit.

More than in Kazakhstan, the public face in Uzbekistan is very much a male one. Women walk the streets but are much less visible than men. Dress also reflects this reality: Women from Bukhara are famous throughout Uzbekistan for wearing traditional clothing, colorful dresses above equally colorful trousers that almost completely cover the body except face, arms, and feet. Very few women, however, veil their faces, and those who do face enormous pressure from police as well as their own kin to stop this. But clothing that uncovers parts of the body or reveals by clinging would equally be considered inappropriate. Men often wear the traditional Uzbek overcoat, the *chapan*. In contrast to, for example, the Ferghana Valley, Western or Russian-style clothing is not very common, except for official situations. Female teachers wear European-style clothes at work but will change as soon as they are back home or when they go visiting in the evening.

Bahodir's family is part of a large network within the village. Numerous first and second cousins settled in Güliston as well as in neighboring villages within a radius of three miles. As a former school director and contemporary molla, the grandfather has special standing within the village, and this is in part transferred to his sons. The younger one also became the director of the school at a relatively early age. The importance of kin is very distinct from that in the Kazakh case. As in Kazakh society, the Uzbek kinship system has a patrilineal bias, but it does not build into a lineage system, at least not for the majority of Uzbeks. Genealogical tracks are usually not kept for several generations, and there exist no groups named after any distant ancestors. In fact, most Uzbeks hardly remember anyone beyond their grandfather. At the same time, the number of known cognates on both sides can be quite extensive. The stress is thus on horizontal rather than vertical connections. Affines play an outstanding role. Very often, they will be in some way related through the mother's or the father's line simultaneously, because marriages with kin, often repeated over generations, are very common. (The government is currently undertaking a campaign against cousin marriage because it is said to increase the chance of hereditary illnesses.) The importance of affines gives women often a crucial position in a household's social network. Elder females are primarily responsible for maintaining social relations and preparing marriage arrangements.

Neighbors and kin frequently visit each other formally, as well as spontaneously if one needs advice or tools or just wants to have a chat. Visiting females will often disappear immediately to help out in the kitchen while the men sit together, discuss local and world affairs, and, eventually, drink vodka. If there is more than one family visiting, the guests will usually be separated by gender and seated in different rooms. There is no strict rule in that respect, but the household will decide, depending on the situation, how to arrange guests. Drinking alcohol at private as well as public parties is hardly less common than in Kazakhstan. The quantities consumed may be quite substantial, constituting a major part of the household's expenditures. Women drink alcohol infrequently, though an occasional nip is not uncommon.

It would be a mistake to attribute the variations from the situation in Aq Zhol solely to a more traditional lifestyle among Uzbeks as compared to Kazakhs. In spite of all the evidence, which seems to indicate a stubborn ignoring of cultural change, Uzbek lifestyles changed fundamentally during Soviet times. This is not only recognizable in drinking habits but also influences much of everyday life habits and attitudes. The last fifteen years, however, have seen a steady decline of many of the facilities of modern life. Uzbeks used to have better access to water and electricity than they have now. This decline has forced them to turn to cultural patterns that look more traditional than they actually are. Thus, many families used washing machines in the past, but today water is too scarce a resource to waste for this. Women have suffered most from the decay of infrastructure, which has eliminated much of the easing of routine labor achieved in socialist times.

CONCLUSION

This chapter has described and compared everyday life in two villages in Kazakhstan and Uzbekistan and tried to address changes since the collapse of the socialist system. We have focused on gender relations in particular. These differed significantly in both places from the pre-Soviet period. In addition, the fact that Kazakh society was more exposed to Russian influence enforced these differences. It is important to note that Kazakhs are fully aware of this greater influence and regard it as part of their cultural heritage. That Kazakh women are freer than their Uzbek sisters is commonly expressed. People usually explain this both by the closeness to Russian culture and the lesser impact of Islamic values.

Both settings, of course, differ in many other aspects, notably economic performance, ethnicity, and social cohesion. Certainly the intentional destruction of traditional structures during the 1930s collectivization period was not without longstanding consequences. Today Kazakh society is plagued by a relatively low degree of cooperation and mutual help, which puts additional stress on the hardships caused by the transformation process. In Uzbekistan, traditional institutions of kinship, neighborhood, and village community were less severely damaged.

In both cases it would be a mistake to think of everyday life only in terms of routines or practices. Certainly, many rules and patterns described above are deeply internalized. People would find it difficult to conduct them in fundamentally different ways. The separation of male and female guests during ceremonies or neighborly visits may serve as an example for this. On the other hand, all of these activities entail an element of negotiation when planned and conducted; they are rarely done without reflection. Therefore, we prefer to think of them as institutions rather than habits. As institutions they constitute a body of rules as well as the expected sanctions should one fail to follow them. On the other hand, people consciously try to manipulate these institutions according to situation and need.

Mental models and social expectations set clear limitations to these negotiations, as may be seen in the story at the beginning of the article. The idea that men would help their wives with washing was, at least to the boys, so strange that they had never thought about this as a possible way of doing things. When the idea had once been brought up, however, it could now be discussed. In all situations described in this chapter, people usually have several choices about how, when, and with whom to do things, and they will choose among these alternatives depending on the concrete situation and other actors involved. As the individuals have different and sometimes opposing views and interests, this inevitably demands some prior discussions about the conduct in question. The scope and the limits of these discussions are determined by the catalogue of what is culturally expected, what is desired, and what is tolerated. With every negotiation, however, the boundaries of what is expected, desired, or tolerated will also change. In this way, everyday life is at the very heart of any cultural change.

The post-socialist situation is one where many everyday life practices have changed fundamentally. Established patterns or institutions have been disrupted. Therefore much of what looks self-evident and natural, or what looks very traditional to an outsider, is in fact a recent adaptation to a new situation. Changes in technology have brought about changes both in the way many things are done and in who does them. And this holds true for more than technologies or the division of labor. Also drastically altered are consumption patterns, as many of the things that were available in the past have become difficult to find. Even the most basic foodstuffs, such as bread, have become a matter of concern, in particular in Uzbekistan. In the past flour was so cheap that people hardly thought of it as an expenditure. Now it is one of the major burdens for most households.

People think and calculate through their everyday lives. Many daily routines are crucial to sustaining a household in the long term. Things have to be planned carefully to make ends meet tomorrow. The same activity, such as drinking vodka, may be a routine and expected behavior on one occasion, or on another may be very strategic (e.g., to bribe someone or establish a firm relationship with him). Such an ordinary activity takes on more the character of an institution, a social frame that can be manipulated, to some degree, to fit one's aims. Some of this manipulation may in fact constitute a part of the institution, as it is anticipated and taken into account. Other variations or deviations may be the beginning of a change of rules, as when, for example, more and more people abstain from drinking for religious reasons. As everyday life is never stagnant and is always negotiated, its institutionalized format is also permanently challenged.

NOTES

1. We have conducted fieldwork in both countries since 1999, for approximately four months in Kazakhstan and one year in Uzbekistan.
2. Youngest sons in Kazakh society are expected not to move out after marriage but to stay with their parents.

REFERENCES

Bacon, E. E. 1966. *Central Asians under Russian Rule: A Study in Culture Change.* Ithaca, N.Y.: Cornell University Press.

Bartlett, D. L. 2001. Economic Recentralization in Uzbekistan. *Post-Soviet Geography and Economics* 42:105–121.

Bourdieu, P. 1977. *Outline of a Theory of Practice*. Cambridge, New York: Cambridge University Press.

Ensminger, J. 1992. *Making a Market: The Institutional Transformation of an African Society. The Political Economy of Institutions and Decisions*. Cambridge, New York: Cambridge University Press.

Eschment, B. 1998. *Hat Kasachstan Ein "Russisches Problem"?: Revision eines Katastrophenbildes*. Köln: Bundesinstitut für Ostwissenschaftliche und Internationale Studien.

Esenova, S. 2002. Soviet Nationality, Identity, and Ethnicity in Central Asia: Historic Narratives and Kazakh Ethnic Identity. *Journal of Muslim Minority Affairs* 22:11–38.

Fierman, W. 1997. Political Development in Uzbekistan: Democratization? In *Conflict, Cleavage, and Change in Central Asia and the Caucasus*, ed. K. Dawisha and B. Parrott, pp. 360–408. Cambridge: Cambridge University Press.

Foltz, R. 1996. The Tajiks of Uzbekistan. *Central Asian Survey* 15:213–216.

Highmore, B. 2002. *Everyday Life and Cultural Theory*. London, New York: Routledge.

Ilkhamov, A. 1998. Shirkats, Dekhqon Farmers and Others: Farm Restructing in Uzbekistan. *Central Asian Survey* 17:539–560.

Kandiyoti, D. 1998. Rural Livelihoods and Social Networks in Uzbekistan: Perspectives from Andijan. *Central Asian Survey* 17:561–578.

Kerven, C., ed. 2003. *Prospects for Pastoralism in Kazakhstan and Turkmenistan: From State Farms to Private Flocks*. London, New York: RoutledgeCurzon.

Knight, J. 1992. *Institutions and Social Conflict: The Political Economy of Institutions and Decisions*. Cambridge, New York: Cambridge University Press.

Krader, L. 1963. *Peoples of Central Asia*. Bloomington: Indiana University.

North, D. C. 1990. *Institutions, Institutional Change, and Economic Performance: The Political Economy of Institutions and Decisions*. Cambridge, New York: Cambridge University Press.

Pine, F. 2002. Retreat to the Household? Gendered Domains in Post-socialist Poland. In *Post Socialism: Ideals, Ideologies and Practices in Eurasia*, ed. Ch. Hann. London, New York: Routledge.

Sancak, M., and P. Finke. 2005. Migration and Risk-Taking. A Case Study from Kazakhstan. In *Migration and Economy: Global and Local Dynamics*, ed. L. Trager, pp. 127–161. Walnut Creek, Calif.: AltaMira.

Schatz, E. A. D. 2000. Framing Strategies and Non-Conflict in Multi-Ethnic Kazakhstan. *Nationalism and Ethnic Politics* 6:71–94.

Schoeberlein, J. 1994. *Identity in Central Asia: Construction and Contention in the Conceptions of "Ozbek," "Tajik," "Muslim," "Samarkandi" and Other Groups*. Unpublished doctoral dissertation, Harvard University.

Subtelny, M. E. 1994. "The Symbiosis of Turk and Tajik." In *Central Asia in Historical Perspective*, ed. B. F. Manz, pp. 45–61. Boulder, Colo.: Westview Press.

Werner, C. A. 1998. Household Networks and the Security of Mutual Indebtedness in Rural Kazakhstan. *Central Asian Survey* 17:597–612.

Zanca, R. G. 1999. The Repeasantization of an Uzbek Kolkhoz: An Ethnographic Account of Postsocialism. Unpublished doctoral dissertation, University of Illinois.

12. Fat and All That: Good Eating the Uzbek Way

Russell Zanca

In many parts of the world where people have known hunger from time to time, foods rich in calories, e.g., fats, and flavor enjoy pride of place in daily diets. Whereas ancient and contemporary peoples almost always have aspired to procure as much meat as possible, many of our archeological and ethnographic data confirm that hunger cannot be satisfied by protein-packed meat alone; animal fat often becomes more sought after, since it delivers so many tasty calories (Richards 1948; Harris 1985; Mennell 1996). Uzbeks and Uzbekistan are no different, especially in the post-Soviet present with most people living poorly. In this chapter I compare favorite dishes and notions of good eating in the country's rural areas and largest cities (Tashkent and Samarkand) to give readers a sense of what people eat every day and what are the kinds of dishes that they consider the very best. In writing about food, I look at the kinds of foods Uzbeks produce, how they shop, prepare, and serve their foods, and when they present their favorite foods. I also look to the notions surrounding gender and the preparation of food, as well as the kinds of foods people prefer to eat at home and those best prepared by professionals in public. The chapter discusses the power of food as *cuisine*, inviting readers to consider how and why culinary research can serve as a well anchored-cultural foundation for ethnic self-awareness and national pride, especially in the wake of the multi-ethnic but nationalism-effacing socialist Soviet Union.

However, I am concerned not only with fat, but also with the characteristics of how and what Uzbeks eat. In turn, I write about what foodstuffs say both about them and about the way they want to be known or understood because of what they eat. Where relevant I make reference to other parts of the world, especially the United States, in order to give readers some idea of cross-cultural similarities and contrasts. Furthermore, the chapter gives me a chance to reflect on my ethnographic experiences and discuss potentially valuable insights into food that also constitute stable and changeable realms of Uzbek ethnic and/or national self-awareness, actually senses that make Uzbeks feel unique or different in Central Asia. This kind of discussion, I believe, forces us to think about whether notions such as "culture," "people," or "group" are still valid.

I want to begin now with a focus on hospitality, a value or lifestyle about which few would deny that Uzbeks are forever self-referential and proud. We will see just how much hospitality can serve to highlight a kind of "us–not us" awareness. For a long while after I returned from my initial field-work in the mid-1990s, and from several other bouts of fieldwork subsequent to that time, I kept wanting to provide myself with an adequate and rational explanation of how a modern people in a fairly modern country with millions of people living in fairly cosmopolitan cities, such as Tashkent, Samarkand, and Bukhara could take such pride and joy in serving foods that seemed fattier than any other cuisine I could think of. It seemed even more than a little baffling, especially as Americans and many European countries were engaged in all manner of campaigns to cut fat out of the diet. From an anthropological perspective, food studies and the very subject of food provide wonderful vehicles through which to stimulate the interests of informants: people love to talk about food. Food interests can also make it possible for researchers to broach sensitive topics in the spheres of political and economic life indirectly, without causing undue discomfort for anthropologists and informants alike. Food research in Uzbekistan helps me to write both about the passion with which people speak about and consume food, and about important perspectives on local politics and economy directly tied into what people eat and what people can/cannot afford to eat day in and day out.[1]

Relative to most inhabitants of the United States or any Western European country, Uzbekistan is impoverished. However, in this comparative sense, its post-Soviet material decline may be difficult for outsiders-as-mealtime-guests to recognize when sitting down to eat with Uzbeks in any part of that country, no matter what the class, status, or type of lifestyle led by the particular folk with whom the outsiders happen to be eating. Stephen Gudeman notes that what and how people eat has entirely to do not only with rules of commensality but also with values of socioeconomic existence (2001:64). As is true of many other peoples throughout Eurasia and the Middle East, Uzbeks spare no expense when it comes to showing hospitality to guests in the form of a meal.

NOT JUST CHICKEN, BUT CHICKEN FAT

The three of us sat storytelling on a sweltering June evening in a friend's kitchen three stories above a residential Tashkent neighborhood. I treated

Samsas sold from a basket in Tashkent.

my friends to beef jerky and a bottle of bourbon. While they enjoyed the soft, chewy jerky, talk turned to a discussion of more robust fare:

"Have you tried chicken *samsas*?"[2] asked Jamshid Q. with a mixture of glee and determination.

"No, I haven't heard about those," I responded, knowing instantly that this would send Jamshid into a snack-resolved, code red frenzy.

"Oh, I'll get you some."

"Are they any good?"

"Just wait till you try them. It's too late to go now, but what about to-morrow? Are you busy?" Jamshid asked, having absolutely no concern for whatever plans I may have had. We were going to eat these chicken sam-sas tomorrow, come hell or high water.

"Where do you buy them?"

"In Chaghatai," Jamshid answered, as if it should have been obvious. Chaghatai is a part of Tashkent's old city revered by locals for numerous private eateries with an emphasis on serving traditional fare for discrimi-nating palates.

"So what makes them so good? The chicken?"

"Well, yes, the chicken! But they're also stuffed with fat. You'll try them, you'll see."

Since making my initial foray into Uzbekistan in 1992, I have never ceased being impressed by two attributes of gastronomic ecstasy that appear far removed from American inclinations—namely, the satisfaction stemming from eating meat with copious amounts of animal fat (either accompanying the meat or in which the meat was cooked), and the importance of drenching rice and sundry vegetables in cooking oils. In the end, it isn't that Americans don't want or don't like fat, they simply want it disguised—sweetened, or overly salted and spiced, in fact. Uzbeks want to praise and consume fats not only in the sense of imbibing the commonsensical good life but also because they see it as an essential part of healthful or nutritious dining. If that notion once held sway in America, it really doesn't any longer.

THE RELATIONSHIP TO FAT

Early on in my first serious fieldwork in rural Namangan, Uzbekistan (a part of the Ferghana Valley), I found that one of the most annoying aspects of trying to accept the cultural practices and values of Uzbeks was the constant barrage of exhortations, urgings, and directives to eat more. Bound up with these fervent expressions of vengeful hospitality was the fact that the food almost always tended to be as rich as imaginable, downright fatty really. If it wasn't the ubiquitous and oleaginous *plov*,* then it was skewers of mutton and beef laced through with hunks of animal fat, full cream yoghurts, heavy cream, and oily soup and greasy soups. For months before I got it, I kept thinking idiotically to myself that my hosts had to know that any person would be very full very fast on such fare, or that once I'd effectively communicated the fact that I'd already had a meal elsewhere, or, more plainly and vastly more stupidly, that I simply wasn't very hungry, they would realize right away that this guy just doesn't want to eat and leave me in peace. What I never understood at the beginning was how to play the host-guest game. Today, whenever I play host to Uzbek friends or guests, who have little familiarity with American culinary practices, I try to remember all of the "rules and regulations" not just about how to eat and how to offer, but, perhaps most importantly, about what kind of fare to serve and in what quantities (Zanca 2003: 8–16).

While I cannot speak with any authority on the latest fads in European cookery and dieting, America characterizes itself by leaping from one food fad to the next. One period it's salt, then it's sugar, then it's artificial sweet-

---

*We know plov as pilaf, a kind of rice stew. It is consumed in less oily ways in Afghanistan and South Asia. The main ingredients for Uzbeks are rice, carrots, onions, mutton or beef, and plenty of salt and cumin.

eners, then we move on to the dangers of carbohydrates, and now the peril
du jour isn't merely fats but transfats. This might be worth discussing in
another context, but it's all a mixture of the boring, the obvious, and the
extreme. In America people want to be less fat, but they cannot bring
themselves to exercise, decrease the size of their portions, and stop their
gluttonous approach to the consumption of processed foods.[3]

I suppose for Uzbekistan to look decidedly more Western or "successful," they will have to face a rapidly fattening society; this is something
we see occurring in countries such as China and India that are rapidly
enriching significant proportions of their citizenries, as commercializa-
tion, fast food, less exercise, and an aesthetic of human chubbiness, especially in children, remains something to attain. In Uzbekistan there are
overweight people to be sure, but not in the numbers that we see in the
West, and excess weight is usually restricted to middle aged and urban
men. An Uzbek man with a potbelly shows not that he is a slothful over-
eater, but rather that he has attained a prestigious degree of material comfort. Frankly, for most Uzbeks a man over fifty who might seem slender
and therefore fit, in the Western sense, probably would seem either ill or
impoverished. Actually, until late in the twentieth century many middle
class Germans and Englishmen, among other Westerners, still associated
the midlife man's paunch with good living (Powdermaker 1997:207). In
Uzbekistan there is still the overwhelming desire not to be fat, necessarily,
but to eat as many fatty foods as possible. Uzbeks remain deeply proud
of their cookery and its most direct appeal to foods promoting their fatty
and oily qualities.

AN EXPLANATION FOR THESE FAT LOVERS?

In this part of the chapter I conjecture about why fat remains so desirable
a part of rural and urban Uzbeks' cookery and commensality, and then
present a number of everyday practices in both rural and urban areas that
deal with shopping for food, eating out, and cooking at home that embody the desire for and appreciation of fat in cookery.

As Uzbekistan moves into the twenty-first century, it seems to worsen
economically with each passing year. Whatever Communism was or was
not, it does seem that by the mid-1980s both rural and urban Uzbeks probably ate as well in terms of nutritional value and caloric intake as they had
at any time in modern history. Here I speak of the population in its en-
tirety. Even the peasants' diets were varied through all manner of crops,
introduced from the 1920s, and all sorts of imported goods, everything
from tomatoes and potatoes to condensed milk and tinned smoked fishes.
One may note this in the modern Uzbek vocabulary whenever peasants
refer to common garden crops such as *gollandskii* (Dutch) for potatoes

and *bolgarskii* (Bulgarian or sweet) for peppers. Yet in this sense, we really have to consider the phases of Soviet power not just in terms of the average urban or rural Uzbek citizen's economy, but also with respect to how she ate at various times. In general, it is hard to speak of anything approaching a modicum of comfort in terms of a European diet until well into the 1950s, and we must not forget that famine characterized many individual years and periods since the Bolshevik Revolution. What I think this means is that Uzbek people have never lost what we might consider a voracious attitude toward rich foods because of the unremitting periods of deprivation that characterized the first half of the twentieth century, and now *a fortiori* owing to the crisis of the post-Soviet period.

I am not necessarily speaking about table manners or eating etiquette per se here, but of the Uzbek emphasis on consuming the most caloric and tasty foods possible when the opportunities arise. Although I will not argue that this is a European medieval peasant outlook, nor necessarily one from a peasant or horticultural society in sub-Saharan Africa, these are comparative studies that would be worth thinking about. Naturally, the Uzbek approach to fat-laden foods is probably typical of the approach taken by almost all poor peoples the world over. On the other hand, there is at least one interesting twist with regard to fat.

Lately, some Europeans, Italians for example, have made fat itself an important part of notions of Italian pride. Take the example of *lardo* in Bergamo.[4] One anthropologist who worked in this region remarks that the consumption of lardo—now incorporated, naturally, into haute cuisine—serves to impart both a sense of regional and national identity in Italy (Kullick and Meneley 2005). Certainly we may find numerous examples of this renaissance of pride in regional oils and animal fats in the Western world as people literally come to their senses in rediscovering a proverbial wheel: the fattiest foods are the tastiest and the most satisfying. This is clearly nothing new in advanced food and cookery studies, but I think that in Uzbekistan the entire nationalization ethos of culture, characteristic through most of the twentieth century, helped enable the Uzbeks to draw from their consciousness of their cuisine something that combined oft-unfulfilled desires and a pride in its fattiness.

Nationalism has to have at least a supposed basis in history; traditions of doing must reside in its core. From a variety of sources that include Soviet-era cookbooks, Uzbeks understand that their meal ingredients and manner of eating are things particular to their nation, and rather than focusing on fat per se, people are wont to talk about the "high calorie" nature of their foods. Such eating among Central Asians of today's Uzbekistan extends as far back as to the court of Tamerlane in the city of Samarkand, when the Spanish ambassador to the court, Ruy Gonzalez de Clavijo, wrote: "He is happiest who is most greasy."

To be sure there, are other Central Asians, such as Kazakhs and Kyrgyz,

Dumba (sheep tail fat) in the kitchen, ready for cooking plov.

who adore fat; but the Uzbeks, especially in terms of their oil-laden plov, stand out against neighbors in Afghanistan, India/Pakistan, and Iran. The one part of Uzbekistan that so many Uzbeks like to think of as very *sui generis*, to put it best, and almost a non-Uzbek entity, to say the worst— Khorezm—is scorned by other Uzbeks because its unique and non-oily plovs are white and flavorless. Think of the Uzbek expression that de-claims, "A good plov is one where the oil drips to your elbow after you eat a handful from the platter."

Lest the reader think that most rural Uzbeks enjoy such frequent oily repasts, it's necessary to understand that most Uzbeks derive the bulk of their calories from grains, especially bread and rice. Apparently, the post-Soviet period marks an increase in the dependence on farinaceous consumption. As readers must realize, this is not taken as a positive de-velopment. Eating and filling one's stomach is one thing, but eating well according to local standards is entirely different. And this is where fat plays a big role.

To return for a moment to the argument that ties the desire for fatty foods into not only a peasant past or primarily rural country, but also an experience of repeated and prolonged periods of nutritional deprivation, Uzbekistan now experiences a very challenging post-Soviet nutritional decline. Writers such as Menell and Braudel examined late medieval patterns of food consumption in Europe to find that the infrequent feasting and explosive consumption of rich, especially animal fat foods took place among peasantries and fat-deprived townspeople because so much of the rest of the diet comprised grain consumption—in the form of gruels, porridges, and breads.

During my own dissertation research, I took time to calculate bread consumption per household and per individual, in the Uzbek village where I worked, based on the weight of raw wheat and wheat flour that families required over a given span of time to feed themselves (Zanca 1999). I will spare readers the details, but suffice to say the grain consumption in rural Namangan was a staggering amount in relation to what you or I probably eat in a given fortnight. Calculations aside, an anthropologist has the advantage of living with a family, and gains a keen sense of what quantities of bread and dough-based foods (noodle dishes, turnovers, pastries, etc.) are prepared and consumed on any given day. This leads me to recall a remark both ribald and bitter that young village men related: *Bizda—non, choi, non, choi va jai, jai, jai!* This last term is onomatopoeic, and the saying means, "All we've got is bread and tea, bread and tea, and then sex, sex, sex!" Similarly, in Tashkent in recent years one of the main means of survival for all of the illegal residents and internal migrants who cannot secure any stable work through normal channels is, apparently, to open up small bakeries, perhaps because of the huge increase in urban bread consumption, especially of the beloved *obi non.*

TO MARKET, TO MARKET . . .

Today in rural Uzbekistan perhaps no site of basic economic activity and transactions is more vital than the marketplaces or bazaars. This marks a big shift from the socialist era, when they served as important centers of rural commerce but were not always jammed with people trying to secure daily necessities and an income. Furthermore, whereas many rural marketplaces operated for perhaps a day or two out of every week, many now operate daily, demonstrating just how necessary they are in the countryside. Given unemployment figures that vary from 40 to 70 percent in rural areas of the Ferghana Valley (to say nothing of the fact that people who are employed are very rarely paid on time), bazaars function as a primary wage-earning institution, whether for the sale of garden produce or of needlework items, such as robes and hats. Understandably, then, if one wants to know how Uzbeks shop in order to get all the items they need to feed themselves, then the importance of visiting and observing marketplace activities and behaviors is essential.

Ben Highmore, a scholar who specializes in thinking and writing about the everyday, takes the position that we must not overlook the basic point

Peasant household garden plot: Essential to the rural diet.

that for millions of people in any given country, everyday life changes rapidly in terms of activities and routines (2001). And this is not just a matter of generational changes; many other phenomena may alter everyday life. I think social science researchers of Eurasia mostly would agree that the political upheaval brought about by Soviet disintegration altered the everyday life of tens of millions of citizens, just as many cultural patterns and routines have endured.

Overall, there are three major sources for food in Uzbekistan's vast countryside, where over 70 percent of the population live. Even small villages have their shops, stocking flour, rice, cookies, tea, canned fruits, vegetables, and meat, and, less frequently, dairy products and sugar. They also have Russian-style bread, juices, water, and alcohol. For fresh foods, there are the garden plots around their homes and the bazaars. The garden plots are essential for many families, as they provide significant portions of seasonal or annual intakes of grains, such as sorghum or rice; nuts, such as walnuts and almonds; fruits, such as quinces, peaches, apricots, cherries, figs, and pomegranates; herbs, such as basil, coriander, and mint; and sundry vegetables, legumes, and tubers, such as peppers, tomatoes, potatoes, black-eyed peas, carrots, and eggplants.

Since the collapse of the Soviet system, however, the roles and sites of these food sources, including the shops selling the staples and the nature of the garden plots, have changed markedly. Observations and interviews tell us that private shops selling expensive foodstuffs, especially imported items, such as canned goods and macaroni, have largely replaced the state stores that sold important bulk items—mentioned above—at subsidized prices. Time investments and intensity of plantings have increased where the necessity of the garden plots is concerned. They are no longer simply sources of supplementary income or a means to preserve favorite homemade foods.

The change in the marketplaces, however, is more significant still. Simply put, the bazaars are a central source of "employment" for the collective farm workers, the *kolkhozniks*, especially if we define employment as making ends meet. In addition to the kolkhozniks, rural people from all walks of professional life, including schoolteachers, musicians, skilled workers, and medical providers, seek vital income in the marketplaces by selling their own produce. And because the rural markets serve as large general stores, there is as much "competition" at the consuming level as there is at the producing level. In addition to all manner of raw foods, markets also specialize in local cooked favorites, including fritters (*khumma*), soups, kabobs, and samsas, so prepared foods play a big role in feeding hungry shoppers—and generally at the cheapest possible prices because, again, the competition combined with the general level of collective poverty is great.

Historically, the kolkhoz or peasant marketplaces in Uzbekistan were the domain of men. Uzbek men, especially, are wont to point this out in discussing how the establishment of Soviet power changed rural culture (Zanca 1999). Today, of course, it is very hard to stand on any reinvigorated patriarchal ceremony, because all hands are needed both to make money and to find bargains. For example, a major part of marketplace shopping is devoted to selling and finding spare parts for all manner of Soviet mechanical and electronics goods, from immersion heaters for boiling water to television and auto parts. People simply cannot afford to replace old Soviet household goods with imports. Frankly, many will choose not to, not only because of the expense but also because they think the imported products— the preponderance coming from China—are of inferior quality. Nevertheless, established patterns dictate that men do the shopping, and then bring the food products home for women to prepare. It is a classic division of labor whereby the men are those who deal with the outside world, while the women stay at home to maintain many of the inner workings of home life. Naturally, it is men's ideal, and any outsider observing modern Uzbek society knows that women are out and about in public life, including shopping in the bazaars, a great deal more than men with newer "traditional" and anti-Soviet values care to admit. Those who do admit to the reality sometimes depict it as just one part of the package of social ills plaguing their society in the early twenty-first century. Curiously, if a man is doing most of the food shopping, from fruits to grains to meats, he also plays a key role in ensuring that his family members and guests eat well in conjunction with his wife's and daughters' culinary efforts. We pursue this idea a little more carefully in the next section.

MEN, WOMEN, THE CONTESTED KITCHEN, AND SOCIAL LIFE

Despite cultural relativist caveats, by and large girls and women in Uzbek society have not achieved the types of freedom, including opportunities, that one finds throughout most of contemporary middle-class American society. One domain of women's power in marriage and family life, however, is the kitchen, and by association much of what we may term the internal feminine spaces—viz., the indoors. By the kitchen we also mean any and all places and products associated with women's culinary control. I make this point because all visitors to rural Central Asia are familiar with the delicious baked products, including breads and turnovers, that are usually a result of *tandir* oven preparation, and the tandirs almost always are found outdoors, within the family's courtyard to be sure, but away from the house itself. As bread is every bit as fundamental and quasi-sacred to Uzbeks as tortillas, for example, are to Mexicans (and also factors large in ideational and psychological realms where the emphasis is on security and peace of mind), partaking in a particular family's bread products leaves a strong and lasting impression.[5] In my experience, people readily identified part of the overall worthiness and decency of any given family by how well they prepared food, especially the basis of all food—the bread. At home, only girls and women bake.

Naturally, even a good cook faces limitations set by the overall quality of the ingredients with which she must work. This applies to flour, eggs, meats, rice, grains, vegetables, and so on. Thus the person who purchases foodstuffs has to be determined about acquiring high quality items, because they reflect on his skills, smarts, and concern for either his own family or his friends and guests. While a dutiful and caring wife or daughter(s) can improve on low quality goods through the magic of her boiling, roasting, frying, baking, etc., there is next to nothing anyone can do for foods that are not transformed via heat, such as fruits, vegetables, dairy products, beverages, nuts, and candies. And because marketplaces are notorious for salespeople who look to take the inexperienced consumer (both through the haggling process and by deception involving the true quality of things that appear to look good, such as melons or potatoes), consistently bringing good things home is an arduous chore.

Ultimately, however, women do most of the daily cooking and men wait to be served. People eat sex-segregated, and men are served first. Surely, the women, girls, and younger children, who ordinarily are relegated to the kitchen or kitchen area when a man entertains distant relatives or friends in the guest room (*mekhmonkhona*), can and do help themselves to plenty of tasty morsels; but by and large the very best victuals of sumptuous dining, including the meat and high calorie substances, must appear on the plates of the men of the house. Some of the good stuff, including hunks of fatty beef or mutton, comes back to its point of origin as leftovers, but even so this does not always mean that the women and girls get to eat their fill as the men do.

As mentioned previously, rotund adult men announce their relatively high status through their very girth. How good or bad a woman's cooking may be is one issue, but a well-fed man truly is a mark of the dutiful wife. By American or Western European standards, the amount of animal fat and vegetable oil that an Uzbek woman adds to her ingredients in making a plov or a soup may seem shocking, but Uzbek sensibilities demand nothing less. Nevertheless, feeding lots of fat to a fatty may not necessarily be a sign of great love or dedicated service to matrimony.[6]

If women face a quotidian oppression in their household labors—with men sharing few to none of the cooking challenges, including drawing water from nearby canals and collecting fuel in the form of dung or dried out cotton plant stalks, aside from their vital roles as food growers and food shoppers—how does the way in which a woman prepares and serves meals greatly affect her husband's status and reputation? Simply, what she brings to the table, especially in the presence of friends or guests, says a great deal both about her basic talents as a cook and, a little more subtly, about her attitude toward those whom she serves. In the end, the man of the house (*khojain*) cannot really control what he eats; he has to trust his wife, so all of the most basic aspects of the nature of the husband-wife relationship are going to be concentrated in how and what a man eats, and in how his social/family life gets represented to his larger village or community. Obviously, Uzbek husband-wife and inter-familial relations are hardly unique in a comparative sense. In terms of wanting to do well by guests, there is probably something nearly universal in how good and bad tastes and presentations affect the status of all couples and families. On the other hand, the forms through which this sort of contested dynamic between husband and wife takes place are specific to the rural Uzbek way of life. The specificity here refers to the progression of a host-guest meal: what sorts of foods will be served, what sort of abundance exists, whether or not all efforts have been made to make a clean, comfortable, and welcoming reclining environment for the guests, and how responsive a man's wife and older children are to basic needs, such as refilling teapots, replenishing plates, and a number of other forms that space constraints will not allow me to discuss. The final point here is neither to show that all relationships are fraught with culinary antagonism nor that the kitchen is some zone of women's liberation in the Uzbek countryside. Rather, within the patrilineal and patriarchal Uzbek villages, the will and ability of men to consciously or unconsciously practice a kind of structural oppression of the opposite sex is tempered by life's most basic requirement—food. Hostility and mistreatment may be met with mealtime sabotage, because women do control most of the preparation of all cooked foods.

DAILY EATING IN THE COUNTRYSIDE

Having said that most peasants and rural people in the countryside now have Spartan diets doesn't mean that people do not eat well, even richly perhaps, once or twice in a week. Even if this means a cottonseed-oil-laden plov served not with beef or mutton but with eggs or chick peas, egg-stuffed dumplings (*tuhum varak*), or assorted *manti* (steamed dumpling) dishes with a bit of animal fat, potato, onions, or squash, poor Uzbeks do eat more than bread and tea. Meat, however, remains the most desirable of foods, and the more infrequently people eat it, the more, obviously, does it become a topic of discussion or obsession. So serious has this become in recent years that a more typical gift to bring hosts, especially if one may be staying the night or for a bit extra, is now a good quantity of mutton or beef, which should include plenty of bone matter and fat. I recollect once telling my host how many people in the United States were turning to vegetarianism as a means toward starting a healthier lifestyle. He chuckled at the notion, and informed me that these Americans would feel very much at home in Uzbekistan because "We're vegetarians now, too."

Although certainly not part of daily eating, at certain times of the year, mainly late summer and throughout the fall, festal dining forms a huge part of common entertainment and takes place almost daily during said times. Whatever the party or occasion, people pull out all the stops to ensure that tens and often hundreds of guests will eat and drink well. And whereas the excess and extent of 1970s Brezhnev-era feasting probably will not be re-experienced any time soon by most rural farmers, various quantities of all those "Golden Age" items, including champagne and candies, still appear (Lubin 1985). However much the economic straps tighten around family budgets, most Uzbeks couldn't face the mortification of not expending all they have to make special occasions food-plenteous.

Feasting occasions in the countryside include religious holidays, national celebrations, life-cycle events, and men's and women's socials. These will begin with a vast array of appetizer offerings, including nuts, candies, turnovers, butter, heavy cream, yoghurt, sharp white farmer's cheese (*suzma*), sliced fruits and vegetables, and various types of fried dough and breads. Hearty meat soups follow with occasional presentations of fried liver or boiled chicken, then perhaps steamed dumplings,

Tuhum Varak (egg-filled boiled dumplings) in yoghurt sauce.

and finally the oily and meat stacked mound of plov. That such occasions are a daily occurrence only at certain times of the year seems well attested by the degree to which people, especially men, gorge themselves at these tables (alcohol may and often does factor prominently here, but that is not subject matter for this chapter). Furthermore, even the toughest cuts or parts of the meat are consumed, no matter the chewing required or the force with which bones must be banged and smashed to extract marrow. These occasions are exercises in gratifying the palate as well as maximizing caloric intake.

Feasting aside, Sundays are reserved for marketing and drinking by many a rural man, as that is the one day that most men take off. Also, one notices many families who go marketing, and the marketplaces are crowded with all sorts of makeshift restaurants and food stands and stalls. Perhaps the favorite marketplace food, and the one people are least likely to prepare for themselves at home, is *shashlik* or kabob. Few types of kabob are more sought after than mutton liver laced with *dumba* (sheep tail fat). Kabobs are spiced with cumin, paprika, and salt. People relish them with raw onions and then sprinkle on vinegar infusions of garlic, coriander, and hot peppers (*kalampir*). More common cuts of meat also make for popular kabobs, but always the chunks of fat are a big part of any skewer. The other marketplace foods that people adore, and that they either rarely prepare at home or do not think they prepare as well, include samsas, turnovers filled with mutton and dumba; laghmon, a bowl of fresh noodles in a spicy and tangy meat broth accompanied by vinegar; mutton-filled manti, served with yoghurt and vegetable oil; and occasional baked chicken served with tangy tomato sauce (*tabak*). Sundays, then, become makeshift feast days for beloved foods rarely served in the domestic setting.

CITY AIR MAKES ONE HUNGRY AND PROUD

As Uzbekistan's largest cities, Tashkent and Samarkand also factor as huge food emporiums, serving a whole variety of imported Euro-American tastes as well as those we might consider to be Uzbek and indigenous—although in this day and age seemingly everything is a product of some globalized hybridity. In addition to the profusion of supermarkets and fast food restaurants that have developed since the mid-1990s in these Central Asian metropoles, from German supermarkets that stock almost exclusively European products to Turkish hamburger and pizza restaurants, culinary excitement comes in the shape of street foods. Impromptu restaurants exist side by side with bubbling cauldrons, braziers, and subterranean tandir ovens (circular clay and wool ovens that exist both above and below the ground's surface, and that are used for baking breads as well as savory pastries).[7] Like all other people inhabiting fast-paced cities, many folks need their meals on the fly.

In Tashkent and Samarkand, it is probably still more common to find people eating out for lunch rather than dinner, although evening restaurant dining has become remarkably ubiquitous in the post-socialist era. It appears paradoxical that so many people try to open restaurants, given the numerous constraints placed on operating private businesses. The turnover rate is exceedingly high. Be this as it may, the most common streetside eateries to be found midday in these cities are plov, shashlik/kabob, steamed dumpling, soup, and samsa stands. While there is variation in how cooks and customers spice and flavor their foods, the most common condiments and flavorings consist of cumin, garlic, vinegar, hot peppers, yoghurt-like sauces, and raw onions. Tashkenters and Samarkandis are not nearly as fond of spicy dishes as are Ferghana Valley folk.

Dishes that cater to slightly more regional or local tastes may be found where most people do their grocery shopping—in the marketplaces or bazaars themselves. Within large and sprawling city markets—Tashkent's Chorsu bazaar, for example—specialty eateries offer not only Samarkand-style plov (which favors chickpeas and raisins over beef, and uses less cottonseed oil or mutton fat), but dishes of more nomadic origin, such as *hasip*, a kind of Uzbek and Kazakh haggis, or *norin*, a Kazakh dish of finely chopped noodles and minced horse meat. People throughout Uzbekistan consider Samarkand the country's culinary star, and the road traveler's first brush with its gustatory greatness occurs upon crossing the city's threshold along one of the country's major highways. Bread sellers barrage travelers at what is almost an obligatory stop for rest, relief, and refreshment, selling wheat's favorite processed product from all manner of wheelbarrows, old baby strollers, and basketed bicycles. Not only do people from all over the country favor the delicious texture and flavor of Samarkand bread, but they also see it as a necessary traveling companion because it is viewed as a blessing (*ne'mat*).

Within the city, Samarkand's vast number of roadside food stands and eateries, many of which still specialize in Russian and Ukrainian fare, uphold the traditions of culinary plenty that have been showcased in writings since the time of Tamerlane. Samarkand may be modern Uzbekistan's second city, but its residents feel that they are far ahead of Tashkent in many ways concerning cosmopolitanism, and the culinary heritage is just one major point of pride in this outlook (Muminov 1969–1970).

Curiously, Uzbekistan's large cities make cuisine an important manifestation of ethnic pride and nationalism. One subtle process occurs simply because many minority groups, such as Russians, have emigrated from the country in large numbers, tilting Uzbek residents toward their own cuisine, despite any desire for diversity when it comes to the palate. National pride in local resources and their processing, in the form of fruit juices, cooking oils, and grains, to name but a few, serves the state and merchants who market their products based on their Uzbek authenticity. One notices this most easily via advertising, whether in the form of television commercials or city billboards. Nevertheless, while prejudices abound regarding Uzbeks' sense that their cuisine is far superior to that of neighboring countries, to say nothing of Russia's and other ex-Soviet European ones, there is a substantial difference in an ethnocentric discourse about cookery and its utilization for violent ends. While it would make no sense to rule such an untoward occurrence as impossible, food employed as a highly chauvinistic ethnic or religious marker so far has not risen to the level of clashes as we have seen historically in India, China, or Indonesia (Goody 1982: 146).

The increase in consumption of foreign and processed foods as well as the ubiquity of all kinds of raw and prepared meats distinguishes urban from rural life. Vast populations of cities, such as Tashkent—over 3 million—and Samarkand—about 500,000—can easily support varied and expensive tastes. Yet shopping remains similar for the bulk of urban residents—lengthy forays to open-air markets to bargain over quantities, qualities, and prices. Save for the major differences of the use of modern kitchens and utensils along with a much greater variety of foodstuffs, home cooking is not all that different in big cities than in rural areas; what quite separates consumption and eating in Tashkent, Samarkand, and Namangan, however, is the popular reliance on restaurants and foods-on-the-go stands for students, workers, and

Author enjoys haunch of mutton.

professionals. Today hot dogs, hamburgers, and pizza have started to become popular, though fast-food American- or European-style restaurants are still too expensive for most families on all but the most special of occasions. Many urban Uzbeks, no matter their ethnicity or nationality, also enjoy European Slavic dishes, such as borscht and beef stroganoff, and Korean specialties (owing to the presence and culinary workmanship of this near 200,000-strong ethnic minority), including types of pickled vegetables and soups. And if these delights fail to satisfy fat cravings, there are always the dense and omnipresent samsas (packed with tail fat) and khumma (the Russian *ponchik*)—a deep-fried fritter, sometimes stuffed with bits of beef fat or meat.

CONCLUSION

This chapter has been both a descriptive and an analytical effort to discuss the enduring importance of fatty foods in the contemporary Uzbek diet as well as the foods that Uzbek people most enjoy eating. Where appropriate, I sought to use comparative examples for readers to gain a sense of what makes Uzbek practices and habits similar and different from others' ways. I argued for the precedent that I think makes fat such a desirable foodstuff, something that goes beyond the mere assertion of fatty foods being the tastiest and most satisfying. I have addressed the speculative notion that Uzbeks continue to be plagued by a fear of want or deprivation in food security, which largely is a product of the economic decline experienced since the dissolution of the Soviet Union. Furthermore, I pointed out that Uzbek foodways play a significant role both in Soviet-era and independence-era collective conceptions of the nation—that is, that the Uzbek diet becomes a prideful expression of national identity, especially because Uzbeks consider their diet to be the best among all neighboring cuisines.

Providing readers with similarities and differences between rural farming diets and culinary practices and those of urban people, I discussed foods and eating practices in both rural locales and cities. The major urban difference has to do with today's emphasis not only on eating imported or foreign-style dishes but also on the trend toward street-food dining, the concentration of regional variations within big cities, and the most recent profusion of fast-food style restaurants.

Generally speaking, Uzbek diets are well balanced insofar as people can afford or have access to a wide range of foodstuffs. For example, nuts, fruits, and vegetables are highly prized in the diet, but given their druthers people will try to eat the foods highest in calories and fat. These are the foods that provide satiation and energy, especially in a country where rural people still do a great deal of demanding physical labor.

NOTES

1. I adhere to the spirited approach to food studies in anthropology promoted by Sidney Mintz. Mintz hopes anthropologists will examine food in a number of different ways, and in so doing try to relate everything from ingredients, preparation, and eating habits to all major realms of cultural life that connect any given people or nation to many others, especially in this day and age of globalization as a phase of contemporary capitalism (2003).

2. These baked or fried savory pastries have been known at least as far back as the tenth century throughout the Arab Middle East and across southern Eurasia, including India—their probable point of origin. (Davidson 1999: 827) The Uzbek *samsa* is very similar to the South Asian *samosa*, but in Uzbekistan they are usually larger meat or potato turnovers with a firm and flaky baked shell. Beef and mutton are the most popular. The most coveted are those stuffed with at least one large globule of sheep tail fat. Uzbeks split them open when hot to add garlic and herb-infused vinegar, and sometimes cayenne pepper. Chicken samsas are a new street food, becoming popular in Tashkent only in the past few years.

3. Recently, a student of the phenomenal aspects of American obesity suggests that while big portions, lack of exercise, and poor nutrition may account for some aspects of American fatness, we must also consider that Americans eat constantly—

as grazers—and on the run, hence often alone when they are less likely to think about how much they are actually eating (Shapin 2006). Fortunately, for most Uzbeks these problems have not arisen in ways closely paralleling the US experience.

4. Lardo is cured pork fat. Often it is cured in marble containers with sea salt and herbs, such as oregano or rosemary. It is thinly sliced and served sometimes as an appetizer in various parts of Italy.

5. In writing about the origins and importance of maize to ancient Mexicans, Sophie Coe points out how similar Aztec beliefs associated with wasting or disposing of tortillas are to those of European peasants regarding old or stale bread (1994: 10–11). Uzbek peasants would never throw away old bread, or bread that accidentally became soiled. They incorporate it into other dishes, soften it in soups, or leave it above the height of a person's head for birds or other animals.

6. This reminds me of an incident related to me by a young Norwegian anthropologist who, in her doctoral work, was studying aspects of family life and women's authority in Tashkent. After watching a woman preparing plov for her husband and his guests and adding copious amounts of animal fat, the young anthropologist said, "My goodness, you shouldn't use so much fat; you're going to give your husband a heart attack." The woman's reply to this dietary health concern: "And what makes you think I don't want to kill him!"

7. Readers will find an excellent synopsis of the tandir or tandoor, including its uses and global range, in Fernandez-Armesto (2002: 15).

REFERENCES

Coe, Sophie. 1994. *America's First Cuisines.* Austin: University of Texas Press.
Davidson, Alan. 1999. *The Penguin Companion to Food.* New York: Penguin Books.
Fernandez-Armesto, Felipe. 2002. *Near a Thousand Tables: A History of Food.* New York: Free Press.
Goody, Jack. 1982. *Cooking, Cuisine and Class: A Study in Comparative Sociology.* Cambridge: Cambridge University Press.
Gudeman, Stephen. 2001. *The Anthropology of Economy.* Malden, Mass.: Blackwell Publishing.
Harris, Marvin. 1985. *Good to Eat: Riddles of Food and Culture.* Glencoe, Ill.: Waveland Press.
Highmore, Ben. 2002. *Everyday Life and Cultural Theory.* London: Routledge.
Kullick, Don, and Anne Meneley, eds. 2005. *Fat: The Anthropology of an Obsession.* New York: Penguin Group.
Lubin, Nancy. 1985. *Labour and Nationality in Soviet Central Asia: An Uneasy Compromise.* Princeton, N.J.: Princeton University Press.
Mennell, Stephen. 1996. *All Manners of Food: Eating and Taste in England and France from the Middle Ages to the Present* (2nd ed.). Urbana and Chicago: University of Illinois Press.
Mintz, Sidney W. 2003. "Devouring Objects of Study: Food and Fieldwork." Indiana University: Text from The David Skomp Distinguished Lectures in Anthropology.
Muminov, I. M., ed. 1969–1970. *Istoriia Samarkanda* (2 vols.). Tashkent: FAN.
Powdermaker, Hortense. 1997. "An Anthropological Approach to the Problem of Obesity," in *Food and Culture: A Reader*, Carole Counihan and Penny Van Esterik, eds. New York and London: Routledge.

Richards, Audrey. 1948. *Hunger and Work in a Savage Tribe: A Functional Study of Nutrition among the Southern Bantu.* Glencoe, Ill.: The Free Press.

Shapin, Steven. 2006. "Eat and Run." *The New Yorker,* 16 January. http://www.newyorker.com/critics/books/articles/060116crbo_books

Zanca, Russell. "The Representation of an Uzbek Kolkhoz: An Ethnographic Account of Postsocialism". PhD diss, University of Illinois.

———. 2003. "'Take! Take! Take!' Host-Guest Relations and All that Food: Uzbek Hospitality Past and Present." *The Anthropology of East Europe Review* 21, no. 1: 8–16.

13. Public and Private Celebrations: Uzbekistan's National Holidays

Laura Adams

Holidays are an important part of any national culture. The significance of national holidays lies in the way that their celebration personalizes abstract ideas about the values of the nation. However, holidays are also spaces for the "practice of everyday life" (de Certeau 1984) where groups of people are free to create their own meanings, which they attach to collective celebrations. For most people in Uzbekistan today, holiday activities are part of a private realm that (unlike during the Soviet period) is no longer of much concern to the government. Although the government of Uzbekistan (much like its Soviet predecessor) attempts to manipulate holidays for its own purposes of nation building and social control, these efforts have very little effect on the daily lives of Uzbekistan's citizens. However, by institutionalizing existing practices, as in the celebration of religious holidays that were banned during the Soviet period, the government has succeeded in opening up cultural space for people to explore and redefine their religious beliefs and practices.

Uzbekistan celebrates a number of official state holidays (see table 13.1), some with great public fanfare, and others more quietly. Uzbekistan's religious holidays are considered to be mainly private celebrations, though some public ceremonies take place on those days, such as the early morning *osh*, or feast, held for government officials and prominent members of the community. International New Year and Remembrance Day are more public celebrations with ceremonies and festivities in which all citizens are invited to take part.

RELIGIOUS HOLIDAYS

Religious holidays, such as the *Hayit* (*Eid* in Persian and Arabic), were officially banned during the Soviet period, but they were one of the main

Table 13.1: Uzbekistan's official national holidays

International New Year	January 1
International Women's Day	March 8
Navruz	March 21
Day of Remembrance and Honor (formerly Victory Day)	May 9
Independence Day	September 1
Constitution Day	December 8
Ramazon Hayiti (feast at the end of Ramadan)	Varies
Qurbon Hayiti (feast of the sacrifice)	Varies

realms of everyday life that people used to continue their religious practices in spite of Soviet repression. Today, religious holidays are marked in some families by religious rituals and prayer at the mosque, but for the vast majority of Uzbekistan's Muslims, the main feature of the day is visiting with family. Various branches of an extended family take turns hosting the feasts from year to year, with members of other households pitching in by bringing food and giving other sorts of assistance. Often visits to friends and neighbors are involved as well, especially if the family has had a wedding, birth, or death in the past year. There are two Hayit holidays celebrated in Uzbekistan: *Ramazon Hayiti* and *Qurbon Hayiti*. Ramazon Hayiti is the three day celebration at the end of Ramazon (Ramadan), the month of abstention that celebrates the revelation of the Quran. Uzbeks observe Ramazon with varying degrees of strictness, but many people have become interested in observing at least some aspects of the fast since the holiday became official again after the Soviet period.

During the month of Ramazon, families who are fasting during the day usually rise before dawn to have a large meal, sometimes returning to bed afterward to catch another hour or two of sleep before going to school or work. During the day, they will not eat or drink anything, even water, and this is one of the reasons the Soviets, who were concerned with promoting both atheism and labor productivity, worked to prevent people from observing the fast (Keller 2001). As the sun sets, families gather to say prayers and break the fast together, first with a sip of water, and then with a large and festive meal. The upside to the daily routine of austerity is that most nights during Ramazon are festive occasions, with family members and neighbors coming together to enjoy the meal. At the end of Ramazon, families prepare for the coming holiday by thoroughly cleaning their homes and by buying a new dress or suit. During Ramazan Hayiti, three days of feasting and visiting friends and relatives are celebrated by everyone, even if they did not observe the fast. This Hayit is also a time when a new *kelin* (bride or daughter-in-law) living in her husband's home invites her family over to see how her new life is going. In order to show how well her husband's family is providing for her, she (with the help of her friends and relatives) will fill tables full of food and she herself will change clothes several times. The Ramazon Hayiti is also a time for visiting families who have lost a loved one in the past year. Over the course of three days, most families pay visits to quite a few homes.

Qurbon Hayiti is the holiday commemorating the biblical story of God's request for Abraham to sacrifice his son as a test of his devotion (God relented at the last minute and the son's life was spared). According to the Muslim version of the story, God asked Abraham to sacrifice his son by his wife's servant, Hagar. This son, Ishmael, is considered the progenitor of the Arabs.[1] Qurbon Hayiti is traditionally celebrated with ritual animal sacrifices at shrines and mosques, but this practice is not nearly as common as it used to be before the Soviet era, when most well-off families would sacrifice an animal whose meat would be distributed to the poor. In part this reluctance to sacrifice animals is due to the influence of Soviet anti-religious propaganda, and in part it is due to the tough economic situation. Apart from this religious aspect to the holiday, Qurbon Hayiti, like all other holidays in Uzbekistan, is celebrated with feasting and family.

SECULAR HOLIDAYS

Most of Uzbekistan's official national holidays are not religious in nature, however. Many are civic holidays marking the formal properties of a modern nation such as Independence Day, Flag Day, and Constitution Day. Most of these modern holidays don't yet have much meaning for many citizens of Uzbekistan, other than being a day off work. The exceptions to this are the secular holidays of the international New Year (*Yangi Yil*, 1 January), the Zoroastrian New Year on the spring equinox (*Navruz*, 21 March), and Independence Day (*Mustaqillik Kuni*, 1 September), which are all celebrated in public as well as in family-oriented ways by most citizens, Uzbek and non-Uzbek alike. On these three secular holidays, the national and local governments sponsor outdoor activities such as concerts and street fairs, which involve all the citizens of Uzbekistan, creating a basis for a civic rather than an ethnic national identity. Although much of the content of these celebrations is related to Uzbek or Central Asian culture and heritage, the way the holidays are celebrated is inclusive of a broader civic community. Of all the national holidays of Uzbekistan, Navruz and Independence Day are celebrated on the largest scale in terms of state spending (more than a million dollars per holiday in Tashkent alone) and have the greatest significance for the public representa-

Dressed for Qurbon Hayiti.

tion of national identity. These holidays were the focus of the research I conducted in Tashkent, Uzbekistan, during 1996.

Navruz, a holiday of the spring equinox, has been celebrated on the territory of today's Uzbekistan since the dominant religion of the region became Zoroastrianism more than two thousand years ago. Even after the majority of the population of the Persian and Turkic world converted to Islam, Zoroastrian practices continued. There are still practicing Zoro-astrians in Uzbekistan, though most of them keep their religion a secret. Navruz, which means "new day" in Persian (*No Ruz* or *Nawruz*), is cele-brated in contemporary Central Asia, Iran, India, and Turkey, by Mus-lims as well as Zoroastrians. In Uzbekistan, as in many regions that cele-brate it, the holiday is not a one-day event. Navruz is more of a season, like Christmas in the United States, and is celebrated in various ways for weeks before and after the day itself. Today Uzbekistan's main Navruz celebration falls on 21 March every year, and it is considered the most pop-ular holiday, at least among those who are ethnic Uzbeks. The Russian-speaking population knows it as a day off from work and a chance to take in some public entertainment, but they do not know much more about its history and traditions than most Anglo-Americans know about Cinco de Mayo. Many Uzbeks are less familiar with Navruz than their grand-parents were, since the holiday was deemed religious by the Soviet au-thorities and consequently banned from being officially celebrated. The one thing everyone in Uzbekistan knows about Navruz is that around the time of the holiday, you eat *sumalak*.

Sumalak, made from flour and wheat juice, is a brown paste the con-sistency of a thick cake batter that tastes like pleasantly toasted malt. But more important than eating sumalak is the collective process of making it. In the family I lived with, it was an occasion for all the women of the extended family and some of the neighbors to get together and socialize while working on the dish. The preparation of the ingredients (sprout-ing wheat and extracting its juice, securing large quantities of flour, etc.) took several days, and the cooking time was more than twenty hours. The cauldron has to be stirred frequently to make sure the flour particles brown but do not burn, so several members of the family stayed up late or got up early to make sure the pot was scraped regularly. Sumalak as a holiday dish appears to be unique to Uzbekistan and Tajikistan, though the process of cultivating a plate of sprouts for ritual purposes on Navruz is common in Iran also (Masse 1954).

The distribution of sumalak around the time of Navruz is an obliga-tory activity for any organization sponsoring a Navruz festival. These lo-cal events take place a few days before or after the actual holiday, since the people who organize and perform in these local festivities are often the same ones who are required to participate in the main holiday concert on the twenty-first. In 1996, for example, each of the twelve districts of Tash-

Recipe for sumalak

30 kilograms flour
1 liter cooking oil
20 kilograms wheat sprouts
30 liters of water

Grind the wheat sprouts, saving the juice. Soak
the remaining wheat pulp in the water and then
strain the water out, pouring it, the wheat juice,
and the oil into a very large cauldron over a
high flame. Stir it all together and then
gradually add the flour, breaking up clumps
with your hands. Add a few large rocks and stir
the cauldron using the rocks to help scrape the
sides. Stir constantly over a high heat for 24
hours, adding water when needed to keep the
mixture stirable. The sumalak should be thick
and a dark velvety brown when it is done.

kent city was assigned a character from Chinese astrology and marched in a carnival-like procession during the performance in Navoi Park. The cultural department of the district was responsible for organizing their part of the procession as well as any Navruz festivities they wanted to have locally, such as an exhibition of schoolchildren's arts and crafts or a dramatized poetry reading in a local park. Because of these multiple obligations spread out over several days, the festive atmosphere of Navruz expands outward around the actual day off work (the twenty-first), with some holiday-related events such as library book displays and special television programming lasting for the whole month of March. Not everyone in a neighborhood can come to the local celebration since these sometimes take place during work days, but one district administrator explained to me that he had persuaded schools and employers in his district to excuse people who were needed for the festivities. The festive atmosphere throughout the city is enhanced by Navruz-related cultural events and the hanging of Navruz banners from lampposts starting about two weeks before the holiday.

So while Navruz is a time for neighborhood fun, scholars and holiday organizers alike are interested in the symbolic aspects of Navruz as a holiday of spring that celebrates the triumph of warmth and light over cold and darkness, the renewal of nature, and the beginning of the agricultural labor cycle. The first aspect, the triumph of light and warmth, is symbolically associated with the equinox and the lengthening of the day, and also with the Zoroastrian symbol of fire, though fire plays almost no role in Uzbekistan's contemporary Navruz celebrations and reference to fire rituals is actively discouraged by the government because they are seen as unIslamic. Some intellectuals also talk about Navruz as a time when the forces of evil rise up and must be put down for another year by the forces of good, but these references to the legendary sources of Navruz are not part of the everyday understanding that I encountered among acquaintances and in popular culture.

The renewal of nature is symbolized by sumalak's sprouting wheat, and sweets are featured as a straightforward message wishing the guest a sweet new year. In Iran, there are even more rituals associated with renewal, such as buying new clothes, cleaning the house thoroughly, jumping over a fire for purification, and the exchange of gifts, such as brightly colored eggs, symbolizing birth and beginning (Boyce 1977; Masse 1954). In Uzbekistan many of these rituals were noted but not observed with much enthusiasm, since buying new clothing and a thorough housecleaning are obligatory among Tashkenters for the Ramazon Hayit, and colored eggs seemed to be associated mainly with Christian Orthodox Easter.

Unlike Navruz, which is being reinvented as part of creating a new national identity, Independence Day is a newly invented holiday without a long history to draw on. In celebrating Uzbekistan's declaration of independence from the rapidly disintegrating Soviet Union in August 1991, the government is trying to create meaningful content that is based both on Uzbek heritage and on the symbols of modern nationhood. Independence Day is celebrated on 1 September, but the holiday begins with a spectacular concert on the evening of 31 August. Common themes in this performance relate to the importance of children and youth to the future of Uzbekistan; the achievements of Uzbekistan in sport, economic production, and international culture; the history of civilizations of the region; inter-ethnic harmony; the military; and pop music. The government encourages the holiday's popularity by giving everyone a day off work on the first, by sponsoring patriotic competitions (such as the annual "Uzbekistan My Homeland" song contest) in the weeks leading up to the holiday, and by throwing a party for the inhabitants of urban areas that begins with the evening spectacle and resumes with city-wide street fairs the following day. On this day other sorts of commemorations might take place as well, such as the honoring of veterans or other patriotic heroes and outstanding citizens.

The Day of Remembrance and Honor (*Xotira va Qadirlash Kuni*) is the new name for the formerly Soviet holiday, Victory Day, which celebrates the end of World War II. Though more than 400,000 Uzbeks died in the war, the holiday is an ideologically complicated one for the current government, invoking loyalties to a defunct Soviet state and supra-national identities that they wish were defunct. Some other former republics of the

Independence Day in Tashkent.

Elder dancing on Independence Day.

Soviet Union, such as Azerbaijan, have dealt with these complications by eliminating the holiday altogether. In Uzbekistan, the scale of the holiday has been reduced since independence and especially since the fiftieth anniversary celebrations in 1995, but it is still an important holiday. In contrast, the government of Uzbekistan eliminated the widely popular May Day holiday soon after independence, even though it was associated with politically neutral themes such as the celebration of spring (in Russia, that is; in Uzbekistan it marked the beginning of really warm weather) and international labor solidarity. Still, as a Ministry of Cultural Affairs official pointed out to me, May Day was primarily associated with Soviet power, and almost all the holidays that Uzbeks could not lay a claim to as "their own" were eliminated or replaced after independence. This logic was not followed in other newly independent states such as Kazakhstan and Azerbaijan, where May Day has continued as an official national holiday.

One Soviet holiday Uzbekistan has not eliminated is International Women's Day, which is celebrated widely on a moderate scale. Women's Day involves nearly everyone on an individual level, at a minimum, since all men and boys are supposed to give small gifts to women and girls. Most people are involved collectively as well, since most schools and workplaces sponsor some sort of holiday program. For example, I was invited to the Women's Day celebration at the Tashkent State Institute of Culture, which consisted of a potluck meal organized mostly by the men, and over an hour of speeches and banter on the theme of women's beauty, grace, and talents (such as raising children and making the workplace more beautiful). At the end of the meal, we women were given flowers and I was presented with a Women's Day pin, in honor of my interest in holidays.

It is interesting that Women's Day is not associated with Soviet power as was the equally popular May Day. My colleagues told me that Women's Day could not possibly be eliminated, since it was "the one day to honor women, and after all, where would we be without women?!" A more structural explanation is that since Women's Day is apolitical, it was not problematic for the government in the same way that May Day and Victory Day are. Additionally, despite the holiday's feminist roots, the way Women's Day is celebrated in Uzbekistan actually promotes traditional gender stereotypes, which the official ideology now supports (see Kamp 2003). There are also two other reasons why Women's Day continues, but the other two holidays do not. First of all, the functions May Day performed are now performed by Navruz, though Azerbaijan celebrates both May Day and Navruz, so it does not necessarily follow that one holiday should substitute for the other. As a holiday of spring, Navruz falls at a climatically more appropriate time of the year for sunny Uzbekistan, and as a holiday that demonstrates the core values of a society, May Day's emphasis on international labor solidarity has become anachronistic in many places, not just Uzbekistan. Navruz fits the bill of a spring holiday much better than May Day by focusing on the renewal of tradition that reinforces the power of the ruling elite, who are seen as restoring lost legacies to the Uzbek people. As much as class was the core of Soviet ideology, national identity is the core of Uzbekistan's ideology.

Second, the way Women's Day has been celebrated lends itself to perpetuation in the absence of large-scale government support. While May Day was equivalent in form to the Anniversary of the Revolution, as well as on the same scale as the current Navruz and Independence Day celebrations, Women's Day is celebrated in a very different way, on a small scale that is meaningful to collectives of people, such as families and colleagues, who share a history of celebrating this holiday together. Thus it is an opportunity for reinforcing small-scale solidarities through pleasurable activities such as shared food, flattering speeches, and gift exchange.International Women's Day is one Soviet tradition that has been thoroughly incorporated into contemporary Uzbek culture. The holiday's perpetuation through small group interactions (as opposed to state-sponsored spectacles and the like) has made it easy to dissociate it from Soviet power, though there is no guarantee it will continue on in the next generation.

A TYPICAL HOLIDAY

On Independence Day, Navruz, Victory Day, and New Year's Day, public sociability is emphasized, though private celebrations are almost always a part of these holidays as well, if on a smaller scale. The people of Uzbekistan, whether ethnically European or Asian, generally enjoy these holidays as they are always glad for an excuse to host a festive meal for friends and family. Part of the private celebration is in a way public, however, as families watch the television broadcast of the holiday spectacles that I will describe in detail shortly. Another part of the public celebration is the *halq sayili*, a term that literally means "public strolling," but which I translate as "street fair" in order to draw an apt parallel with activities Americans engage in on some holidays. The sayil involves several elements: dressing nicely, doing a lot of walking around the city, buying food and drink from vendors especially set up for the occasion, and watching entertainment on the city's public squares. Most of the entertainment and vendors are oriented toward families and children.

A typical sayil in the capital city of Tashkent will start out with a family's subway trip to the center of the city, where they merge with the thronging crowds out on the streets, many of which are closed to traffic. The city has been decorated; ten-story banners hang from buildings and the government billboards are decorated with holiday slogans. All of the city's beautiful fountains are turned on and water spouts from fountain jets in the Anhor

River. National flags and small, colorful banners flutter everywhere. The holiday program is published in advance on posters, but these programs are rather unevenly distributed throughout the city, and it is hard to know in advance where a particular musical group will be playing.

The family sets out from the metro station, perhaps for the plaza in front of the Navoi Theater, where children's entertainment is usually held on holidays. After watching a puppet show or a children's dance ensemble, the family will probably head up the pedestrian mall, *Sayilgox* (Persian for strolling street, but more commonly known in Tashkent as "Brodvey," after the New York street famous for its entertainment). Broadway is a place of everyday festivity in Tashkent, where people go to see and be seen, to have a bite to eat at their choice of chic outdoor cafes or dodgy pilaf stands, to hear bands perform in the courtyard of the famous Zarafshan restaurant, to see what the artists and craftsmen are selling along the sidewalk, or to sing karaoke at a walk-up machine right out on the street. Broadway's everyday liveliness is amplified on holidays with throngs of people clogging the street and crowding the tables of the cafes, and occasionally dancing to the songs of live bands playing popular Russian and Uzbek pop music. The family will probably avail themselves of the relatively inexpensive kabobs, pilaf, and sweets available before making their way to the other end of the street, Independence Square.

On the square are more stands run by local government-owned grocery stores selling basically the same things at the same price as they would on an ordinary day. Soda pop and cookies are especially popular with the crowds, soap and canned vegetables understandably less so. The family might get some ice cream and move on to the small stage (on the steps of the Cabinet of Ministers building) where "ethnic" ensembles are performing: perhaps the Uyghur dance troupe, or a folklore group from Bukhara, or even the republic's premier Uzbek national dance and music ensemble, Bahor. While the younger kids are drawn toward the circus performers (strong men and tightrope walkers) in the middle of the square, the older kids are eager to move on to the larger stage from which emanates music so loud the folk music cannot quite drown it out. The larger stage (by the Tashkent equivalent of Red Square's mausoleum—a red granite monument upon which an enormous statue of Lenin used to stand) is reserved mainly for "international" culture, and there the family can listen to anything from Russian pop ballads to Uzbek rap. After a few hours in the hot sun, the family will probably take a rest along the cool banks of the Anhor river, which runs along one side of Independence Square. Along the parkway, various regions of the city have set up temporary cafes to show their hospitality. The night before, these tables were reserved for important guests of the neighborhood officials and served as an arena for the display of social status. Today, anyone who wants to pay a small amount for a *somsa* (meat pastry) and a bottle of Coke can have a seat.

If the kids are not too tired, there are other things for this Tash-kent family to do and see. Other city squares have performances by re-gional stars of popular and classical music, displays of handicrafts, per-formances by local amateur groups in a variety of languages, and more places to stroll and snack. The city's larger parks have fun things to do, such as row-boating and carnival rides (which, like the activities on Say-ilgox, are available every day). Or the family could go back to their own neighborhood to see what kind of festival their local park is putting on, to fly a kite and socialize with neighbors or schoolmates. Or perhaps they are expected at their parents' house to help prepare dinner for twenty relatives.

One thing most families cannot do on a holiday is go see the multi-million dollar spectacles on the city's main squares. Attendance is by in-vitation only and the seating is limited to 10,000, making a ticket a very precious thing indeed. The holiday itself is a street fair for the masses, but the holiday spectacle is a show first and foremost for the elite, and only via television broadcast for the rest of the country. This kind of cele-bration is relatively new in Uzbekistan, introduced in an era of global-ization where the Olympics opening ceremonies serve as a model that Uz-bekistan's holiday planners strive to emulate (Adams 2003). Before the Soviet era, Navruz was celebrated in the marketplaces, city squares, and main streets, not unlike contemporary sayils (Qoraboev 1988, 6; *O'zbekiston Respublikasi Entsiklopediya* 1997, 540–541). The entertainment consisted of clowns, musicians, storytellers, and games such as *ko'pkari*, a game of horse-manship, also known jokingly as "goat carcass polo." Now the clowns, musicians, and storytellers entertain from an elevated stage in a carefully planned and rehearsed performance, and Uzbeks see ko'pkari *performed* more often than they see it *played*.

The Navruz spectacle takes place every year in the Alisher Navoi National Garden, located in Tashkent's central district. Framing the staging area are five dramatic backdrops: three impressive modern buildings (a "wedding palace," a concert hall, and the parliament building); a 200-year-old reli-gious building that served as a museum of atheism during the Soviet pe-riod; and a hill, upon which a wide staircase leads to a large, newly built blue-domed gazebo housing a statue of the fifteenth century poet, Alisher Navoi. Along with the president, prominent political and religious figures, and the international diplomatic community, the seating area holds 10,000 more ordinary audience members lucky enough to obtain an invitation to the event. The seats are in a U-shape around the staging area, and those seated in the center section have the ideal position for viewing the back-drop of the hill.

In addition to the physical characteristics of the staging area, there are similarities in production from year to year. The crest of the hill is lined with young men holding colorful banners that blow in the breeze. Streaming down the staircases on the hill are young women in whimsical costumes—

some in rainbow-colored hoop skirts and others dressed to look like red tulips. Off in the distance, from behind the hill, hot air balloons are launched, sending off a series of rockets that produce trails of colorful smoke as they rise slowly into the air.

Taking an example from the 1996 show, the center stage is crowded with young women dancers in diaphanous green costumes designed in the style of women in Persian miniatures, the typical costume for professional women's dance ensembles.[2] The dance style is modern: geometric patterns embellished with stylistic elements of Central Asian hand and head movements. On the outskirts of the stage is the Uzbek National Chorus: middle-aged men wearing tuxedos and middle-aged women, some of whom are wearing European chiffon dresses, others wearing long Central Asian velvet robes. The chorus is mouthing words to a majestic sounding song celebrating the coming of Navruz, which had been recorded for the spectacle's soundtrack a week or two before (there are no live performances in Uzbekistan's holiday spectacles; everything is lip-synched). The song itself, blasting from the loudspeakers, is the genre known as national orchestral music: European-style music played by Uzbek national instruments, accompanied by the choir, which is also an imported music genre.

Surrounding the central stage are four smaller stages that are also occupied by dancing girls in beautiful costumes. Between the stages are lanes through which performers can enter and exit the main stage, and visible in the background are the puppets and costumed performers waiting to take the stage for the next number. The lanes are lined with artificial flowers (it is still too early in the season for real flowers) donated by Sovplastital, the local Italian-Uzbekistan joint venture plastic factory. For now the lanes are empty, but they, too, become part of the staging area later in the show when residents from each of Tashkent's neighborhood districts parade through, carnival style, dressed in all sorts of costumes, only some of which play on the official theme of animals from the Chinese zodiac. Also still to come are more background effects that constantly draw the viewers' attention to something new and interesting: high wire acts; fountains; twenty-meter-tall, brightly colored balloons that are in the shape of horses, bulls, and roosters; kites flying; children on roller skates zooming through the staging area; young men dressed as Timurid-era soldiers (fourteenth century) marching or doing tricks on horses; expensive Mylar balloon strings, imported from Moscow, being set free to decorate the sky with their snaky rainbow trails. There are probably few events anywhere in the world that approach the scale, the extravagance, and the visual chaos of Uzbekistan's holiday spectacles. The government spends millions of dollars on the Navruz and Independence Day holiday concerts each year, and each year persuades more than 10,000 participants to dance, sing, and parade for its vision of the new national identity.

Whether celebrated with mass spectacle or privately in the home, holidays are a significant marker of the cyclical time of everyday life. However, this cyclicity does not imply mere repetition, since holidays in Uzbekistan have served as sites of cultural and ideological contestation for many decades. Holidays frequently serve as an ideological battleground for modern nation-states (Petrone 2000; von Geldern 1993; Ozouf 1988; Lane 1981; Binns 1980), but the case of post-Soviet holidays in Uzbekistan demonstrates the relative weakness of even an authoritarian state when it attempts to transform the private realm through public culture. Throughout the post-Soviet world, new holidays that are designed to reinforce a particular image of the state (such as constitution days) still have little meaning in the private lives of citizens. Other holidays, especially those that revive pre-Soviet religious and folk traditions, are embraced by the population and have taken on a variety of meanings in everyday life. While government actions had a large impact on religious celebrations (by officially sanctioning them without dictating how they should be celebrated), government attempts to manipulate and control national identity through the celebration of civic holidays has been largely ineffective. This brings us back to an important point made by other studies of everyday life: even strong states can only set the parameters of lived culture; they cannot control its content.

NOTES

1. The Jewish and Christian version of this story has Abraham sacrificing his son by his wife, Sarah. This son, Isaac, is considered to be the progenitor of the Jews.

2. This costume typically consists of a solid-color long dress with a wide, flowing skirt; sleeves that are narrow at the shoulder and wide at the cuff; a tailored bodice covered by an embroidered velvet vest in a complementary color; and a flowing head scarf or colorful skullcap. The typical costume for women in folk ensembles is the shapeless dress made of multi-colored *atlas* (*ikat*) silk that is referred to in everyday life as "Uzbek national dress." For examples, see the author's video about the 1996 Independence Day concert (http://www.youtube.com/watch?v=9Pbj2txia-s). Videos are also available about Navruz (http://www.youtube.com/watch?v=DyoMu_DYyiU) and the making of sumalak (http://www.youtube.com/watch?v=i4tIELlJcz0).

REFERENCES

Adams, Laura L. "Globalization without Capitalism: Modernity and Cultural Form in Central Asia." Paper presented at the American Sociological Association Annual Meeting, Atlanta, Ga. 2003.

Binns, Christopher A. P. "The Changing Face of Power: Revolution and Accommodation in the Development of the Soviet Ceremonial System: Part I & II." *Man* 14/15, no. 4/1 (1979/80): 170–187.

Boyce, Mary. *A Persian Stronghold of Zoroastrianism.* Oxford: Clarendon Press, 1977.

de Certeau, Michel. *The Practice of Everyday Life.* Trans. Steven F. Rendall. Berkeley: University of California Press, 1984.

von Geldern, James. *Bolshevik Festivals, 1917–1920.* Berkeley: University of California Press, 1993.

Kamp, Marianne. "Between Women and the State." In Pauline Jones Luong, ed., *The Transformation of Central Asia.* Ithaca, N.Y.: Cornell University Press, 2003.

Karabaev, Usman. "Iz Istorii Massovykh Prazdnikov v Uzbekistane." In E. Ia. Zazerskii, ed., *Mesto Massovogo Prazdnika v Dukhovnoy Zhizni Sotsialisticheskogo Obshchestva.* Leningrad: Ministerstvo Kul'tury RSFSR, 1981.

Keller, Shoshana. *To Moscow, not Mecca: the Soviet campaign against Islam in Central Asia, 1917–1941.* Westport, Conn.: Praeger, 2001.

Lane, Christel. *The Rites of Rulers: Ritual in Industrial Society—The Soviet Case.* Cambridge: Cambridge University Press, 1981.

Masse, Henri. *Persian Beliefs and Customs.* Trans. Charles A. Messner. New Haven, Conn.: Human Relations Area Files, 1954.

O'zbekiston Respublikasi Entsiklopediia. Tashkent: Qomuslar Bosh Tahririiati, 1997.

Ozouf, Mona. *Festivals and the French Revolution.* Cambridge, Mass.: Harvard University Press, 1988.

Petrone, Karen. *Life Has Become More Joyous, Comrades: Celebrations in the Time of Stalin.* Bloomington: Indiana University Press, 2000.

Qoraboev, Usmon. "Navrozi Olam." *Guliston* 3 (1988): 6–7.

———. *Ozbekiston Bayramlari.* Tashkent: Oqituvchi, 1991.

14. Music across the Kazakh Steppe

Michael Rouland

Song opened the doors of the world to you.
Song will see you off in earthly dust and mourning.
Song is the eternal companion of joy on earth.
So heed it keenly and value it, beloved.

—Abai Kunanbaev (1888)

Since independence in 1991, music has flourished in the everyday life of Kazakhs. With the combination of new commercial opportunities and the quest for a post-Soviet cultural identity, Kazakh music has occupied an essential place in the public sphere. Shifting from Soviet tautologies and engendering new patterns of self-discovery, music has remained the key medium of Kazakh national consciousness and self-expression. Kazakh society has broadly supported the undertaking to preserve traditional Kazakh music from the past and to support increased production of new music.

Although these efforts fill a vacuum left by the failed Soviet experiment, using music to frame identity is not a recent phenomenon. Music played a central role in the national and cultural formation of Kazakhs during the 1920s and 1930s, and it is natural that it has been rediscovered as a basis for post-Soviet identity. Kazakh music has expanded in two predominant directions. The first is traditional music grounded in history, art, and poetry. The second is popular music based on Soviet traditions, the world music scene, and new images of national identity. The result of this enthusiasm has brought Kazakh music to concerts on the world stage, expanded the number of local music festivals, and infused music into everyday life.

A KAZAKH CONCERT

In early 2005, two orchestras from Kazakhstan arrived in the United States and gave concerts at the Kennedy Center in Washington and Carn-

egie Hall in New York. Functioning as part of a diplomatic mission to celebrate a "long-time strategic partnership" between the United States and
Kazakhstan, these orchestras played the role of cultural ambassadors for
the Kazakh Embassy. This was the latest stop on a tour that included Tokyo,
Paris, Vienna, and London and exemplified Kazakhstan's mission to share
its culture and accomplishments with the world.

While such concerts are common on the international stage, this concert
had a different resonance for Kazakhs. Based on the Soviet festival tradition
of the "national arts," music has served as an ambassador for the Kazakh
nation throughout the twentieth century. This reflects the continuity of
Soviet-era policies in the post-Soviet political arena. While new diplomatic
realities have provided the opportunity to expand these festivals beyond the
Soviet sector to the global stage, the form has remained the same.

During this concert, "Melodies and Songs of the Kazakh Steppes,"
Kazakh music was offered in its two primary symphonic forms, classical
and folkloric. The classical style attested to Kazakh mastery of a globally
recognized musical genre, while the folkloric represented their cultural
and historical past. Led by the Kazakh State Chamber Orchestra, or "The
Academy of Soloists," the first half of the concert was dedicated to a classical
repertoire, including works from Brahms, Mozart, Tchaikovsky, and Grieg.
In addition to the European classical repertory, Tles Kazhgaliev's "Konzert-
stucke for Piano and Orchestra" was added to exhibit native classical compositions. This part of the concert concluded with Ivan Frolov's "Concert
Fantasy on Themes from Gershwin's 'Porgy and Bess'." The artistic director,
Aiman Musskhodzhaeva, who performed on a seventeenth-century Stradi-
varius violin purchased for her by the Kazakh government, provided the
solo highlights. Despite their efforts, the classical concert did not impress
American music critics. One reviewer noted that the concert included "so
many forgettable lollipops from the standard repertory."[1]

The critic's tone, however, changed in describing the second half of the
concert. Repeating clichés of the earlier Soviet press, the reviewer expressed
admiration for the folk concert. Knowledge of the Kazakh language was not
essential, the review argued, since "the language barrier didn't dull [the
musician's] message even slightly."[2] The contrast between rejecting the familiar musical language of the classical genre and celebrating the foreignness of the Kazakh folk genre was repeated in the Kazakh official discourse.
Ambassador-at-Large Duissen Kasseinov asserted, "It's unlikely we will
impress Americans with chamber music or with our chamber ensemble,
but they were really impressed and excited by the performance of our folk
musicians and folk orchestra."[3]

The Kazakh State Kurmangazy Orchestra, under the direction of Aitkali
Zhaimov, provided the music for the second half of the concert. It was clearly
more intriguing for an American audience eager for the exotic. Traditional
costumes in bright blue hues and elaborate designs along with unfamiliar

musical instruments provided a visual and musical experience that transported the audience to a different time and place. The music chosen for the folk concert offered diversity for the aural palette rather than a clearly articulated message. The folk music highlights included: "The Song about Beautiful Khusni and Khorlan," sung in baritone; "Freedom is My Call," played on *dombïra* (described below) with voice accompaniment; "Teasing Melody," rendered on dombïra; and "Nightingale," sung in soprano.

The printed literature that corresponded to the concerts underlined the entwining of music with everyday life. This view suggests that music offers a cultural repository, musicians possess vital social positions, and musical instruments have particular societal functions. From their nomadic past to their modern present, Kazakhs perceive music as their most refined artistic form and musicians as their philosophers. Indeed, Kazakh legend even argues that music was invented on the Syr-Darya River, which winds through southern Kazakhstan.

MUSIC IN EVERYDAY LIFE

Until the twentieth century Kazakhs had a largely nomadic society, in which their culture, religion, and political discourse were transmitted through music. And with the upheaval brought by Russian and Soviet conquest, music remained a vital link among Kazakhs. Looking back at the transformation of Kazakh music across the steppe, we see traditional cultural forms sustained despite the changing venues and contexts: from professional bards traveling the steppe to the emergence of stage performance, radio, and television. The importance of music has been so mythologized that contemporary popular belief asserts that Kazakhs traditionally greeted each other in song when encountering each other on the steppe.

Throughout Kazakh history, music has provided a repository of legends, politics, literary culture, and folklore and a cultural edifice for modern Kazakh identity. On a performative level, music offered the essential entertainment for community and family events. Conveyed in various forms, music accompanied dancing, storytelling, family gatherings, and community celebrations. Kazakh music was played by family and community members themselves or by professional bards invited for special occasions.

As the music shifted from narratives of myths and legends to modern expressions of national origins and innovative compositions, folklore continued to be vital to music. Even the origins of Kazakh instruments are expressed through musical narration. An early Turkic legend shared by Kazakhs relates the story of Korkït-ata, the composer, poet, and shaman, who was traditionally viewed as the creator of the *kobïz* instrument (described below) in the ninth century.[4] Kazakhs today understand him as the creator of modern music. According to the legend, Korkït was a young boy who was given his name, "the terrible one," as a result of the ominous storm that coincided with his birth as well as his ability to read the future. One night in his dreams, the legend details, an old man told him that he would die prematurely, and so he set out into the woods to escape death. But as he tried to flee he began to observe death everywhere. Overcome by this terror, he transferred his soul into the strings of the kobïz and traveled widely across the steppe.[5] The eerie human sound of the instrument combined with Korkït's ability to prophesy made the kobïz the prototype musical instrument for Kazakh shamans.[6] Popular legends such as this are inextricably linked with music in the Kazakh tradition. Whether offered as lullabies to children or learned as part of a wider cultural education, Kazakh music possesses an anthology of history, legends, and heroes. The Korkït legend is important to Kazakhs as they see themselves at the center of the origins of modern world music.

In addition to its significance in oral culture, music plays a central role at Kazakh social functions. When a guest is invited into the home, or friends gather for an evening, the dombïra is often brought out following the meal. Traditional and popular songs are sung collectively at the table, and revelry often passes late into the night. The younger generation, growing up after the Soviet era, listens to popular music on compact discs and the radio during their social gatherings. Significantly, popular musicians preserve a critical link between the generations by incorporating traditional song lyrics into newer musical genres. Whether through the acoustic influences of the Beatles or the recent trends of electronic and world music, professional Kazakh musicians influence the broader musical sensibilities of their generation.

Three celebrations, commemorating birth, marriage, and death, predominate in the life of Kazakhs. And musical performances take center stage in the banquets of these highly ritualized events within Kazakh communities. One of the most memorable scenes of Kazakh music in everyday life occurs during the wedding ceremony. For particularly lavish ceremonies, professional musicians are invited to perform for the guests, either in the traditional or modern style. In events without professional entertainers, the traditional songbooks are brought out and family members themselves participate in the musical incantations. In the traditional form, a singing competition between the bride and groom's retinue develops in the ritual. The focal songs, *"Zhar-zhar"* ("Loved One, Loved One"), *"Sïnsu"* ("Bride's Farewell"), and *"Betashar"* ("Unveiling of the Face") describe the ritual itself, which is a blend of folk, Islamic, and modern traditions.[7] While the styles and arrangements are relatively flexible for Kazakhs, it is essential that music highlights the celebration of life along the steppe.

KAZAKH INSTRUMENTS IN CONTEXT

The modern development of Kazakh music can be explained through the emergence of two predominant instruments and their divided social functions: the kobïz, a two-string bowed instrument similar to the violin or fiddle, and the dombïra, a two-string lute.[8] The kobïz belonged to the spiritual and healing power of shamans, while the dombïra emerged alongside the popularization of folk music among the nomadic Kazakhs.[9]

The kobïz is fashioned from one piece of wood (usually birch or mulberry) into a body, a neck, and a hollow basin. A piece of camel skin, often from the camel's throat, covers the lower basin of the instrument. Two strings made from camel or horse hair link a high bridge with the top of the instrument. Since there are no frets, fingers press the string against the neck in order to produce the particular notes or a variety of overtones along with the movement of a bow.[10] In this fashion, the sound of the kobïz resembles the human voice. Traditionally, the kobïz is played by itself, though it may occasionally be accompanied by vocal performances.

The kobïz has historically functioned as a sacred instrument that reportedly possessed special powers against evil spirits, disease, and death. It was the primary instrument utilized by Kazakh shamans. In Kazakh lore, ordinary Kazakhs feared even to touch the kobïz as it was viewed as a portal to the ancestral world and as a tangible link to their destiny. Kazakhs traditionally believed in the spiritual capacity of the instrument, and bestowing the instrument on a shaman was considered a great honor. According to Alma Kunanbaeva, a scholar of Kazakh music and folklore, "Kazakh musical instruments are an acoustical embodiment of the traditional 'three worlds' of the Kazakh shamanistic universe: upper, middle, and lower."[11] Their musical sounds and motifs represented the journey from birth to death and beyond, while the shaman could travel freely between these three worlds.

Legend has it that shamans developed the kobïz in order to preserve the sound made from the friction of two hunting bows. To emphasize the totemic quality of the instrument, they fashioned its handle in the form of horns or a bird's head. They also attached rattles to the instrument reflecting those worn on the shaman's own clothing and drums. Mirrors were sometimes placed in the basin of the instrument in order to reflect the participants of the ritual and thereby draw them into the power of Kazakh music.[12] During the nineteenth century, however, the musical-religious influence of the kobïz waned as the dombïra emerged as a secular instrument. By the early twentieth century, the extant kobïz instrumental pieces lacked the religious and magical characteristics traditionally associated with this instrument. With the creation of the Kazakh folk orchestra in the 1920s, the kobïz was used as the lone bowed instrument and was critical to arranging music on European symphonic models. The kobïz returned to prominence as a solo performance instrument, divorced from overt religious significance, during the 1980s.

The dombïra (*dombra* in Russian) is a stringed long-necked lute, tuned to a fourth (or sometimes fifth) with frets, often fashioned from pine or birch. The instrument is played using a middle finger strum, which contributes to its technical difficulty. Images of similar instruments have been found in the Buddhist Subashi Temple with Tocharian inscriptions (dated between the sixth and eighth centuries) as well as in the Kizil Caves, both in the Kuqa region of China. While only shamans could possess the kobïz, the dombïra was available to all Kazakhs. As a result, the demystification of music, along with the popularization of the dombïra during the nineteenth century, expanded the networks of Kazakh music beyond the control of religious and social elites. The dombïra essentially stimulated a musical revolution among Kazakhs. Experimentation, public performances, competitions, and diverse styles emerged to create a vibrant music scene. If you can imagine a nation whose primary artistic outlet was the guitar, a rich musical culture would not be surprising. A Kazakh proverb says that "a true Kazakh is not a Kazakh; a true Kazakh is a dombïra"; and it is still common today to find a dombïra in homes.

TRADITIONAL KAZAKH MUSICIANS

Although proficiency in music has traditionally been widely shared across the Kazakh population, certain exceptional musicians have always been revered for their performative talents, technical skill, and panache. The major professional musicians in traditional Kazakh music are the *zhïrshï* (epic storyteller) and *akïn* (bard). Through their voices, legends and values crossed the steppe and supported strong cultural bonds among Kazakhs by establishing a collective body of work. Due to the lack of written musical notation, musicians learned to play by hearing and repeating. They were therefore expected to have a good ear and auditory memory as well as a deep knowledge of traditional music.

The zhïrshï (sometimes *zhirau*) traditionally played the kobïz to accompany their songs. Their repertoire included heroic epics, philosophical reflections that ranged from comical to denunciatory, sermons, and panegyric odes to the glory of the khan or war hero. The success of the zhïrshï depended on their oratorical and improvisational skills as well as their knowledge of political affairs and legends. They would sing before battles in order to invoke the spirits of ancient warriors to help them to victory. Many were the official oral chroniclers for their clan or tribal group.[13] At the end of the seventeenth century, when Islam expanded its influence among the nomadic Kazakh populations, zhïrshï abandoned the kobïz for the dombïra. This change in instrumentation symbolized the shift from the predominance of shamanism to Islam in the oral culture of the Kazakhs. By the late eighteenth century, even epics lost their dominant place in Kazakh oral literature.

With the declining influence of the zhïrshï, the akïn emerged as the most significant figure in the history of Kazakh instrumental music. Akïns were less involved in political and military events than the zhïrshï and performed instead at important social events such as weddings, celebrations, and funerals. Akïns maintained traditions developed centuries earlier by traveling storytelling musicians, who gave dramatic recitations of verse tales and epic poems in the form of songs. The key event for the akïn was the *aitïs*, the music and poetry contest, which staged a performative duel between two akïns or amateur musicians in front of an audience of fellow musicians and other cultural elite.[14] It was usually held in association with large festivals including other competitions such as wrestling matches, horse races, and games. There were several types of aitïs: battles of the sexes, religious debates, riddle competitions, and duels of professional bards.[15] Only through success in numerous competitions against experienced akïns could a musician earn the title of akïn.[16]

In Kazakh society, respected musicians acted as mediators and *aksakals* ("white beards," or elders). Their ability to move across social boundaries, their relative freedom from tribal attachments, and their esteem within the community provided a unique opportunity to settle legal and property disputes. They effectively served as advisors to the political elite and khans. These roles only served to enhance the position of music within traditional Kazakh life. Today, while more modern institutions have replaced their legal and political functions, Kazakh musicians are widely respected as elders and cultural emissaries.

KAZAKH MUSIC IN THE TWENTIETH CENTURY

The most influential Kazakh musician at the end of the nineteenth was Abai Kunanbaev (1845–1904). He was born into a well-connected family and was given an Islamic education in a madrasa as well as a brief education in a Russian school in Semipalatinsk. He created lyrical songs in a style that infused Kazakh folk traditions with Russian song melodies.[17] In addition, he rendered Kazakh translations of Russian and European Romantic works. Abai personally sought to introduce European and Russian ideas into Kazakh culture, as well as to promote education and social reform. His song, *"Segiz aiak"* or "Eight Lines," from the 1890s, presents an example of his increasing social activism, exhorting the Kazakh people to improve themselves through self-education. Abai served as a link between the musical styles of the nineteenth and twentieth centuries.

While traditional musical life continued relatively uninterrupted until the 1930s, even with massive literacy campaigns and the development of a Kazakh literary culture, music remained at the center of the Soviet cultural transformation in Kazakhstan. Kazakh singers played an important role in establishing modern poetic verse in Kazakh as oral culture was translated to the written text and to the stage performance. Amid massive social changes, the ideology of socialism, and the radical imposition of a new economy, music continued to provide a stable cultural link to the traditional world that was being rapidly transformed.

Seeing the centrality and vitality of music, scholars and musicians embarked on a program of cultural exploration. Aleksandr Zataevich (1869–1936) led a massive campaign to collect and to classify Kazakh music; Akhmet Zhubanov (1906–1968) emerged as the primary music historian and created a Kazakh folk instrument orchestra; and Turmagambet Iztleuov (1882–1939) rendered folkloric sermons into the Kazakh literary language.

Official discourse on national music, particularly in Central Asia, stated the ideological aims for the music of Soviet nationalities: combating feudalism, promoting atheism, establishing national identities, and encouraging cultural development.[18] Yet there was an additional element of interest and enthusiasm that coincided with the official cultural policy. By the 1930s, the fusion of traditional dombïra instrumentalism and nineteenth-century Russian Romanticism made manifest the mantra of "national in form, socialist in content" in Kazakh music. Additionally, the official program of "building music culture" as part of socialist construction reached full force. Composers were expected to participate in the building of socialism with enthusiastic and triumphant melodies celebrating past victories, present optimism, and future glory. This enthusiasm resulted in a vibrant era of rediscovery of traditional Kazakh music. And several of the most respected Kazakh musicians in history worked during this time.[19] Ultimately, a Soviet stamp was imposed upon Kazakh music with the arrival of Evgenii Brusilovskii, who arrived in Alma-Ata (Almaty) in the early 1930s, ostensibly to help Kazakhs write their first operas.

Following the Second World War, Soviet music promoted the use of the Russian language, post-war patriotism, and the All-Union concept of "brotherly cooperation" that temporarily undermined local Kazakh efforts to explore and to expand traditional musical techniques. Increasingly, a kind of kitschified Kazakh music based on Russian Romanticism replaced folk traditions deep into the steppe. The learning of newly harmonized songs, popular in Kazakh musical theater, even erased folk performances that could be traced for centuries. Nevertheless, the official sanctioning of folk music, often replacing traditional lyrics with new ideological ones, celebrating universal and abstract themes such as world peace, still helped to preserve Kazakh music and to maintain its presence in everyday life.

An increasing sense of musical unity was emerging in Kazakhstan: whereas earlier musicians tended to remain in their native regions, by the 1960s musicians identified with Kazakhstan as a whole, and their music was shared more broadly.[20] In the early 1960s, musicians brought back the tradition of the aitïs, which had virtually disappeared under the influence of Soviet cultural norms, by combining competitions with official celebrations of political and celebrity anniversaries.

Alongside the official Soviet promotion of Kazakh folk music, the broader international popular music scene increasingly influenced Kazakh music in the 1960s and 1970s. In particular, a young group from Alma-Ata, Dos Mukasan, became popular in 1968, and their electric guitars and brash folk style drew comparisons with the Beatles.[21] They toured Europe and the Soviet Union and won a gold medal at the Berlin World Youth Festival in 1973. Despite their international appeal, Kazakh lyrics and traditional song standards remained at the core of their musical identity, as evidenced by their popular favorites "*Kudasha*," a song about love, and "*Toi zhyry*," a wedding song. In the late 1970s and 1980s, Roza Rymbaeva arrived on the Kazakh popular music scene with her strong voice and strident personality to expand the outreach of Kazakh music as a major Soviet pop artist.

During the same period, stars such as Ermek Serkebaev and composers such as Talghat Sarybaev and Tles Kazhgaliev continued to blend classical and folkloric musical genres for orchestra, opera, and ballet. In the second half of the twentieth century, the survival of Kazakh folk music depended on this link between tradition, the conservatory, and the national stage. Otherwise, artists preserved traditional texts by weaving Soviet political messages into folk songs. More recently, Edil Khuseinov's performance on the mouth harp has given him world renown as a "one-man orchestra," and even provided a source of inspiration for Yo-Yo Ma's *Silk Road Journeys*.

This process ultimately conditioned younger artists to blend international pop music genres with their recently resurrected folk music heritage. By the 1980s, cheap cassette tapes began to flood across the Soviet Union, and Russian, American, and European music inundated Kazakh youth culture. Alongside political independence, however, a more vibrant and popular local music scene emerged in Kazakhstan in the 1990s. More recently, Kazakh-language music has integrated folk styles and instrumentation with contemporary approaches to rock music as well as mixing and backbeats. Ruslan Kara and his group, Roksonaki, use an electric *shan-kobïz* along with jazz and rock elements to complement Kazakh folk songs. The groups Urker, a self-described "pop-folk" group, and Ulytau have rendered Kazakh traditional music attractive to the world music scene. Another strain of contemporary Kazakh popular music borrows from Russian and Kazakh musical styles as well as languages of performance. As a result, musicians Batyrkhan Shukenov, Tolkyn Zabirova, and

Iapurai

Zhaz bolsa, zharqyraghan kolding beti, ai,	With summer, the lake shore glittered,
Kogerip tolqyndaidy, iapurai, arghy sheti, ai.	Turning blue-green, Iapurai, the opposite shore rose in a wave,
Dirildep tolqyn basqan moldir betin, ai,	A vibrating wave transparent to the other side
Shaiqaidy zhas baladai, iapurai, zhelding lebi, ai.	Like a young child swaying to and fro, Iapurai, the wind's interjection.
Altyn bu aq kobikpen betin zhabar,	Gold steam and white foam cover the side,
Sudan bu kokke tonip, iapurai, marzhan taghar.	From water's steam the earth lunges, Iapurai, pearl attaches,
Esime aq erkemdi alghan kezde,	When I remember my beloved,
Aq marzhan zhylt-zhylt etip, iapurai, zherge tamar.	Glistening like a white pearl, Iapurai, my tears fell to earth.

Iapurai. *Istoriia kazakhskoi muzyki v 2-x tomakh,* vol. 1. Almaty: Ghylym, 2000: 66.

the Russo-Kazakh duet of Musicola evoke the bilingual identity and cultural compromise in modern Kazakhstan. Rakhat Turlykhanov's international pop-music style, on the other hand, evidences the ability to translate dance and ambient music into any language.[22]

THE MUSIC

Beyond heroic epics, love stories, and tales of musical origins, a great deal of Kazakh music depicts daily life. The innovation of the *kiii,* a purely instrumental piece lasting from one and a half to three minutes, shifted musicians from anonymous chroniclers of legends to original composers of music in the nineteenth century.[23] As a result, musicians introduced a diversity of themes that were conveyed solely through musical expression. An entire genre of Kazakh song arose to address the pastoral experience.

Strong regional characteristics reflected the simplicity, precision, liveliness, and *joie de vivre* of the music of the south alongside the tender and sincere lyrics, narratives, and epics of western Kazakhstan. While there was no unified Kazakh style, music rendered a rich complexity of emotions to portray the challenges of steppe life. Kazakh music was often performed with verve to contrast the open-air acoustic spaces and was always revered for its beauty and technique by audiences.

Lyrical songs about nature, such as *"Iapurai,"* paint poetic landscapes and evoke the experience of everyday life on the Kazakh steppe. Iapurai is an onomatopoetic word that expresses a wistful sorrow, conveying the sense that "those were the days." It is an elegiac song about lost love and youthful memories. The beauty of its music and the melancholy of its words are typical in Kazakh song. The lush images of Kazakh life are also characteristic in this song. Rather than the barren landscape of the empty steppe, a common image of the region by outsiders, the text evokes a glistening lake and the gentle crests of its waves. The distressing memory is transposed with summer abundance and relaxation.

Elegies were not only used to express pastoral beauty but also served a social function in daily life. Elegiac farewell songs were performed at various occasions, such as embarking on journeys and commemorating family members.[24] Drawing from this tradition, *"Elim-ai"* or "Oh, My Country," appeared as an early anthem for the Kazakhs. This celebrated historical song recalled the memory of Kazakhs driven from their ancestral lands and their plight before the twentieth century.[25] It is a song of regret, frustration, and displacement that challenges Kazakhs to hold onto their homeland. Today, this song remains a touchstone for Kazakhs. Always in the repertory of the folk orchestra, it inspires a strong sense of patriotism for the Kazakh audience. Despite the pessimism of its text and the memory of suffering, *"Elim-ai"* is perceived in proud terms, with the Kazakhs ultimately triumphing over their suffering.

COMPETITIONS AND FESTIVALS

Since the 1990s, there has been an explosion of interest in traditional and popular Kazakh music as well as an increasing diversity of styles. The Kazakh non-profit organization Asyl Mura, for example, has led recent efforts to preserve traditional music recordings and make them freely available on the Internet.[26] A more visible showcase for Kazakhs has been the proliferation of music competitions and festivals throughout Kazakhstan. These events bring together youth, amateurs, and professionals to compete in the oldest venue of Kazakh culture: the aitïs.

In these singing competitions between groups or individuals, music and lyrics are improvised, and the more dynamic improviser is declared the winner. Facets of daily life, well-known legends, polemical debates, or mock love duels provide the inspiration for lyrics.[27] In the instrumental version of the aitïs, the *tartïs*, perfection is achieved by transforming the musical moment into an eternity, holding long high notes, which creates a meditative and emotional connection with the audience. Employing this style, two musicians, sometimes a man and a woman, challenge each other's intellect, rhythmic skills, and performative panache through a competition of technique or a musical dialogue.[28]

Elim-ai!

Qarataudyng basynan kosh keledi, ei!	From the summit of Karatau, nomads stagger, oh!
Koshken saiyn bir tailaq bos keledi, Ei, elim-ai, elim-ai!	One empty foal for deserving nomads goes along, Oh, my country! My Country!
El-zhurtynan airylghan zhaman eken, ei!	Our people appear deprived and suffering, oh!
Qara kozden moltildep zhas keledi, ,Ei elim-ai, elim-ai!	Tears overflowing from black eyes, Oh, my country! My Country!
Myna zaman qai zaman? Baghy zaman, ei!	What is this time? Days of yore, oh!
Baiaghydai bolsaishy taghy zaman, Ei, elim-ai, elim-ai!	If it becomes again the time as before, Oh, my country! My Country!
Atadan ul, eneden qyz airyldy, ei!	Father's son, mother's daughter are dispossessed,
Kozding zhasyn kolghylyp aghyzamyn, Ei, elim-ai, elim-ai!	I let tears from my eyes form a lake, Oh, my country! My Country!
Myna zaman qai zaman? Qysqan zaman, ei!	What is this time? Time of suffering, oh!
Baqyt qusy alashtan ushqan zaman, Ei, elim-ai, elim-ai!	The bird of fortune flew away in Alash's time, Oh, my country! My Country!
Kok aspannan topyraq pen shang borady, ei!	Soil and dust blew in from the blue sky, oh!
Kuni suyq qantardan, qystan zhaman, Ei, elim-ai, elim-ai!	Colder than the days of January, poor winter encampment Oh, my country! My Country!
Qosh aman bol, Qaratau, atam olkem, ei!	Pleasant protection remains in Karatau, my father's province,
Tort tulik pen el eken zherding korki, Ei, elim-ai, elim-ai!	Four breeds and peoples appear in this beautiful land, Oh, my country! My Country!
Baq, bailyqpen dangqty alash uly, ei!	Orchards and riches are the glory of Alash's sons,
Qaisy zhurttyng bolar-au kelekesi, Ei, elim-ai, elim-ai!	Who will inherit this shelter? Oh, my country! My Country!
Qosh aman bol, Qaratau, el olkesi, ei!	Pleasant protection remains in Karatau, people's province,
Zherding keter el ausa berekesi, Ei, elim-ai, elim-ai!	If they leave this country, they will lose their prosperity, Oh, my country! My Country!

Khanzadadai, khanshadai osken ul-qyz, ei!	Offspring of the khan, daughters of the khan grew into sons and daughters!
Qaidan endi tabady berekesin, Ei, elim-ai, elim-ai!	From where can prosperity be found now? Oh, my country! My Country!

Elim-Ai (O, My Country!). *Qazaq anderining antologiiasy: eki tomdyq,* vol. 1 (*Khalyq anderi men khalyq kompozitorlarynyng anderi*) (Almaty: Oner, 1991): 14–15.

These competitions were tremendously common in the nineteenth century, although they varied in formality from major regional fairs to private interludes of an individual clan. In the twentieth century, however, aitïs became increasingly less common as Kazakh traditional life was affected by Sovietization. The major aitïs in 1913, 1927, and 1943 tended to coincide with major social upheavals and thus exuded a sense of normality in times of instability. Music culture in the 1990s signaled a return to the earlier aitïs tradition, now financed by local and national authorities. Cars were being given away to winners in the nearly weekly Almaty music competitions in 2005, as traditional music blended with postmodern commercialism.

International events such as the "Voice of Asia" (*Azia Dauysy*) Contest held annually in Almaty since 1991 have raised the profile of Kazakhstan as a world music capital. The format is similar to the European Music Festival in which national pride and musical styles are on display for the entire continent. While the move toward musical *estrada,* or Soviet-style vaudeville, reflects a generational shift in tastes, Kazakh music has shown itself to be resilient as well as experimental in its expression of national identity. In its function as a spiritual, social, artistic, and political medium, Kazakh music not only has demonstrated its historical significance but also has played a fundamental and persistent role in the daily life of Kazakhs.

Bekbolat Tleukhan, a Kazakh deputy and performer with the Kurmangazy Orchestra, maintains that music is for everyone. Walking through Kazakhstan today, you can hear this sentiment playing all around you. Music of the Central Asian "Madonna," Yulduz Usmanova, fills the cafes, streets, and markets. A rock beat from Ruslan Kara and Roksonaki offer Kazakhs a new modern identity with a new kind of poetry. New state projects seek to surpass the Soviet aesthetic for largesse. Huge folk ensembles, philharmonic orchestras, and the new President's Orchestra are celebrated as new symbols of national vitality. Music remains fixed at the core of Kazakh identity and everyday life.

NOTES

I would like to thank Natalie Rouland, Alma Kunanbaeva, Richard Stites, James Millward, and Izaly Zemtsovsky for their helpful comments and suggestions. An earlier version of these ideas was addressed in my dissertation, "Music and the Making of the Kazakh Nation, 1920–1936" (Ph.D. dissertation, Georgetown University, 2005): 109–154. Research was funded by the International Research and Exchanges Board and the American Council's ACTR/ACCELS program with funds provided by the National Endowment for the Humanities, the United States Information Agency, and the U.S. Department of State, which administers the Russian, Eurasian, and East European Research Program (Title VIII).

1. Andrew Lindemann Malone, "The Kazakh Steppes," *Washington Post* (3 February 2005): C10.

2. Andrew Lindemann Malone, "The Kazakh Steppes," *Washington Post* (3 February 2005): C10.

3. Nikola Krastev, "Kazakhstan: U.S. Gets Rare Opportunity to Hear Rare Kazakh Folk Music," *Radio Free Europe/Radio Liberty* (8 February 2005).

4. Edige Tursunov, *Istoki tiurskogo fol'klora: Korkyt* (Almaty: Daik, 2001); S. Aiazbekova, *Kartina mira etnosa: Korkyt-ata i filosofiia muzyki kazakhov* (Almaty, 1999); H. B. Paksoy, "Introduction to Dede Korkut" *Soviet Anthropology and Archeology* 1 (1990); Bisengali Gizatov, *Sotsial'no-esteticheskie osnovy kazakhskoi narodnoi instrumental'noi muzyki* (Alma-Ata: Nauka, 1989): 7–16 and V. Bartol'd. *"Eshche izvestie o Korkyte,"* *Sochineniia* 5 (1968).

5. Mukhtar Auezov and Leonid Sobolev, *Epos i fol'klor kazakhskogo naroda* (Alma-Ata, 1953): 228.

6. This contrasts with the drums and tambourines of Siberian shamanistic practices.

7. These songs are transcribed and texts given in Viktor Beliaev, *Central Asian Music: Essays in the History of the Music of the Peoples of the U.S.S.R.* (Middletown, CT: Wesleyan University Press, 1975): 54–57.

8. Bolat Sarybaev has argued that there were initially twenty-five Kazakh instruments but only the kobïz and dombïra remain significant today.

9. In addition to these instruments, the *sïbïzgï*, a reed flute, and the *komïz* (or *shan-kobïz*), a mouth harp or Jew's harp, also play a smaller role in Kazakh musical history. Still other Kazakh musical instruments are rarely played today. The *zhetïgen* is a seven-stringed instrument similar to the harp. The *daulpaz* is a percussive signaling instrument with a wooden base and leather cover used for hunting. The *dongïra* is a percussive instrument similar to a tambourine. The *kopïrau* is a set of bells attached to a wooden staff. The *asataiak* is a wooden staff-shaped percussive instrument with chimes attached. Lastly, the *saz sïrnai* is a three or four holed wind instrument fashioned from clay in the shape of a goose egg. From the fifteenth to eighteenth centuries, there is evidence of a Kazakh military orchestra that consisted of *surnais, karnais* (bass horns), and *daulpaz*. All of these instruments were found throughout Eurasia as a legacy of the interactions of the Silk Road and its Turkic and Mongolian heritage. In the Kazakh tradition, each of these instruments has a special history and each played a significant role in society. The kobïz and the dombïra, however, have emerged as the preeminent Kazakh instruments and have possessed the deepest cultural significance.

10. The kobïz is similar in sound and appearance to the Kyrgyz *kiak* and the Mongol *khur,* which are also capable of *glissando* (the rapid sliding along the musical scale), *vibrato* (the slight and rapid alteration of pitch), *harmonics* (affecting the

tone produced by vibrating a nodal point), and *legato* (the smooth transition between notes).

11. Alma Kunanbaeva, *The Soul of Kazakhstan* (New York: Easten Press, 2001).

12. See the discussion of shamanism: Marjorie Mandelstam Balzer, ed., *Shamanism: Soviet Studies of Traditional Religion in Siberia and Central Asia* (Armonk, New York: M. E. Sharpe, 1990).

13. Akhmet Zhubanov, "*Muzyka kazakhskogo naroda do Velikoi Oktiabr'skoi sotsialisticheskoi revoliutsiia*," in *Ocherki po istorii Kazakhskoi muzyki* (Alma-Ata: Kazakhskoe gosudarstvennoe izdatel'stvo khuzhestvennoi literatury, 1962): 10.

14. See N. Smirnova, ed., *Istoriia kazakhskoi literatury*, vol. 1 (Alma-Ata: Nauka, 1968): 324.

15. Kunanbaeva. The *tartïs* is an instrumental variation of the *aitïs* that has two styles: in the first, musicians take turns playing until they exhaust their repertoires; and in the second, one musician plays a küi while the other is expected to repeat the küi without error.

16. M. Auezov, "*Kazakhskii epos i dorevoliutsionny fol'klor*," in Leonid Sobolev, ed., *Pesni stepei: antologiia kazakhskoi literatury* (Moscow: Khudozhestvennaia literatura, 1940): 16.

17. Varvara Dernova, "Pesni Abaia," in *Muzykal'noe tvorchestvo Abaia* (Alma-Ata, 1954).

18. Theodore Levin, "Making Marxist-Leninist Music in Uzbekistan," in Regula Burchhardt Qureshi, ed., *Music and Marx: Ideas, Practice, Politics* (New York: Routledge, 2002): 190.

19. Dina Nurpeisova (1861–1955), Estai Berkimbaev (1868–1946), Kenen Azerbaev (1884–1976), Kosymzhan Babakov (1891–1954), Isa Baizakov (1900–1946), Manarbek Erzhanov (1900–1966), Garifulla Kurmangaliev (1909–1972), and Zhusupbek Elebekov (1904–1977). Recorded live performances from many of these musicians can be found on the Asyl Mura website (http://www.asylmura.kz/english/index.php).

20. *Istoriia kazakhskoi muzyki v 2-x tomakh*. Volume 1. (Almaty: Ghylym: 2000): 212–213.

21. Dosym Suleev, Murat Kusainov, Kamit Sanbaev, Sana (Aleksandr) Litvinov, who comprised the first band members, lent their names directly to the group.

22. Many of these groups have websites with free music to download.

23. The word *küi* signifies both instrumental and vocal music. This term originated in the fourteenth century, yet the instrumental style gained primacy over words only in the nineteenth century. Küi styles are named for the animal sounds they produce such as the swan (*aqqu*), the goose (*kaz*), the nightingale (*bul-bul*), and the camel (*nar*). Kurmangazy Sagirbaev (1806–1879) was the grand master of the küi. His notable works include, "*Serper*," or "The Gust," regarding his confinement and flight from prison in Orenburg; "*Sary Arka*," or "The Golden Steppe," lamenting his exiled wandering across the Kazakh steppe; "*Kishkentai*," or "Little," relating a nineteenth century Kazakh uprising; and "*Kobik Shashkan*," or "Raging Billows," mourning the tragic flooding of the Aral Sea. What is important about these instrumental works is that they formed a new canon of modern Kazakh music to complement the earlier epics.

24. *Koshtasu* means "to bid farewell."

25. *Qazaq anderining antologiiasy: eki tomdyq*. Volume 1 (*Khalyq anderi men khalyq kompozitorlarynyng anderi*) (Almaty: Oner, 1991): 14–15.

26. See http://www.asylmura.kz/english/index.php.

27. Thomas Winner, *The Oral Art and Literature of the Kazakhs of Russian Central Asia* (Durham, N.C.: Duke University Press, 1958): 29–34.

28. N. Gotovitskii, "*O kharaktere kirgizskikh pesen*," *Zapiski Turkestanskogo otdela obshchestva liubitelei estestvoznaniia, antropologiia i etnografiia*, vol. 1 (Tashkent, 1879).

PART FIVE

Nation, State, and Society in the Everyday

Popular and scholarly conceptions of the everyday direct us towards the personal, the private, the mundane. Broader and larger concepts and institutions nonetheless intervene in almost all aspects of daily life. As across much of the world, nation and state have emerged as two of the most important structures in modern Central Asia. Both evolved from a complex interplay of local traditions and international innovations. Central Asian intellectuals began to imagine national communities in the late nineteenth century as a result of contacts with philosophies and practices across Europe and Asia. Moscow imposed a highly invasive model of the modern state on the region. Both legacies permeate Central Asia today. Ordinary citizens at once support, accommodate, and resist policies, initiatives, and identities imposed by national and state agents. The divide between public and private, the extraordinary and the everyday, emerges as extremely blurred in the contributions that follow.

Before the arrival of tsarist troops, the peoples of Central Asia identified themselves with their religion, kin group, neighborhood, or village. Such affiliations confused Western observers, who sought to apply nineteenth-century models of European nationality, based on a common language, culture, and broader territory. Clusters of Central Asian intellectuals, many of whom became known as *Jadids*, or "new-method thinkers," saw European nationhood as a source of strength for a region that had been so easily conquered. Jadids sought to blend Western-style education, knowledge, and philosophies with local practices and reformist ideas circulating across Asian and Islamic regions in the late nineteenth century. As Shoshana Keller and Victoria Clement show, Jadids sought radical changes in everyday life, from the way people communicated to the way they educated their children and considered themselves part of the wider world. Jadids remained a small minority, however, distrusted by imperial authorities and condemned as impetuous youth by Islamic religious leaders.

Opportunities for modernist Central Asian thinkers came with the Bolshevik Revolution of 1917. Russian socialists shared Jadid dreams of creating "modern" citizens in Central Asia. The state became a tool for the transformation of local societies and cultures. Bolsheviks, Jadids, and other local representatives planned to introduce national identities to supercede other forms of affiliation considered backward. Investigations of regional languages, customs, and economies led to official recognition of the five nations—Kazakh, Kyrgyz, Tajik, Turkmen, and Uzbek—that have become the basis of today's nation-states. The national delimitation of the 1920s, as previous authors have noted, was a confused and complicated process. Madeleine Reeves discusses how the assignment of national affiliations and, particularly, the drawing of boundaries, has had a profound impact on everyday lives for people in mixed border regions, especially now that these nation-states have gained independence and consider border posts and visa regimes essential symbols of state sovereignty and control. Although recent research has challenged views that national delimitation was a simple "divide-and-rule" strategy imposed by central Bolsheviks, Central Asians became acutely aware in the 1930s of the extent to which Moscow sought to direct changes in their everyday lives. Marianne Kamp and Douglas Northrop have, in previous articles, discussed the effects of policies designed in the center not only to direct economic development and crush dissent, but also to alter traditional culture, religion, and gender roles. Clement and Keller report other changes beginning in the 1930s that showed the increasing desire of Bolshevik planners to draw Central Asian nations into a Russian, and Russified, orbit. Millions of Russians came to the region to direct economic and social transformations. Central planners demanded all national languages, only recently changed from the Arabic to a Latin script considered more simple and modern, now be written in Cyrillic, as was Russian. Jadids and other intellectuals who had worked to design national cultures suffered in the great purges, making way for a new generation of local Communist elites considered more loyal to Moscow. As Keller notes, Moscow's influence after the 1930s filtered down to the everyday level of school textbooks, as Uzbek students were taught a national history and culture whose myths and values closely paralleled those of Russia. After many fits and starts, education in Soviet Central Asia—from academics to sports—grew to have more in common with European models than the Islamic practices that had dominated the region in previous eras.

After World War II, when the Soviet Union began to pump more resources into Central Asia, residents started to see benefits of the Communist state in their daily lives. Along with universal education came housing, medical care, employment, vacations, and other social benefits.

Women gained increased opportunities in public life; the Soviet-reared family that Reeves describes at the beginning of her article seems like the realization of gender roles envisioned by the writers of the 1930s journal *Bright Life* discussed in the essay by Marianne Kamp. As Kelly McMann argues, the "nanny state" was far more important in the everyday fabric of Central Asia than Communist engines of repression. Favorable views of the Soviet state's role in everyday life that McMann documents in her extensive survey data seem to show that Central Asians do not take into account Communist legacies that have led to current difficulties in the newly independent countries. Keller argues that former Communist Central Asian officials, many of whom are still in power today, used the Soviet state to engage in massive graft and corruption schemes. Efforts to compete for resources from Moscow encouraged regional and "clan-based" networks that undermined loyalties to nation as well as state. Moreover, with few exceptions, the central government placed its most advanced industries in the western USSR, leaving Central Asian regions to develop agricultural and primary goods. The Soviet system collapsed before it became clear that economic planning was insufficient and social spending unsustainable given the growing population of Central Asia. Such legacies plague Central Asian states and affect the everyday lives of their peoples today, as we see in articles throughout the volume.

One aspect of Soviet rule that did evoke protests in the 1980s was continued Russian dominance. An unanticipated aspect of the largely successful attempt to implant national identities was a growing demand across Central Asia for greater rights and privileges to be given to the "titular" national groups. As Clement demonstrates, Turkmen in the Turkmen Soviet Socialist Republic sought to have their language, instead of Russian, privileged in official circles. A sense of national belonging and privilege, as McMann shows, continues today. Being a member of the titular nationality is the strongest indicator as to whether Central Asians feel that current, post-Soviet states meet their daily needs.

The stress of the post-Soviet transformation has nonetheless meant that even members of the titular nationality consider the Moscow-directed "nanny state" of the past superior to the current situation. Current governments, ostensibly in the name of giving greater freedom to citizens and the market, have retreated, to varying degrees, from social and cultural spheres. All of the authors discuss how contemporary state policies and priorities have complicated the lives of ordinary citizens. Keller writes about families desperately searching for effective teachers, whose dreadfully low salaries parents must supplement; Clement discusses an elder Turkmen woman now made virtually illiterate by state policies to shift Turkmen from a Latin to Cyrillic script; McMann highlights a Kazakh man who, despite successfully making a living as an independent farmer, regrets the loss of social services, from subsidized daycare to free concerts; and Reeves travels across the

Uzbek, Kyrgyz, and Tajik borders with a local friend whose journey to see family, once a simple car or bus ride is transformed into a harrowing expedition involving deception and multiple bribes. Uncertainty has replaced the sense of security and stability that Central Asians felt in their everyday lives in the late Soviet period.

The contemporary emphasis on national origins and the changing role of the state has nonetheless created opportunities for many. We read in this section about those who have used national affiliation, linguistic and technical skills, as well as entrepreneurship to find paths to success in the post-Soviet world. Central Asian citizens have opportunities for study, travel, and work abroad that were all but forbidden in the Soviet era. These individual success stories, however, come tinged with troubles for contemporary states and societies. McMann's successful farmer notes the growing problem of inequality between rich and poor. Keller finds that well-educated, privileged students are seeking opportunities not in their own lands, but in Europe or North America. A growing sense of distance and frustration seems to characterize individuals' everyday negotiations with the state. Random acts of personal kindness and informal exchanges, as Reeves notes, as well as reliance on family or other group networks, perhaps give a sense of community to society, but only as it attempts to replace or deceive a state perceived as absent or harmful to the rhythms and practices of daily life. Leaders of the post-Soviet Central Asian states use their own patronage networks to stay in power, to various degrees sanctioning, tacitly if not openly, any number of schemes to simultaneously extract revenues and squelch opposition from their citizens. As the post-Soviet states have retreated from offering services to society, so is society retreating from offering allegiance to its sovereign entities, attested to by a 2005 revolution in Kyrgyzstan and increased popular unrest in Uzbekistan.

15. The Shrinking of the Welfare State: Central Asians' Assessments of Soviet and Post-Soviet Governance

Kelly M. McMann

A farmer in Kazakhstan summed up life before and after the collapse of the Soviet Union as follows: "We are freer now. Before the KGB monitored with whom we spoke. Freedom is freedom, but people need to live and we have not reached a good level yet."[1] The farmer's comment suggests that the political liberties many people of the former Soviet Union have acquired do not compensate for the greater economic hardships they now face. New governments have emerged from the Soviet state and introduced political and economic changes; however, these new governments have not necessarily improved everyday life. As a result, citizens consider their current governments inferior to the Soviet one. This might come as a surprise to outsiders, who remember the Soviet state foremost as an oppressive government.

It is particularly interesting that Central Asians view Soviet rule in a relatively positive light. One might expect that they would remember the Soviet era unfavorably because ethnic Russians and other Slavs, not the local peoples, held the most powerful positions in the Central Asian republics. One might also anticipate that Central Asians would harshly judge the Soviet government for damaging the region's environment. By trying to make deserts into cotton fields, the Soviet regime contributed to the desiccation of the Aral Sea, the salinization of the drinking water, and the resulting increases in typhoid and hepatitis, particularly in Uzbekistan and Turkmenistan. In Kazakhstan a legacy of forty years of nuclear testing continues to threaten human and animal life.[2]

Why do Central Asians consider their current governments inadequate relative to the Soviet one? To explore this question, I first examine the role of the Soviet state in citizens' everyday lives. By everyday lives I mean "those most repeated actions, those most traveled journeys, those most inhabited spaces that make up, literally, the day to day."[3] I then describe how current governments have withdrawn from citizens' lives and the problems that have ensued for two residents of contemporary Kazakhstan, the farmer introduced above and a scientist from a large city. These accounts represent two of the 101 in-depth interviews I conducted in rural and urban Kazakhstan in the summer of 2001. Using survey data I ask to what extent are these two individuals' perceptions of declining state responsiveness common throughout Kazakhstan, as well as neighboring Kyrgyzstan and Uzbekistan. In each country, colleagues and I surveyed a random sample of 1,500 adults in late 2003. A detailed description of the field and survey research appears in the appendix. I conclude by examining the impact of my findings on the study of everyday life and prospects for improved governance in Central Asia.

THE SOVIET STATE IN EVERYDAY LIFE

Whereas Westerners recall how the Soviet government deviated from their own democratic ones, Central Asians remember the role that the Soviet state played not in their political but in their everyday lives. Over the years Westerners have portrayed the Soviet government primarily as a repressive regime that restricted freedom of speech, the practice of religion, free movement, and the expression of ethnic identity. During the Cold War the term "evil empire" became part of American political rhetoric. In the late Soviet era, during Mikhail Gorbachev's policy of *glasnost*, Western media reported on revelations about the Stalinist purges. Today professors continue to introduce their students to the totalitarian model, which attributed to the Soviet Union a "terroristic" police and communications monopoly, among other features. Because the horrors of Soviet rule, such as political imprisonments and executions, directly touched only a portion of the population, few Central Asians consider the Soviet Union an "evil empire."

Instead, Central Asians remember the Soviet "nanny state" that met essential needs. Led by the Communist Party, the state provided extensive social services to the population. The system was far from perfect; there were shortages of some goods and many consumer products were of poor quality. Nonetheless, Soviet citizens could expect basic cradle to grave support. With the birth of a child, families received supplemental income. The state then provided free, or highly subsidized, day care, education, and recreation for the child, and upon graduation the child, now an adult, received a job assignment from the state. Through this state job, the individual not only earned income, but also acquired housing, received health care, took part in vacations, and had access to credit for consumer purchases.

CONTEMPORARY STATES IN EVERYDAY LIFE

Sit down today with a Central Asian at his or her kitchen table and the conversation quickly turns to how the new government does not address the problems that the Soviet state used to resolve. Or, more abstractly, people complain about the reduced role of the state in their lives.

Post-Soviet states provide few, if any, of the benefits the Soviet state did. Post-Soviet governments that have undertaken market reforms have intentionally reduced the role of the state in the economy. Typically these states provide free elementary and secondary education but few of the other services. The state no longer serves as the primary employer, landlord, health care provider, entertainer, and banker, having devolved these roles to private entities. Post-Soviet governments that have not pursued market reform, as well as many of those which have, have reduced state services because of shortages of funds. With the demise of the Soviet Union, many newly independent countries lost subsidies from Moscow and had difficulty producing goods for export to world markets. As a result, government coffers quickly became depleted. Frustration over the reduced role of the state is common among men and women, in villages and in cities. However, rural residents and urban dwellers face different problems, as the following stories of Almaz and Anara depict.[4]

ALMAZ, A FARMER

Living in a village in southern Kazakhstan, Almaz was in his mid-seventies at the time of the interview. Like most rural residents of the former Soviet Union, Almaz had worked since he was a young man on a *sovkhoz*, a farm controlled by the state. Because the newly independent government of Kazakhstan stopped supporting the sovkhoz, Almaz's standard of living and economic security have declined precipitously. The governments that emerged from the Soviet Union have tended to close or privatize these farms or allow them to go under. As a result many people have lost their jobs and many services are no longer available.

The sovkhoz where Almaz worked was founded in the mid-1930s and focused primarily on breeding livestock. The Soviet state provided all the inputs for the sovkhoz, including fuel, fodder, and vaccinations, and purchased its products. The disintegration of the Soviet Union made it more difficult to obtain the many inputs that came from other former republics. The economies of Soviet regions were highly specialized so that often it was possible to obtain a good from only one location. Independence for the fifteen Soviet republics introduced new borders, currencies, and paperwork, hampering the movement of goods. These new obstacles to trade also made it difficult for the sovkhoz to sell the livestock it bred to buyers in other former republics. Sales further decreased because guaranteed state purchases evaporated. Moreover, the sovkhoz had to cope with an end to state subsidies—a result of the government's plan to move to a market economy and reaction to the general economic crisis facing the country. In the burgeoning market economy, the sovkhoz faced the added challenge of paying freed, skyrocketing prices for energy. Eventually the government disbanded the state farm by auctioning it off to the workers. Yet, the farm had little value, as equipment and animals were dispersed to pay off debts for fodder, fuel, and salaries. Most employees who received animals in lieu of salary sold the livestock in order to meet immediate financial needs.

The obvious impact of the demise of the sovkhoz, the main employer in the village, was that most people lost their jobs. This was a severe shock to people as the Soviet state had guaranteed employment for citizens, finding them jobs and rarely firing them. The sovkhoz, where Almaz had worked as a livestock tender and then an accountant, once employed 780 individuals. The new collective farm has only eleven employees.

Almaz left the sovkhoz in 1998 because he, like many workers, was not receiving his salary. But unlike most former employees who today work odd jobs and practice subsistence farming, Almaz has managed to develop a commercial wheat farm that supports him and his wife and his three children's families. He received a tractor from the state farm in lieu of his salary, and he has used his pension and savings to rent land from the collective and purchase inputs.

Almaz's relative financial success highlights another significant change in people's lives—increasing socioeconomic inequality. Whereas the Soviet state minimized wage differentials and controlled access to luxury goods, the new government of Kazakhstan has adopted market principles that have resulted in significant inequalities in standard of living. As Almaz noted, "Before, 99 percent lived equally; now some people are millionaires while others cannot stand on their feet . . . All five fingers are the same but they all live differently." Due in part to this growing inequality, resentful villagers have accused Almaz of using his former position at the sovkhoz to his advantage in building his business.

Almaz has lost the economic security he had been accustomed to for the previous seven decades, and his relations with some villagers have deteriorated. Although he and his family are better off than many in the village, they have, nonetheless, also witnessed a steep decline in their standard of living. Quality of life has worsened because the sovkhoz and village government no longer provide services to the community. Drawing the edge of his hand across his forehead to indicate abundance, Almaz said, "We lived well in the sovkhoz," but today "everything is ruined here." In the Soviet era, the state funded the village school and hospital, and profits from the sovkhoz went to other services, such as free home repairs, subsidized day care, and a village club that housed a library and offered free concerts. The sovkhoz sent young residents to study in the republican capital Almaty, paying for their education and hiring them when they completed their studies. The farm also contributed to the costs of residents' gas and water and subsidized villagers' vacations.

Today, the village offers few services and those it does provide are expensive. Primary education is no longer free. While the government continues to pay the salaries of teachers at the village school, parents pay for textbooks, provide coal for heating, and contribute building materials for renovations. The hospital now charges for all services and can no longer care for patients overnight or transport them by ambulance. Moreover, patients must obtain all medicines on their own. Almaz reflected on coping with discontinued medical services: "Now when my head hurts I know what medicine to take here at home. If it hurts badly, I go to [the county seat]. Before I would call the doctor and he would come to my house . . . I tell my family, my grandchildren, 'Try not to get sick, try not to get a cold.' "

The collective farm does not offer services as the sovkhoz once did. The daycare center closed, and the village club is now a private disco that charges admission. The farm cannot afford to send youth to study or guarantee them employment once they have graduated. Almaz's grandson has to work as bank guard in Almaty and study through an evening program, even though his family is one of the wealthiest in the village. Private firms provide electricity and gas at higher rates. Furthermore, the gas company has turned off the gas to the entire village because some people have not paid and it is not profitable to supply gas to only some residents. With the economic deterioration in the village, all but one of the stores closed.

ANARA, A SCIENTIST

Like Almaz, Anara, a fifty-nine-year-old widow living in a northern city with her daughter, has faced greater economic uncertainty and declining state services since Kazakhstan became independent. As an urban resident, however, Anara has more possibilities for earning income and has a wider selection of goods and services. As her daughter clarified, "Everything is in stores. Now the problem is money." While urban residents no longer face Soviet-era deficits in goods, they do have difficulty earning sufficient income. In cities, unlike in villages, jobs are available, but finding high-paying, stable work in one's field of expertise is difficult.

Anara had a career as a chemist until she retired in 1997. Late in her career she and her fellow scientists began to use their laboratory's technical equipment for commercial barter. In collaboration with a metallurgical plant, they developed inputs for Chinese firms in return for consumer goods. Anara obtained clothing, a television, and a videocassette recorder through these transactions. Anara and her colleagues' involvement in the market was not unusual, as declining salaries for scientists forced many of them into trade. This group of researchers was fortunate to be able to profit from its scientific knowledge. Many intellectuals have had to completely abandon their laboratories and books for the daily grind of selling macaroni and slippers in the local bazaars.

As a pensioner, Anara has also experienced economic insecurities. Delayed and unpaid pensions have been a problem throughout Central Asia and most of the former Soviet Union. In Kazakhstan, the promise of substantial pensions in a declining economy encouraged many people to retire early. At the same time, newly privatized companies concerned with their bottom lines failed to contribute to the pension system, and local officials used pension funds to pay other social benefits.[5] Prior to the government's reform of the pension system in the mid-1990s, people often waited three months for their pensions. This was quite a shock to citizens, who remembered their parents' steady and relatively generous retirement benefits. Today Anara nearly always receives her pension on time or, at worst, one month late; nonetheless, her retirement funds do not go far. She receives 8,000 *tenge* per month and uses all but 2,000 of it to pay utilities for her apartment.[6]

For urban residents the end of free and subsidized utilities is a daily reminder of the reduction in state services. Utilities are no longer guaranteed but depend on a person's ability to pay for-profit companies for service. Fearing that they would not be able to pay their bills, Anara's neighbors began to refuse to let the electric companies' representatives into their apartment, forcing the firm to move its meters to the hallways. Anara recounted how the electric company has confiscated personal property and cut wires to apartments of residents who have not paid. Anara and her daughter do not fear having the wires to their apartment cut. As her daughter explained, she and her mother have made utilities a high priority, outranking other items, such as certain foods. "We just decide to pay the bills on time. Then no apples or no oranges."

In Kazakhstan, as in much of the former Soviet Union, the state has also withdrawn from the landlord business. In the Soviet era, urban residents received housing from the state based largely on their position in the workforce, and the state was responsible for repairs. Kazakhstan privatized apartments, so today Anara owns and maintains hers. She no longer receives free government maintenance but must make repairs herself or pay the government or a private firm to do so. She has opted for a maintenance contract, costing 326 tenge a month, from the communal services committee, which is run by the government.

Anara could not afford utilities and repairs to her apartment, not to mention food and clothes, were it not for her daughter's salary. Her daughter, in her twenties, works as an English-language instructor at a private language institute. Unlike government organizations, the institute pays its instructors on time and also provides pay advances when needed. As an urban resident Anara's daughter had the option of studying English and finding work as a language instructor. Other lucrative career options in the fields of law and business are also more readily available in the cities than the countryside.

Despite these benefits of urban living, Anara and her daughter still struggle economically. They earn enough for food, clothes, and utilities, but they cannot buy extras, such as new, warmer winter coats. They also have not been able to save money. There are unexpected expenses, like medicine for Anara's mother, and they have lost money in banks, causing them to abandon such institutions. Instead, Anara has invested money in a private financial venture, which sounds suspiciously like a pyramid scheme. She sells certificates to friends and acquaintances, and after selling a certain number she will supposedly receive more back than she contributed. She has confidence in the program because a friend already received money. As the state has reduced its monopoly over banking functions, citizens of Kazakhstan have increasingly faced challenges in trying to save and invest money.

GOVERNMENT RESPONSIVENESS: THEN AND NOW

The stories of Almaz and Anara illustrate how contemporary governments play a smaller role in everyday life than the Soviet government did. As a result of this withdrawal of the state, residents of Kazakhstan, as well as Kyrgyzstan and Uzbekistan, consider their current governments less responsive than the Soviet state.

In each of the countries, our study asked 1,500 adult respondents to react to the statements "The Soviet government responded to citizens' needs" and "The [current] government responds to citizens' needs." Across the three countries a considerably larger percentage of people agreed with the statement about the Soviet government than with the statement about the current government. And, conversely, a substantially larger percentage of respondents disagreed with the statement about the current government than with the statement about the Soviet government.

Although considerably fewer respondents in each country assess their current government as responsive relative to the Soviet state, there is variation across the three countries. Of the three groups of respondents, residents of Uzbekistan are most positive about the current period. This is likely due to the government's attempt to maintain extensive welfare services, reminiscent of the Soviet era. For example, mothers continue to receive payments for the birth and care of their infants. However, state subsidies are sometimes delayed and the number of recipients and level of benefits have

Table 15.1. Country Differences

The government responds to citizens' needs.
(percentage of respondents; 1,500 per country)

	Kazakhstan		Kyrgyzstan		Uzbekistan	
	Soviet	Current	Soviet	Current	Soviet	Current
Strongly Agree/ Agree	49.7	9.1	70.3	16.9	48.1	28.1
Somewhat Agree/ Somewhat Disagree	32.7	36.7	16.7	33.7	22.1	28.9
Disagree/Strongly Disagree	9.9	47.6	6.3	42.9	6.9	28.5
Difficult to Answer	6.6	5.7	6.3	6.3	21.4	13.9
Decline to Answer	1.0	.9	.5	.2	1.5	.7
TOTAL (percentage rounded)	100	100	100	100	100	100

declined over time. The fact that Uzbekistan has fewer ethnic minorities might also increase the percentage of people evaluating their government positively: as this chapter later suggests, titular groups find their government more responsive than ethnic minorities do. It is less likely that the lack of a public discourse about declining standards of living inflates the percentage of positive responses. Uzbekistan's more authoritarian system does make public criticism of the government riskier, yet officials are open to complaints about everyday life. Also, people discuss economic difficulties with friends and family, and these conversations prime people for assessing government responsiveness across eras.[7]

Compared to people in Uzbekistan, fewer residents of Kazakhstan and Kyrgyzstan believe their current governments measure up to the Soviet regime. This difference likely reflects more extensive market reforms, including the dismantling and privatization of state services, in Kazakhstan in Kyrgyzstan. Governments of both countries have also reduced services in reaction to fiscal constraints. As a forty-year-old woman in a village in Kazakhstan explained, "The state has distanced itself . . . we live on our own strengths, no one else's . . ." The larger percentages of ethnic minorities in these countries might also account for the difference.

Surprisingly, within each country unemployed people, women, and rural residents are generally not more negative about the current government than employed people, men, and urban dwellers. (See table 15.2.) We would expect that a higher percentage of people who lack employment and face the challenge of finding a job would assess their current government negatively relative to the Soviet one, which provided an employment guarantee. Yet in Kazakhstan there is almost no difference between the assessments of the unemployed and employed; in Kyrgyzstan and Uzbekistan the differences are relatively small.

Women have suffered the brunt of economic decline and reforms. They have had to cope with reduced maternity and children's benefits and shuttered child care centers. They are also typically the first to be laid off because, despite decades of Soviet ideology about gender equality, they are viewed as less productive because of their responsibilities to their families, and their breadwinning is seen as secondary to men's. Having lost their jobs, many have had to work in the local bazaars, reselling products they have purchased from others. Yet, women's assessment of the state in each country differs little from men's. For many women, their experience as entrepreneurs has given them a sense of satisfaction. One middle-aged woman in a city in Kazakhstan began trading in dry goods in 1992 while continuing to work as an engineer. She used the profits from her business to purchase a home for her family. She recounted, "At work I told people I bought a home, and I just cried . . . I earned money slowly, but it was honest money."

With fewer job opportunities available in villages, we would expect rural residents to feel that the government has done less to respond to their needs. Yet in Kyrgyzstan and Uzbekistan, rural residents are slightly more likely to evaluate the state as being more responsive. In Kazakhstan rural and urban dwellers differ little in their assessments of the state.

The difference in urban-rural assessments in Kyrgyzstan and Uzbekistan versus Kazakhstan might reflect ethnicity patterns. In Kyrgyzstan and Uzbekistan rural residents are more likely titular peoples, with minorities residing mainly in cities; whereas in Kazakhstan ethnic minorities are common in the countryside and outnumber Kazakhs in urban areas.

Ethnic identity, in fact, has a significant influence on people's assessment of state responsiveness. Across the three countries, it is not unemployed people, women, or rural residents who are most negative about the state. Instead, members of the non-titular ethnicities are the demographic group that finds it least responsive. Whereas 51.0 percent of non-Kazakhs disagree or strongly disagree with the statement that the state responds to citizens' needs, only 43.8 percent of Kazakhs disagree. Opinions diverge even more in other countries, with 50.9 and 37.7 percent for non-Kyrgyz and Kyrgyz and 36.9 and 26.4 percent for non-Uzbeks and Uzbeks. (See table 15.3.)

Minority groups in each country are likely more negative about the current governments because they do not view sovereignty as a benefit. With the independence of the Central Asian republics, Russians and other

Table 15.2. Demographic Differences

The government responds to citizens' needs.
(percentage of respondents; 1,500 per country)

	Kazakhstan		Kyrgyzstan		Uzbekistan	
	Unemployed	Employed	Unemployed	Employed	Unemployed	Employed
Strongly Agree/Agree	7.0	9.0	16.8	15.3	26.4	28.9
Somewhat Agree/Somewhat Disagree	37.1	38.4	37.8	34.0	26.0	29.5
Disagree/Strongly Disagree	50.3	46.6	38.3	44.9	36.0	28.1
Difficult to Answer	5.2	5.7	6.6	5.6	11.6	12.8
Decline to Answer	.3	.3	.5	.2	0	.7
TOTAL (percentage rounded)	100	100	100	100	100	100
TOTAL (number)	286*	633	392*	483	250*	688

	Kazakhstan		Kyrgyzstan		Uzbekistan	
	Female	Male	Female	Male	Female	Male
Strongly Agree/Agree	9.6	8.4	15.1	19.2	26.3	30.1
Somewhat Agree/Somewhat Disagree	38.0	35.1	35.7	31.3	29.4	28.3
Disagree/Strongly Disagree	46.0	49.6	43.1	42.5	27.8	29.3

	Kazakhstan		Kyrgyzstan		Uzbekistan	
	Rural	Urban	Rural	Urban	Rural	Urban
Difficult to Answer	5.4	6.2	6.0	6.6	15.4	12.1
Decline to Answer	1.0	.7	0	.4	1.1	.3
TOTAL (percentage rounded)	100	100	100	100	100	100
TOTAL (number)	820	680	832	668	803	697

	Kazakhstan		Kyrgyzstan		Uzbekistan	
	Rural	Urban	Rural	Urban	Rural	Urban
Strongly Agree / Agree	10.1	8.0	18.8	13.3	31.3	22.3
Somewhat Agree / Somewhat Disagree	32.8	40.5	33.7	33.7	25.9	34.1
Disagree / Strongly Disagree	48.9	46.3	40.2	48.0	26.6	31.7
Difficult to Answer	6.9	4.6	7.0	4.9	15.6	10.9
Decline to Answer	1.2	.5	.3	0	.6	.9
TOTAL (percentage rounded)	100	100	100	100	100	100
TOTAL (number)	740	760	990	510	958	542

* Unemployed refers to those people who are currently out of work and are looking for jobs. People who are unemployed for other reasons, such as retirement, illness, education, or child care, are not included in either category.

Table 15.3. Ethnic Differences

The government responds to citizens' needs.
(percentage of respondents; 1,500 per country)

	Kazakhstan		Kyrgyzstan		Uzbekistan	
	Kazakhs	Others	Kyrgyz	Others	Uzbeks	Others
Strongly Agree/ Agree	10.1	8.1	21.4	10.0	29.0	24.1
Somewhat Agree/ Somewhat Disagree	39.0	34.6	34.4	32.7	28.6	29.8
Disagree/Strongly Disagree	43.8	51.0	37.7	50.9	26.4	36.9
Difficult to Answer	5.9	5.6	6.3	6.3	15.3	8.1
Decline to Answer	1.1	.6	.2	.2	.7	1.0
TOTAL (percentage rounded)	100	100	100	100	100	100
TOTAL (number)	712	788	924	576	1205	295

Slavic peoples lost their privileged standing in these societies. Prior to the Soviet period, Russians moved to Central Asia seeking land and jobs building the railroad and mining natural resources. The Soviet government sent Russians and other Slavs to serve in government and industrial management positions. Other groups, Uzbeks in Kyrgyzstan and Tajiks in Uzbekistan, became minorities in these countries because of the borders drawn by Soviet planners. With the demise of the Soviet Union, titular groups grew dominant in the governments and began to introduce policies and informal practices to advantage their own countrymen. As a result, ethnic minorities have found it more difficult to live in these countries. Whereas enthusiasm for sovereignty dampens titular groups' frustration with their current government, it does not reduce minorities' irritation; in fact, it most likely contributes to it.

PROSPECTS FOR GOVERNANCE

With the demise of the Soviet welfare system, citizens of Central Asia and other post-Soviet states have had to take additional responsibility for their lives. The state no longer supports one from cradle to grave. This is especially true in market-oriented countries where individual responsibility is part of the new ideology.

These changes in the former Soviet Union offer a different perspective on everyday life. The study of everyday life has emphasized repetition and boredom in people's private lives, particularly in capitalist societies.[8] In the post-Soviet context, the withdrawal of the state from the economy represents a step toward capitalism; however, capitalism has brought neither repetition nor boredom to Central Asia. Instead, capitalist development has transformed everyday life. In part, as states play smaller roles in their economies, people's private lives have expanded relative to their public lives. Now most economic activity falls within the private realm, where state welfare guarantees are largely absent. Overall, this chapter suggests that everyday life is a useful subject of study even in societies experiencing upheaval, such as initial capitalist development.

While Central Asians have adapted to these new conditions, they remember the role of the Soviet state in everyday life fondly and assess their current states' responsiveness as inadequate. Ethnic minorities evaluate their states even less positively. They have experienced not only a reduction in welfare services, but also a drop in their status in society. Improved economies are unlikely to alleviate their dissatisfaction because they are also suffering from the trauma of becoming second-class citizens. Yet, the ethnic divide is not great; many members of the titular group are disgruntled as well.

From the perspective of some foreigners and Central Asians, increasing contentment with existing government is not the top priority. Instead, according to this viewpoint, these governments need to be replaced in order to provide better services and guarantee freedoms. There are signs that Central Asia will obtain more responsive governance. The survey results in this chapter suggest that citizens have a sense of entitlement to good government, and protests in Uzbekistan and the Tulip Revolution in Kyrgyzstan indicate that citizens have not grown politically passive. Only through engagement with their states will citizens of Central Asia initiate change, either gradual or dramatic, in government to improve their everyday lives.

APPENDIX

In the spring and summer of 2001, I conducted 101 interviews in Kazakhstan. These in-depth interviews were with three sets of people: 1) average citizens who are coping with economic problems, 2) individuals who might be helping people survive economically, and 3) individuals who have background information about economic problems and assistance. This chapter draws on two interviews from the first set. This set of interviews took place in a northern city and its satellite towns, a southern province, and a village in that region. The purpose of the interviews with average citizens in Kazakhstan was to inventory problems no longer resolved by the state, to catalog people's coping mechanisms, and to begin to understand how coping experiences shape attitudes toward and relationships with the state. For this reason, I did not select the individuals randomly. I chose to interview members of households to get a broad overview of problems no longer resolved by the state.

With the assistance of BRIF, a private research firm in Almaty, Kazakhstan, and in cooperation with Pauline Jones Luong, I conducted mass surveys in Kazakhstan, Kyrgyzstan, and Uzbekistan in late November and early December of 2003. The surveys were face-to-face interviews lasting approximately an hour and in Kazakh, Kyrgyz, Russian, or Uzbek. The sample for the mass survey in each country was a multistage stratified probability sample of the country. In each country the mass survey questionnaire was administered to 1,500 individuals, age eighteen and older. In each country, macroregions were defined—14 for Uzbekistan, 14 for Kazakhstan, and 8 for Kyrgyzstan, including the capital cities as macroregions. Strata were distributed among the macroregions based on each macroregion's proportion of the total population. Primary sampling units (PSUs) were administrative districts. PSUs were selected randomly using probability proportional to size. Within each PSU, households were randomly selected. One respondent was randomly chosen from each household. If a potential respondent declined to participate, another was selected randomly from the PSU.

NOTES

The author would like to thank Henry Hale, Jeff Sahadeo, and Russell Zanca for their comments and Philip Kehres, Sarah Tremont, and Brittany Williams for their editorial assistance. Grants from the National Council for Eurasian and East European Research, the National Endowment for the Humanities, and the International Research and Exchanges Board funded this research.
    1. The KGB or the Committee of State Security was the Soviet secret police.
    2. Erika Weinthal, "Beyond the State: Transnational Actors, NGOs, and Environmental Protection in Central Asia," *The Transformation of Central Asia: States and Societies from Soviet Rule to Independence,* ed. Pauline Jones Luong (Ithaca, N.Y.: Cornell University Press, 2004), 246.
    3. Ben Highmore, *Everyday Life and Cultural Theory: An Introduction* (New York: Routledge, 2002), 1.
    4. Almaz and Anara are not their true names. I use these names to protect their privacy.
    5. W. Baldridge, "Pension Reform in Kazakhstan," *Central Asia 2010: Prospects for Human Development* (The Regional Bureau for Europe and the Commonwealth of Independent States, United Nations Development Programme, 1999), 177.
    6. At this time 8,000 tenge was approximately fifty U.S. dollars.
    7. In the administration of the survey, interviewers reported that these sur-

vey questions were not troubling to respondents in the three countries. Therefore, differences in results across the countries likely reflect true differences in experience and opinion and not fear on the part of Uzbekistanis.

8. Henri Lefebvre, *Critique of Everyday Life*, vol. 1 (New York: Verso, 1991). David Crowley and Susan E. Reid, "Socialist Spaces: Sites of Everyday Life in the Eastern Bloc," *Socialist Spaces: Sites of Everyday Life in the Eastern Bloc* (New York: Berg Publishers, 2002), 7.

16. Going to School in Uzbekistan

Shoshana Keller

June 20, 2003—It's a warm graduation night at the Alisher Navoi Humanities Lyceum, an elite liberal arts high school (grades 9–11) in Tashkent, Uzbekistan.[1] The school's outdoor courtyard is decorated with lights, red carpets on the walls, and a banner saying "*Oq yol, aziz birodarlar!*" (Bon voyage, dear friends!) There are tables and stools for the hundred or so graduates and their families, and a sound system blasting pop music. The girls have spent days selecting their long ballgowns and getting their hair and makeup just so, complete with liberal amounts of glitter. They won't dress this way again until the day they get married, if then. The boys are sloppier, with their white shirts refusing to stay tucked into their black pants.

After much milling around, the music is turned off and the teachers seat themselves in a rather stern line at the head table—the ceremony begins. In many ways it is similar to an American graduation rite, although the atmosphere is more relaxed, and at times even a little chaotic. The Uzbek flag is raised and everyone stands to sing the national anthem. The school's director walks up to a microphone and small table in the middle of the courtyard and congratulates the students on their achievements. He says that because of young people like them the great, independent republic of Uzbekistan, guided by President Islam Karimov, has a bright future. He then calls up the lyceum "stars" (*yulduzlar*), the top three graduates, and gives the two girls and one boy special sashes and awards. While boys and girls sit on separate sides of the courtyard, there is no sense that they are treated differently. The rest of the graduates are called up one by one to receive their diplomas and a handshake, accompanied by clapping and occasional hoots from friends and family. Not only does every student get his or her photograph taken receiving a diploma, two men with large video cameras roam around filming things. After the first few students the music comes back on, and the girls at my table start quietly singing along to favorite tunes while still applauding their friends and taking each others' pictures.

Once the diploma-giving is done, the kids take over. They present flowers and gifts to all of the teachers, publicly thank their parents, and take turns reciting poetry from a collection the girls have written. A boy and girl sing together about fond school memories, and all the girls get up to do a little karaoke number, swaying and clapping along to the rhythm. Then it's party time, with music and dancing late into the night.

The Alisher Navoi academy is not a typical Uzbek high school. This lyceum draws top students from all over Uzbekistan to study foreign languages, sciences, history, and the arts. The students here all intend to go to college, provided they can pass the brutal entrance exam awaiting them on August 1, and many of them want to study abroad as well. One of the three "stars," Mavjuda Erkinova, wants to study English and Spanish at the Tashkent University of World Languages. She's also an accomplished poet and an avid user of the internet and MP3s. Her best friend, Alina Abdullaeva, speaks quite good English already and dreams of someday visiting New York City.

Mavjuda, Alina, and their friends are the products of a century of struggles over education, struggles that have affected the lives of students and teachers and the direction of Central Asian states and societies. Until the 1860s traditional Islamic teaching methods had worked well for the purposes of producing people who knew how to farm, run small businesses, and behave properly according to their station in society. The late–

Mavjuda Erkinova and Alina Abdullaeva, Tashkent, Uzbekistan, 2003.

nineteenth-century Russian conquest forced Central Asians to realize that the old ways could not protect them from foreign domination, and that Russia's scientific and technical knowledge was a key component of its military strength. The ease of the conquest and their absorption into a foreign, Christian empire set off decades of arguments among Central Asians over why they were so weak and how best to fix that weakness. Education was a focal point of these arguments: was traditional Islamic learning part of the problem, or was it the solution? Central Asians were not alone in raising these questions. The entire Islamic world was having similar discussions as European imperialism spread around the globe. In the Soviet era, officials continued to look west, to Great Britain, France, and Germany, for educational models, all the while hoping to teach new ideologies that would challenge Western supremacy. Following a period of instability, the USSR managed after the end of World War II to train a critical mass of teachers, and new generations of Central Asians understood that they would benefit from studying and working within the Communist system. Knowledge filtered down from intellectuals and politicians and transformed Central Asians' ways of looking at themselves and the outside world. Now, however, neglect instead of interest marks the attitude of the independent state of Uzbekistan towards schooling. While the parents of today's lyceum graduates still push their children to do well in school, they have good reason to fear that theirs may be the last generation to receive such a high level of education.

In modern countries, going to school every day is not just about learning basic skills. The daily routine of schools creates a sense of national identity, of cultural continuity through time, and of loyalty to the state. Children learn proper behavior and thoughts as they read, take tests, and have class discussions. Clubs and silly games are as important as studying history and literature in shaping a sense of citizenship, because they train children in ways of thinking and patterns of behavior in a low-key way: "the great mundane flow of everyday experience at school, which uneventfully, but inexorably, shapes the lives of millions."[2] Schools are also local models of society, where students' interactions with teachers and with each other reflect social and political tensions around them. This essay will show how Soviet school structures not only created national identities, but also enforced class and ethnic status. Meanwhile post-Soviet Uzbek schools are mired in the corruption and decay that is dragging down the entire country.

TEACHING TURKISTANIS IN THE RUSSIAN EMPIRE

Tsarist Russian officials, more interested in economic exploitation than in cultural Russification, did not at first try to change the traditional Islamic school system in Central Asia. However, as time went on, Russian governors and some Central Asian elites believed that everyone would benefit if native children learned the Russian language and basic sciences. The *Jadids*, a group of Muslim educational reformers, sought to go further, overturning standard Islamic teaching methods and replacing them with European/ Russian subjects and methods of study. While neither the Jadids nor the Russian governors had sufficient resources to build many new schools, their efforts still sparked opposition from Muslim elites who feared any change in what children knew and any threat to their power. Several school systems competed in late imperial Central Asia, though most children had access to only five years of education at best.

The traditional Islamic system featured two main types of schools: the elementary *maktab* and the higher seminary for clerics, the *madrasa*. The maktab taught rote memorization of important religious texts and poetry rather than phonetic literacy. Students learned the names of the letters of the Arabic alphabet, but not how to sound out new words from those letters. A student did not pass through grades in a regular sequence, but sat on the ground and recited from one book until the teacher decided he could go on to the next. Discipline was rough. When a father took his son to school for the first time he addressed the teacher with the ritual phrase "You can beat him as long as you don't kill him; the meat is yours, but the bones are ours."[3] Girls also received elementary education, but in separate maktabs or from private women teachers called *otins*. The goal of the maktab was to produce someone who could recite the correct phrases from the Quran or the classics of Central Asian or Persian poetry in the appropriate contexts. Since Turkistani culture was mainly oral, there was little need for people to read or write. Because maktabs were small and mobile, Russian officials were never able to make an accurate count of them, but all of their estimates were in the thousands.

Students who continued to the madrasa received an extensive education in literature and Islamic law, although only a small percentage of Central Asian men completed the course there. Foreign observers (both Russians and travelers from Europe and the United States) condemned the madrasas as backward, anti-scientific institutions, but most of the Central Asian educational reformers who worked in the late nineteenth and early twentieth centuries were madrasa graduates, so the madrasas could not have been completely intellectually hopeless.

These reformers, the Jadids or "New Method men," advocated combining European methods of teaching phonetic literacy, mathematics, and basic science with the study of history and original Islamic texts (instead of subsequent clerical commentaries on those texts).[4] Bukharan writer Abdurrauf Fitrat hoped to use Western teaching tools to raise a new generation of "perfect Muslims and well-trained patriots"—loyal to a Turkic nation, not the Russian Empire.[5] New method schools, which opened in Russian Turkistan

in 1893, and about fifteen years later in Bukhara, introduced new pedagogical ideas that challenged fundamental social and cultural traditions
of everyday life. Reformers believed that schools with neatly aligned rows
of tables and chairs should offer texts suitable to students' level of understanding. Beating was not seen as the best way to drill knowledge into a
slow student. The schools were open to girls as well as to boys, although
few girls attended. As a result of their radical ideas, Jadids, despite their
small number of schools—in 1903 Tashkent had around twenty of them,
the highest concentration in Central Asia—attracted a great deal of hostility from Russian officials and conservative Muslim clergy.[6] Russians
viewed new-method schools as potential carriers of revolutionary ideas,
which was in fact the Jadids' hope. Clergy, feeling their monopoly on education threatened, condemned the schools as introducing infidel culture
and ideas to subvert Islam.

Russian imperial authorities designed their own educational system
for Central Asian Muslims, aimed at attracting elites to Russian culture
and instilling loyalty toward the tsar. At the same time, tsarist officials
understood that open challenges to Islam in education would generate
great local hostility.[7] In 1884 Governor-General N. O. Rosenbakh sponsored a system of native-language elementary schools that combined
much of the traditional maktab curriculum (taught by mullas) with instruction in basic Russian, arithmetic, geography, and other subjects. The
schools also developed a modernized local language for instruction that
improved native-language literacy. The Russian-native school system grew
slowly, but by 1909 enough families saw the value of Russian education for their children that the number of schools had risen from four to
ninety-eight.[8]

On the eve of the 1917 revolutions, three school systems with incompatible goals operated in Central Asia. The largest by far, the traditional
system, reached tens of thousands of children. The smallest in size, but
perhaps the largest in political influence, was the network of approximately one hundred Jadid schools, where many of Central Asia's future revolutionary leaders studied for at least a short while.[9] The state-
sponsored Russian-native schools, even as they grew in number, were
plagued by the problem of children dropping out the moment that they
had mastered enough language and math skills to work in their parents'
businesses. Most Central Asians saw advanced formal education as a low
priority on the scale of their everyday concerns.

REVOLUTIONARY EDUCATION

Once the 1918–1921 Civil War ended, the Bolsheviks made educating the
Russian and non-Russian "backward masses" a high priority, but lacked

the resources to implement ideas of revolutionary education. In Central Asia, to create a good, Communist school system, the Soviet government needed to train secular teachers and write textbooks in multiple languages, build adequate buildings, persuade parents to send their children (daughters as well as sons) to the new schools and destroy the rival Islamic system. They might have experienced early success had they been able to spend huge amounts of money and time on the project. However, the infant state was trying at the same time to build a new, revolutionary economy, political structure, and culture at a breakneck pace. They did manage to lay a small but solid educational base for future growth, which was amazing enough under the circumstances.

As soon as they could, the new Soviet government of Turkistan, following the 1917 revolutions, founded trade schools, Russian-language primary schools, and Turkic- or Tajik-language primary schools that also taught Russian. The Turkistan Commissariat of Enlightenment trained teachers, translated textbooks into local languages, and published an educational journal called *Maorif (Enlightenment)*. By 1920 Turkistan could boast over two thousand secular primary schools, although many lacked adequate textbooks or teachers. Communist authorities compromised with local mores, allowing sex-segregated schools and some religious instruction. Severe cuts to Turkistan's school budget in the 1920s, due to the fiscal austerity of Lenin's New Economic Policy in 1921, forced local governments to rely upon the traditional Muslim system of funding schools through charitable land endowments, known as *waqfs*. Waqf money went to fund not Soviet schools but traditional or reformed (Jadidist) maktabs. The militantly atheist Soviet government found itself supporting Muslim as well as secular schools.[10]

In 1927, the Communist Party, under Joseph Stalin, started to confiscate waqf properties and their income as part of a larger effort to eliminate Muslim social institutions, including all kinds of schools, a process that continued for over a decade. However, it took longer to train new teachers and build secular schools than to shut down the old system, leaving many Central Asian children with little access to any education. In 1927 Uzbekistan, the largest of the new Central Asian republics, had an estimated 1,548 primary schools serving 83,963 students, 55 secondary schools with 24,680 students, and 49 technical schools with 6,790 students, out of a total population of 4.6 million people. Finding teachers to staff these schools was exceedingly difficult, because so few Russian teachers knew local languages and so few Central Asians had the necessary European education. Of the roughly two thousand Uzbek secular teachers available in 1927, only 5 percent had studied beyond elementary school themselves.[11]

Soviet policies in the 1930s relegated education to a secondary priority. Even as the USSR passed a "Universal Compulsory Primary Education" initiative, mandating that all children attend secular primary schools, the government made clear to local officials that their priority was to pursue collectivization and industrial projects, such as building irrigation canals, throughout Central Asia. In some rural areas, village leaders declared that they had never even heard of the compulsory education law.[12] Typical of the chaos of the First Five Year Plan period, Soviet officials were changing the alphabet of the Uzbek language at the same time they were requiring Uzbeks to rapidly enroll all children in primary schools that had not yet been built or staffed. In 1923, as part of a drive to improve general literacy, Turkic intellectuals, with Soviet state support, had implemented a simplified version of the centuries-old Perso-Arabic script used for Central Asian languages, which only scholars could read. Beginning in 1927, the government converted Turkic and Tajik languages to a Latin-based alphabet, partly on the grounds that Latin characters were easier to learn to read than Arabic ones, and partly to make it harder for people to read Islamic texts. The change meant that the few Uzbek school textbooks that had been printed had to be scrapped and replaced with books written in the new alphabet. In 1939 the USSR mandated another change for Turkic languages, to a Cyrillic-based alphabet to facilitate the learning of Russian. Educators knew that these changes interfered with achieving the Soviet goal of universal literacy, but this was another area of life in the USSR where ideology trumped efficiency.

Despite these obstacles a secular school system grew slowly through the 1930s. The Commissariat of Enlightenment introduced standard textbooks across the USSR in 1933–1934, translated from the original Russian into local languages. A central pedagogical institute for training Uzbek teachers opened in Tashkent in 1935 and was soon joined by branch institutes in Bukhara, Andijon, Termez and other cities. In March 1938 Russian language instruction was made obligatory in all schools, although the acute lack of textbooks and teachers meant that the decree was impossible to realize. By the eve of World War II the number of primary schools had grown to almost five thousand.[13] Schools in Central Asia were still quite poor compared to those in Russia, but the Soviets had built an educational base big enough to launch an impressive growth spurt after the war was over.

THE FLOWERING OF THE SOVIET SCHOOL

Hitler's invasion of June 1941 disrupted education everywhere in the USSR. Even though Uzbekistan was far away from the front lines, schools closed due to a lack of funds and pupils, since many local children stopped attending. The arrival of 85,000 refugees from war zones further strained resources. When the war finally ended in 1945, the surviving population was eager to resume a normal life. It was in the postwar period, especially after Stalin's death in 1953, that education finally stabilized enough for going to school to become a major part of the daily life of Uzbek children.

The number of Uzbek schools returned to pre-war levels only in 1950, although during the war the government had continued to build teacher training institutes. Rural areas, where most Uzbeks lived, continued to suffer shortages of schools and teachers—villages were still trying to implement universal compulsory primary education in the mid-1950s. Even where schools existed, parents frequently removed their children after fourth grade to join them in working the cotton fields.[14] This was especially the case for girls, who were still expected to marry young and devote their lives to raising children. The Soviet government itself encouraged these attitudes with its continual pressure on the Uzbek SSR to meet cotton production quotas.

The problem of Uzbek parents not valuing advanced schooling was rooted in the contradictions of the Soviet system. The state wanted both high levels of production at low cost, and the creation of a well-educated population of modern Uzbek Soviet citizens. Children could not learn to be these new Soviet citizens without spending more years in school, but Central Asian citizens saw few incentives to have children to stay after grades 1–4, the elementary level. A lack of economic opportunities hardly made prolonged Soviet education, which disrupted traditional family life, worth while. Even if more parents had wanted to see their children continue, there still were not enough schools, teachers and textbooks to meet demand. Bringing the reality of ordinary citizens' lives more into line with Soviet propaganda of a universally advanced, educated society would require putting fewer resources into heavy industry and more into "soft" goods such as textbooks. Nikita Khrushchev (Communist Party head 1955–1964) in particular, as well as his successor Leonid Brezhnev (premier 1964–1983), understood that proving Soviet superiority over the capitalist West in social as well as military terms would require advanced learning even more than it required cotton.

The post-Stalin decades saw the full development of a modern curriculum in Uzbekistan. This curriculum was designed both to create an Uzbek national identity and to create a sense of citizenship in the Soviet Union. Boys and girls alike were to be fluent in Russian and Uzbek, knowledgeable in basic science and mathematics, proud of Uzbek writers such as Alisher Navoi and Ghafur Ghulom along with Pushkin and Chekhov,[15] and comfortable with Russian children's pastimes like joining model airplane clubs and dancing around in bunny costumes with Grandfather Frost (the Russian Santa Claus).[16]

Teachers struggled to balance "Uzbek" and "Soviet" identities, as much because of the politics involved as the complexity of the task. Children acquire a sense of national identity partly through the study of history, the story (*hikoia*, the tale, as Uzbek educators wrote) of what their people have done in the past. The difficulty was that Uzbekistan was a new nation, and

Soviet Communist history was not only a new discipline, but one that changed frequently as the political line from Moscow shifted. Historians struggled to decide when "Uzbek" history had begun, who could be included and excluded from the story, and how Uzbeks fit into the Marxist model of historical progression through class struggle. Most tricky was the issue of tsarist Russia's relationship with Central Asian peoples. Scholars in the 1920s were free to repeat Lenin's line that the Russian Empire had been "the prison house of peoples," but by the mid-1930s Stalin preferred to emphasize that Russian rule had been benevolent and "progressive" for all non-Russian peoples. Every once in a while a historian could slip a mild criticism of Russian colonialism past the censors, but it was always a gamble. Several attempts to write national histories of the Central Asian peoples during Stalin's time foundered on politics. School textbooks for non-Russian history did not exist.[17] All Soviet children received history lessons that focused overwhelmingly on Europe and Russia. Their rigorous curriculum began with Greek and Roman civilization. History of the "fatherland" (*vatan*) meant Russian history. Only after Khrushchev broke the spell of the Stalin cult in 1956 could educators think about developing a stable curriculum for Uzbek or Turkmen or other national histories.

In 1958 professional historians published the first one-volume history of Uzbekistan in Uzbek. At a whopping seven hundred pages, the *History of the Uzbek SSR* was never intended to be a school textbook, but since no Uzbek history textbooks existed and Khrushchev was in a hurry to boost the school system, the *Teachers' Newspaper* (*O'qituvchilar gazetasi*) instructed teachers on exactly what pages out of the book to teach and exactly how to teach them.[18] Textbooks are essential for creating a uniform curriculum and continuity in what students learn from year to year. Any state that wants to inculcate a particular worldview and set of values needs books that children can memorize from, study the pictures in, and handle every day as they grow to be adult citizens. A textbook that a child has scribbled in has become an invisible tool shaping the assumptions that child makes about the world.

The foundational themes set out in the 1958 book shaped every school history text that followed. The authors begin their story with the ancient Eurasian nomads called the Scythians, who fought against the invading Achaemenid Persian Empire (sixth century BCE). Then they describe the Abbasid Arab overlords of the eighth century CE, who brought Islam to Central Asia; the tenth century flowering of intellectual culture with Ibn Sina and al-Biruni; the Mongols in the thirteenth and fourteenth centuries; and Timur and his astronomer grandson Ulugh Bek in the fifteenth century.[19] Finally after two hundred pages they get to Shaybani Khan, who led the nomadic people called Uzbeks from the Caspian steppe region into Central Asia in 1499.

This book takes a very different narrative strategy from most Western national histories. A United States history textbook written along these lines would focus on events in North America, beginning with the arrival of people from Siberia thirty thousand years ago, rather than emphasizing, as many do, the Jamestown settlers or the Continental Congress or earlier forces that led to the European conquest of the New World. U.S. history is taught mainly as the story of northern Europeans and their descendants in a new land. In contrast, Stalin had defined nations partly by territory, so "Uzbek history" consisted of everything that had happened in the region that in 1924 became Uzbekistan. It was not the story of the Uzbek people as a distinct ethno-linguistic group wherever they happened to be living.

At the same time, "Uzbek history" had to conform to the larger narrative of Soviet history. The 1958 *History of the Uzbek SSR* and the school texts that descended from it tell a story of heroes and villains. Marxist history—in the crude form that the Soviets taught it—is a story with a beginning, middle, and end, and with clearly marked opponents: class exploiters and exploited. The problem for Soviet historians was that these criteria were very difficult to apply to any of the peoples east of the Black Sea. Assorted khans, emirs, and bois were obvious oppressors, but there wasn't much of a dialectic happening (such as eighteenth century peasant resistance against land enclosure in England), and bourgeois capitalism had not yet developed. Lacking identifiable Luddites or anti-clerical heroes such as Giordano Bruno,[20] historians of Central Asia chose to extol the valor of *native* resisters to *foreign* invasion, both of which proved to be problematic concepts.

Fourth graders from the 1960s to the 1980s learned that foreigners had invaded their fatherland for 2,500 years, but working-class natives had always risen up against the oppressors. Heroes included a Scythian shepherd named Shiroq, who pretended to guide an invading Persian army in the sixth century BCE to his people's main camp. But the cunning Shiroq really led the Persians into the desert to die, and he died with them. The story ends "He was killed, but his glory is immortal."[21] Scythian warrior Spitamenes sought to repel Alexander the Great in 329 BCE, swearing to the gods "I love my kin and my country . . . my people—my brothers." Alexander prevailed, but buried Spitamenes with kingly honors. According to the textbook, when the Arabs invaded in 709 CE "local tribes resisted manfully. But there was no unity among them."[22] The textbook narrative here is actually mapping Russian history onto "Uzbek" history. The Russian Primary Chronicle records that in the ninth century CE "there was no unity" among the Slavic tribes, and so they had to invite the Vikings in to rule over them. The story of Shiroq and the Persian army closely parallels the tale of Ivan Susanin, whose sacrifice to protect the tsar from a Polish army in the seventeenth century was celebrated in Mikhail Glinka's opera *A Life for the Tsar*. Love for "the people" is a long-standing Russian theme, but these textbooks did not explain that in Central Asia "the people" were mostly the descendants of previous generations of invaders.

The coming of Islam gave Soviet historians particular problems, because one of their tasks was to celebrate Uzbek secular cultural achievements. The leading intellectuals of medieval Central Asia were all products of Muslim philosophy and science, and worse, they were not ethnically Uzbek. The great architecture that students went on field trips to admire was Persian in design and built for religious purposes. The Central Asian scholar most recognized by Muslims, al-Bukhari (d. 870), had to be ignored entirely because his major work was to compile and authenticate the sayings of the Prophet Muhammad. School texts praised al-Biruni and Ibn Sina for criticizing Islam; they were cast as enlightened free-thinkers as well as patriots. Textbooks did not assign ethnic identifications to their medieval heroes and downplayed the fact that these men spent most of their lives in Persia or Baghdad.[23]

Difficulties with the foreign invader vs. noble patriot narrative increased after the Mongol era. Fourth grade textbooks decried the Central Asian-born Timur as a brutal despot, but admired his military prowess. Explaining that Uzbek tribes drove out the last Timurids was apparently too complicated for young students; textbooks abruptly digressed into cultural achievements and then skipped to the seventeenth century and "progressive" trade connections between the Bukharan emirate and Russia. Books for older students (seventh–ninth grade) did discuss the origin of Turkic-speaking groups northeast of Central Asia and the arrival of the Uzbek leader Shaybani Khan, but stated that the nomadic Shaybanids gradually merged with settled Uzbeks and Tajiks who had *already* been living there for centuries: "They were a new element, entering into the developing structure of the ancient Uzbek people here in the eleventh–twelfth centuries."[24] In one form or another, Uzbekistan had always existed, even if people calling themselves Uzbeks were late arrivals and the Uzbek SSR was only forty-seven years old. Like their good friends the Russians, cultured Uzbeks had always fought oppression, and together with the Russians they would create a socialist society. The textbooks did not commit many outright fabrications, but deliberately fudged boundaries of time and geography to create an ancient history for the nation.

Textbooks are certainly not the only way to teach history. From the early 1950s students created classroom historical exhibits, including models, panoramas, small monuments to revolutionary heroes, and newspapers posted on the wall. In one school, students organized their own history museum and acted as tour guides for visiting classes and parents. The museum included a small library and items loaned from the Lenin Museum in Moscow.[25] Schools sponsored "Young Historians" (*yosh tarikhchilar*) clubs that read books and sponsored discussions, put up more wall newspapers, and organized after-school activities. A "Young Archeologists" (*yosh arxeologlar*) club set up a public exhibition on the ancient peoples of Central Asia, which included excavation demonstrations by the students.[26] In Ferghana, a middle school set up a museum with exhibits on women's role in defending the fatherland against Muslim invaders in the eighth century and anti-Soviet guerillas (*basmachi*) in the twentieth, on how the October Revolution liberated Uzbeks from oppressive khanates, and on the "superphosphate" (*superfosfat*) and other factories in Kokand.[27] The museum, which included busts of female heroes, contrasted Islamic misogyny and economic backwardness of the past with Soviet liberation and progress of the present, and showed that Uzbeks had always fought on the side of liberation and progress. In the later 1950s teachers were encouraged to take their students on field trips to view museums, historical sites, and architecture. Movies and film strips started to become available at this time as well, although the "historical films" that teachers could use were limited to Russian topics such as Peter the Great or the Civil War hero Chapaev.[28]

Keep in mind, however, that many rural Uzbek schools still did not have electricity, that textbooks continued to be in short supply, and that in the 1960s the state was struggling to build schools fast enough to accommodate the growing population. Most teachers still lacked schooling beyond seventh grade. For every Uzbek child pictured in newspapers and magazines using scientific equipment or playing the piano, several more were spending much of their school time working in the cotton fields. Children who attended trade schools spent part of their day just doing factory work. In February 1964, tenth-grader Mavjuda Rasuleva of Andijon got her picture in the newspaper *O'qituvchilar gazetasi* for stitching 120 percent of her quota for *doppas*, traditional Uzbek hats.[29] The school system was increasingly successful at teaching basic literacy and arithmetic skills, but it did not provide an equal education to all levels of society.

For students in the post-war decades school meant more than formal classes, and instruction in how to be a Soviet Uzbek occurred outside as well as in the classroom. After school clubs involved kids with learning both European and Central Asian classical music and dance, reading books and poetry, or playing chess. There was even a "Young Tourists" club! Girls as well as boys played basketball, ran track, and learned to swim, which required completely abandoning traditional Muslim modesty in dress and behavior. Younger children had song and dance hours, where they would learn "folk songs" such as "Lenin is Our Honored Grandfather," or "Hello school," and dance to music from Grieg, Tchaikovsky, or the Central Asian repertoire. Even Pioneer (a Soviet youth organization for younger children) summer camps sponsored "we love books" festivals along with "Spartakiad" athletic contests and camp songs and crafts. In or out of school, Uzbek children learned European and Central Asian traditions, but the Uzbek identity they were taught had been cut to fit a European model. Certainly there's never a simple correspondence between what a teacher says and what students believe or do in response, but over decades schools fostered an understanding of Uzbekness that had distinctly Russian features and was very different from forms of national identity elsewhere in the Islamic world.[30] By the 1970s the schools had also achieved a goal that all Soviet citizens could take great pride in: near-universal literacy.

POST-SOVIET DECLINE

Another feature of daily life in the USSR, especially in the 1970s–1980s, was corruption. The delivery of basic services, such as plumbing repair, had broken down to such an extent that even the most honest citizens had to pay bribes to get their pipes fixed in a reasonable amount of time. While slogans on billboards exhorted the masses to toil joyfully on Lenin's road, the real ethos of the Communist elite was to hoard money and privileges and ignore the needs of ordinary citizens as much as possible. Uzbek government officials in this period were from the first generations to grow up in a stable, good-quality school system. They had learned their arithmetic, their Navoi and their Pushkin; they had also learned how to fake local cotton accounts to steal millions of rubles from Moscow. This was the leadership that took and maintained control over Uzbekistan after 1991. While they continue to proclaim support for education, like many other aspects of Uzbek life schools have deteriorated sharply under their rule.

The roots of the problem are money and political choices over how to allocate that money. All of the former Soviet countries faced major expenses in rewriting textbooks and updating pedagogical methods, for which they have received significant international help.[31] Nonetheless, while UNICEF reported in 2002 that the population of school-age children in Uzbekistan was roughly 6.3 million, new history textbooks have been printed in inadequate runs of 20,000 to 200,000.[32] It is too early to say whether an innovative textbook-rental plan supported by the Asian Development Bank will be able to solve the problem.[33] Teacher salaries are extremely low, usually the equivalent of U.S. $30 a month. Low pay and poor conditions have driven many experienced teachers, especially men, from the profession. Some schools can no longer teach all of the subjects they are supposed to for lack of personnel. While being a teacher commanded respect in the Soviet Union, the job is increasingly becoming a low-skill ghetto for neighborhood women who have no professional stake in their performance. As one relatively affluent mother told me, when parents in her neighborhood find a good teacher, they pool their own funds to supplement her salary so that she'll stay at the school.[34]

The Uzbek government is not ignoring these dire conditions, but their programs tend to look better on paper than in reality. In 1992 the Supreme Parliament (*Oliy Majlis*) reduced the Soviet system of compulsory education from eleven years to nine. In August 1997 the parliament passed an additional "National Skills Formation Directive" that more formally divided school structure into nine years of compulsory education followed by a variety of elective technical colleges or liberal arts lyceums. At the end of nine years students are examined in Uzbek and Russian, mathematics, sciences, Uzbek history, physical fitness, and a unique subject called "Concepts of national independence and the foundations of spirituality" or "Feelings toward the Fatherland."[35] Many urban schools also teach English or other foreign languages. If students continue until the eleventh grade (as only one-third do) they must pass extraordinarily tough subject area exams in order to enter a university. Inadequate textbooks, teachers, and school facilities, especially in the countryside where 70 percent of the Uzbek population still lives, create a barrier that prevents many children from advancing to higher education. The government provides aid such as free books and warm clothing to poor students, but this cannot compensate for all of the deficiencies in the system. In a 2002 survey, UNICEF found that 60 percent of Uzbek schools do not have toilets or running water.[36] Recently the Ministry of Education made life harder for teachers by decreeing that they must wear uniforms approved by (and purchased from) their school management. This decree, which includes a ban on makeup and jewelry, is ostensibly to enforce standards of modesty. However, the uniforms can cost two-thirds of a teacher's monthly salary, leading to protests and more teachers quitting their jobs. Why the government has done this is unclear.[37]

Children of the upper class are still getting an excellent education, however. Those who attend higher schools like the Alisher Navoi Humanities Lyceum or the specialized arts and sports schools that still exist from Soviet times have access not only to the best teachers and materials, but to computers and the internet as well. In addition to the traditional subjects, lyceum students study English, world history, and electives like Chaghatay Turkic. In 2002–2003 they began for the first time to learn about AIDS, a growing problem in Uzbekistan. They also have fun. For the great Navruz spring festival, Alina Abdullaeva and Mavjuda Erkinova's class spent all night in school with their teachers, making the traditional spring treat *sumalak*. Other times they've held carnivals or disco nights. One day the students became the teachers, and Alina spent an hour teaching an English literature class while her teachers listened. Even this educational island is not without problems, however. There are not always enough math and science teachers, and many students skip classes and don't care about their work.[38] How can this be, given the ferocious set of exams that stand between them and a university? The exam regime itself is destroying motivation to work hard.

On August 1, 2003, some 300,000 prospective university students sat for examinations in history, literature, mathematics, physics, and other topics. The history test alone consisted of 848 multiple choice questions divided into twelve sections, including "In France beginning in the twelfth century manufacturing centers for coarse cloth and linen were in which precise places?"; "The second stage of Amir Timur's military activity conquered which precise countries?"; and "Which precise president of the United States began aggression against North Vietnam?"[39] Even the top lyceum students would struggle with this material, but students with money don't need to—they can just buy an answer key for 100,000 *som* (equivalent to $100, well beyond the reach of most Uzbeks). One report states that during the 2002 exams half the students in a testing auditorium were openly using the crib sheets.[40]

Corruption has become a large problem at many levels of the educational system. Parents must pay under-the-table fees to enroll students in kindergartens and schools that are ostensibly free, and buy gifts, really salary supplements, for teachers. At higher levels students from wealthy families can buy places in a university and grades for classes, while doing minimal studying. This leaves them with a degree, but also with no real skills or knowledge. Poor but bright students are all but locked out of higher education, and even those who do make it through have trouble finding a decent job afterwards. As in many developing countries, more than half of Uzbekistan's population is under the age of twenty-five, but most of those young people are unable to find ways to realize their ambitions.[41] It was not surprising that, when I spoke to a group of prospective college students in Tashkent, almost every one of them wanted to move to Europe or North America. This is a tragic situation, not only for them but for the future of Uzbekistan. As for Mavjuda and Alina, they passed their exams and entered the University of World Languages in Tashkent. After her first year, Marjuda decided to transfer to a business university, which should give her slightly better job prospects. These young women have the education and the talent to serve their country well, but the question remains whether their country will let them.

NOTES

Research for this article was supported by a grant from ACTR/ACCELS. The author wishes to thank Ergash Umarov and the Payziev family for their help and hospitality.

1. Alisher Navoi (1441–1501) was the first person to write high quality poetry in Turkic, rather than the standard literary language of Persian. He is called the father of Uzbek literature, even though he lived in Herat (now northern Afghanistan) before the Uzbeks arrived in Central Asia.

2. Alfred Kelly, "The Franco-Prussian War and Unification in German History Schoolbooks," in Walter Pape, ed., *1870/71–1989/90: German Unifications and the Change of Literary Discourse.* (Berlin: Walter de Gruyter, 1993), 42.

3. Adeeb Khalid, *The Politics of Muslim Cultural Reform: Jadidism in Central Asia.* (Berkeley: University of California Press, 1998), 22.

4. Central Asian Jadids were inspired by the ideas of Ismail bey Gasprinskii,

a Crimean Tatar who promoted a unified Turkic language and a phonetic method of teaching it as a first step in allowing Turkic peoples to express new ideas, raising their cultural and intellectual level and eventually creating a unified nation strong enough to stand up to a Christian power. Wayne Dowler, *Classroom and Empire: The Politics of Schooling and Russia's Eastern Nationalities, 1860–1917.* (Montreal: McGill-Queen's University Press, 2001), 156–160. Sergei Zenkovsky, *Pan-Turkism and Islam in Russia.* (Cambridge, Mass.: Harvard University Press, 1967), 31–35.

5. Khalid, 177.

6. Khalid, 164–165.

7. Daniel Brower, *Turkestan and the Fate of the Russian Empire.* (London: RoutledgeCurzon, 2003), 68–69.

8. Khalid, 159. Kiriak E. Bendrikov, *Ocherki po istorii narodnogo obrazovaniia v Turkestane, (1865–1924 gody).* (Moscow: 1960), 70. Shoshana Keller, *To Moscow, Not Mecca: The Soviet Campaign Against Islam in Central Asia, 1917–1941.* (Westport, Conn.: Praeger Publishers, 2001), 15.

9. Brower, 70. Bendrikov, 379.

10. Keller, 39–40.

11. M. Stambler, "Voprosy narodnogo prosveshcheniia v Srednei Azii," *Za partiiu* no. 2 (November 1927): 91–92. Douglas Northrop, *Veiled Empire: Gender and Power in Stalinist Central Asia.* (Ithaca, N.Y.: Cornell University Press, 2004), 10 n. 9.

12. Keller, 209–210. Kuznets, "Predvaritel'nye itogi smotra vseobucha v Srednei Azii," *Partrabotnik* no. 5–6 (March 1931): 24. E. Thomas Ewing, *The Teachers of Stalinism: Policy, Practice and Power in Soviet Schools of the 1930s.* (New York: Peter Lang, 2002), 58–61.

13. Sheila Fitzpatrick, *Education and Social Mobility in the Soviet Union, 1921–1934.* (Cambridge: Cambridge University Press, 1979), 230–231. Peter A. Blitstein, "Nation-Building or Russification? Obligatory Russian Instruction in the Soviet Non-Russian School, 1938–1953," in Ronald Grigor Suny and Terry Martin, eds., *A State of Nations: Empire and Nation-Making in the Age of Lenin and Stalin.* (Oxford: Oxford University Press, 2001), 260–261. M. A. Akhunova and B. V. Lunin, *Istoriia istoricheskoi nauki v Uzbekistane.* (Tashkent: n.p., 1970), 76. I. K. Kadyrov, *Narodnoe obrazovanie sovetskogo Uzbekistana.* (Tashkent: Uzbekistan, 1964), 17.

14. "Umumii majburii ta'lim planini to'la amalga oshirish uchun," *O'qituvchilar gazetasi* 7 January 1954, p. 4. R. Sharafutdinova, *Shkol'noe obrazovanie v Uzbekskoi SSR.* (Tashkent: Gosizdat, 1961), 22–26. Kadyrov, 26.

15. Ghafur Ghulom (1903–1966) was a poet who survived by writing extravagant praises of Stalin. Ghulom became a leading Soviet Uzbek writer; generations of Uzbek children memorized his poems. Alexander Pushkin (1799–1837) is still revered as the greatest of all Russian poets, and the plays and short stories of Anton Chekhov (1860–1904) have entered the canon of world literature. While Alisher Navoi is the Uzbek equivalent to Pushkin in status, Ghulom is not far behind.

16. *O'qituvchilar gazetasi,* 9 January 1952: 4. This page features a photo of costumed children in the "Stalin" Pioneer unit with Ded Moroz/Qor Bobo and a New Year's tree.

17. Lowell Tillett, *The Great Friendship: Soviet Historians on the Non-Russian Nationalities.* (Chapel Hill, N.C.: University of North Carolina Press, 1969).

18. Iahya Gh. Ghulomov, Rashid N. Nabiev, M. Gh. Bahobov, *O'zbekiston SSR tarixi (bir tomlik).* (Tashkent: n.p., 1958). "4-sinfda SSSR tarixi o'rganish masalalariga doir," *O'qituvchilar gazetasi* 7 August 1959: 2.

19. Ibn Sino (980–1037), known to Europeans as Avicenna, was the greatest philosopher and physician of his day. Al-Biruni (973–1048) was a leading mathematician. Timur or Tamerlane (1336–1405) was one of the last terrible invaders out of Central Asia, who cut a swath of destruction from India to southeastern Europe.

20. The Luddites were skilled weavers in nineteenth-century England, who smashed the steam-powered looms that were destroying their livelihoods. Giordano Bruno (1548–1600) was burned at the stake by the Catholic Church for supposing that the universe might be infinite.

21. Kamil Akilov and Nina Teikh, *Istoriia Uzbekskoi SSR. Rasskazy dlia 4-ogo klassa.* (Tashkent, 1963), 9. Iahya Ghulomov and Rashid Nabiev, *Istoriia Uzbekskoi SSR. Uchebnoe posobie dlia 7–8-ikh klassov shkol Uzbekistana.* (Tashkent, 1971), 16, cites "a Greek tale" as the source for this story. Post-Soviet Uzbek textbooks still discuss Shiroq, and credit the story to a second century BCE Greek historian named Polyaenus. A. S. Sagdullaev, V. A. Kostetskii, and H. K. Norkulov, *Istoriia Uzbekistana 6,* (Tashkent: Sharq, 2000), 153–155. The *Cambridge History of Iran* dryly describes Polyaenus as a second century CE "author of a miscellany of stratagems selected on merit rather than authenticity." (Cambridge: Cambridge University Press, 1985) 2: 220.

22. Akilov and Teikh, 10, 11.

23. Iranians also claim Ibn Sino and al-Biruni, as great Iranian and Muslim "sources of pride." That two countries, speaking two very different languages, claim the same honored ancestors as exclusively their own is awkward, but not uncommon when history is used as a tool for national identity development. Golnar Mehran, "The Presentation of the 'Self' and the 'Other' in Postrevolutionary Iranian School Textbooks," in Nikki R. Keddie and Rudi Mathee, eds., *Iran and the Surrounding World: Interactions in Culture and Cultural Politics.* (Seattle, Wash.: Univ of Washington Press, 2002), 236.

24. Ghulomov and Nabiev (1971), 59.

25. A. Sultonov and A. Ziyoev, "Tarix muzei qandai tashkil qilindi?" *O'qituvchilar gazetasi* 4 April 1963: 4. This was a major project that lasted for at least four years; obviously, the students had a great deal of help from adults.

26. N. Iunusov, "Maktabda o'lkashunoslik muzei," *Sovet maktabi* no. 6 (June 1964): 31–32.

27. A. Sultonov and A. Ziyoev, "Tarix muzei qandai tashkil qilindi?" (How Was the History Museum Organized?) *O'qituvchilar gazetasi* 4 April 1963: 4. This was a major project that had begun in 1959; obviously, the students had a great deal of help from adults. "Maktabda tarix muzei" (A History Museum in School), *O'qituvchilar gazetasi* 17 July 1959: 4.

28. "Maktabda tarix kabineta," *O'qituvchilar gazetasi* 20 January 1954: 3. Muhametzianova, "Tarix darslarida ko'rgazmali qurrolar bilan ishlash," *O'qituvchilar gazetasi* 25 March 1958: 3. N. Remeev, "Tarix bo'icha to'garak ishlari," *Sovet maktabi* No. 8(August 1963): 33–36. In 1963 two teachers from Andijon expressed appreciation of the films they had, but suggested that it would be really helpful to have historical movies in the Uzbek language, so children could understand them. *O'qituvchilar gazetasi* 8 August 1963, 4.

29. Letters complaining about textbook shortages in *O'qituvchilar gazetasi* 10, 27 January and 14 February 1963, from several regions of Uzbekistan. B. Mavlonov and M. Abdullaev, "O'qituvchilar 6 tonna paxta terdilar," *O'qituvchilar gazetasi* 18 September 1957: 6. B. Rahimov, "Xorazmda maorifi," *Sovet maktabi* no. 9 (Sept. 1964): 28 brags about the cotton-picking abilities of students and teachers. Children elsewhere in the USSR were also frequently recruited to help gather the fall harvest. *O'qituvchilar gazetasi* 6 February 1964: 4.

30. Examples from issues of *O'qituvchilar gazetasi* and *Sovet maktabi* 1954–1961. Sadly, there was no photograph of children dancing the "Andijon polka" in November 1959.

31. The Asian Development Bank, several United Kingdom educational foundations, and the government of Japan, among others, have donated money, train-

ing, and equipment. Asian Development Bank news release No. 241/02, 6 December 2002. http://www.adb.org/Documents/News/2002/nr2002241.asp, accessed 15 June 2004. *Times of Central Asia* 18 June 2003, 4.

32. *Srednesrochnyi obzor: Stranovaia programma sotrudnichestva 2000–2004.* Pravitel'stvo Respubliki Uzbekistan Detskii Fond Organizatsii Ob"edinennykh Natsii (UNICEF). Tashkent: November 2002, 22. *O'zbekiston tarixi 9,* (Tashkent: O'qituvchi, 1994). *Istoriia Uzbekistana 6,* (Tashkent: Sharq, 2000). *O'zbekiston tarixi 7,* (Tashkent: Abdulla Qodiriy Nomidagi Xalq Merosi Nashriyoti, 2001). Great thanks to Anvar S. Zakirov and Jamoliddin K. Fazilov of the Ministry of Public Education of Uzbekistan, who were immensely helpful in providing me with documents and tea.

33. Tony Reed, "Overcoming Textbook Misery in Uzbekistan," World Bank Group Research Report September 2002. http://www.worldbank.org/transitionnewsletter/julaugsep02/pgs41–42.htm, accessed 19 May 2003.

34. Personal conversations with students and parents in Tashkent, July 2003. When a research librarian learned that I was investigating education in the Soviet period, she muttered, "It was a lot better then than now." An October 2002 report on the Uzbek website *Zamon* (*Time*), found similar complaints in other parts of the country. http://www.internews.uz/zamon/zamon238e.html, broadcast #238. Report no longer accessible.

35. *O'quvchi ma'naviiatini shakllantirish.* (Tashkent: Sharq, 2000), 19. The Uzbek is literally translated as "Directive on the preparation of national cadres," which reveals how Soviet the government's thinking still is. "Ob obrazovanii v Uzbekistane," unpublished report prepared for the author by the Main Administration of General Secondary Education, July 2003, 5.

36. "Nowadays in our country every third child studies at the secondary school or gets trade experience at the high and secondary special schools and trade institutions." *Education in Uzbekistan,* at the state-sponsored website http://www.tashkent.org/uzland/educate.html, accessed 23 August 2004. *Srednesrochnyi obzor,* 22–23. *O'quvchi ma'naviiatini shakllantirish,* 23–25 October 2002 *Zamon* report. Turkmenistan also reduced its compulsory education to nine years, and then gutted the remaining schools by firing 12,000 teachers and dropping core subjects in favor of memorizing from President-for-Life Saparmurat Niyazov's *Book of the Soul.* "Brain Dead," *The Economist* (22 July 2004).

37. Gulnoza Saidazimova, "Uzbekistan: New Laws Ban Everything from Motorcycles to Movies," Radio Free Europe/Radio Liberty, 13 April 2005. http://www.rferl.org, accessed 13 April 2005.

38. Personal conversation with Mavjuda Erkinova and Alina Abdullaeva (pseudonyms), 6 August 2003. *Sumalak* is a pudding-like concoction of wheat flour, water, and ground nuts, boiled for up to twelve hours. It is eaten cold in the spring, and is supposed to have great nutritional value.

39. *Abiturientlar uchun Tarix. Fanidan 2003 yil testlari toplami.* Tashkent: 2003, no. 67: 9; no. 15: 16; no. 1: 33

40. B. Zohida, "Ishonch, hadiq, umid," *Mohiiat* 1 August 2003, 1. *Mohiiat* is the only independent Uzbek-language newspaper. Ol'ga Lisitskaia, "Testy: zapominat' ili uchit'?" *Narodnoe slovo* 16 July 2003, 1–2.

41. Esmer Islamov (pseud.), "Uzbekistan's corruption-ridden educational system seen as a source of frustration," *Eurasia Insight* 29 April 2004. http://www.uzland.uz/2004/april/30/09.htm Accessed 18 June 2004.

17. Alphabet Changes in Turkmenistan, 1904–2004

Victoria Clement

While visiting with a Turkmen friend in Aşgabat in 1997, I asked her to write her address for me. Even though we had been speaking her native Turkmen language, my friend, Ogulbibi,[1] wrote in the "Russian alphabet." Turkmen had used the Cyrillic, or Russian, alphabet for more than fifty years, but when the country gained independence in 1991, it adopted a new writing system. As an elementary school teacher, Ogulbibi used the new "Turkmen National Alphabet"[2] every day in the classroom. The change in script had been an important symbol of Turkmenistan's post-Soviet independence, marking Turkmen identity in opposition to Russian or Soviet. Why was this ethnic Turkmen woman not taking advantage of the symbolism offered her by the new alphabet? Why would she continue to write with the letters that Moscow had imposed on her culture?

When the Soviet Union ended in 1991, Turkmenistan's government changed its flag, currency, national anthem, as well as street and city names. Symbols of Turkmen national identity rapidly replaced those from Soviet culture. Script became one of these important markers. As a result the look of public texts changed dramatically: newspapers, textbooks, street signs, maps, even license plates exhibited a radically new alphabet. People went to sleep registered at Улица Первога Мая (May First Street, in Russian, honoring the socialist holiday) and woke up on Gorogly Sha-ýolu ("Goroglu Avenue," named for the Turkmen folk hero) with a new street sign. It cost the government a lot of money to import new signs, obtain new textbooks, refit publishing technologies, and change over all administrative materials. Plus, Turkmenistan's citizens had to learn a whole new system for writing; for some this was the third of their lifetime.

Why did the state spend time, energy, and money to alter so many mundane facets of everyday life? Most adults knew how to read and write in the Cyrillic alphabet. Adults already working in jobs, regularly reading the newspaper, able to help their children with homework, and capable of dealing with official documents had to learn a whole new system that challenged their literacy at the most basic level. Ogulbibi explained that although she knew the Latin alphabet, she was *accustomed* to writing in Cyrillic. For her, questions of national identity were secondary to ease and functioning in daily life. She, like many of her friends and co-workers, had learned the new script and used it at work. Still, in their personal lives they privileged comfort over national symbolism. They wrote in the alphabet they had learned as students: Cyrillic.

Speech communities around the world have experimented with script change. That is, one or more groups within the society determined that changing the system of writing among their people would bring some material or symbolic gain. In the modern era such change was often linked to expressions of national identity. Alphabets and writing systems can be powerful symbols. However, alphabet change also places the literacy of an adult population in jeopardy. Daily tasks of complying with tax notices, knowing what the schoolteacher wrote on the board during a parent meeting, or understanding the headlines in television news became serious challenges. Many adults would never learn the new alphabet and thus became illiterate overnight. Why would a government put its people's literacy and ability to function in society at risk? In an effort to shed light on these questions, this chapter examines how political and intellectual elites have employed alphabet to shape Turkmen society. Along the way, we will trace the experiences of Ogulbibi's family, noting specifically how representatives from different generations have dealt with alphabet change.

STATE, SOCIETY, AND SCRIPT IN THE IMPERIAL
AND SOVIET ERAS

The people of Turkmenistan have written with four different alphabets over the past one-hundred years: Arabic ca. 1000–1928, Latin (I) 1928–1939, Cyrillic 1940–1993, Latin (II) 1993–present. Ordinary people themselves did not choose to change their writing systems. Rather, intellectual or political elites decided at specific moments in history that a particular alphabet would symbolize changes that the society was experiencing in those moments. Change often entailed a complete break with the past. The reformers could have chosen clothing or men's beards, as Russia's Peter I did in order to Westernize eighteenth-century Russians. Art or literature might have expressed social transformations. For the Turkmen, language, including vocabulary, orthography, and educational instruction, became expressions of identity.[3]

Ogulbibi grew up in a Yomut village near Nebit Dag. Born in 1957, she was a student when the Cyrillic script and the Russian language were basic features of modern Soviet life. Although her family spoke a Yomut tribal dialect, she learned the standard Turkmen literary language and Russian in school, where Turkmen was the language of instruction. Later she studied at the University in Aşgabat, where she learned to drop the regional peculiarities from her daily speech, adopting the standardized national dialect. She married a fellow university student. He was from the Teke tribe, but Ogulbibi continued to wear the Yomut style *yaka* or embroidered neckline and headscarves with patterns that mark her tribal heritage. The slight differences in their dialects, which they spoke freely at home, betrayed their tribal affiliation but did not interfere with comprehension. In many ways, Ogulbibi was representative of her generation. She lived as a Soviet-educated city girl but held fast to her family and village roots.

Like all students, Ogulbibi had learned the Cyrillic script in school. However, unlike many of her urban peers, Ogulbibi had also learned the Arabic script from a village elder. After independence, she studied the new Turkmen National Alphabet in a summer class offered to teachers by the Ministry of Education. Later, when the state emphasized the need for workers to conduct business in Turkmen, not Russian, she taught night classes to those who did not know Turkmen. The alphabet was always the topic of the first lesson. Most of her students were non-Turkmen— Russian, Armenian, maybe Ukrainian—but a few Turkmen appeared in each class. These were typically the Sovietized Turkmen who had not learned to speak fluent Turkmen or could not read it because they had spent their educational and then working years using the Russian language. Although many grew up in villages, they had not learned Turkmen as Ogulbibi had. Their parents were like many others in the Soviet Union who did not school their children in the local language (Moldovan, Turkmen, Evenki) because Russian was the language of industry, medicine, education, and the state. These non-Russians likely studied at elementary schools where the language of instruction was Russian rather than Turkmen. Most could understand and probably speak some Turkmen, but it was less likely that they could read or write in it. That Ogulbibi had learned to read, write, and speak well in both Russian and Turkmen put her in good stead for the post-Soviet era.

About one hundred years earlier, the small number of literate Turks who had lived in the Russian Empire used an Arabic script, employing it as a practical tool but also as a marker of their ethnic and religious identity.[4] The Quran had been recorded in this script, as had much science and literature. Thus, Arabic writing was an important aspect of the cultural and intellectual heritage shared by all Muslims that also differentiated them from non-Muslims. Before and during the Russian empire, small numbers of Turkic children (mostly boys) studied in traditional *maktabs* (elementary schools) and *madrasas* (secondary schools).[5] In traditional Islamic maktabs, the *ulema* (*mullas, ishans,* and *ahuns*) acted as teachers.[6] In these schools, students sat on the floor or on low benches in a half-circle with the instructor in the center, close enough so his *taýak* or stick could reach each student, disciplining or encouraging them as they repeated his recitations. Students learned the letters of the Arabic script and to recognize and pronounce words. However, they did not study reading and writing for functional use. Most of the time was spent reciting and memorizing texts, including the Quran and other religious books that introduced the basics of education and Islamic *terbiýe* (upbringing). In the late nineteenth century, the methods of these traditional schools would become a lightning rod for Muslim modernists throughout Central Asia.

Ogulbibi's early study of Arabic language and writing with the village mulla took on a similar appearance. In fact, throughout the Soviet era informal teaching persisted, despite attacks by local Turkmen reformers and Soviet officials. Ogulbibi's teacher did not have any professional pedagogical training, but he had graduated from a maktab, knew how to "read" the Quran, impart terbiýe, and write in the Arabic script. The village recognized him as the most religious and learned person in the village; thus he oversaw religious rituals such as marriages, funerals, and circumcisions. He gathered the children everyday before school to practice reciting and writing the Arabic letters, rapping their knuckles with the taýak if they made a mistake. The mulla oversaw the children's Islamic education somewhat informally because there was no other organized source for such learning. The Soviet government had spread universal education throughout the Soviet Union, but it did not provide for confessional studies at the elementary level. Parents were responsible for teaching their children *Türkmençilik*, or how to live as proper Turkmen and good Muslims. But the custom of entrusting the children to a village elder or mulla for study of *adat* and *edeb* (customs), prayers, basic literacy (in the Arabic script), and religious texts continues today.

Ogulbibi took me to her village, and she made a special point of visiting Atamurad *pahir*.[7] Over ninety years old, he was still busy teaching the village children. He endeavored to impart wisdom and terbiýe to all he met, including this non-Muslim American female. Like many teachers throughout Central Asia, this mulla had never actually organized a formal maktab. He worked only from his home, where his door was always open and visitors seeking erudition or services for a Muslim rite frequently appeared. He did not work as a professional pedagogue, but rather served Allah and his community.

In the late nineteenth century, when the mulla's parents and Ogulbibi's grandfather were still trying to fight off Russian military incursions, peoples worldwide were discussing "modernity." Intellectuals from all nations shared ideas about nationalism and the place of traditional customs in a rapidly changing world. Turks too became concerned with problems of literacy, education, and social reform. Turkmen learned of these ideas from Tatars, Azerbaijanis, Ottomans, and Uzbeks who had already begun experimenting with reforms as part of their quest for broad social change. These reformers (*Jadids*) targeted traditional schools and teaching methods as outdated and in dire need of revision. To this end, they began a movement known as jadidism, from Arabic *usul-i jadid* or "new method."[8] Jadids saw traditional pedagogy, such as the rote memorization of religious texts, as flawed. They believed that a "new method" of teaching, one focused on reading for comprehension, would aid Turkic youth in interacting with the modern world. Reformers targeted functional, mass literacy, and the education of girls, as key to development of a "modern" Turkic society.[9]

The new method aimed to make learning easier and more accessible to greater numbers of Turkmen. However, the traditional Arabic script did not fully reflect every spoken Turkic sound; Turkic languages had more vowel sounds than the Arabic script had symbols to represent. Traditional Arabic symbols ى, و, ا [10] (even with aids that extended these short vowels into long ones) could not differentiate between *all* of the Türkmen sounds: [a], [ä], [e], [i], [o], [ö], [u], [ü], [y]. It was this disconnect between the spoken and the written language that was thought to make learning to read and write more difficult.[10] Turkic reformers decided that the best way to address this problem was by expanding the alphabet to include more letters. They created a reformed Arabic script by adding diacritics above and in front of these vowel letters to mark a greater number of vowel sounds.

A small number of Turkmen, such as Muhammed Geldiew, Muhammetgulu Ataba ýew, and Durdu Gylyç, studied at new method schools with Uzbek or Tatar teachers and then returned home to apply progressive ideas in Turkmen society. Turkmen built upon broader jadid ideas to create a local reform movement, writing their own poetry, textbooks, and grammars to ensure that teachers had materials and the populace had access to the ideas. Only a handful of new method schools opened in Turkmen lands. Still, they did graduate students and make an impact on Turkmen modern identity. As these students went on to become influential playwrights and literary figures, Turkmen began using the terms "old method" and "new method" to describe institutions, teachers, books, and the respective Arabic scripts.[11]

The 1917 Bolshevik revolution shook up the political system. Despite the many changes the new Communist system brought, the Central Asian debates over culture and modernity carried over into the new Soviet era (1917–1991). The enthusiasm of Turkmen alphabet and education reformers initially merged with early Soviet cultural goals, especially under the influence of *korenizatsiia* (nativization).[12] Efforts to spread the socialist, Soviet culture among the many different peoples within the USSR brought local intellectuals, including jadids, into Soviet institutions.[13] Many contributed to the "liquidation of illiteracy," an important strategy in the Bolsheviks' building of socialism. Moscow and Turkmen intellectuals endeavored together to promote literacy and the people's integration into the modernizing world by producing new textbooks, dictionaries, codified grammars, and standardized scripts. Turkmen such as Orazmammet Wepaýew published poems and articles in the journals— *Turkmen Ili* and *Tokmak*—designed to bring socialist ideas to ordinary Turkmen *in the Turkmen language.*

Initial Soviet progress was uneven. In these years, the late 1920s, Ogulbibi's mother, Jemal, began studying in the village elementary school. She still had to help her family with chores such as cotton picking and hosting visitors, so she sometimes missed classes. This irregular attendance, however, was not unusual in the villages, especially among girls. After age nine Jemal no longer attended the maktab, but was taught basic reading and writing by a knowledgeable aunt. While this provided Jemal with some rudimentary literacy skills, it did not afford her an education. Her experience, typical of the times, was the kind of situation that jadids hoped to change. They wanted both girls and boys to have access to a broad education.

While traditional Islamic maktabs struggled with questions of teaching methods and changing the Arabic alphabet,[14] parents were learning about alphabet reforms from *Turkmen Ili*. Not many Turkmen could read and write in these years, but elites, including Geldiew, Atabaýew, and Wepaýew, reached out to the community first with jadidist writings and then with Soviet journals and adult literacy classes paid for by the central government in Moscow.[15] Meanwhile, their children's schools and textbooks were changing rapidly. The state began funding schools and paying salaries; government drummed the *ulema* out of the teaching corps—the state desired only teachers with formal pedagogical training; new texts reflected a secular-based education; and students sat at Western-style desks. A teacher would not be *mulla,* a clerical instructor in Islamic schools, but *mugallym,* signifying a secular teacher in a job that was being professionalized.

In 1921, Ogulbibi's grandfather read aloud to her family the news of the *Türkmen Bilim Heýaty* (Turkmen Academic Commission) that Moscow had funded. Developing out of both Moscow's concerns and local interest in educating Turks, this three-man committee aimed to "liquidate illiteracy" among Turkmen. But first they needed to have a stable, standardized writing system. The problem was that the many regional dialects of Turkmen meant that words were pronounced differently in different regions: "'father' had multiple variants (*kaka, ata, däde, aba, eke,* and *akga*)."[16] Newspapers and textbooks reflected the dialect of the writer or editor. Both Turkmen elites and Moscow were frustrated by the variations. In 1924, Moscow drew borders through Central Asia, creating the Soviet Socialist Republic of Turkmenistan. Certainly such an entity needed to have stability in its newspapers and textbooks. The committee set to standardize the literary language so all Turkmen would study one pronunciation and all newspapers would use the same spelling. Within a few years the committee introduced a refined version of the Turkmen-jadid (Arabic) script, followed by grammars and rules about spelling.

In 1926, not long after the alphabet and spelling reforms were published, four Turkmen, including Geldiew, traveled to Baku for the first conference of the New Turkic Alphabet Committee (NTAC). Representatives from around the Turkic-speaking world gathered at this Moscow-funded conference to discuss the possibilities of adopting a Latin-based script in place of the Arabic writing, changing spelling rules, and generally stabilizing the written representation of spoken dialects. Ultimately, the NTAC recommended scrapping the Arabic script (even in its modified forms). Latin was seen as simpler, easier to learn, and more modern. Another possible reason for Moscow's support of this change could be that the central government might have wanted to separate Muslims from their cultural heritage: "The significance of the [script] decree was manifold. Overnight it produced an instant crop of millions of illiterate Muslims who found that a wall had been erected between them and their pre-Soviet cultural heritage. Another major impact was the elimination of a vital channel of communication with the Islamic *umma* [community] outside the Soviet Union . . ."[17] The Quran was written in the Arabic script. To many, giving up that writing system was the same as giving up an aspect of their Muslim identity. Still, there was "a lack of serious [Turkmen] opposition" to the Congress's proposal.[18]

Whatever reasons actually lay behind the change in script, the fact is that Turkmen literacy was once again challenged. Not long after the 1926 Congress, the Turkmen Academic Commission gave up trying to perfect the Arabic script for spoken Turkmen. Scholars continued work on an alphabet to reflect spoken Turkmen, but now with the Latin script. Practical social needs pressed in on them. Schools needed new books, again, and the rationale behind the change had to be explained to the people. The newspaper *Türkmenistan* published alphabet charts and polemics of linguists and politicians who debated the benefits of the new script. Beginning in 1926 the paper slowly shifted from the Arabic script to the Latin. First the title appeared in the new alphabet, then a new section appeared: *Täze Elipbiýi Bölimi* (New Alphabet Section). This special section showed alphabet charts, discussed ideas behind language reform, and eventually included everyday news as the Latin alphabet spread to all the pages.

In the 1930s, the political climate in the USSR shifted from an atmosphere of compromise between the state and local intellectuals to one in which the centralized state firmly took control of Soviet cultural policy. Stalin's regime attacked the intellectuals who had been educated during the Imperial era. Instead, it favored younger cadres who had been trained by the Party and were considered loyal to the government. The regime sought to purge the system of potential "nationalists" or intellectuals who were perceived as expressing sympathy for their ethnic group over the interests of "the workers." The Communist Party accused regional cultural reformers of possessing "chauvinistic" goals that threatened socialism. Arrests and executions spread through the Soviet Union. In Turkmenistan, Kümüşaly Böriew, Turkmen Education Commissar and Director of the Turkmen Cultural Institute, was jailed in 1932; Abdülhekim Gulmuhammedow, editor of the newspaper *Türkmenistan*, took his own life; Muhammed Geldiew and other well known intellectuals and political leaders, such as Gaýgasyz Atabaýew, were branded "bourgeois nationalists" and *halk düşmany* (enemies of the state).[19] Their names were stripped from history unless as an enemy of the state; their professional and intellectual achievements went largely unacknowledged.

Ogulbibi's father-in-law, a contemporary of these men, was a writer of fiction in the 1930s. Because his stories focused on Turkmen rather than Soviet heroes, the Party classified him as a "bourgeois nationalist" and jailed him in 1938. Still, he was luckier than some of his colleagues: he was never sent to a labor camp and he was released after Stalin's death in 1953. In 2001 I attended the annual *Hudaý ýoly* or *hatyra günü* his children held in their father's memory. It marked the occasion of his death with the respect he had been denied during his life.[20] Today Ogulbibi's father-in-law's works are found in private libraries but are not widely known among the younger generation. His works were printed in the Latin alphabet, but by the time he was freed from jail a new alphabet was in place. His works became unmentionable for political reasons, but even after his rehabilitation they were absent from libraries and the literary canon due to alphabetic circumstances.

Turkmen officially used the Latin alphabet in schools, newspapers, state documents, literature, and public signs from 1928 to 1940.[21] The years up to and even after the 1928 alphabet reforms had reflected some degree of cooperation between local Turkmen and central Soviet representatives. However, in 1940 authorities in Moscow decreed that the Turkmen, along with many other Soviet peoples, would shift to a Cyrillic writing system. People had to learn a script astoundingly different from their own. Textbooks, typesettings, and state documents changed again. But with this change little discussion took place, and there are few records of state announcements. There were no explanations or exhortations from the intelligentsia. In this way, the alphabet symbolized a larger political shift: cultural control, centralization, and Russification. Language and education became vehicles for a Soviet-wide shift away from local peculiarities to cultivation of a common, Soviet people.

The Cyrillic alphabet expressed "the unity of the great Soviet people, brotherhood, and Stalinist friendship."[22] Local dialects remained the language of elementary education and the family, but Russian became the language of administration, science, technology, and higher education.

Everyday life was divided into linguistic spheres; though no longer into alphabetic spheres, since Turkmen now shared the Russian alphabet. Over the following decades Russian-language speakers came to hold most positions of authority. Ethnic Turkmen could progress in most areas of the Soviet system only if they had facility in Russian.

Ogulbibi was able to study at the university because she had learned Russian. But as a student, she explained to me, she did not know it well and preferred to speak Turkmen. In those years, "Russian was the language of everything, Turkmen was [considered] uncouth, and people laughed at us if we spoke it on a city bus." Only in her twenties then, Ogulbibi had already learned two languages and three alphabets. Life in the Soviet Union did not require her to know the Arabic script, but it was a valued part of her heritage. Her ability to express familiarity with Islamic texts and learning brought her respect among her Turkmen friends.

THE END OF THE USSR, AND A NEW NATIONAL ALPHABET

Alphabet reform again arose as an aspect of Turkmen identity with Mikhail Gorbachev's attempt to reform Soviet systems. As part of these attempts, a 1988 central Party resolution guaranteed "the free development and equal use by all the Soviet Union's citizens of their own language and the mastery of the Russian language."[23] Accordingly, on 24 May 1990 Turkmenistan passed the "Law on Language" that raised Turkmen to the status of the state language.[24] Many ethnic Turkmen hailed this law as an appropriate reflection of social shifts taking place under *perestroika.*[25] Instead of Russian, the Turkmen language became the conduit to political, economic, and social power. But it was still written in the Cyrillic script.

Public debate about everyday language began to flourish not only among linguists and educators, but also in the general public. The new status of Turkmen led to discussions of further sociocultural reforms, including a script change. Throughout the USSR, ethnic groups began talking about renouncing the Cyrillic script. Turkmenistan's populace joined in public debates over whether the script should change, and how. Citizens published their opinions regarding the representation of foreign words, especially ubiquitous Russian terms. One newspaper article elicited a great deal of public response. It asked why the Turkmen alphabet should contain the letters *ш* [sh], *щ* [shch], *ж* [zh] and soft/hard signs, *ь* and *ъ*, explaining that these letters were useless to the Turkmen language because they appeared only in foreign words such as *жандарм* (gendarme) and *журналист* (journalist). The authors argued that these signs should be eliminated because they only symbolized the authority that Moscow had over them for seventy years.

Turkmen linguists P. Azymow and B. Çaryýarow suggested in a scholarly article, which was of such interest that it was reprinted in the popular press, that in addition to the five above listed letters that the Cyrillic letters ё [yo], ю [yu], я [ya], ц [ts], and ч [ch] should also be eliminated. Some Turkmen agreed; some disagreed vehemently. Other articles expressed concern that it was an inappropriate time in Turkmenistan's history to bother with alphabet reform. The country's economy was weak and the bureaucracy was still organizing itself. One citizen asked, "In this [time of] paper shortage, why should we waste time, spend lead, use up the paper we do have, just to play with people's nerves [with alphabet change]?"[26]

Although the populace expressed its opinions, the state took ultimate responsibility—organizing, paying for, and implementing language and alphabet reform after the disintegration of the USSR. Turkmenistan declared its independence on 27 October 1991. This new era began with a dramatic backlash against the Soviet experience. One of the government's first initiatives was to jettison Cyrillic and design a new Latin alphabet. Both the president and scholars made clear that they saw the culture and language as parts of the larger questions Turkmenistan faced in its new political configuration. Linguists and state representatives worked together to produce the symbols of Turkmen independence.

On 21 January 1993, Turkmenistan's government created a high-profile, six-man advisory Alphabet Delegation of intellectuals and state administrators to carry out the details of (re-)Latinization. President Saparmurat Niyazov (Saparmyrat Nyýazow) was chair, and Professor Myratgeldi Söýegow, director of the Academy of Sciences Turkmen Language Institute, was the lead academic. The Turkmen Language's New Alphabet State Advisory Commission created a thirty-letter alphabet. The commission then recommended the reform to the public via the press, stressing that it was imperative to change from the Cyrillic to the Latin script in a manner that "preserved comprehension." After all, a great deal of the population was literate primarily in Russian. Alteration of the script would not only create social change, it would affect the economy as well; some citizens would gain jobs, some would lose them. This was one reason for the state's decision to undertake alphabet reform in an unhurried manner, planning implementation over the period from 1993 to 1995.[27] The commission began with street signs and newspaper mastheads and broadened slowly from there. The schools began with the first grades and, each subsequent year, expanded the focus to include the upcoming class, keeping pace between classroom-instruction, teacher training, and development of new textbooks.[28] Government offices were the final targets for reform.

Turkmenistan's government engineered the transition to a new alphabet, informing the populace through newspapers and television. Beginning in 1992, various authors communicated their support of the new Latin-based writing system in the press. Despite the costs incurred, many ethnic

Turkmen perceived the new alphabet as an appropriate symbol of the new country because it asserted distinct national identity. In eradicating Soviet Cyrillic, Aşgabat signaled an anti-Russian cultural stance that was moving swiftly throughout the former Soviet Union. Still, literacy was a real concern. Unlike in earlier periods, the concern involved how to maintain the degree of literacy reached during the Soviet years.

On 12 April 1993, the *Mejlis* (Assembly of Deputies) passed a resolution in support of the law adopting the new Latin-based script in place of the Cyrillic. The president explained that the Cabinet of Ministers, in cooperation with the Academy of Sciences and regional officials, would oversee the creation and implementation of a new alphabet for the Turkmen language. In June he provided his rationale for reform, underscoring his expectations that the new alphabet would enhance Turkmenistan's cultural revival, increase its ability to communicate with other countries, and expand citizens' access to information technology and computers.

The president made a separate presentation to the Mejlis in which he discussed the highlights of Latinization. He devoted a third of that speech to discussion of information technology and the idea that a Latin alphabet would facilitate use of computers. President Nyýazow said that alphabet change would aid Turkmenistan in catching up to global standards. He even explained that one of the underlying reasons for the transition from the Cyrillic alphabet to a Latin-based one was that, "as usage of the Cyrillic alphabet had made it easier for Turkmen to learn Russian, so would a Latin script assist them in learning English, the international language of technology."[29] To that end, the President himself insisted that all letters in the new alphabet be taken from signs found on typical keyboards. For example, *instead of* borrowing letters from the Turkish alphabet, the Turkmen alphabet committee chose "universally recognized signs": $, ¢ [sh], £ [zh], ¥, ÿ [й], Ñ, ñ [ng]. Turkmen citizens slowly gained access to computers imported from Dubai and Abu Dhabi and internet connections via the state internet provider *Turkmentelekom*. Though admittedly limited, users viewed this access to information and the larger world as an important aspect of their new independence

The 1993 New Turkmen National Alphabet made clear President Nyýazow's insistence that the new alphabet accord with Western technology. However, the intellectual community did not agree with all the details. In 1995, Professors M. Söýegow and B. Öwezow explained in a newspaper article that the alphabet commission had decided to modify the 1993 alphabet. The sign "$" would no longer represent [sh]. Instead the commission chose Ş, a letter found in the Turkish alphabet, stressing that this alphabet would better correspond with computers.[30] A year later the commission also replaced £, ¥, ñ with ž, ÿ, and ň. Not long after that they again changed ÿ to ý.

It is understandable that a new country faced for the first time with

ТУРКМЕН ЭЛИПБИЙИ

A a	*α*	N n	*к*
B b	*б*	Ñ ñ	*нg*
Ç ç	*г*	O o	*о*
D d	*g*	Ö ö	*ө*
E e	*э*	P p	*n*
Ä ä	*ә*	R r	*p*
F f	*ф*	S s	*c*
G g	*г*	Ş ç	*ш*
H h	*x*	T t	*m*
I i	*u*	U u	*y*
J j	*жg*	Ü ü	*ц*
£ ſ	*ж*	W w	*в*
K k	*к*	Y y	*ы*
L l	*л*	Ÿ ÿ	*й*
M m	*M*	Z z	*з*

The Latin-Based Turkmen Alphabet shown as printed and handwritten. Taken from Myratgeldi Soyegow and Nyyazberdi Rejebow, *Taze Turkmen Elipbiyi* (Asgabat: Ruh, 1993), 14.

the responsibilities of managing a modern national system would accomplish some tasks in fits and starts. The changes in the alphabet illustrate that Turkmen were adapting as quickly as they could to circumstances around them. It cost time and money to modify the alphabet. Books with the 1993 version became obsolete in just two years time. Public signage, purchased from a company in Moscow, changed again and again. Teachers had to keep up and ensure that students were learning the new letters. The state began printing packages and labels for products in the new alphabet. In the case of a local brand of sugar cubes, the packaging had been printed according to the first alphabet proposal in 1993. The letter *ñ* appeared in the word *Türkmenistanyñ*. However, after the 1996 reforms the letter *ň* replaced *ñ*. The factory had to correct thousands of boxes of sugar by covering the old *ñ* with tiny stickers showing the letter *ň* to spell: *Türkmenistanyň Altyn Asyr önümi* (Turkmenistan's Golden Era product). The symbols of independence did not come cheaply.

Ogulbibi does not know English. She does, however, know the new Turkmen Latin Alphabet very well, and in her spare time she teaches Turkmen language. Her two daughters flourish in their study at universities in Aşgabat and hope to find work involving the foreign languages they have learned. Her husband knows the new script, but he too shows the habit of continuing to write in Cyrillic. Unlike Ogulbibi's own mother, Jemal, his mother, Altyn, never studied an alphabet other than Cyrillic. Altyn says she will never learn the new alphabet. She used to read the paper every day in Cyrillic. But since they are now only printed in Latin she gets her news from neighbors or the radio. She enjoys reading and has several decades' worth of Soviet published novels in her home library; some are in Turkmen, some in Russian. She is a bright woman, but must take her granddaughter with her to handle ordinary tasks such as paying the telephone bill or reading her medicine at the pharmacy. Even Jemal, despite her early introduction to reading in both Arabic and Latin scripts, shows the signs of alphabet fatigue. She too is uninterested in reading current news since in addition to letters much of the vocabulary has changed to support the new post-Communist environment.

The family story brings us back to the question of why a government would risk the literacy of its citizens. Does alphabet change create illiteracy? With each major political shift Turkmen adopted new songs, new slogans, and often, a new script. Political conditions required the people to remake themselves. The history of alphabet change reflects the ways that politics shape identity. Most of the reforms intended to expand upon each of these and to encourage the Turkmen society's greater integration into a global community. The change to Cyrillic, however, aided in defining Turkmen as part of the Soviet community, with only limited ties to other peoples. The post-Soviet reforms, in contrast, set in motion a decade of change that intended not only to reverse Russification, but also to assert Turkmenification. In neither case did the government set out to *create* illiteracy. But the political objectives, such as marking a new national identity, were sought at such price that the cost to adult knowledge was acceptable.

The script reforms discussed here challenged the Turkmen people's identity as well as their literacy. Many citizens who wrote about language or alphabet in the press were concerned with Turkmen identity and the symbolic nature of alphabet and language status. However, they were equally or perhaps more concerned with the influences of such change on everyday life. President Nyýazow's post-independence announcements about script change emphasized the "everyday" concerns of being able to get a job and keep up with a global economy as much as national identity considerations. In many respects, defining Turkmenistan will be an ongoing project. Ogulbibi and other Turkmen know who they are, but the various methods of symbolizing that identity to the world—in some cases, through alphabet—will continue to be a challenge as Turkmen society evolves.

NOTES

1. Ogulbibi is a composite character based upon several Turkmen women I spent time with in Turkmenistan 1997–2004.
2. The Turkmen government adopted the Latin-based Turkmen National Alphabet [*Türkmen Milli Elipbiýi*] on 12 April 1993.
3. The term "Turkic" refers to the shared cultural and linguistic heritage of Turkic-language groups.
4. Paul B. Henze, "Politics and Alphabets in Inner Asia," in *Advances in the Creation and Revision of Writing Systems*, Joshua A. Fishman, ed. (The Hague: Mouton, 1977), 374.
5. Girls also studied, but often in separate areas and with a female teacher.
6. *Mulla* indicates a person with an elementary education; a graduate of a maktab. *Ishan* or *ahun* designates a person with a higher education; graduate of a madrasa. *Ulama* (pl.), *alim* (s.), a title for a religious scholar or leader.
7. A Turkmen form of respect for an honored elder.
8. Adeeb Khalid, *The Politics of Muslim Cultural Reform: Jadidism in Central Asia* (Berkeley: University of California Press, 1998).
9. Hakan Kırımlı, *National Movements and National Identity among the Crimean Tatars (1905–1916)* (Leiden: E. J. Brill, 1996).
10. Ideas about phonetic teaching and perceptions about reflecting the spoken word in the written were popular in Europe and Russia in the nineteenth century. See Ben Eklof, *Russian Peasant Schools: Officialdom, Village Culture, and Popular Pedagogy, 1861–1914* (Berkeley: University of California Press, 1986).
11. Tagangeldi Täçmyradow, *Türkmen edebi diliniň Sovet Döwründe ösüşi we normalanyşy* (Aşgabat: Ylym, 1984), 160.
12. *Korenizatsiia*, or nativization, was a program aimed at defining and strength-

ening ethno-linguistic groups in the 1920s and 1930s. For a general study of this Soviet policy see Terry Martin, *The Affirmative Action Empire: Nations and Nationalism in the Soviet Union, 1923–1939* (Cornell: Cornell University Press, 2001).

13. *Iazykovoe stroitel'stvo*, language construction, was the language planning part of *sovetskoe stroitel'stvo* [Sovietization].

14. Not all teachers/mullas supported reform. See Khalid.

15. See Myratgeldi Söýegow, *On çynar: Ilkinji Türkmen Dilçileri ve Edebiýatlary Hakynda Oçerkler* (Aşgabat: Kuýash, 1993) and Tagangeldi Täçmyradow, *Muhammet Geldiewiň ömri ve döredijiligi* (Aşgabat: Ylym, 1989).

16. Adrienne Lynn Edgar, *Tribal Nation: The Making of Soviet Turkmenistan* (Princeton: Princeton University Press, 2004), 149.

17. Ayşe Rorlich, *The Volga Tatars: A Profile in National Resilience* (Stanford, Calif.: Hoover Institution Press, 1986), 151.

18. Edgar, 141.

19. Söýegow, 21–66.

20. *Hudaý ýoly*, or path to God, is the Turkmen name for a Muslim tradition commemorating the death of a family member. Some families hold these "thanksgivings" on the first anniversary, some on the tenth, but some gather every year.

21. "Karary 268 san," *Türkmenistan*, 4 January 1928: 1. At this time, Moscow feared that Cyrillic alphabets would seem imperialistic and create resentment among Turks.

22. John Perry, "Script and Scriptures: The Three Alphabets of Tajik Persian, 1927–1997," *Journal of Central Asian Studies* 2, no. 1 (Fall/Winter 1997): 8.

23. Text in *Izvestiia*, 24 September 1989.

24. On Gorbachev's reforms and post-Soviet alphabet reform throughout Central Asia, see Jacob Landau and Barbara Kellner-Heinkele, *Politics of Language in the ex-Soviet Muslim States* (Ann Arbor: The University of Michigan Press, 2001).

25. *Perestroika* translates loosely as "restructuring." It referred to Gorbachev's goal of reforming the state bureaucracy in an attempt to save it from its inherent problems. Perestroika also allowed for *glasnost,'* or openness, which gave citizens permission to critique the system and its administrators.

26. P. Azymow and B. Çaryárow, "Türkmen diliniň elibpiýini kämilleşdirmeli," *TSSR YA habarlary. Gumanitar ylymlaryň seriýasy*, 1990, no. 3: 3–11, reprinted in *Mygallymlar gazeti*, 28 November 1990, 1.

27. There was also the problem of attaining textbooks—most were sent by Turkey—and training teachers.

28. Interview with Dr. Myratgeldi Söýegow, Professor of Turkmen Language and Literature, International Turkmen-Turkish University, Aşgabat, Turkmenistan, 2 June 2004.

29. Türkmenbaşy, 33–34.

30. B. Öwezow and M. Söýegow, "Täze ýazuwymyz: Düşündiriş berýäris," *Türkmenistan*, 11 January 1995, 1.

18. Travels in the Margins of the State: Everyday Geography in the Ferghana Valley Borderlands

Madeleine Reeves

"You see, then we were *free*. You could travel anywhere you wanted, get on a train and ride to Moscow if you wanted without even taking your passport with you! Now you just try! Now I become a criminal every time I want to visit my mother. What kind of freedom is that?" Saodat-opa thumbed her green Uzbek "citizen's passport" nervously as she spoke.[1] The pages, full of the stamps that traced her movement through the newly bordered routes of the Ferghana Valley, were soft at the edges from frequent checking.

We were waiting for the pages to be scrutinized once again. I was making the journey with Saodat-opa and the youngest of her seven children from the village where she had spent her married life to the childhood home where her parents and brothers still lived. When Saodat-opa and her husband, Ilkhom-aka, had married thirty years previously, the two-hundred-kilometer distance separating their respective families was considered large, but not excessively so. Both husband and wife were in the first generation of their respective families to get a university education; they had met as foreign language students in Leninabad (today Khujand, Tajikistan) and had taken pride in holding a "komsomol" wedding, blending Brezhnev era innovations (a white dress for the bride, vodka at the wedding feast) with much older features of the Tajik culture to which they both subscribed.[2]

As custom dictated, Saodat-opa left her family home in the small industrial town of Komsomolsk, in the Tajik SSR, to live with her husband's family in his native village in Sokh *rayon* (district), in the neighboring Uzbek republic. Neither of their families considered the fact that they were from different union republics an obstacle to marriage. Indeed, as *peredovye kadry* ("foremost cadres") who would be among the first to teach foreign languages in rural Tajik medium schools, their marriage brought pride to both of their families as a sign of their progressiveness: they had married for love, after getting acquainted at the university. Ilkhom had waited for Saodat to finish her studies before asking for her hand. They were both members of the Communist youth league, and the fact that Ilkhom had chosen a wife from beyond his own locale was celebrated as a spur to his district's development. "I was," he commented with pride, "one of the first in Sokh to take a bride who was educated. Before Saodat started teaching, there were very few female teachers here. We were incredibly dedicated to Sokh's development. They gave us all kinds of awards (*nagrady*) [. . .] We thought of ourselves as Soviet then."[3]

Soviet internationalism now has a nostalgic ring for Ilkhom-aka and his family. Saodat-opa finds herself in a situation where she and her natal family are citizens of independent states, Tajikistan and Uzbekistan, operating a visa regime with one another that is legitimated through a discourse of "security."[4] At the time of our journey, a visit such as Saodat's would officially require her relatives across the border to issue a letter of invitation, certified through their local office of internal affairs. Saodat, in turn, would have to travel to Tashkent where, ten days later and upon payment of a consular fee (a considerable sum on her teacher's salary), she would be issued a visa to enter Tajikistan.[5] An analogous situation faces citizens of Tajikistan wanting to enter or cross into Uzbekistan. In practice, the time, uncertainty, and expense involved in such a process means that for those, like Saodat-opa, wanting to snatch a quick visit to relatives amid her huge load of domestic responsibilities, to attend a life-cycle ceremony (*toi*) or funeral, this official route is never even considered, with families whose kin networks straddle the border preferring instead to "negotiate" a bribe (*pora*) with the border guards and customs officers at the relevant posts. Saodat-opa's sweat-softened passport-cover, her nervous flicking of its pages, spoke of the tension, uncertainty, and humiliation that this informal route involved.

This chapter seeks to gain an analytical grasp on such transformation of everyday geographies in the Ferghana Valley by focusing on a single valley journey, made at the time of the spring new year (*Navruz*) celebration between a married and a maternal home. Saodat-opa's journey is chosen neither because it is especially dramatic or unusual, nor because her particular predicament as an Uzbekistani Tajik wanting to travel to relatives in Tajikistan is in any way exceptional. It is narrated, rather, because her journey and the elements it contains (checkpoints, admonishments, categorizations, bribes . . .) are repeated in myriad forms by men and women, young and old, Kyrgyz, Tajik, and Uzbek, going about their normal lives in the Ferghana valley. State borders have become part of everyday reality for thousands of people in Central Asia. By focusing on *practice*, retracing Saodat-opa's journey, we can begin to get an insight into the micro-encounters through which this normalization occurs.[6]

MOVEMENT, CLOSURE, AND THE TRANSFORMATION OF
EVERYDAY GEOGRAPHIES

The idea, as Saodat-opa expressed it, that the Soviet Union was "free" and
that the current post-Soviet condition is, by contrast, one of *restricted* mobility, perhaps rings unusually to Western ears. Dominant narratives of
post-socialist "transition," captured in the compelling image of the Berlin
wall being torn down by crowds of East Germans longing to rejoin the
"West," have tended to presuppose that an era of restricted movement has
given way to a period of greater mobility, un-freedom to freedom, the foreign transformed into the familiar.[7] Such images have been invoked as met-
onyms for the much broader collapse of Cold War ideological antagonisms,
bolstering a discourse of post-Communist "transition" that has often been
both teleological and triumphalist.[8]

Anthropologists working in post-Communist states, including Central
Asia, have been some of the most vocal in critiquing simplistic narratives
of transition, encouraging instead a ground-up approach sensitive to what
Morgan Liu has called "the actual processes of how values like entrepreneurship or citizenship take root (or fail to take root) at the level of mundane life."[9] However, while this approach has successfully helped us train
our sights upon the micro-level, phenomenological dimensions of border
openings that are typically approached from the "top down,"[10] there has
been comparatively less discussion of the reverse side of this phenomenon:
the *contraction* of everyday, experiential geographies in the wake of Soviet
collapse;[11] the transformation of places once familiar, once "ours," into sites
which remind of changed status—comrade into alien, fellow-citizen into
foreigner; or the myriad daily performances of border-guards, newsreaders,
teachers, and village functionaries that construct difference, create an exception, imbue the abstract category "citizenship" with salience and emotion, with the state's terrifying magic.[12]

The lack of ethnographic attention to globalization's Janus-face in the
post-Soviet space—to the appearance of *new* boundaries, new points of exclusion, at the same time that they are being dismantled elsewhere—is also
characteristic of contemporary anthropologies more generally. As a discipline historically focused on small-scale and seemingly static communities,
anthropology has undergone a radical disciplinary shift in recent decades
toward accounting for "flows" and "displacements" of people, projects,
concepts, and practices that cannot easily be contained within traditional
analytical categories, nor grasped with the timeworn tools of village fieldwork.[13] This has prompted a rich and productive strand of theorizing, but it
risks generating its own scholarly lacunae: the reality in many sites around
that increasing globalization has fostered its own forms of closure. As Yael

Navaro-Yashin has argued in the context of the heavily bordered Turkish Republic of Northern Cyprus, "[a]nthropologies of globalization [. . .] fail to study the ways in which the very processes of transnationalism which supposedly promote mobility and flexibility also engender the opposite: immobility, entrapment, confinement, incarceration."[14]

This omission is significant for our understanding of everyday life in Central Asia. For less visible and less triumphal than the dramatic reopening of borders is the reality that for many citizens the collapse of Communism has actually entailed a de facto *decrease* in mobility, whether through the vagaries of newly installed visa regimes, dramatic hikes in fuel prices, or the collapse of state-run transport systems. It has transformed travel within neighboring republics into a nervous attempt to avoid the document check (*proverka*). It has also meant that distant sites to which one formerly traveled as citizen are now encountered in a different guise—as labor migrant, guest-worker (*gastarbeiter*), even, in popular discourse, slave (*rab/kul*)—the latter term capturing not just new contours of economic dependence, but radically transformed status in sites where one would formerly have been "one of ours" (*svoi*).[15]

Nowhere is this more true than in Central Asia's Ferghana Valley, a broad fertile zone (22,000 square kilometers) that is encircled by the by the Tien Shan and Pamir Alay ranges to north and south to create a distinct, densely populated ecological and cultural zone. Inhabited by Uzbeks, Kyrgyz, Tajiks, and a number of smaller ethnic groups who migrated or were deported as part of the great Soviet modernizing project, the valley has historically been marked by a high degree of ethnic interdependence, with shared bazaars, trade routes, sacred sites, and canal systems, coupled with elaborate unofficial mechanisms for regulating water use between upstream and downstream communities.[16] Following the national-territorial delimitation of 1924, the valley was divided administratively between Kyrgyz, Uzbek, and later Tajik union republics in a complex and contested process that was crucial in mobilizing and crystallizing identities along "ethnic" lines.[17] As well as marking out the exterior contours of the new Union republics, the delimitation process and subsequent adjustments to the borders during collectivization created a series of enclaves— "islands" of territory belonging to one union republic entirely enclosed within the territory of another; yet these, like all borders in the Ferghana Valley, unmarked and frequently unknown in their precise contours, had little salience for locals, even for those living at their edge. It was to one of the larger of these enclaves, Sokh, that Saodat-opa moved on getting married, joining her husband to live in his parents' home. A mountainous district of twenty-three *mahallas* (neighborhoods) watered by the Sokh river, it is administratively part of Uzbekistan, entirely encircled by Kyrgyzstani territory and with an ethnically Tajik population.[18]

Sokh's challenge to a nationalist logic in the Ferghana Valley—a logic in which ethnic and administrative boundaries are seen as ideally co-extensive, ambiguity is eliminated, and cultural diversity seen as inherently threatening—was of little significance for locals when, as one elderly schoolteacher put it, "You could travel with the same passport from here to Murmansk [in northern Russia]." In the geographical imaginary of Sokh residents, the administrative status of "enclave" has gained salience only in the *post*-Soviet period. In the evocative image of a former music teacher turned car mechanic, who traced out the new boundary with an oily thumb for added emphasis, "We have *become* an island. In Soviet times we never thought of ourselves as living separately from our neighbors [in Kyrgyzstan]. Do you see? It's like we're stranded, an island in the sea."

Images of "islands" and "oases" recur frequently in the descriptions of Sokh presented by its residents, as do rather bleaker allusions to spatial confinement in the form of military garrisons and prison cells. It is not difficult to see why. In recent years internal USSR borders between Tajik, Uzbek, and Kyrgyz republics have been transformed into militarized international boundaries, backed up by an elaborate system of visa controls regulating population movement and customs regulations to limit cross-border trade.[19] For those living in border regions, one-time "lines on a map" have now become salient as sites where the "state" must be negotiated on an everyday basis: to get to local markets, to visit friends, to reach relatives in neighboring villages who happen to have become citizens of a different state, or to reach ancestral burial grounds. It also renders villagers acutely conscious of the extent to which local livelihoods depend on the play of politics between the "big ones" (*chongdor/kattalar*) in Tashkent, Bishkek, and Dushanbe. As one NGO activist had put it to me a few months previously, "At moments of tension, it is the border regimes that are tightened, and it is we who [are] taken hostage in our own states." Ideas about what is "local" and "foreign" are being transformed, discourses and practices of citizenship are taking on new significance in an area where other modes of identification (according to settled or nomadic lifestyle, ethnicity, region of origin or religion) were historically far more salient; and a whole host of new agents and technologies of governance are being introduced into border towns and villages.

The result of these processes in the Ferghana Valley has, however, been more complex than a simple contraction of space, a "retreat" to the village, a reconfiguration of identities along nation-state lines. For one thing, there are too many cross-cutting family ties, too much resource interdependence, for everyday geographies to fit easily within the new boundaries of nation-state. People, stories, rumors, television broadcasts, and jokes move across borders and re-embed in new contexts just as much as goods and currency and contraband do. For another, the very fact that the three states into which the valley falls are experimenting with widely divergent economic and political programs means that the fortunes of valley residents are also beginning to stratify along a far greater continuum than was imaginable

Man at Ferghana valley border crossing between Kyrgyzstan and Tajikistan. Sign reads: "Unity, friendship, peace."

in Soviet times—a process which itself generates new patterns of cross-border movement and relations of dependence.[20] It is in this context of simultaneous crossing and closure, subversion and control, that movement itself becomes politicized. By traveling with Saodat-opa and her daughter through an area that has, in the words of Pierre Bourdieu, been "taken over by a thought of the state,"[21] we can begin to trace some of the ways in which the divergent interventions of territorializing states are being mediated at the local level and incorporated into the everyday.

A BORDERLAND JOURNEY

We climbed out of the small Damaz minivan that runs between the center of Sokh and the enclave's westernmost border post and gathered our three small bags by the side of the customs building. Having deposited us, the Damaz sped on along its route toward the outlying villages at the mountainous south of the enclave, the driver turning and bowing deeply in a gesture of respect to the border guard manning the exit barrier so as to avoid having to stop his engine and show his documents. The border guard obliged: the Damaz had local, Uzbekistani number plates and the driver was a regular on this route. It was, as the young soldier at the barrier shouted out to his superior further back, "one of ours," and as such could be spared the time-consuming registration and customs checks that would add minutes, even hours, to journeys begun further afield in Kyrgyzstani cars.

To the unsuspecting passenger seeking to travel between Kyrgyzstan's southern oblasts, the border posts at either end of the Sokh enclave are a strange and unwelcome anomaly—proud assertions of the state's territoriality, its impulse to control, its fear of intrusion in a remote, rural space that is otherwise scarred with all the signs of the state's hasty post-Soviet retreat: abandoned mercury mines, roads with cavernous potholes, abandoned *kolkhoz* machinery rusting with disuse, schools long in need of new roofs. Many are the times when, traveling west along Kyrgyzstan's southern flank with weary Kyrgyz shuttle-traders, heavy-laden with goods from the huge wholesale bazaars in Osh and Kara-Suu, the Sokh border posts prompt otherwise nonchalant passengers into angry soliloquies— the absurdity of the controls just to pass from one piece of "our" country to another; the unfairness of it ("They never check anyone with an Uzbek number plate. Why? Do they think terrorists won't sit in an Uzbek car?"); the expense involved in bribes and favors to get through without a full customs check; the extra time added to an already long journey when a queue of cars and trucks builds up.

For Saodat-opa, however, the feelings invoked by the post were rather different. The large metal customs cabin, decked out proudly in the blue, green, and white colors of the Uzbek flag, beside which we now sheltered, marked the boundaries of the familiar. It was the journey beyond that provoked concern. We had disembarked there in the hope of flagging down a car to take us to the small Kyrgyz town of Batken, an hour away to our west. Sokh and Batken are no longer connected by a regular bus service, though there at the post we knew that if we were to wait long enough we could pick up the old, overworked Ikarus bus that connects the southern Kyrgyz towns of Osh and Batken in an eight-hour bone-jerker of a ride as it is stopped for the regular passport and customs checks. The customs officer sauntered over to eye the strange trio that had been deposited outside his post: Saodat-opa, in her early fifties, shy little Zulaikho, the youngest of her seven children, and me, an English anthropologist who had been living in Sokh for the previous four months. "Where are you going?" he asked. "Botken," Saodat-opa replied on our behalf, pronouncing the word in Tajik. In response to the officer's raised eyebrow she added, in Uzbek, that I had asked her to accompany me to the family with whom I had lived several months previously in Batken for the spring Navruz holiday.

Like many border exchanges, Saodat-opa's story contained a partial truth, a reflex rendering of reality to forestall the questions and accusations that would follow any mention, in this politicized space, of Tajikistan. We would, indeed, be going to Batken, and staying overnight with the Kyrgyz family with whom I had lived earlier in the year before setting off at dawn the following morning for Tajikistan. But Batken was not our final destination, and the journey in question was not entirely my initiative. Saodat-opa was planning to be with her parents in Komsomolsk in time for Navruz, and to stay a few days beyond to attend the huge ceremonial feast, *sunnat toi*, that was to be held to mark a nephew's circumcision. Batken was merely a stopping point for us. But Saodat-opa knew from bitter experience that it was better not to mention Khujand or Komsomolsk at the border here: unlike the familiar destination of Batken, where Sokh residents could legally travel without visas, to mention a destination in Tajikistan would be to invite a thorough search of one's bag, a series of unwanted questions, and possibly the payment of a bribe—the guards' "take" (*stavka*) for turning a blind eye to a journey that was technically illegal.

Several cars passed us heading toward Batken, but all were full, heaving with passengers and with young saplings tied precariously to their roofs, for this was the start of the planting season. Every car doubles as a taxi in these parts and most already had a full load of clients. The large Kamaz trucks that run the "detour route" (*ob"ezd jol*) north of Sokh speak, in turn, of the informal economy that feeds the valley, and which the customs services can make only a token gesture to contain: clothes and household wares from the Kyrgyz bazaars further east in Osh and Kara-Suu, the cheapest in the region because of their imported Chinese goods; contraband petrol from Uzbekistan, on sale throughout Kyrgyzstan's southern regions; base metals obtained from rusting factories for export to Xinjiang; livestock and apples making their way from the higher plains to the cities in the valley's heartlands; Uzbek cotton for illegal processing in Osh, where a far higher price will be paid. To stand at the border and to watch the passing traffic is to glimpse the valley and its life-force in microcosm—the density of production, the trade that links the corners of the valley into a single whole despite the border controls, the risks that are taken to squeeze a profit from the different economic regimes that operate, and the unofficial deals that bind state functionaries into relations of mutual dependency with the traders whose movement they nominally control.[22]

With car after heaving car passing on its way, we waited outside the customs post for the Ikarus to rumble up—there is no schedule, and at this far end of its journey, its arrival time is hard to predict. In between the cars, we chatted with the border guards about their aspirations—most of them *kontraktniki*, contract soldiers here for a six-month posting, happy with their pay but disappointed by the lack of drama that characterizes their day. I pointed to the mug shots of terrorist suspects that were posted on the wall of their cabin behind us. "Have you come across any of these?" I asked. "Not yet. But I'm sure we will one day. When the fighters (*boeviki*) tried to enter Uzbekistan in 1999 and 2000, they nearly got as far as Sokh."

The Ikarus gradually swung into sight, rolling down the smooth dip that marks the western side of the Sokh Valley before pulling up in front of the first of the two large cabins. The passport check that followed was a speedy affair, a familiar routine for border guards and driver and passengers alike, and many of the latter drew a visible sigh of relief when a soldier hopped on board and asked the passengers simply to hold their passports in the air for a quick, visual check. That would mean no unbundling of goods, no long registration process, no frantic squabbles, altogether a shorter journey. Everyone on the bus knows that the scale of scrutiny on these large public buses is a litmus test of interstate relations, an index of the sincerity of "brotherly friendship" that is proclaimed in official Kyrgyz and Uzbek discourse. When relations turn stormy, bus passengers are some of the first to feel the thunder.

Within moments we were on our way toward Batken, Saodat-opa smiling at me with a mixture of excitement and fear. As the bus lunged through the grey, stony wasteland that opens out west beyond the Sokh Valley—the Soviet Union collapsed too soon for grand plans for a reservoir in these parts to be realized, though soon enough for whole villages to be resettled in anticipation—I sensed that Saodat-opa was scanning the landscape for signs of difference. It is a habit I have often noticed when residents of one Ferghana valley settlement have the chance to call on, or even just drive past, the homes of those across the border. In Batken I was quizzed on lifeways in Sokh; in Sokh, it was Batken that was of interest: "Does everyone there have television? What do they watch? Do they have piped gas like us? How much does it cost?" In such questions difference is calibrated—the different economic policies that the two states have introduced, converted into meaningful units of tarmac and pension levels and petrol prices. We passed through three kilometers of waterless land before meeting the Kyrgyz border post at Kyzyl-Bulak, a disused railway wagon parked on an empty stretch of road. It was a smaller and seemingly more temporary affair than the Uzbek post we had just left, but the red Kyrgyz flag painted on to the camouflage background reminded that this, just as much as the more impressive set of buildings that marked the edge of Sokh, was state space *par excellence*—a random assertion of its claim to monopolize legitimate violence and legitimate movement, a point of entry and control, a reminder of the state's territoriality, its "spatializing" impulse.[23]

A soldier climbed on board, asking of the driver, *"Tajikter barby?"* ("Are there any Tajiks [on board]?") The question caught both our ears, and though it was said without aggression, in the matter-of-fact way that one might ask whether there were children present, it made us both glance at each other and slip instinctively deeper into our seats. Was he enquiring about citizenship? Or ethnicity? And did it matter? For a moment we just waited as he paced up the bus eyeing the passports held out. Virtually all were turquoise, the color, here, of belonging, for the passengers were mostly from Batken and beyond in Kyrgyzstan, weary after their long journey. My heart instinctively started to beat faster at the soldier's question, and I sensed from Saodat-opa's sideways glance that hers was too. "But this is silly!" I thought. "We have every right to be here, I have a Kyrgyz visa; Saodat-opa doesn't need one." The soldier came over to us, our passports giving us away even if our appearance—my glasses, Saodat-opa's gold-speckled scarf done up the typical Sokh way, with two ends dangling behind her—didn't. He flicked the pages nonchalantly, scrutinizing the pictures, my series of visas and our respective passport covers for some sign of fault. I instinctively started rehearsing the story that Saodat-opa had given earlier in my head: we were going to Batken; where I had taught English for several months; we needed to be there for the forthcoming Navruz celebration; Saodat-opa was my guest. . . But we did not need to—he thrust our passports back into Saodat-opa's hand, calling out to the driver, "*Kettik!*"—("Let's go!") and the old Ikarus engine spluttered into action again.

It is in such micro-encounters as these that the power of the border regime is contained, that the "border" itself becomes salient not just as abstract geopolitical fact—a line on a map to be traced and memorized in geography lessons—but as a materialization of power that carves itself into the consciousness of valley populations. We had not been hurt or abused or mocked, we had merely been picked out and *classified*—reminded by an eighteen-year-old with a Kalashnikov on his back that whether we were from Sokh or from England, we were, in this parched corner of Kyrgyzstan, *equally* foreign; that the Kalashnikov was there because foreignness is threatening. The salience of the border for locals lies less in its overt violence, less in the shots that are occasionally fired or the landmines that have been scattered at various sensitive border-points, maiming children who roam too far with their cattle and killing livestock, than in the threat that is implicit. It is the unstated *possibility* of violence, the capacity to mark an exception, to create a category, to fix the political bodies inside and out in spaces still remembered as "common," that is significant. From the ethnographic perspective it is in such myriad everyday encounters—in the very *banality* of the passport check—that borders, together with the citizenship regimes they would enforce, "become" real for the Ferghana Valley residents.

With evening just beginning to set in, we arrived in Batken, the cows roaming along its main street giving it the feel more of an oversized village than a regional (*oblast*) center. This settlement of 20,000 had been designated the regional capital after the notorious "Batken events" five years earlier, when an incursion of Islamic militants across the Alay mountains to the south had suddenly focused the attention of the government and international organizations on the region's isolation and relative deprivation. It still had the feel of a settlement struggling to adjust to its sudden shift in status: the thrusting monument to *Erkindik*, freedom, that had been mounted a few months earlier, a copy of the monument found in

Bishkek's central Ala-Too square, still looked rather out of place among the squat low houses and dusty streets above which she presided.

Our arrival at the home of Turat-aka and Jamilya-eje, the Kyrgyz family with whom I had lived the preceding year, was unannounced. Telephone connections as much as road communication have been transformed by the nationalization of space in the Ferghana Valley, and a call from Sokh to Batken is not just costly, but dependent on a fragile link with the Uzbek "mainland." As we approached the recently whitewashed wall of Turat-aka's house, a moment's nervousness—would Jamilya-eje be at home? Was it acceptable for me to roll up at this late hour with guests from Sokh?—gave way, with hugs and smiles and the presenting of *sumalak*, ritual spring food, into the relief of coming "home."

Saodat-opa and Jamilya-eje started chatting to one another in the heavily inflected Uzbek that serves as a cross-border *lingua franca* in the Ferghana Valley, Saodat-opa's speech dotted with Tajik idioms, Jamilya's with Kyrgyz. As we sat eating *plov*, the rice dish traditionally served to guests throughout much of Central Asia, and watching a home video of a recent circumcision feast, the conversation slipped into discussion of weddings, the cost of flour, the parlous state of schooling as increasing numbers of teachers left to work on building sites in Russia, and, as ever, the border regime that has carved the valley up. Jamilya-eje recalled having traveled regularly to Sokh in her youth: "We would go there to the bazaar, sometimes even just to have lunch. The *chaikhanas* were much more civilized than ours ever were, really cultured (*kul'turnye*), even in Soviet times. Then it was all easy, we were all one country." Jamilya has not stopped there now for years.

The following morning we set off early for what we knew to be the most unpredictable part of our journey. Dilapidated yellow buses still ply the route from Batken to Chor-Tepa, just across the border in Tajikistan, but they take several times longer than a share-taxi on the twenty-kilometer journey, stopping at all the villages dotted along the way. Saodat-opa was eager to reach Chor-Tepa as soon as possible. "From there," she said, "we will be okay. No more checks." As we sat waiting at the bus stop for an additional pair of passengers to make the requisite foursome for a share-taxi, a group of tenth-graders passed us on their way to school. All four were wearing jeans, one had a stars-and-stripes scarf tied, bandana-style, around her head. This change in dress-style, according to Batkeners, has just taken root in the last few years, a reflection of the settlement's shift up the civilizational ladder from a mere "village with urban features" (*poselok gorod-skogo tipa*) into a fully fledged town. I recalled a Batken University teacher having commented to me with pride several months before that "our girls have become just a little bit urban (*shaardyk*)," their style now having more in common with the capital city, Bishkek, than with that found in villages just a few kilometers away. The change in style was not lost on Saodat-opa as she watched the girls walking confidently past: "Look how cultured the girls are here. It'll be decades before our girls dress like that. In Sokh it's considered shameful if you let your girl out without covering up, even if she is Zulaikho's age."

After a short wait, a red Audi rolled up at the bus stop, its gleaming exterior contrasting with the dilapidated Soviet *Moskvich* cars that are more commonly seen in Batken. "Anyone for Chor-Tepa?" the driver called out, adding, as emphasis of his credentials, "*inomarka*" ("foreign car"). The car was, it turns out, the driver's pride and joy, the trophy of two successful seasons' work in Russia, driven back from a second-hand car market in Moscow. We piled in gladly, along with a pair of men who had been waiting with us at the bus stop. The road between Batken and Chor-Tepa is lined with the apricot trees on which both communities depend for their livelihood, just beginning, on this sunny mid-March morning, to open into stunning white blossoms in the more sheltered fields. "The apricot tree is like a woman," our driver joked, "very beautiful but totally unpredictable." As the owner of some of the trees just outside Batken—he pointed them out with pride—he well knew that if a frost were suddenly to strike during the next two weeks, he would be without a harvest.[24]

As we neared the border with Tajikistan, beyond a half-completed park honoring the epic hero Manas, we could see the beginnings of a new border post being constructed, this time a much grander and more permanent-looking building than the single disused railway wagon that marked the "edge of the state" further east toward Sokh. Piles of radiators stood in stacks in the sun alongside sheets of futuristic plate glass. Like other Central Asian border posts that have metamorphosed in recent years from disused railway wagons to grand multi-story complexes (invariably to be followed by a much more haphazard trail of money-changing kiosks, mini-markets, and taxi stands), this relatively quiet stretch of road looked set to be transformed by the grand new building that was taking shape at its side.[25]

For the time being, however, the border post we were set to cross between Kyrgyzstan and Tajikistan was still of the informal "wagon" variety, and within moments the first of the two wagon-posts swung into view. A Kyrgyz soldier peered in the driver's window and asked for passports. Saodat-opa and I exchanged brief glances and extracted ours to hand over for inspection. Our driver turned around, his eye initially caught by my document, and then by Saodat-opa's. "What? You've got a *green* passport, *here?* That's not good for us . . ." He instinctively slid out of his seat to try to speak to the border guard outside the car, for in the unwritten rules of border exchange at this end of the valley, the driver answers for the passengers' documents in the first instance. Nobody mentioned citizenship. Nobody needed to: in the color-coded world of state bureaucracies, a passport cover is enough to signal citizen or foreigner. As the soldier scoured our documents, one of our fellow passengers, a Tajik from Chor-Tepa, turned to Saodat-opa and commented in Uzbek, "I thought you were one of ours (*bizniki*), from Chor-Tepa. You look to me like you are Tajik!" "I am," responded Saodat-opa, "but I live in Uzbekistan." And she sketched to him her life trajectory: born in one republic, living now in another, entirely enclosed within a third. "A true valley person, then," laughed our fellow passenger. "Crazy valley (*duratskaya dolina*)!" Saodat-opa answered back, glancing over nervously to the soldier as she did.

The border guard beckoned me to the wagon. "Registration," he said. I went in, to find another pair of soldiers playing cards to while away the time. A buxom blonde in traditional Russian costume smiled out from an election poster on the wall above their heads advertising the Agrarian Party of Russia—a small, intimate reminder in this ultimate "sovereign space" of the multiple ties that continue to link livelihoods in Central Asia with the former Soviet center. The wagon was sparsely decorated: bunk beds, a small cooking stove, a table with the books to register comings and goings, and that ultimate instrument of bureaucratic power—the rubber stamp. It is in the elaborate play of stamps that movement is regulated and tribute extracted. On several occasions I have witnessed passengers being waved through a border post without having their document stamped by one guard, only to be stopped a few kilometers further along their journey for a "spot check" by another guard from the same shift. The unlucky passenger is forced to pay a "fine" in order to continue along his or her journey, ostensibly for having entered the country without the stamp to prove it, thereby having broken the law on the border. According to locals, this is a common scam, based on a tacit agreement (*dogovor*) between the soldiers involved, in which both take a cut of the bribe, with the rest going to the officer in charge of the post (*nachal'nik zastavy*).[26]

My conversation in the stuffy border post wagon was jovial and lighthearted: one of the card-playing soldiers had remembered me from a crossing through the post a year before, and we spent time chatting about our lives in between. I declined an offer of tea, and the chance to join in a hand of their game: foreigners from the "far abroad" are a rarity here, and they were eager to find out about life "over there." How much do border guards earn there? What do people know about Kyrgyzstan? How difficult is it to get a visa to Britain? But the friendly tone immediately changed when they turned to asking about Saodat-opa. "Is that lady traveling with you?" they probed. I explained that we were colleagues, that Saodat-opa was born in Komsomolsk, that all she wanted was to return to her home for the brief spring break that accompanied Navruz. "Please don't give her a hard time," I commented, anticipating the hassles that her Uzbek passport were likely to cause at this border. "Go and call her in," was the noncommittal reply, with one of the two adding quietly, "and you just wait outside." Any deal that was to be negotiated was clearly to be conducted in private.

I climbed down from the wagon and beckoned to Saodat-opa to enter. For the ten minutes that she was gone, I stood outside the wagon, joining my fellow passengers in their conversation about Sokh. As Chor-Tepa Tajiks, they, too, were interested to know how their "brothers" in Sokh lived, for the territory there was as much off-limits to them as Tajikistan technically was for Saodat-opa.[27] "The *Sokhskie* used to travel all the time through Chor-Tepa. Their best and brightest would study in our cities, you know— Dushanbe had one of the union's finest medical schools, and dozens of them would be studying in Leninabad at any one time. Now they're all studying in Uzbek, there's hardly any of them left here now."

Saodat-opa emerged from the wagon, her hands plunged deep into the pockets of her long cardigan. Her brow was strained in thought. "How much?" one of our passengers asked in Tajik, the context obviating any need to elaborate how much of what had been presented to whom. All knew that an Uzbek passport here would mean a certain bribe: the only question was how strong Saodat-opa's bargaining position had been. "Six thousand" was her answer—six dollars' worth of Uzbek *sum*, and almost a quarter of her monthly teacher's salary. "They asked for ten [thousand sum], but I told them that I just wouldn't be able to get home then. Even now, I don't know how we're going to make it to Komsomolsk and back. I can't afford to give any more." "And that wasn't even the Tajik post!" commented our driver. "The rate (stavka) for your passport will be double that there." Saodat-opa described how they had forced her to pay up, holding their stamp poised over her passport with the comment, "A mark from here will create problems for you back home," until she had laid out sufficient notes on the table in front of them to concede and withdraw their weapon. Saodat-opa wasn't sure whether a Kyrgyz border stamp would really have created problems for her in Sokh, but she was not willing to take the risk: she well knew that an "unusual" stamp, even one marked in another country entirely, could be the excuse for hassles at future border crossings. Her eldest son, who traveled regularly to Russia to work on building sites in Siberia, had often recounted how even Russian and Kazakh border guards would scrutinize one's passport, scouring its pages for the slightest unusual mark. "You should have paid in Kyrgyz money. They might have taken less then," was the driver's comment as he restarted his engine. "Well, shall we get going? We've still got another one to get through and we've already wasted twenty minutes here." Saodat-opa nodded silently.

The Tajik post was in sight of the Kyrgyz, distinguished from the latter only by the flag, now faded slightly, painted on its side. The outward signs indicated that a repeat of the ritual of stately verification awaited all of us. Yet, as we pulled up by the Tajik post, there was a discernible shift in dynamic. Farkhod, the passenger sitting next to me, gestured to Saodat-opa not to get her passport out again. We were inches into Tajik territory, and his manner was signaling that here he knew himself to be local and would be taking charge of the situation. *"Assalomualeikum,"* he called out in greeting to the border guard now bending in at the open window, holding out his hand. "You'd better register this foreigner," he said matter-of-factly, pointing to me, "and this is my wife," he added, gesturing nonchalantly to Saodat-opa. The soldier glanced over at Saodat-opa. It was plausible—her features and dress suggested she was Tajik, and there was no reason why she shouldn't pass as the wife of this middle-aged Chor-Tepa man. The border guard nodded, indicating to me that I should go and register.

I willed the process to be over as soon as possible, for we were not off the hook until we were all back in the car, speeding on along our way to Chor-Tepa. The process was slow: three grand ledgers had to be filled by hand, in considerable detail, a procedure slowed all the more by a flurry of questions that blurred the boundary between the soldiers' official and unofficial personae. Indeed, it is precisely in the oscillation between these two personae that the power of the border encounter is maintained: officious scrutinizing of documents is interspersed with familiar, domestic questions; stern reminders that this space is charged with the full force of the state's monopoly of legitimate violence are coupled with jokes that gently mock the very powers these officers would serve. To my great relief, however, the questions did not turn to Saodat-opa, and the guards did not suspect that we had ever met before this morning's journey. Passport safely back in hand (though without the all-important stamp: it had apparently been taken by one of the guards on military service the year before and they were still waiting for a replacement to be sent), I climbed out into the sunlight and we were left to drive off along our journey, without so much as a glimpse of Saodat-opa's "dangerous" document.

"Thank you, husband!" she joked, turning to Farkhod, "you saved my skin! I'd have no money at all now if they'd seen my passport." And then, reclaiming the landscape and the day as normal, she rolled down the window, stuck her arm out as though to touch the apricot trees that rolled past, and added, jovially, "welcome, at last, to my motherland (*rodina*). I'll buy you all ice-cream when we get to Chor-Tepa."

COMMENTARY: BORDER ENCOUNTERS AND THE REMAKING OF THE "EVERYDAY"

Saodat-opa's journey, and the thousands like it traced everyday through the borderlands of the Ferghana Valley, are a salient reminder to the champions of global ethnoscapes, borderless flows and "cosmopolitan ethnography"[28] that the end of a bipolar world and increasingly rapid capital flows do not, *ipso facto*, result in borders becoming any less salient or space being marked with any less intensity. For many residents of the Ferghana Valley, whose kinship networks straddle newly nationalizing states, the spatial and temporal contours of everyday life have been profoundly transformed in the last decade, and with them the experiential significance of such categories as "citizenship," "independence," "homeland," and even "family." From the actor-centered view privileged by anthropology, we see that for Saodat-opa the distance between natal and married homes has become *greater*, not smaller, as a result of independence, and the regular cycle of visits has collapsed into much longer periods of absence. The cost and stress of "going home" mean that, experientially, time and space have expanded, not compressed in the ways that classic accounts of globalization would suggest.[29]

In addition to this very obvious impact of border regimes for those who live in the state's margins, there is a more subtle, though no less consequential, effect that the classificatory logic of nation-state is having on inhabitants of the Ferghana Valley. This has to do with what might be called the "location of threat": the fact that border posts, and the more general étatization of space of which they are just one manifestation, foster a perception that "otherness" (whether a difference of ethnicity or citizenship) is inherently threatening, such that contact must be regulated, contained, seen, and thus *managed*.[30] The internalization of this threat produces a particular kind of border subjectivity, a heightened awareness that "protection" is territorially defined and that crossing a border means entering a space "beyond law."[31] As Parviz, an exceptionally insightful former teacher, commented as we crossed the border at Sokh's southern end, where Tajik and Kyrgyz villages back onto one another in a dense knot of streets, "You see, the problem with all these border controls is that they work on our unconscious, they start to make us react differently without even noticing it. When I am able to cross this [Uzbekistani] post without any checks because I'm Sokhskii, but I see that Kyrgyz from Tuz-Bel (a Kyrgyzstani village at Sokh's southern border) are stopped and checked, it sends out a signal to me: "They must be dangerous," I start to think. And the reverse is also true. I will be stopped at a Kyrgyz post and they won't be. At an unconscious (*podsoznatel'nyi*) level, we come to see each other as threatening, for why have a post between us if not?"

The attempt of the state to assert its territoriality is not lost on borderland villagers like Parviz, both in Sokh as elsewhere throughout the valley. His remarks, based on a decade of border controls around his district, echo Bourdieu's profound observation that it is through the elicitation of such "doxic submission" rather than simply the imposition of "ideology" that the state comes to appear to us as natural: "State injunctions owe their obviousness, and thus their potency, to the fact that the state has imposed the very cognitive structures through which it is perceived."[32] Yet the experience of Saodat-opa on her journey home also demonstrates that the new set of classifications that the border regime would impose is neither immediate nor unambiguous in its impact. Former modes of identification are not somehow suddenly erased by the establishment of passport controls or the increased cost of local transport. That Saodat-opa and Jamilya-eje were able immediately to strike up conversation was possible because they could tap into a large reservoir of common experience and shared cultural practice. The passenger who saved Saodat-opa from a bribe did so by invoking an idiom of relatedness that directly challenged two states' attempts to impose a line of exclusion between them. These random gestures of kindness are *also* part of the valley's everyday, just as much as the exclusions are; the reassuring sight of apricot trees in spring is as much part of its experiential reality as the visceral nervousness, the adrenalin rush associated with a checkpoint suddenly emerging into view. Indeed, the analytical challenge for an account of "everyday" experience in the Ferhgana Valley borderlands is to capture precisely this duality—the simultaneity of familiarity and threat, of movement and constraint, incorporation and exclusion. Everyday life here, shot through as it is with globalism's "Janus-face," has challenged, just as much as it has been transformed by, the border-fixing impulse of three vigorously nationalizing states.

NOTES

1. The names of all people and places other than regional (oblast) centers and administrative districts (rayons) have been changed in the text.

2. Discussion of the Soviet transformation of wedding ceremonies in Sokh can be found in Urunboi Sufiev, *Traditsii i innovatsii v svadebnykh obychayakh i obriadakh tadzhikov doliny r. Sokh.* Unpublished candidate of science dissertation, Leningrad filial, Institute of Ethnology and Anthropology of the Soviet Academy of Sciences, Leningrad: 1991.

3. This and subsequent quotes from Ilkhom-aka and his family are taken from fieldnotes and interviews during fieldwork in Sokh from November 2004 to March 2005.

4. On "security" as a legitimizing discourse, see David Campbell, *Writing Security* (Minneapolis: University of Minnesota Press, 1998); on its application to the contemporary Central Asian context, see Nick Megoran, "The critical geopolitics of danger in Uzbekistan and Kyrgyzstan." *Environment and Planning D: Society and Space* 24 (3), August 2005: 555–580.

5. Detailed analysis of the normative acts regulating movement between different states of the Ferghana Valley can be found in A. T. Ismailov et al. (eds.), *Putevoditel' "puteshestviia po Ferganskoi doline"* (Osh: Ferghana Valley Lawyers Without Borders, 2006).

6. In doing so I have been influenced by Michel de Certeau's discussion of the "innumerable and infinitesimal transformations of and within the dominant cultural economy" that make up the "practice of everyday life," and by Sheila Fitzpatrick's application of this approach to the analysis of everyday life under Stalinism. See Michel de Certeau, *The Practice of Everyday Life,* translated by Steven Rendall

(Berkeley, Calif.: University of California Press, 1984), and Sheila Fitzpatrick, *Everyday Stalinism. Ordinary Life in Extraordinary Times: Soviet Russia in the 1930s* (Oxford and New York: Oxford University Press, 1999).

7. See, for instance, Gale Stokes, *The Walls Came Tumbling Down* (New York and Oxford, Oxford University Press: 1993).

8. See, for instance, Francis Fukuyama, *The End of History and the Last Man* (London: Hamish Hamilton: 1992).

9. Morgan Liu, "Detours from utopia on the Silk Road: Ethical dilemmas of neoliberal triumphalism," *Central Eurasian Studies Review* 2(2), 2003: 2–10. For anthropological critiques of teleological accounts of post-Socialist "transition," see Daphne Berdahl et al., eds., *Altering States: Ethnographies of Transition in Eastern Europe and the Former Soviet Union* (Ann Arbor: University of Michigan Press, 2000); Caroline Humphrey, *The Unmaking of Soviet Life: Everyday Economies After Socialism* (Ithaca and London: Cornell University Press, 2002). For an application of this critique to accounts of Central Asia, see especially Deniz Kandiyoti and Ruth Mandel, eds., *Market Reforms, Social Dislocations and Survival in Post-Soviet Central Asia*, special issue of *Central Asian Survey* 17 (4), 1998.

10. See especially John Borneman, *After the Wall: East Meets West in the New Berlin* (New York: Basic Books, 1991); Daphne Berdahl, *Where the World Ended: Reunification and Identity in the German Borderland* (Berkeley: University of California Press, 1999).

11. Though note, in the Central Asian context, the important contribution of Nick Megoran, The Borders of Eternal Friendship? The Politics and Pain of Nationalism and Identity Along the Uzbekistan-Kyrgyzstan Ferghana Valley Boundary, 1999–2000. PhD dissertation, University of Cambridge, 2002, 164–208.

12. Michael Taussig, *The Magic of the State* (New York and London: Routledge, 1997); Eleni Myrivilli, The Liquid Border: Subjectivity at the Limits of the Nation-State in South East Europe. Ph.D. dissertation, Columbia University, 2004.

13. See, programmatically, Arjun Appadurai, "Global Ethnoscapes: Notes and Queries for a Transnational Anthropology," in Richard Fox, ed., *Recapturing Anthropology: Working in the Present* (Santa Fe: School of American Research, 1991), 191–210; James Clifford "Traveling Cultures," in Lawrence Grossberg, Cary Nelson and Paula Treichler, eds., *Cultural Studies* (New York: Routledge, 1992), 96–111. For explorations of the methodological implications of this critique, see especially the essays collected in Akhil Gupta and James Ferguson, eds., *Anthropological Locations: Boundaries and Grounds of a Field Science* (Berkeley: University of California Press, 1997).

14. Yael Navaro-Yashin, "'Life is dead here': sensing the political in 'no man's land'." *Anthroplogical Theory* 3(1), 2002: 107–125: 108.

15. For references to slavery in relation to the new labor migration from Central Asia, see Ulugbek Babakulov, Natalya Domagalskaya, Asel Sagynbaeva, and Aitken Kadirbekov, "Kyrgyz 'slaves' on Kazakh plantations," *Institute of War and Peace Reporting Central Asia*, no. 222, August 5, 2003.

16. Usto Jahonov, *Zemledelie tadzhikov doliny Sokha v kontse XIX—nach. XX v. Istoriko-etnograficheskoe issledovanie* (Dushanbe: Donish, 1989).

17. Sergei Abashin, "Naselenie Ferganskoi doliny (k stanovleniiu etnograficheskoi nomenklatury v kontse XIX—nachale XX veka)," in S. N. Abashin and V. I. Bushkov, eds., *Ferganskaya dolina: Etnichnost', etnicheskye protsessy, etnicheskii konflikt* (Moscow: Nauka, 2004); Arne Haugen, *The Establishment of National Republics in Soviet Central Asia* (London: Palgrave-Macmillan, 2003).

18. Indeed, the *Sokhskie* are eager to point out that they are the only remaining "truly Tajik rayon" in Uzbekistan, where schools and technical colleges teach

entirely in Tajik. Although there is a Kyrgyz minority in several of the villages in Sokh district, the younger Kyrgyz are much more comfortable speaking Tajik and Uzbek than Kyrgyz, and are closer to their fellow Sokh youth in terms of dress, religious practice, gender dynamics, and everyday practice than to young people living in neighboring Kyrgyz villages.

19. On obstacles to cross-border trade in the Ferghana Valley, see A. Iusupova, "Khozhdenie za tri granitsy, ili o tom, kak mozhno proiti uzbekskie pogranposty," *Vechernii Bishkek*, August 20, 1999; UNDP, *Bringing Down Barriers: Regional Cooperation for Human Development and Human Security* (Bratislava: UNDP, 2005), 51–67. On border violations as a result of restriction on movement, see Dolina Mira, *Analiz situatsii po perekhodu granits v Ferganskoi Doline* (Osh: Dolina Mira, 2005).

20. Beginning in the spring planting season, for instance, it is possible in border villages throughout the Ferghana Valley to find informal, illegal labor exchanges in which poorer villagers, predominantly from Uzbekistan and Tajikistan, sell their labor to the more land-wealthy of the Kyrgyz farmers. In the spring and summer of 2004, Kyrgyz farmers from Batken would regularly talk about "picking up a dozen Tajiks" from the informal roadside labor market near Chor-Tepa to work on their fields. This overwhelmingly female labor would cost their temporary employer 35–40 Kyrgyz *som* ($.90–$1.00) per employee per day, and its presence was a source of considerable local tension, indexing for the "selling" population the extent to which divergent policies toward land distribution were impacting upon the relative well-being of neighbors just a couple of kilometers away. The extent and precise dynamics of this micro-stratification deserve further research, and the degree of difference in economic well-being should not be overstated. Many Kyrgyz villages are characterized by considerable poverty and land shortage, and the phenomenon of labor hiring seems to be localized to areas where privatization resulted in a greater area of land being redistributed. Nonetheless, the ethnographically significant point is that villagers in Uzbekistan and Tajikistan *perceive* the difference in well-being to be linked to the fact of land privatization *per se*. Many times I heard comments analogous to that from a housewife in Sokh who, when asked whether she would be better off if land there were privatized, gave the typical Central Asian gesture of material abundance: a hand swept along the top of her neck. "We'd live like that!" she said, "we'd live like the Kyrgyz!"

21. Pierre Bourdieu, "Rethinking the state: genesis and structure of the bureaucratic field," in George Steinmetz, ed., *State/Culture: State Formation After the Cultural Turn* (Ithaca, N.Y.: Cornell University Press, 1999), 53.

22. According to traders in Sokh, a single *Kamaz* truck must pay 100,000 sum (approximately $100) in bribes to pass through the six border posts separating the enclave from the oblast center of Ferghana. See also Sveta Lokteva, "Nachal'nik zastavy: sam sebe 'krysha'," *Vechernii Bishkek*, August 13, 2002

23. On the state's claim to monopolize legitimate movement, see John Torpey, "Coming and going: on the state monopolization of the legitimate 'means of movement.'" *Sociological Theory* 16 (3) 1997: 239–259.

24. Indeed, just days after our conversation, temperatures that had been pushing the mid-20s centigrade suddenly plunged to cover the whole of Kyrgyzstan in a blanket of snow. Snow enters the apricot blossom, preventing the fertilization that would result in fruit. Jamilya and her family lost their entire harvest, depriving them of over a ton of apricots, their single main source of income. "It's God's will" was her response to her feelings about this loss. "Perhaps it will be better next year."

25. For a striking account of one such border transformation, see the depiction

of the "friendship" (*dostlik/dostuk*) border post between Uzbekistan and Kyrgyzstan just west of Osh in Morgan Liu, Recognizing the Khan: Authority, Space and Political Imagination Among Uzbek Men in Post-Soviet Osh, Kyrgyzstan. Ph.D. dissertation, University of Michigan, 2002, 36–43.

26. The real extent of an upward flow of tribute throughout the border control system is extremely difficult to assess. It is widely rumored that the "tax" to become a head of a lucrative (*khlebnyi*) post in the Ferghana Valley is several thousand dollars.

27. Indeed, anyone wanting to travel from Tajikistan eastward through southern Kyrgyzstan is obliged to bypass the Sokh enclave altogether, traveling along a rocky "detour route" (*ob"ezdnaya doroga*) that is only passable in summer.

28. Appadurai, 197–210.

29. David Harvey, *The Condition of Postmodernity* (Cambridge: Blackwell, 1989).

30. An impulse, I would argue, that is also reflected in a number of internationally sponsored projects committed to conflict prevention in the Ferghana Valley. See Madeleine Reeves, "Locating danger: *konfliktologiia* and the search for fixity in the Ferghana Valley borderlands." *Central Asian Survey* 24 (1), 2005: 67–81

31. See Mirivili, 247–274, for a fascinating analysis of such "border subjectivity" in the contemporary Balkan context.

32. Bourdieu, 69.

PART SIX

Religion

Faith in the supernatural and the communitarian rituals that form a key part of worship are elements as universally human as feasting and marriage. Attitudes towards and practices of religion form an essential part of our investigation into everyday Central Asia. In approaching religion from the perspective of the people living in these authoritarian countries, where governments and, now, militant religious organizations seek to channel and control spiritual thought as well as practice, our authors illustrate, through careful and empirical research, that the citizens of such countries are, far from unquestioning automatons, people who may conduct themselves cautiously or covertly but who nevertheless choose to worship or not in myriad ways that often have little or nothing to do with positions advanced by governing or spiritual elites.

Two primary issues motivate our desire to convey religion as viewed and engaged by Central Asians in everyday life. First, we want to engage popular and scholarly views that Islam, in the Soviet era, was either essentially neutralized, on the one hand, or driven underground, where it galvanized a sense of opposition to modernization and sovietization, on the other. Our authors discover a far more complicated dynamic. Second, we want to confront the role of religion in the wake of an upsurge in international Islamist terror activity, which has led to violence in Afghanistan, Kyrgyzstan, Tajikistan, and Uzbekistan.

Many Western scholars of Central Asia in the Soviet era believed that the Islamic nature of these societies would prevent their full integration into the officially atheist European- and Russian-dominated USSR. Such advocates surmised that the predominantly Muslim identity of Central Asians could not be fully assimilated to a Soviet identity, and that on this simple basis Central Asians would always reject the Soviet dominance, with its particularly Marxist, hence anti-religious, positions. Furthermore, scholars felt that the Soviets created a paradoxical situation for themselves by helping to develop national Muslim majority republics, mini-Soviet Unions with their own national and cultural characteristics. This fact in and of itself may have prevented a more general assimilationist policy. After all, if assimilation and the creation of a Soviet person had been the goal, why make statelets that enjoyed at least a legal autonomy from the central power of the Soviet state in Moscow? Certainly there was much to recommend the predictive thinking of these scholars, save for two vital issues: a) they conducted little on-site research by our post-1990 standards, and b) when they traveled to Central Asia they tended to focus on the viewpoints of intellectuals and anti-Soviet scholars who did not necessarily represent the voices of millions of fellow Central Asians. Two developments in late Soviet history partially belied these pre-breakup notions of Western scholars. First, during the Soviet war in Afghanistan, Central Asian soldiers, despite predictions, largely remained loyal instead of joining the Afghan *mujahideen*, despite religious, cultural, and ethnic affinities between themselves and the northern Afghans. Second, when popular polls and referenda were taken in 1990 and 1991, vast majorities of Central Asians voted against breaking up, let alone destroying, the USSR.

Even if anti-religious policies had eroded common religious knowledge and daily practices, some Westerners considered that religiosity was being kept alive by underground associations of Sufis, itinerant Muslim brotherhoods (*tariqat*) dispersed throughout the region. This notion, though not based on substantial first-hand evidence, certainly was accurate to a degree. Less reasonable, however, was the conviction that continued belief would pave the way for some type of wider Islamic rebellion against Soviet power. Islam operated in more complicated ways that Westerners are only now beginning to understand. The picture that has emerged over the past decade is less a matter of basic dichotomies and more one of startling complexities.

A rise in radical Islamist activity in the late 1990s, from kidnappings by the Islamic Movement of Uzbekistan to the rise to power of the Taliban in Afghanistan, led all of us to reconsider the role of religion in Central Asia. The signal event of 9/11 strengthened the commitments of those of us studying the region to consider the degree to which religious militancy had risen in the wake of the collapse of the USSR. We were also determined to challenge the facile views, spread by Central Asian governments as well as many Western observers, of a dangerous expansion of Islamism in the post-Soviet era. Since we are well aware that the political and politicized aspects of Islam make headlines and sell books these days, we remind our readers that the preponderance of believers in Central Asia are no more motivated or interested in politics than you yourselves may or may not be. We investigate religion and daily life from the perspective of how Islam or, to a far lesser extent in Central Asia, Christianity, informs culture and creates social and spiritual meaning for individuals. Our goals remain to understand specifically how religious orientations and the adoption of religious values create new meanings, including freedoms and oppressions, in peoples' lives. Our authors' fieldwork presents them, and us, with a very important basis for drawing conclusions about the role and purpose of religion in daily life. Furthermore, we see that historical research shows perhaps even more in the way of patterns of religious continuity than any radical breaks with past traditions.

Our contributors on religion focus for the most part on social life and Islam. In a deeply personal narrative, Eric McGlinchey combines fieldwork techniques from anthropology with a political scientist's awareness of Islamism. In close, personal, and often poignant encounters, exchanges, and observations, McGlinchey explores Islamic radicalism from the viewpoint of those accused of "terrorist" actions by a Central Asian state anxious at once to play up and rein in religious-based opposition. McGlinchey convincingly reveals the state's role in terrorizing its own population in pursuit of relatively small numbers of radical Islamists. More importantly, he presents his informants' ideas about devotion and militancy in such a way as to show that it can be very dangerous simply to be a practicing, dedicated Muslim in Uzbekistan.

David Abramson and Elyor Karimov embark upon a study of contemporary Central Asian worship through an examination of local traditions that stretch back centuries and combine Sufi Islamic beliefs with those associated with more ancient and non-monotheistic Central Asian values. Abramson and Karimov dissect the phenomenon of visits to religious sites, or shrines, central to local Islamic practice. Journeys to shrines, often difficult, have different and multiple meanings to their visitors. Shrine visits often exist in an antagonistic relationship with Islamist adherents, who consider these ritualistic visiting acts blasphemous to their understanding of orthodoxy. The continued popularity of shrines displays the important local component to Islam that insulates the population to outside Islamist blandishments.

David Montgomery examines the variety of religious thoughts and acts in the Ferghana Valley. His fieldwork uncovers locals who see themselves as Muslims, but are often unsure or self-conscious about what is and isn't Islamic. His subjects debate over what makes "good" and "bad" Muslims, ideas that incorporate local and international ideas and rituals. Montgomery's investigation of the everyday world of religion finds highly syncretic and personal forms of belief and practice, once more providing an important corrective to views of Central Asian Muslims as one undifferentiated mass, with the potential to follow a radical message.

Sean Roberts' study of the *Zarya Vostoka* neighborhood of Almaty, Kazakhstan, looks at varieties of devotion to Islam among the minority Uyghur population, who live mainly in the Xinjiang region of China. He also finds great variety of belief based on factors such as age and time of immigration from China to Kazakhstan. Roberts employs the ideas of French scholar Pierre Bourdieu, that people's practices in daily life greatly affect their sense of themselves, thus creating their own sense of what comprises "normal" society. Daily life events integrate religious practices into profane and spiritual affairs, from the community dedication of a new soccer stadium to a wedding celebration. Roberts' study also allows for an examination of the link between religion and ethnicity in this minority community.

Sebastien Peyrouse provides a historical and demographic framework to understand changes in everyday life faced by the region's largest religious minority. Christians, primarily but not exclusively Orthodox Russians, settled in the region during tsarist colonization. Soviet atheism blurred differences between religious communities, but the post-Soviet period has posed multiple challenges for Christians, including mass emigration of Russians and other Europeans from Central Asia. Peyrouse reveals the tensions between Russian Orthodox leaders, who actually have a comfortable relationship with Muslim clerics, and the present influx of foreign Christian missionaries. In addition to explaining varieties of Christianity in Central Asia, Peyrouse discusses how issues of freedom of conscience are being tested in the more authoritarian Central Asian states.

19. Divided Faith: Trapped between State and Islam in Uzbekistan

Eric M. McGlinchey

Though I had been working with Islamic activists in Uzbekistan for several months, I had yet to accompany any of my colleagues to Friday prayer. It was not that I was avoiding prayer services out of principle. I study religion and politics and am a frequent visitor to mosques, churches, and temples in the United States. And although mine is more an intellectual than a spiritual pursuit, I have always felt welcome by the American Muslim community. Islam in Central Asia, however, is not Islam in the United States. I feared that, here, moving from outside observer to inside fellow traveler might not be so easy.

At the same time, I knew that the only way to begin to understand Islam in Uzbekistan was to become a participant in Uzbek society and not simply a consumer of the state-controlled media. The post-Soviet Uzbek government attempts to manage Islam much as it attempts to manage many other aspects of Uzbek life. The Uzbek National Press Agency regularly writes about Islamic "bandits" and "extremists," and the Uzbek president, Islam Karimov, warns of a "huge evil—international terrorism, extremism, and fanaticism—which has been posing a threat to our peaceful and calm life over the past few years."[1] The Uzbek state, though, is by no means omnipresent and all-powerful. The more I traveled throughout Uzbekistan the more I learned that the state's alarmist rhetoric, along with its policies, laws, and directives, are often ignored at the local level. And thus, it is at this local level—in conversations with friends and colleagues at the mosques, the markets, in family homes, and during Friday evening gatherings—in short, in the experiences of everyday Uzbek life, that I focus my study of Islam in Uzbekistan. Much as the historian Stephen Kotkin notes in his analysis of state-society relations during 1930s Soviet rule, so too in today's Uzbekistan "there is no substitute for letting people speak as much as possible in their own words."[2]

Listening to Uzbeks' own words allows us to explore the strengths and limits of authoritarian rule. That is, although the state's strategies of control may be apparent, we can understand the effectiveness of these strategies only in their application, only by investigating how a "society resists being reduced" to the will of the state.[3] In this chapter I detail Uzbek society's attempts—some successful, some not—at such resistance. In section one I use the lens of the neighborhood mosque to illustrate how imams and congregants often ignore the Karimov regime's attempts at control. In section two I shift my focus from the neighborhood mosque to individuals' and families' attempts to resist government intimidation. More specifically, I study social activists' successful attempts in resisting false charges of Islamic extremism. The Karimov regime has proven adept at manipulating Islam, at using such charges to intimidate and imprison its perceived opponents. In section three I conclude with one failed attempt at resisting state repression. I share the story of Rustam Klichev, a popular imam whom the state recently imprisoned on charges of Islamist extremism. Unfortunately, Uzbek society occasionally does succumb to the will of the Karimov regime. And, as my Uzbek colleagues emphasize, these cases of failed resistance need to be recounted as well.

THE NEIGHBORHOOD MOSQUE AND THE LIMITS OF UZBEK STATE CONTROL

A common refrain among Uzbek Muslims is that separation of religion and state, though provided by the constitution, does not exist in practice. The committee for religious affairs, Uzbek President Islam Karimov's gatekeeper for all things spiritual, decides which religious groups can or cannot be registered. Several groups—those the government perceives as extremist—are blacklisted and classified as criminal organizations. Any association with these organizations can lead to lengthy jail stays—punishments that, I discovered in my conversations with practicing Uzbek Muslims, can become life sentences.

The Uzbek leadership has been the most fervent of all Central Asian governments in its prosecution of Islamic activists. Since the Soviet collapse in 1991, Uzbek security services have jailed more than seven thousand Muslims.[4] Some of those currently in jail indeed are, as the Uzbek government asserts, Islamist extremists. Most notably, the Islamic Movement of Uzbekistan (IMU) has repeatedly taken civilian hostages and mounted armed attacks against government forces in its avowed quest to build an Islamic caliphate in Central Asia. Moreover, militants thought to be connected with the IMU targeted President Karimov in a botched assassination attempt in February 1999 and engaged Kyrgyz and Uzbek troops in the Ferghana Valley in the summers of 1999 and 2000.[5] In 2004 suicide bombers attacked Tashkent's central bazaar, the government prosecutor's office, and the Israeli and U.S. embassies. That all of these attacks are coordinated actions of a militant Islamist opposition—as the Karimov government claims—is not certain.[6] What is clear, however, is that President Karimov faces steady opposition. And this opposition, coupled with sporadic violence, has created an atmosphere of suspicion and unease from which few are immune.

An early casualty of government suspicion was Muhammad Rajab, an imam in the Ferghana Valley city of Kokand. A local court imprisoned Rajab in 1994, charging him with narcotics possession, though the state's real grievance, city residents told me, was Rajab's popularity.[7] One decade later, Rajab's mosque remains padlocked. Kokand's residents, however, have found a new charismatic leader, and it was his mosque my colleague, Botir, and I were now entering.[8]

Inside we join hundreds of worshippers tightly packed in the central prayer hall. Grateful to be out of the cold rain, Botir and I remove our shoes and, along with other new arrivals, squeeze in for the start of the afternoon service. Young men and boys don *kufi*, knitted prayer hats, while older Uzbeks remove wet plastic coverings from their *doppi*, the traditional four-sided Uzbek skull cap. From where I sit, I count fifty rows of people lined shoulder to shoulder, twenty-five across. Outside in the courtyard hundreds more gather in partially enclosed alcoves to listen to the imam's sermon. This, though, is a small crowd. Botir assures me that during better weather the congregation spills into the surrounding streets.

That this one mosque should be so popular might appear odd to the casual observer. Several other mosques, many of them more centrally and conveniently located, are spread throughout the city, yet most of these mosques are sparsely attended during Friday prayer. Rather, it is this out of the way mosque here on the edge of town that attracts the largest crowds. Muslims in Kokand and the surrounding villages come here, Botir explains, because the mosque's imam—the spiritual leader—is one of the few who does not mix politics with religion.

Uzbekistan's Muslim Spiritual Board, also known as the Muftiate, exercises considerable control over the country's Islamic leaders. Though the Muftiate is formally independent of the secular government, in reality it is controlled by the state administration and used both to populate and to police Uzbekistan's Islamic clergy.[9] Particularly disliked by practicing Muslims, the Muftiate acts as a propaganda arm of President Karimov. It drafts the text of Friday prayers in the state capital, Tashkent, and distributes these official state sermons every week to imams throughout the country. Thus, an Uzbek attending Friday prayer in the green foothills of the Tien Shan Mountains in the far east of the country will hear the same sermon as an Uzbek at Friday prayer one thousand kilometers to the west, in the arid Kyzyl Kum desert. Often, the text of these prayers does not please the mosque congregants. In October 2001, for example, the Muftiate instructed

Uzbekistan's imams to praise U.S.-led military actions in Afghanistan, despite the concerns many Uzbeks had that the bombing campaign might result in the deaths of many innocent Muslims.[10]

Importantly, not all Islamic leaders toe the government line, and this is what distinguished the popular Kokand imam from his local colleagues. The previous evening I had spoken with Abdulhaviz-qori, the head imam of Kokand city. Abdulhaviz-qori, a slight man in his fifties, acknowledged the Muftiate's influential role. At the same time, however, he emphasized that he personally had no complaints and that he could not understand why other Islamic leaders ran afoul of the Muftiate and the government.[11] Many other imams I spoke with shared Abdulhaviz-qori's sentiments. Indeed, Ismail Raikhanov, the head imam of Karshi, a city just north of the Afghanistan border, concluded that the Muftiate's direction was helpful; without it he would need to consult multiple Islamic texts so as to prepare his own Friday prayer.[12]

In one sense, Abdulhaviz-qori's and Ismail Raikhanov's sentiments are understandable. Working with rather than against—or even independently of—the Muftiate makes one's life considerably easier. What it does not do, however, is give Islamic leaders legitimacy in the eyes of the broader Uzbek Muslim community. In Uzbekistan all Islamic leaders face a tension between the top-down dictates of the government and the bottom-up demands of the population. How an imam resolves this tension—his choice to serve either government or society—has profound effects on his popularity and, often, his personal safety. And it is not just imams and religious elites who face these difficult decisions. Uzbek citizens must also choose whether it is worth pursuing personal beliefs and convictions and risk attracting unwanted government attention. While it is impossible to quantify how many people the Karimov government has charged with Islamic fundamentalism, the stories of ordinary Uzbeks suggest the regime perceives small, even symbolic challenges to government-controlled Islam as a threat to state authority.

FAMILY LIFE AND STATE INTIMIDATION

To some degree, that Islam has become so politicized in Uzbekistan is surprising. In other countries oppositionists do use Islam—and religion more broadly—to mobilize support against state authority. In divided societies, for example, competing groups often politicize religion in their struggle for power or independence. Thus, Chechen separatists employ Islam to mobilize support, both locally and internationally, against Russian rule. Similarly, the Irish Republican Army stresses its Catholic identity in its fight against British rule in Northern Ireland. And Sunnis and Shiites continue to fight one another in post-Saddam Hussein Iraq. In

Uzbekistan, though, in contrast to Russia, Northern Ireland, and Iraq, even in contrast to neighboring Central Asian countries, religious divisions are few. Eighty-eight percent of Uzbekistan's 26 million people are Muslim and the overwhelming majority of these are Sunnis.[13] Yet, despite this comparative social homogeneity, the Karimov government continues to raise the specter of radical Islam at every turn.

President Karimov's fear of Islam is, to some degree, a legacy of Soviet rule. Karimov rose to power in the late 1980s and continues to maintain power today by balancing competing regional elites against one another.[14] Patronage politics—distributing state wealth among this regional elite—provides the foundation for Karimov's authoritarian rule. The sudden emergence of new standards with which to measure a leader's legitimacy, though, has eroded Karimov's distinctly Soviet strategy of rule. Revealingly, for example, in September 1991 thousands of protestors took to the streets in Kokand to demand Karimov's resignation and his replacement by the Islamic scholar and head mufti of Central Asia, Mohammad Sodik Mohammad Yusuf.[15] That the Karimov government pressured the popular mufti to flee Uzbekistan in 1993 is an indication that the Uzbek leader may indeed see in Islam a real threat to his authority.

Importantly, though, the Uzbek government's steady warnings of Islamist extremism are equally instrumental. The Karimov regime manipulates the specter of militant Islam so as to cow domestic activists as well as the international community. Raising the threat of radical Islam serves as an expedient justification for authoritarian rule, for the expansion of the police state into the everyday fabric of Uzbek life. Radical Islam, in short, is the Karimov government's equivalent of a universal search warrant. It allows the state to stop and search whomever it wishes.

Walking past the Israeli embassy in August 2004, for example, I found my path blocked by several Tashkent police bearing Kalashnikov assault rifles. My Uzbek friends joked that the police likely questioned me because of my appearance—my facial features are strikingly similar to those of a Chechen. Street interrogations for me are a minor nuisance. In recent years the United States and Uzbekistan have increased military cooperation and, in contrast to the harassment I occasionally experienced in the mid-1990s, police now are reticent to bother anyone with an American passport. For my Uzbek colleagues, however, interactions with the police rarely end so amicably. Indeed, as I discovered walking the Tashkent and Kokand city streets with my bearded colleague Botir, deviations from what the state considers "normal" appearance invite unwanted and sustained police attention.

In addition to looking stereotypically Chechen, other perceived markers of deviant or radical Islam are the *hijab*—headscarf—for women and the beard for men. For Botir, his beard, much like the hijab for many Uzbek women I met, is as much a symbol of resistance as it is a sign of his religious devotion. Botir refuses to allow the state to dictate his personal appearance. This principled independence, an independence that extends beyond questions of personal appearance, unfortunately has resulted in repeated state-led intimidation against him and his family.

In November 2004 I spent several days with Botir in Dungar, his home village in the densely populated Ferghana Valley. Botir is an immediately recognizable figure in Dungar. In addition to being one of the few bearded men in the village, Botir's gymnast physique, conditioned from years performing with the Tashkent circus, cuts an unusual profile among his friends. It is his knowledge of Islam, though, more than his appearance, that most distinguishes Botir. In the fifteen years since the Soviet collapse in 1991, Botir has become a self-taught religious scholar, well versed in Uzbek and Arabic, as well as Russian and English, commentary on the Quran.

His study of Islam has not come without cost. The Dungar police, like police in villages and cities across Uzbekistan, keep close watch over those who pursue Islam outside of state-sanctioned mosques and madrasas. The deceptively titled 1998 *Law on Freedom of Conscience and Religious Organizations* (hereafter 1998 *Law on Religion*) prohibits the "private teaching of religious principles."[16] Botir, in short, because of his outward appearance and because his Islam is self rather than state taught, is suspect in the eyes of the local police. Indeed, following the March 2004 suicide bombings in Tashkent—bombings the government claims were conducted by militant Islamists—Botir, his family, and several of his friends were caught in the Uzbek government's dragnet for Muslim radicals. That Botir himself is not a militant was of little consequence. The simple fact that he is bearded, educated, and independent was enough to elicit the unwanted attention of local state authorities. In early April Botir—then working in Tashkent—received a troubling call from his wife. The Dungar police had arrived late at night, woken her and her four children, and proceeded to search their three-room house for evidence connecting Botir to the Tashkent bombings. They took Botir's English language video collection (consisting largely of Clint Eastwood movies) and warned ominously that they would study the tapes for any signs linking Botir to Islamist extremism.

Botir's was not the only house the police targeted. Indeed, Botir fared comparatively well. His friend Erkin, in a neighboring village, received a similar visit, only in Erkin's case the police allege they found a Kalashnikov ammunition cartridge during their search, evidence they claim links Erkin to militant Islamists. Botir and I met with Erkin on a Saturday evening in November 2004. Over the course of the evening I saw first hand the devastating influence police intimidation can have on family life.

Saturday evenings in Uzbekistan are reserved for *gap* (literally, "talk"), for gatherings in which men of the same age or school cohort gather in groups of ten to fifteen to exchange important news and share advice. The gap which Botir and I attended at Erkin's house was unusual, however, in that Erkin's father-in-law was also present. He had just arrived from Bukhara, a city seven hundred kilometers to the west of Dungar, and from the look of anger and concern on his face, I could see immediately that this would not be the customary relaxing Saturday night gap session.

The evening began pleasantly enough; after introductions, Erkin's father-in-law, whom Botir and I respectfully call *Otazhan*—father—described the success his birds were having in Bukhura's cockfighting tournaments. Following the main course of rice and lamb *plov*, however, conversation turned to the recent visit police visit to Erkin's house. Why did the police search turn up a Kalashnikov ammunition cartridge, Otazhan demanded? Why was Erkin associating with Islamist militants? How could Erkin risk putting Otazhan's daughter in so much danger? Otazhan threatened he would force his daughter to divorce, that she and the children would move back to Bukhara. Erkin tried to appease his father-in-law. Erkin assured he was not a militant, he was not even a devout Muslim. The police, Erkin explained, were using their Islamist extremism charges as a way to punish him for talking with a BBC reporter about the abuse his brother had earlier suffered while in police custody. Otazhan seemed little pleased with this explanation. Nor was he moved when Botir joined the conversation in support of Erkin's explanation. Botir, Erkin, and I were from a different generation than the father-in-law. Otazhan had been a Soviet bureaucrat. He trusted the state. And he was suspicious of Botir who, with his beard and his fluent speech, sounded and looked like an imam. He was suspicious of me, an American who disconcertingly resembled a Chechen. And, most of all, he was suspicious of Erkin, his son-in-law, whom the local police had just been found to be in possession of Kalashnikov bullets. Fearing that we were only adding to Erkin's difficulties, Botir and I left, politely explaining that we were expected at another gap back in Dungar. On our walk home Botir reflected: if Islam is any threat, it comes not from practicing Muslims, but from the state and its false charges of extremism.

THE STATE'S MANIPULATION OF RADICAL ISLAM

If the Uzbek state uses false charges of religious extremism to intimidate ordinary Uzbeks, it perhaps is no surprise that the Karimov regime is equally willing to raise similar charges of extremism against the independent-minded religious elite. Most Uzbek imams accept this and are wary not to antagonize their government handlers. A few imams, however, though they may not directly oppose the government, may also choose not to extol the Karimov regime. Choosing such independence, as the case of imam Rustam Klichev illustrates, can cost one his freedom.

I have said goodbye to Botir and am now headed to Karshi, an Uzbek city a hundred miles north of the Afghan border. This will be my second visit. Three months earlier I had flown to Karshi to meet with Nodira, a young Muslim activist in her early thirties.[17] I am taking a car this time, splitting the fare with three others I met at Tashkent's long distance bus station. My flight out in August taxied past the wreckage of a recently crashed Yak-40—uninspiring. And besides, I need the extra four hours the car ride takes to reflect on my visit with Botir and to prepare my thoughts for what awaits in Karshi.

The sun catches the compact disc dangling from the rearview mirror. We are driving west, and the evening light dances on the Islamic talisman. The Arabic script, black on the disc's silver cover, reminds me of Nodira's fears, and of her hope that, perhaps through me, her story can reach an audience outside of Uzbekistan. This is the reality of Central Asia: reports of government intimidation and repression are freely circulated only beyond the state's borders.

Nodira is no stranger to the Uzbek police. Her husband, a recovering drug addict, is serving a ten-year sentence for narcotics distribution. Nodira found Allah and a supportive community in the years since her husband has been in prison. She is a devout Muslim who, along with other women in her neighborhood, attends weekly meetings to read the Quran and to study Arabic. Similar to Botir's experience in Dungar, here in Karshi the local authorities monitor her comings and goings. And where Botir was deemed suspect because of his beard, Nodira is harassed by the *mahalla* (neighborhood) officials for wearing the hijab. For Nodira this harassment is little more than a nuisance. She has invited me to Karshi not to discuss the chauvinism Muslim women confront in daily life; rather she has asked me to meet with the mother and the followers of Rustam Klichev, a young imam who has just been sentenced to fourteen years on charges of religious extremism.

Islam is resurgent in Uzbekistan. Its symbols are everywhere, from the prayer beads in my traveling companions' hands, to the new and newly restored minarets rising above squat, Soviet-era architecture, to the colorful hijabs a small but growing number of women like Nodira and her friends now choose to wear. Does the Uzbek government really think it can control this Islamic renaissance? And, more troubling, what would it take for the Karimov regime to control and direct the future of Islam in Uzbekistan?

We arrive in Karshi at sunset. Tulkin Karaev, an independent journalist, human rights proponent, and my host, meets me outside the heavy sheet-metal gate to his home. The adjoining single-story Uzbek houses, their whitewashed walls forming an unbroken barrier between family court-yards and the public roadway, belie the communalism suggested by the address, Workers' Street. Unlike the newer Soviet apartments with their balconies facing out, here Uzbek homes are inward looking, giving the visitor the sense that Communism perhaps did not pervade all aspects of private life so thoroughly.

After showing me in, Tulkin excuses himself for his evening prayers. During his student days, Tulkin confided during my visit to Karshi last August, he was not a practicing Muslim. In the mid-1980s, however, as opportunities to study Islam increased under the Soviet leadership's *perestroika* reforms, Tulkin took a greater interest in religion. His two teenage sons, however, appear more interested in the internet than they are in Islam. Within minutes of my arrival they are transferring music files from my laptop to the family computer. Tulkin finishes his evening prayers to the power chords of Green Day's new album and his sons' cheers of delight.

Over a dinner of pickled tomatoes and plov, Tulkin and his wife, Tahmina, update me on the local government's latest attempts to silence Imam Klichev's supporters. Tulkin and twelve others traveled to Tashkent in October to protest the imam's imprisonment—only to be forcibly sent back to Karshi on a state-chartered bus. Tulkin's colleague Edgar Turulbekov, head of the Karshi office of the Organization for Human Rights, was jailed for two weeks for organizing an unsanctioned demonstration. Nodira, also a participant in the Tashkent protest, was dismissed without warning from her administrative job at a local clinic. In short, neither the government nor, I sensed from the look on her face, Tahmina were pleased with the coordinated protests against Klichev's imprisonment.

Like the old Soviet regime, the new Uzbek government employs multiple levers to deter what it perceives as excessive independence among practicing Muslims. Tahmina has witnessed this first-hand—the police have repeatedly detained and interrogated her husband, posted patrol cars outside the family home, and threatened Karaev with charges of collaborating with Islamic fundamentalists. Tulkin's outspokenness has even jeopardized Tahmina's own work as a reporter for a local state-run newspaper. Although she respects her husband's determination and his conviction that Imam Klichev was wrongly convicted, Tahmina, like most Uzbeks, seems unsure if principled determination is worth the potential sacrifice in her own family's welfare.

Imam Klichev was, until recently, a model for the Uzbek government's next generation of young Islamic leaders. Klichev attended state sanctioned madrasas and, with the Uzbek Spiritual Board's blessing, he interned in and ultimately became the imam of a state-approved neighborhood mosque. In 2002 Klichev won Karshi's competition for most learned Quranic scholar.[18] And Klichev was widely praised for his efforts to deter young Uzbek men from joining fundamentalist groups such as *Hizb ut-Tahrir.* And for those found guilty of militancy and fundamentalism, Klichev traveled to the jails and urged them to return to Uzbekistan's traditional and moderate form of Islam.

I spoke with Klichev's mother, Buston Boltaeva, my second day in Karshi. Although clearly proud of her son's achievements and the great esteem congregants of the neighborhood mosque held for her son, I quickly get the sense that Boltaeva would have preferred her Klichev had become an engineer rather than a member of the Muslim clergy. Boltaeva quickly noted the irony of her son's situation: Klichev worked tirelessly to deter fundamentalism and is now serving fourteen years for his own alleged fundamentalism.

Like Nodira, Buston Boltaeva wears the hijab. Her knowledge of Islam, however, she notes early in our discussion, is not extensive. She had only a passing interest in religion prior to her son's becoming a deputy imam in 1999. Pointing to her hijab she explains: "I wear this more for him than for me."

As with many Uzbek families, three generations live side by side in the Klichev household. The family moved to their present residence in 2000 when the Spiritual Board elevated Rustam from deputy to head imam of the Navo mahalla mosque. Boltaeva tells me she regrets the move. This, she comments, pointing to the bare walls around her, never felt like home. And now that her son is in jail, it is as if all life has disappeared.

Boltaeva, understandably, wavers between joy and despair. When she discusses her son's achievements, her face lights with pride, making her appear considerably younger than her fifty-one years. When she recalls Rustam's arrest, however, her energy fades and conversation becomes difficult and painful. I find myself contrasting the subdued Klichev household to Tulkin Karaev's vibrant family and, for a moment, am distracted by a sobering thought that Tulkin might one day face a situation similar to Rustam's.

Tulkin poses less of a threat to the Karimov regime, however, than does the young imam. Although Tulkin is an internationally respected journalist and a prominent human rights defender, his beliefs do not resonate with ordinary Uzbeks in the same way that Rustam Klichev's do. Imam Klichev is an example of what the autocratic Karimov government fears most—independent and charismatic leadership. None of the Klichev supporters with whom I spoke believed that the young imam nurtured political ambitions. Nonetheless, government officials came to see Klichev's growing popularity in Karshi and in the surrounding cities as a political threat.

When I visited the Navo mosque in August 2004, I saw few remaining indications of Klichev's popularity. I arrived just before afternoon prayer and, except for a handful of elderly men, the mosque was empty. There was little about Navo itself that would indicate Klichev was, until his recent imprisonment, the most admired imam in Karshi. In contrast to the towering minarets of the city's central mosque, Navo was a humble, indeed half completed, affair. Bricks lay in piles on the foundation of what was to be a new prayer hall. My self-appointed guide, a white-bearded man in his eighties, explained that the original hall, even with the addition of a terrace, could no longer accommodate the crowds that came to hear Klichev's Friday sermons. In the space of four years Klichev had transformed Navo from a neighborhood mosque into the most widely attended place of worship in Karshi. Most troubling for the Spiritual Board's chain of command, Navo was regularly filled to overflowing on Fridays, while the city's central mosque was all but deserted.

I meet with Nodira and several of her friends the day after my interview with Imam Klichev's mother. We gather at Tulkin's house. Even though Tulkin's house is monitored by the police, his links to international organizations such as Human Rights Watch and the Institute for War and Peace Reporting afford a measure of security Nodira and her friends can find nowhere else. As I listen to the young women, I begin to understand why the Navo mosque is deserted save the few octogenarians I saw during my visit. The younger men either have fled or, worse, have been jailed for religious extremism alongside Imam Klichev. One woman in a sky-blue hijab noted her comparative luck—her husband left for Russia to work illegally and to maintain a low profile until the Klichev affair blows over.

The previous night Buston Boltaeva recounted how the police claimed to have found extremist *Wahhabi* pamphlets in her home following her son's arrest. Wahhabism is a conservative form of Sunni Islam widely practiced in Saudi Arabia. Klichev made the *Haj* in 2002 and, Boltaeva explained, was befriended by several Saudis during his pilgrimage. The Saudis, wealthy businessmen, were impressed with the young Uzbek imam's devotion and his mastery of Arabic. They gave Klichev several religious texts and, even after his return to Uzbekistan, continued to act as benefactors.

In the first years of independence, Uzbek imams eagerly welcomed Saudi partners. The dazzling minarets and azure-tiled domes of the Kokcha mosque in Tashkent, for example, were built with a million-dollar donation from a wealthy Saudi benefactor in the early 1990s.[19] The Karimov regime, however, quickly cooled to Saudi philanthropy. Fearing petro-dollars would disrupt its patronage control over the Uzbek religious establishment, Karimov made it clear to the religious elite that cozy relations with wealthy Saudis was no longer acceptable. The term Wahhabi became invective in government-speak, synonymous with extremism and fundamentalism. In a radio interview in 1998, for example, Karimov warned that unchecked Wahhabism would lead to civil war. To prevent such an outcome, the Uzbek leader told his listeners, "such people must be shot in their foreheads . . . I'll shoot them myself, if you lack the resoluteness."[20]

Klichev, his mother had told me, paid little attention to President Karimov's rants. Neither did he listen to the directives from the Spiritual

Board. Klichev was popular, Nodira and her friends explained, precisely because he was not a bought man. In contrast to other imams in Karshi, Klichev did not deliver the Spiritual Board's canned, pro-governmental Friday prayer. Nodira noted that, although Klichev was by no means an oppositionist, neither was he a mouthpiece for the Karimov regime. And this, Nodira emphasized, was the reason why people not only in Karshi but in the surrounding villages and cities traveled every Friday to hear the young imam at the Navo neighborhood mosque. Klichev was an independent imam who preached an Islam that, instead of propaganda, promised guidance for the challenges of daily life. Klichev, now serving his sentence, is paying dearly for this independence.

CONCLUSION

Imam Klichev's story captures the multiple forces which shape state-society relations in Uzbekistan. In Klichev's growing popularity we see the threat that Islam indeed does pose. Importantly, though, this threat is not one of religious extremism. Rather, it is a threat of competing legitimacy, of local religious leaders who enjoy growing grassroots support and of a central leadership whose one power is its promotion of an environment of fear.

Beyond the immediate violation of human rights, this environment of fear raises equally troubling concerns for Uzbekistan's and the Central Asian region's future stability. The Karimov regime's manipulation of Islam, its labeling of social activists as religious extremists in its attempt to legitimate repression, may indeed engender a militant opposition united by, among other things, a strong belief in Islam. As scholars of revolutionary movements demonstrate elsewhere, ordinary citizens may become militant oppositionists when they perceive "no other way out," when a tipping point is reached where authoritarian states become so repressive that the only effective means of resistance is violent protest.[21]

Uzbekistan may be nearing just such a tipping point. In May 2005 two dozen armed men, several of whom indeed were Islamist militants, clashed with government forces in Andijon in Uzbekistan's Ferghana Valley. The Karimov state responded with disproportionate force, both killing the militants and firing indiscriminately into crowds of demonstrators who had gathered in Andijon's central square to protest authoritarian rule. Predictably, President Karimov blamed the Andijon uprising on "extremists" and "fundamentalist groups."[22] Independent accounts from watch groups such as Human Rights Watch and Freedom House have found that hundreds of the protestors killed in Andijon's city center were unarmed civilians.[23]

The Andijon protestors will likely not be the last casualties of the state's manipulation of Islamist extremism. Importantly, though, as the everyday acts of resistance discussed in this chapter suggest, the Karimov government's attempts to label all activists and oppositionists as Islamic militants will remain only partially effective. Ultimately, terror, absent any coherent ideology, provides a weak foundation for sustained rule, and it is only a question of time before the Karimov regime itself collapses under the weight of growing social discontent.

NOTES

1. "Uzbekistan Keeps Threat of Terrorism from the Door—Leader's New Year Message," BBC Monitoring International Reports, 1 January 2003 (from Uzbek Television first channel, 31 December 2002), available online on LexisNexis.

2. Stephen Kotkin, *Magnetic Mountain: Stalinism as Civilization* (Berkeley: University of California Press, 1995), 21.

3. Michel de Certeau, *The Practice of Everyday Life* (Berkeley: University of California Press, 1984), xiv.

4. Human Rights Watch, *Creating Enemies of the State: Religious Persecution in Uzbekistan* (New York: Human Rights Watch, 2004), 1.

5. For more on the 1999 Tashkent bombings, see Abdumannob Polat and Nikolai Bukevich, "Unraveling the Mystery of the Tashkent Bombings: Theories and Implications," *Demokratizatsiy* 8:4 (2000).

6. Polat and Bukevich suggest, for example, that forces within the Uzbek government may have had a hand in the 1999 Tashkent bombings. Raising the militant Islam threat, these authors reason, could help legitimate Karimov's authoritarian leanings.

7. Author interview with an Islamic scholar in Kokand, November 2004 (name withheld at interviewee's request).

8. Name changed to preserve the privacy of my colleague.

9. For more on state control of the Muftiate and Islam, see Igor Rotar, "Uzbekistan: Total State Control over Islamic Faith," *Forum 18 News* (20 May 2003), available online: http://www.forum18.org/Archive.php?article_id=58.

10. Author interviews in Dungar, Uzbekistan, November 2004. See also Rotar, "Total State Control."

11. Author interview with Abdulhaviz-qori, head imam of Kokand, 18 November 2004.

12. Author interview with Ismail Raikhanov, head imam of Karshi, 24 November 2004.

13. *CIA World Factbook,* January 2004 estimates.

14. For more on Karimov's post-Soviet balancing act, see Pauline Jones-Luong, *Institutional Change and Political Continuity in Post-Soviet Central Asia: Power, Perceptions, and Pacts* (New York: Cambridge University Press, 2002), 120–130.

15. "Uzbekistan Muslims Demonstrate Against Communist Leadership," Russian Television 1700 GMT, 22 September 1991, BBC Summary of World Broadcasts, 24 September 1991, available online at LexisNexis.

16. Article 9, "Religious Schools," *1998 Law on Freedom of Conscience and Religious Organizations,* available online: www.pravo.uz.

17. Name changed to preserve privacy.

18. Author's interview with Buston Boltaeva, Imam Klichev's mother, 23 November 2004, Karshi, Uzbekistan.

19. Author interview with Rakhmatulla-qori Obidov, imam of the Kokcha mosque. Tashkent, Uzbekistan, 17 November 2004.

20. Uzbek Radio Second Program, "Uzbek Head: I'll Shoot Islamic Fundamentalists," BBC Worldwide Monitoring, 2 May 1998. Available online at LexisNexis.

21. Jeff Goodwin, *No Other Way Out: States and Revolutionary Movements, 1945–1991* (New York: Cambridge University Press, 2001).

22. Press Service of the President of the Republic of Uzbekistan, "Islam Karimov: No One Can Turn Us from Our Chosen Path," (16 May 2005). Available online: http://www.press-service.uz/en/content.scm?contentId=8908.

23. Human Rights Watch, "Uzbekistan: Killings Demand International Inquiry" (20 May 2005), available online: http://www.hrw.org/english/docs/2005/05/20/uzbeki10989.htm; Freedom House, Uzbekistan: Violence Could Lead to Larger Conflict (17 May 2005); available online: http://www.freedomhouse.org/media/pressrel/051705.htm.

20. Sacred Sites, Profane Ideologies: Religious Pilgrimage and the Uzbek State

David M. Abramson and Elyor E. Karimov

Islam has been a defining aspect of life in Central Asia, and sacred places, most predominantly saint shrines, have played a key role in the everyday spiritual life of Muslims for much of the region's history over the last twelve centuries. After many decades of life under Soviet socialism, Islamic rituals, such as pilgrimages to sacred sites, are gaining popularity in Uzbekistan and in the region. While many of the ritual practices observed today have centuries-old roots, they also have new, contemporary meanings for the region's Muslims, who are struggling to make sense out of the remarkable social, economic,[1] and political changes affecting their lives (DeWeese, 1988: 45–83). Those meanings are often made in the context of large-scale events. However, they are shaped more directly by everyday conflicts over, for example, what constitutes authentic ritual observance, how people talk about the value of sacred sites in their lives, the architectural designs of those sites, and even how people define what it means to be Muslim.

In examining each of these areas of conflict, we argue that Islam's renewal in Uzbekistan today is a dynamic, multi-faceted phenomenon that entails, among other things, the accumulation and deployment of political, economic, and social capital. Just as importantly, it also entails spiritual renewal and the search for forms of moral authority alternative to those prescribed by socialism and nationalism. Moreover, our research on practices surrounding sacred sites has yielded a rich set of intriguing observations that are shedding light on the nature of moral authority and how culture (particularly debates centered on Islam) is being shaped and is shaping the stage on which national and local politics unfold.

The story told in this chapter is based on archival information on more than 2,000 sacred places out of an estimated 3,500 sacred sites in Uzbekistan, and on fieldwork conducted in five regions of the country—Tashkent, Bukhara, Khorezm, Kashkadarya, and Navoi. Several observations are particularly significant. First, since independence, the number of people who are making pilgrimages (*ihson*) to sacred sites has grown significantly. This newfound popularity of sacred sites (*ziyaratgoh*) is reflected partly in the demographic diversification of visitors to shrine sites. While categories of visitors used to consist primarily of, women, children, and elderly men with less education and of a lower social status, they now also include men of all ages and people representing all levels of education, wealth, and social status. The growth in the number and categories of pilgrims has been accompanied by a vastly increasing influx of money through donations (*sadaqa*), the purchasing of souvenirs and talismans, written verses from the Quran, literature about local saints, and entrance fees.

Sacred sites, or shrines, have also become the focus of renewed saint veneration, which in some cases has brought people who had no prior relationship to a sacred place to seek to establish a genealogical connection to it, often for political (legitimacy), economic (profit), and/or social (status) reasons. The increasing number of pilgrimages and amounts of money and the growing social importance of these sites are also reflected in and influence the architecture of new and restored sacred sites and shrine complexes. In addition to restoring old sites, individuals have begun to build mausoleums and monuments around existing tombs, as well as to place their own graves and sometimes mausoleums adjacent to saints' tombs.

Lighting lamps or candles and tying shawls or pieces of cloth on tree branches are the main practices pilgrims engage in at sacred sites. Historically these practices derive from pre-Islamic traditions, but today they bear significance for Muslims in Uzbekistan that is inseparable from Islam. The official Islamic establishment (e.g., the Mufti of Uzbekistan and Muslim clerics such as imams credentialed in Tashkent) now reject many of these practices as being inconsistent with Islamic tradition. This position is communicated most often in mosque sermons but is also seen on instructive plaques sometimes placed at holy sites. At the same time, religious authorities facilitate such practices by supporting sacred sites and encouraging visits. Besides mosque attendance, pilgrimages are one of the most visible manifestations of popular interest in Islam and are a considerable financial source for religious communities.[2]

Finally, supporters of some Islamist trends in Uzbekistan condemn the institution of saints (*avliya*) and saint veneration as un-Islamic and, in some cases, have vandalized saintly shrines because they are deemed un-Islamic. These actions and other claims about what is or is not Islamic exploit the ambivalence of some Muslims about the Islamic authenticity of shrine use. In this way, they seek to challenge the official Islamic establishment supported by the government.

These developments are interesting because each one expresses a particular tension between cultural continuity and change, tension expressed in both practice and discourse about the role of sacred sites in Central Asian Islam. In this chapter, after providing the basic elements that constitute a "sacred site" in the Central Asian context, we explore each of the above trends and the conflicts embedded in them and, in conclusion, suggest ways in which they influence and are influenced by larger societal dynamics.

DEFINITION OF A SACRED SITE

What is a sacred site? In the Central Asian context, a sacred site can consist of anything from a natural site, such as a water source, to an extensive complex including mosque (*masjid*), religious school (*madrasa*), tomb (*mazar*), cemetery (*qabriston*), and additional buildings for administration, artisanship, and even tourist facilities. While the actual form of the site can vary (e.g., a water source, tree, stone, mosque, mausoleum, the saint's tomb), most sites consist of at least a tree, a water source, and a tomb, all of which are considered sacred because of their affiliation with the site and miracle stories (*karomatlar*) about the interred saint. The telling and retelling of miracle stories by shrine caretakers and other devotees essentially reenact the miracles themselves and intensify the experience for audiences in search of a saint's good will, grace, or blessing (*baraka*).

Sacred places are commonly understood to serve the spiritual needs of all kinds of people, including the sick and childless, who visit shrines to ask for the help of a saint. We can divide sacred sites in Uzbekistan into four somewhat distinct categories: 1) sites known throughout the Muslim world and visited by pilgrims from other countries; 2) sites known only within a particular region in Uzbekistan; 3) sites visited primarily by people of a particular occupation; and 4) new sites, which have not yet acquired renown.

While sacred sites draw pilgrims for multiple reasons and at any time, there are generally five types of visits. Everyday visits are characteristic of people who live near a shrine and regularly attend mosque.[3] Visitors leave sadaqa, usually a small sum of money in the range of 25–100 *som*,[4] in a standard set of places close to the site, such as under stones and trees or by tombstones. In the past, before inflation drove coin currency out of circulation, visitors would also throw coins into a sacred water source near the shrine. Typically income from the donation is small, but it may vary in accordance with the sacred site's popularity, ranging from zero to 4,000 som per day, from 100 som to 25,000 som per week, and averaging 80,000–100,000 som per month. These considerably lucrative sources of income are often neither documented officially nor taxed, and monies are distributed to a wide range of beneficiaries, from the local shrine attendant to the Muftiate in Tashkent.

Thursdays, Fridays, and Sundays are considered to be special days for visiting shrines and tend to bring larger numbers of visitors who come from further away. On these days, people usually make more elaborate preparations, often with the goal of requesting special favors from God. Typical requests include children (if a woman is having difficulty getting pregnant), a son (if a couple has only female children, since boys are generally more highly valued than girls), a cure for an illness (to supplement other efforts, or when other efforts have failed), and economic or social success. Depending on the saint's status, sometimes the saint's descendant may be present on these days. Historically, these descendants (*ishan*) would oversee maintenance of the mazar, although teacher-clerics (*imam-hatib*) of adjacent or affiliated mosques, fortune-tellers and seers (*folbin*), spiritual healers (*tabib*), and others are more typically on hand to serve as proprietors of the shrine. In many cases, one will find local or national government-appointed imams or shrine administrators (*mutawali*), who may not have any blood ties to the saint.

Depending on the shrine's remoteness from population centers, visitors may come alone, as a family, or in groups of as many as twenty to thirty people, in which case a bus is chartered for the trip. Preparations are made in advance for making animal sacrifices (*kurbonlik*), slaughtering of chickens or rams or giving between 50 and 200 som. Visitors also give a donation to the site's proprietor, averaging 2,000 to 5,000 som weekly for lesser-known sites, and 1,000–25,000 som weekly and 40,000–100,000 som monthly for more popular places. According to tradition, only the designated proprietor of a sacred site may take the money.

The third category consists of sacred sites that are famous and may be deemed to have a special power that supplements visits to other lesser-known sites. Usually, these places are more easily accessible by roads and can receive large numbers of visitors, varying from 50 to100, at lesser-known sites, to 150 to 800 people per day. On traditional pilgrimage days, one can find visitors from all social strata, including high-level government officials, wealthy businessmen, and famous artists and performers. Non-monetary forms of sadaqa are more typical at these sites, including the slaughtering of cattle, carpets (*gilam*), carpet mats (*kigiz*), prayer rugs (*joynamoz*), and Central Asian velvet, silk, or cotton mattresses (*korpacha*). Those who choose to give money tend to give 100–500 som, while wealthier visitors might give 10,000 som or more. Income from donations can average 50,000–200,000 som weekly. It is worth noting that the income ranges according to season, being lowest during the winter and highest during the summer, when most people are on vacation, and the autumn, when people earn more money from harvests.

Entrance to Zangi-ota mazar, outside Tashkent. The sign says "Dear Pilgrims. Praying at the grave for fertility or to be freed of concerns, bowing to the grave, and tying cloth on trees are considered sins in Islam."

Special occasions (*mavsumiy ziyoratlar*)—such as before making the *hajj* or *Umra* or in connection with the harvest—mark another reason for making pilgrimages to sacred sites.[5] As a rule, people choose the most popular sites and make visits on the traditional days of the week. These visits are typically treated as holidays and involve commemorative rituals and feasts for up to ten acquaintances at the sites themselves. Guests bring sadaqa, which they donate to the site. While it is difficult to estimate the amount of these donations, in some cases stacks of 100- or 200-som notes were given to the site, thus totaling 10,000 or 20,000 som. Clearly, only wealthy visitors are in a position to make such large donations.[6]

It has also become popular for newlyweds, accompanied by their wedding party, to express respect for local traditions or to visit the most respected and popular local sacred sites. At the sites, they follow the same ritual practices that others do when making a pilgrimage—circumambulating the site and touching it—even if some of the selected sites are not considered sacred. In the past, couples who got married in Tashkent would visit Soviet monuments to the Great Patriotic War (World War II) such as the Eternal Flame or the Tomb of the Unknown Soldier as part of their wedding pilgrimage.

In many cases, people also give sadaqa without actually entering a sacred place, often stopping while driving by cemeteries that are located alongside main roads and giving money to people who sit at the edge of the road for this very purpose. In an observation period of just fifteen minutes, donations totaling 300–600 som were given in this manner by passersby. This practice was observed at several sites near Zangi-ota, Qo'ylik-ota and other big mazars along busy roads on the outskirts of Tashkent.

SHARED SHRINES, CONTESTED PRACTICES

The following descriptions of rituals people perform at sacred sites will provide the reader with a picture of what takes place at shrines on a daily basis.

The Shrine of Ughlanjon-ota, Kamashin Rayon, Kashkadarya Viloyat:[7]

The tomb, decorated inside and out with designs made from clay, stands as an isolated structure in an arid desert. On one side is a tree tied with numerous handkerchiefs and strips of cloth. Women, often barefoot and in a trancelike state, slowly circumambulate the tomb an odd number of times. As they walk, they make wishes, ask to be cured of an illness, or make other kinds of supplication. They concentrate on the ritual and do not interact with one another. Some women touch their hands to the walls of the tomb as they pass and then touch their eyelids. Only a small girl, perhaps the daughter of one of the women, was looking around at other visitors who were not engaged in the ritual.

Next to the grave is a special separate place for lighting candles and, more commonly, *piliks,* which are flammable objects made of cotton wool wound around a small stick and wrapped in raw cotton. Only an odd number (3, 7, or 11) of candles or piliks are lit. The pilgrim then says a prayer and places a small amount of money next to the piliks.[8] The practice of lighting piliks has ancient pre-Islamic roots whose complexity is reflected in the fact that there is no consensus about the practice's Islamic legitimacy. At the same time, lighting candles in conjunction with prayer at sacred sites is one of the most common Muslim practices in Central Asia.

Not far from the tomb is a tree on which pilgrims are tying pieces of cloth and handkerchiefs and making wishes. One of them leaves the clothes someone was wearing at the time he was bitten by a rabid dog.[9]

The Tomb of Bahauddin Naqshband, Bukhara Rayon, Bukhara Viloyat:[10]

The tomb of Bahauddin Naqshband stands amidst a complex which includes a mosque, a madrasa, a cemetery, a man-made pool (*hauz*), a well, a very large old tree, and various other buildings. According to a well-known legend, which the sites's imam-hatib Bobojon Rahmonov related, Bahauddin Naqshband's walking stick turned into the sacred tree that one can see there today. Pilgrims walk around the tree an odd number of times and make a wish.[11] Other pilgrims are relaxing in a nearby garden. Also, nearby is the tomb of Bahauddin Naqshband and adjacent to it sits a mulla under a mulberry tree, leading a group of people in prayer. In front of him is spread a tablecloth where pilgrims leave cookies and various sweets. After the prayer, the pilgrims stand up and give money to the mulla or put it in a dedicated charity box (*ehson*). There is also a well nearby from which pilgrims draw water and drink or fill bottles for relatives.[12]

At several other sites, there is evidence of objects that have roots in pre-Islamic animistic traditions, mixed in with more traditional Islamic objects. At the mazar and mosque Langar-ota in Kamashin Rayon, Kash-kadarya Viloyat, several objects were found in a chest on the site. These included a Hand of Fatima (*panja*), which traditionally had topped a long pole (*tugh*) placed in mazars or laid on top of graves, horns from an *ahrar* (a mountain goat native to Central Asia), and various musical instruments used by ascetics for *zikr-i djahr* and *sa'ma*.[13] In the mazar of Sayid Ibn Abu Vakkos-ota (Sa'ad Ibn Malik az-Zuhri) in Shahrisabz Rayon, Kashkadarya Viloyat, mountain goat horns lie under a carpet that was draped over the tomb. Similar objects, especially the horns, can be found in open graves at most sites in Kashkadarya. According to tradition, local mountain goat horns are believed to protect sacred places, and the people who make pilgrimages to them, from misfortune and evil. Local imam-hatibs often not only sanction but also actively work together with seers (*folbin*) to ensure that these symbols comprise the ritual experience for visiting pilgrims.

The combined elements of prayer and recreation, Islamic and pre-Islamic symbols, independent and clergy-assisted practices, and the variety of ritual practices that people engage in when making pilgrimages illustrate the varied levels of knowledge and expectations that Uzbeks and other visitors have of saint cults in Uzbekistan, which doubtless affect the kinds of relationships that they have with the divine. What they share, however, is the religious understanding that Islam plays a central role in their lives, in being Uzbek, and that sacred sites are integral to their religious imagination.

This conclusion cannot be taken for granted given decades of Soviet rule and its extensive, and at times intensive, efforts to remake that imagination. One legacy of such efforts, which we shall discuss below, is a lingering coexistence of and apparent contradiction between officially sanctioned and actual practices. One example can be found in the commemorative complex of the fifteenth-century religious figure Khoja Ahrar, which is located near Samarkand (Karimov 2003: 48).

In 2002, the government of Uzbekistan hosted a commemorative six-hundredth anniversary of Khoja Ahrar, who is known for having insti-

Pilgrimage drive-through at Zangi-ota mazar, outside Tashkent.

tutionalized Naqshbandi Sufism in Central Asia (Karimov 2003: 42). The primary significance of this is that the government has identified Naqsh-bandism as the Islamic tradition that resonates most closely with Uzbeki-stan's cultural traditions. At the entrance to the complex is a depiction of a man with the caption "Khoja Ahrar." For adherents to some orthodox forms of Sunni Islam, images of people, especially spiritual figures, are blasphe-mous, but the use of such images in Central Asia, including on gravestones, is quite common and usually is not contested. To the left of the picture is a plaque, most likely erected since 1991, with the instructions "Rules for Vis-iting Cemeteries" (*Qabristonni ziyorat qilish odobi*). While the first few rules, including reciting from the Quran and dressing appropriately, are widely known, the last five in particular are worth noting:

- Do not kiss the grave and bow down before it
- Do not light candles or twigs
- Do not put money on the gravestone
- Do not tie scarves or cloth strips on the trees
- Do not ask of the Saint herein to resolve personal problems or to pro-vide help in other ways. These can be asked from Allah.

Despite these posted rules, the abundant ashes and cloth strips constituted enough evidence to prove that people were not complying with these proscriptions. Such inconsistencies between dogma and practice abound. Visitors to shrines have been engaging in all of the above-mentioned proscribed practices for centuries. For example, at the shrine complex of Zangi-ota near Tashkent (Karimov 2000: 32–33), which commemorates a well-known leader of Yasavi Sufism (Karimov 1999: 40), small spirit houses sit atop the graves. These houses were constructed in an identical fashion to those for lighting fires at other gravesites—two vertical bricks standing side by side with a horizontal brick on top forming each wall of the house, with two additional bricks forming the roof. At this particular site, the graves on which these "houses" were erected were new because the tombstones had not yet been delivered—typically, tombstones are not put in place until one year has passed after a person's death. The spirit houses, however, are erected within forty days after a person's burial, based on the belief that the dead person's soul is still with the body for forty days.

The Zangi-ota cemetery attendant (*domla*), a university graduate with a degree in Arab philology, was responsible for carrying out religious functions at the site. In response to an interview question about the small houses on the graves, he said, "Illiterate people do this, because of their ignorance" (*Bu savodsiz halq bilmasdan qiladi*), highlighting the importance for practicing Muslims of having knowledge of Arabic in order to read the Quran, rather than simply knowing Central Asian Islamic practices. While the attendant may have been promoting his own credentials as an Arabic language specialist, he was also expressing the widely shared position among establishment clergy that observance of universal Islamic principles is more important than respect for local practices.

In many other cases, however, when the local imam-hatib or other custodian is not schooled in Tashkent or not sponsored by the Islamic establishment, distinctions regarding religious literacy are less likely to be drawn. At the same time, there may be more than one person associated with a particular site claiming authoritative knowledge of the history of or appropriate ways of paying respect at that site. These claims can sometimes come into conflict and may involve the custodian, self-appointed financiers, or frequent visitors themselves. Tensions arise not merely over knowledge about a shrine's sacredness, but also over decisions concerning architectural design in a given restoration project. Given their growing cultural importance and increasing financial income, it is hardly surprising that the exercise of worldly power would extend to sacred sites. The following discussion addresses precisely this worldly aspect of shrine cults, demonstrating that materialism and spirituality are in many ways inseparable and at the same time very much situated in historical and social contexts (Karimov 1991: 80–82).

SACRED SITES AND PROFANE PRACTICES

The following has been excerpted from a conversation about a construction project at the Zarkent-buva shrine (Parkent Rayon, Tashkent Viloyat) that took place in June 2002 between our interviewer and the custodian of the site. Atypically, the custodian refused to be photographed, citing religious reasons.

> *EK:* Who is building the mazar? [meaning the edifice over the grave (*maqbara*)]
>
> *C:* Formerly, this place belonged to a Soviet Pioneer youth camp. After- ward representatives from the mayor's office (*hokimiyat*) came and sepa- rated this place off. Now the elder brother of the chairman (*rais*) of the "Uzbekistan" collective farm (*kolkhoz*) is rebuilding it. This place is sacred . . . Zarkent-buva came here, spoke with some local elders, and then walked around the spring and disappeared. That's why nobody knows if he died here or not.
>
> *EK:* Is there a grave here?
>
> *C:* A grave is here, but we don't know who is in it.
>
> *EK:* Was there an old tombstone (*qabrtosh*)?
>
> *C:* There were old tombstones made of marble.
>
> *EK:* Were there any trees?
>
> *C:* Yes, there were.
>
> *EK:* Why isn't the tombstone visible?
>
> *C:* Because of the buildings and because we covered it with gravel (shaghal) to protect it from water erosion.
>
> *EK:* Who cut down the trees?
>
> *C:* I did. I am allowed to do it, because I am from a line of Khojas who have lived here for centuries.[14]
>
> *EK:* Oh, you are from this lineage. So why is the chairman of the collective farm in charge of the construction?
>
> *C:* I don't know. Other people made that decision. They have spent a lot of money on it. Such construction requires a lot of money. And people from all places come here: from the [Ferghana] Valley, from Khorezm. . . At first, they come to Zangi-ota, then to Turkistan-buva,[15] and then here. People who made the Haj were asked if they had been to Zangi-ota, Turkistan-buva, and Zarkent-buva, and they explained that only after making pilgrimages to these three places would they be allowed to make the Haj.[16]
>
> *EK:* Was there a large mosque here before?
>
> *C:* Yes, there was, but then the Russians came and burned it down. . .
>
> *EK:* Were there any books?
>
> *C:* All the books that were kept here were burned. But the documents were saved and taken away to Tashkent.[17]
>
> *EK:* You are the custodian of this place. Do you maintain it?
>
> *C:* I clean the creek (water source) three times a year.

EK: Did somebody entrust the building to the chairman's elder brother or did he do it on his own initiative?

C: The chairman of the collective farm's brother oversaw it. He came here and said that he would build it himself.

EK: And who built the mosque?

C: Another chairman (rais), Ermon Holmonov from Chatkal, built it.

The shrine's custodian conveyed that he understood that there was a division of labor between those local leaders who would handle the administrative and financial aspects and his own custodianship, including responsibility for maintenance and spiritual oversight of the site. This conversation reveals that members of the local political elite—municipality and collective farm leaders—were clearly in charge of the decision-making process surrounding the rebuilding of this shrine. It also seems likely that someone had ordered the custodian to make certain changes to the site, such as clearing away trees, covering up the tombstone, and making significant alterations to the old site's general appearance. Nevertheless, the role of the custodian, who is recognized as, or at least claims to be, the most recent representative of a sacred lineage, is key to the changes that were underway at the shrine, including communicating the site's uncertain history. While we do not know what specific factors motivated these local-level decision-makers, other cases described below narrow the possibilities down to an identifiable cultural pattern that suggests a post-Soviet realignment of leadership with Islam as the dominant legitimating force in local, if not national, politics.

As some Islamic practices have been more openly tolerated and embraced since Uzbekistan's independence, not only have more people in Central Asia expressed a new and public appreciation for Islamic sacred sites, but Muslims from abroad have sought to build ties to kindred spirits. Take the mazar of Khoja Mir Kulol (or Amir Kulal), a famous representative of Naqshbandi Sufism.[18] Located in Bukhara Rayon, Bukhara Viloyat, the shrine, according to residents, was restored in 1995. In fact, older photographs show that it was completely demolished and rebuilt without regard to its original design. After Uzbekistan became independent, the number of pilgrims to the shrine, including many disciples (*murids*) of the Naqshbandi movement, increased after independence. Among them was a murid from Pakistan who came to Bukhara in 1994, claiming to be a descendant of Khoja Mir Kulol. At that time, the site was not being maintained. Using his own money, the Pakistani worked with the local administration to construct a mausoleum for the tomb and a separate mosque named after Khoja Mir Kulol. While the mausoleum's design differed remarkably from the local style, it nevertheless provided the necessary conditions for pilgrims, such as access to water and a shady place to pray, prepare food, and rest.

A different example illustrates the way in which local politicians and businessmen cultivate links to local shrines as a means of garnering political capital. Outside of the town of Otrar in southern Kazakhstan (in a region adjacent to Uzbekistan) is the grave of the saint Arslan-baba, one of the spiritual teachers (*pir*) of Ahmad Yasavi, after whom another of the Central Asian Sufi movements was named (DeWeese 1996: 192). The gravestone bears an inscription indicating that Arslan-baba lies there (Karimov 2000: 30–35). Not far from the grave is a second grave indicating that it belongs to a descendant of a Kazakh khan. Throughout much of the region's history, there was a tradition of burying members of the ruling dynasty close to the graves of saints. For example, the grave of Amir Temur, or Tamerlane (Bartold 1964: 446), rests at the foot of Said Baraka's tomb in Samarkand; members of the Shaybanid dynasty were buried behind the tomb of Bahauddin Naqshband in Bukhara; the Kungrats lie near the grave of Pahlavan Mahmud in Khiva; and there are many other examples of political leaders who chose to be buried or whose followers chose to bury them and their relatives on already sacred ground.

Not far from Arslan-baba's grave, next to the above-mentioned grave, a descendant of a Kazakh khan resides in the much newer grave of Uzbekali Janibekov. As the local attendant (*chiroqchi*)[19] proudly explained, brandishing an obituary from the local newspaper as a helpful prop, Janibekov was a member of the Central Committee of the Communist Party and Kazakh Minister of Culture, etc. As Janibekov was from Otrar, he wanted to be buried there. The luxurious beauty of the tomb entirely suited a former minister of culture, even if it made the surrounding tombs, including that of Arslan-baba, pale by comparison. The practice of burying political figures next to saints is new for the last few generations in Uzbekistan who lived under Soviet rule and reflects the widespread recognition that Islam as a cultural model is a growing and important source of moral authority in Uzbekistan. Furthermore, in order to visit the site of Arslan-baba/Janibekov, even pilgrims are required to purchase tickets, which is extremely rare at sacred sites that are not also tourist destinations.

If political legitimation and the establishment of an enduring social legacy comprise one rationale for restoring and reconstructing sacred sites, then economic gain, even involving money laundering, is another. The more expensive the building, the more money can be laundered. Consequently, sacred sites have attracted patrons who would not necessarily have taken an interest, in the past, when pilgrimages to such sites were of little concern to the state. For example, at the site of Etti Tugh in Kashkadarya Viloyat, a man named Rahmatulla Urokov helped finance construction of a marble mausoleum around the grave, since 1991 and independence from the Soviet Union. The assistant of the imam-hatib of Etti Tugh praised the good works of Urokov, a man from the local village , and asked visitors to pray for his soul. He

Sacred Sites, Profane Ideologies / 331

explained, "Everyone here benefited from Urokov's kindness and charitable activity." As it turned out, according to other sources, Urokov had been a director of the Karshi animal and vegetable fat factory. In 2000, he was kidnapped and killed. Kidnapping for the purpose of ransom is highly uncommon, so the more plausible explanation is that someone simply wanted to kill him to get his money. Moreover, the official salary in Uzbekistan of the director of a fat factory was never sufficient to build such a mausoleum. After his death, Urokov was buried in a grave adjacent to the saint's mausoleum. Apparently, animal fat production has become grounds for sainthood!

As Islam becomes a source of moral authority in Uzbekistan today, expressions of religious piety that do not explicitly challenge political authority are increasingly difficult to question. In fact, creative efforts to fuse moral and political authority, particularly in morally problematic situations where the latter needs some shoring up, in the uncertain climate of the post-Soviet transition, are quite welcome. Saint shrines, which Central Asian Muslims will only continue to visit and honor in greater numbers due to their unquestioned sacred status, are ideal sites for the conversion of gradually delegitimized socialist values into those that might constitute a new model for morally grounded social relationships. Even if pilgrims view certain aspects of a shrine, such as its maintenance, to be exploited or mismanaged by the living, they continue to believe that its sacredness transcends the material present, and therefore is incorruptible.[20]

RETHINKING RELIGION IN THE POST-SOVIET WORLD

One of the major weaknesses in the study of Islam in contemporary Central Asia has been the scholarly assumption that Islamic belief and practice is a discrete category that requires an unassailable purity of intentionfor it to be considered legitimately religious. Without that purity, religious practice has been regarded as being either inauthentically Islamic (i.e., an amalgam of religious and non-religious local customs) and the product of ignorant adherents who do not know their own religious heritage, or as insincere, even hypocritical, and the product of practitioners who have lost or never had a profound appreciation for the idea of a moral community based on otherworldly concerns. In his extensive and deeply informed review of Yaacov Ro'i's book *Islam in the Soviet Union*, DeWeese (2002) illustrates these and other pitfalls that few scholars have managed to avoid in characterizing the social significance of Islam in Central Asia.

Our chapter on the growing popularity of pilgrimage to sacred sites in post-Soviet Uzbekistan does not traverse the same broad scholarly territory DeWeese's review covers so well; rather, it builds on his recommendation that the study of Islam transcend the frozen typologies of previous generations of scholars. We therefore analyze how some actual customs of Central Asian Islam—namely, the shrine cult and shrine pilgrimage—relate to lived and experienced political and social conditions. In taking this approach, we set aside the categories of "official" and "unofficial" Islam commonly used in Soviet, sovietological, and post-Soviet studies, for the very reason that they mostly just echo political struggles over Islamic authenticity (Karimov 2000: 3–4; Karimov 2003: 2–4), rather than contribute to understanding the sources and forms of everyday religious knowledge. Such analytically stale and politically embedded claims reduce Islam to a political phenomenon, burying its social relevance as something that is lived, is experienced, and possesses the power to transform social life.

Since ours is not a theological discussion, this study does not address what constitutes "genuine" Islam. Rather, we are concerned with what people know about Islam in Uzbekistan, how such knowledge is applied in everyday life, and how it shapes the way certain aspects of everyday life are experienced. Thus, categories such as official and unofficial Islam, or traditional and orthodox Islam, and debates over religious authenticity are relevant here mainly because their presence in everyday speech influences to some degree local Islamic practice and Islam's place in the social and political imagination (Karimov et al., 2004).

The categories "official Islam" and "unofficial Islam" are also useful methodologically in that they serve as guides to approaching different kinds of ethnographic sites—i.e., they reveal something about the way people imagine their religion, including the political and social constraints on and motivations behind Islamic practices. For example, official sites, including mosques, which are often closely monitored by the state, tend to be more difficult places at which to conduct interviews and to observe behavior that has not been influenced by state surveillance. Many less well known saint shrines and other sacred sites are not monitored and generally have not been cast as places that either pose a threat or are deemed useful to the legitimization of the state's interpretation of authentic Central Asian Islam. Therefore, we were privileged to observe some individuals (with considerable local influence) exercising leadership by appropriating Islamic traditions for political, economic, and social ends in sites where the state's presence was either weak or absent.

Soviet state policies did not uniformly seek to rid socialist society of Islam and in many ways were consistent with tsarist policies, which redefined Islam in such a way as to separate and isolate its doctrinal from its lived aspects. As a number of historians and social scientists of religious and other forms of identity in Soviet policy now argue, the twentieth century-religious imagination that helped to shape state policies was culturally grounded. Even across the Soviet Union's huge and diverse expanse of land and peoples, these policies drew more and more on shared, European-oriented understandings of piety and practice (Abramson 2002; Abramson 2004). The doctrinal (i.e., absolute, ideal) dimension could then be placed on an intellectual pedestal while institutions were eradicated and practices defined as products of ignorant or irrelevant social behavior or cultural forms (DeWeese 2002).

Meanwhile, the representatives of Soviet-retained Islamic clergy studied Islam abroad in Saudi Arabia and Egypt, thereby further distancing themselves from Islam as it was experienced and practiced in Central Asia. The spiritual and social needs of local communities, once met by multiple individuals filling specialized roles, were reassigned to "clergy," such as imam-hatibs, who were expected to provide multiple services while specializations were eliminated. The training of Muslim clergy in an Islamic theology divorced from local traditions is not unique to Soviet Islam—indeed, the consolidation of clergy, including those with specific ritual roles to play, and the fixation on a state-trained clergy are very much part of a common pattern in the modern nation-state. The multiple attacks by the state on Islamic institutions and local knowledge, however, had a perhaps unprecedented effect on the popular Islamic imagination, both among Muslim elites and among non-elite practitioner-believers.

CONCLUSIONS: ISLAM AND THE ANTHROPOLOGY OF SOCIAL CHANGE

The renewed interest in Islam in Central Asia is undoubtedly a product of numerous factors, which we cannot realistically hope to capture in any comprehensive way in its development and without additional research. However, we do suggest a few important connections that link practices surrounding saint shrines (e.g., how people talk about the sites and the pilgrim-saint relationships) with Islamic discourses produced in other cultural locations (e.g., the debate over what constitutes authentic Islam). These connections will form the basis for further research and our analysis of survey results of ritual practice and ethnographic interviews, much of which we have already collected. Future stages in our collaborative research will include further investigation into the following relevant topics:

- The new economics of donations (*sadaqa*) given to sacred sites, including an examination of capital accumulation, sites of accumulation, how this capital is spent, and its role in enhancing the cultural "currency" of Islam.

- The stories told about saints' lives and about the miracles saints performed, in the lived process of honoring and commemorating sacred figures, and what these stories reveal about the emergent popular Islamic imagination, such as parallel constructions of moral authority in both spiritual and social worlds.

- The inspiration behind pilgrimages to sacred sites and the process whereby people decide that such visits will play an important role in their lives, including the decision of students to make pilgrimages to sacred sites to pray for success in taking university entrance exams.

- Architecture in the construction and restoration of sacred sites and its role in debates over Islamic authenticity, including an examination of extreme Wahhabi-influenced viewpoints that saint shrines are categorically un-Islamic.

The combined study of these various dimensions to Central Asian Muslims' relationships to sacred sites is critical to understanding the role of sacred sites in the Islamic revival, and the revival itself, in contemporary Uzbekistan. The long-term struggle within Islam in Uzbekistan centers on ideological debates over what constitutes "authentic Islam," without ever questioning the premise. The Islamic establishment's sporadic support for the "traditional" practice of visiting sacred sites and honoring saints is keyed to broader debates about state legitimacy, which, out of political necessity, are couched more and more in Islamic terms.

Debates over religious authenticity in contemporary Uzbekistan tend to focus precisely on what is naturally or culturally indigenous to Central Asia versus a more universal Islam seen by many to be imported by "foreign extremists" whose ideas lead local Uzbek Muslims astray. This is how the debate is generally framed in Uzbekistan today. The significance of this research is that it reveals how shrine usage offers competing versions of true, authentic Islam. The variety of types of sacred sites—from those of only local interest to those of international renown—is evidence that sacred sites such as the shrines of saints have resonance beyond local forms of Islam. Moreover, it suggests that contested claims over what constitutes "authentic" Islam are not limited to local versus imported truths. Similar debates are taking place "out there" in the world as much as they are taking place locally. In other words, what some perceive or consciously claim to be a debate between national and foreign ideas is really a global debate that is taking place locally and in response to local conditions and concerns. This article has attempted to show that Islamic shrines constitute a key ethnographic site of these debates. Shrine cults have played an indisputably prominent role in Central Asian Islam. Given their growing popularity in post-Soviet Uzbekistan, a better understanding of how Muslims in Uzbekistan experience them is one way to assess the role of Islam as a reemerging force in Uzbek society on multiple levels—spiritual, social, economic, and political.

These ideological struggles raise questions of individual agency and the unintended consequences that result from widespread and changing social practices throughout the Muslim world. For example, as state support for social welfare dries up and the economy deteriorates, people more and more seek economic resources, moral authority, and leadership outside existing state structures. As people turn to the spiritual world for moral guidance through what is seen as traditional Islamic practice, their actions open up new possibilities for local elites to step in and fill the gap, whether through the sometimes opportunistic misappropriation of sacred sites through fabricated ties of kinship to sacred lineages or through financial support for the restoration of sacred sites. The increasingly widespread realization by both elites and non-elites that such efforts can be advantageous is evidence that local Islam has become a foundation for establishing new kinds of social relationships.

NOTES

Dr. Elyor Karimov is a historian of Islam in Central Asia and member of the Uzbekistan Academy of Sciences. Dr. David Abramson is a cultural anthropologist who has conducted research on Uzbekistan since 1991. This chapter is based almost exclusively on field research Dr. Karimov conducted or supervised during 2000–2004. This multifaceted and ongoing project has involved research on close to 1,400 sacred sites in five regions of Uzbekistan. We are grateful to the following group of researchers who worked with Dr. Karimov in conducting fieldwork for this project: S. Gayupova, K. Kalonov, K. Jabbarova, G. Babajanova, and A. Sherov. This project was supported by grants from the French Institute for Research on Central Asia (IFEAC) and from the Kennan Institute of the Woodrow Wilson International Center. Additional thanks go to George Washington University's Institute for European, Russian, and Eurasian Studies and to Georgetown University for providing opportunities to present and obtain feedback on this project.

1. Like other Central Asian Sufi orders (*tariqats*), the Naqshbandi tariqat engaged in economic activities since the time of Saiddina Bakharzi, who died in 1261. In Bukhara Bakharzi was the proprietor of an important *waqf* endowment, which subsequently passed into the hands of his spiritual and familial descendants over the course of five centuries (DeWeese, 1988: 47, 49).

2. The economic aspect of rituals at sacred sites is an ongoing part of our research.

3. Typically, only the largest and most famous sacred sites and cemeteries have an affiliated mosque located nearby. At tombs without mosques or attendant imam-hatibs, pilgrims pray on their own.

4. It is important to have a framework for understanding the value of donations to sacred sites. At the time the research was conducted, the official exchange rate was about $1=1000 som; however, a thriving black market rate was 30–50 percent higher than the official rate. Officially, government salaries range

from 5,000 to 30,000 som per month, and individuals spend a minimum of 100,000–200,000 som per month in Tashkent, the country's most expensive location, although in rural areas one can live on much less. It is important to note that those who live and work on government-run farms (formerly known as collective farms) often receive government payment in goods, rather than cash, when they get paid. Both poor and wealthy pilgrims give donations, thus the extreme variation in amount.

5. Planting and harvesting are very important features of life in Uzbekistan, where agriculture plays a central role in the nation's economy.

6. Students who are about to take university entrance exams comprise a special category of visitors to sacred sites. Before taking the exams (which are given usually in August), thousands of young people visit sacred sites.

7. Besides translating the terminology from Russian into Uzbek, Uzbekistan generally has preserved the territorial administrative units of the former Soviet Union. Thus, *viloyat* is approximately the equivalent of a province or state and *rayon* of a county.

8. The practice of leaving money by the candles is based on the popular belief that one must "throw seven coins to spirits" (*ruhlarga etti tanga atasñ*) in order to be unburdened by life's problems.

9. According to legend, the tomb of Ughlomgon-ota could cure people who were bitten by rabid dogs. As one local ishan explained, a person would be entirely cured of both the wound and rabies if one visited the tomb over the course of forty days after being bitten. He also explained that if one leaves clothing ruined by the dog at the shrine, it will become intact again. Actually, no one touches the left clothes and they eventually decompose.

10. This is one of the most famous religious sites in Central Asia, certainly in Uzbekistan. Bahauddin Naqshband was a legendary figure after whom the Khojagon-Naqshbandi tariqat (Sufi order) was named and who according to local Islamic legendary tradition is said to have contributed several principles to the body of sacred principles (*kalimat-i qudsiya*) of the twelfth-century Sufi scholar Abdulkhalik Gijduvani and, moreover, organized the movement's teachings (DeWeese 1996). The fifteenth-century shaykh Khoja Ahrar elevated Naqshbandi Sufism as a spiritual movement to the level of a political-religious ideology, which sealed its fate as the predominant form of Islam for most of the rest of Central Asia's history, until the region fell under Russian tsarist rule at the end of the nineteenth century. It was not until the Central Asian republics became independent from Soviet rule that Naqshbandi Sufism was revived in Uzbekistan as the version of Islam seen as being most compatible with local religious traditions.

11. Pilgrims believe that circumambulating this tree will purify them of sin.

12. One of the authors visited the Naqshbandi site twice during the same season—in 1996 on a Friday, which is one of the most popular visiting days of the week, and in 2002 on a less popular day. There were many more pilgrims in 2002, on the off day, than in 1996 on the Friday.

13. *Zikr-i djahr* (*djali*, '*alaniya*) and *sa'ma* are two distinct kinds of ritual events, often involving song and mystical poetry, performed variously by the adherents of the Sufi movements popular in Central Asia.

14. It is prohibited to remove objects from, alter, or destroy part of a sacred site, including its natural surroundings; only people from an appropriate lineage are permitted to do so.

15. The Ahmad Yasavi shrine is in the town of Turkistan, Kazakhstan.

16. Beliefs about whether visits to highly revered shrines can be equated to making the Haj or Umra pilgrimages are numerous, contested, and variable by region. The Muftiate does not recognize such claims. At the same time, the custodians of

the most sacred shrines sometimes promote these beliefs, which add significantly to the popularity of a given shrine.

17. These are papers that document the line of descent from the saint and/ or custodians of the site, possibly over several centuries—a deed for sacred property. It was not clear where the documents were kept in Tashkent and who possesses those papers now.

18. Khoja Mir Kulol, who lived from 1287/1288 to 1370, is believed to have been a teacher of Bahauddin Naqshbandi. Because Khoja Mir Kulol is the patron saint of potters, his tomb is, among other things, a popular pilgrimage site for potters (Manoqib-i Amir Kulol Rukopis' IV; Karimov 2000: 10).

19. A *chiroqchi*, or *shirahchi*, is a man who traditionally looks after tomb sites and assists the imam. Literally, it means lamplighter. In southern Kazakhstan, a chiroqchi is usually the sole attendant at a site.

20. This is supported not only by complaints by some pilgrims and shrine custodians, but also by the comments of a former high official of the Muftiate in a personal communication, May 3, 2004.

REFERENCES

Abramson, David. 2002. "Identity Counts: The Soviet Legacy and the Census in Uzbekistan," in David Kertzer and Dominique Arel, eds., *Census and Identity: The Politics of Race, Ethnicity, and Languages in National Censuses*. Cambridge: Cambridge University Press, 176–201.
———. 2004. "Engendering Citizenship in Postcommunist Uzbekistan," in Kathleen Kuehnast and Carol Nechemias, eds., *Post-Soviet Women Encountering Transition*. Baltimore: Johns Hopkins University Press, 65–84.
Bartold, V. V. 1964. "O pogrebenii Timura" [On the burial of Timur], in *Sochineniia*, Volume 2, Part 2, Moscow.
DeWeese, Devin. 1988. "The Eclipse of the Kubraviyah in Central Asia," *Iranian Studies* 21(1–2): 45–83.
———. 1996. "The Masha'ikh-i Turk and the Khojagan: Rethinking the links between the Yasavi and Naqshbandi Sufi Traditions?" *Journal of Islamic Studies* 7(2): 180–207.
———. 2002. "Islam and the Legacy of Sovietology: A Review Essay on Yaacov Ro'i's *Islam in the Soviet Union*," *Journal of Islamic Studies* 13(3): 298–330.
Karimov, Elyor E. 1991. "Nekotorye aspekti politicheskoi i religiozno-filosofskoi praktiki tariqata Naqshbandioa v Maverannahr XV veka," [Some political and religio-philosophical aspects of Naqshbandi practice in fifteenth century Maverannahr], in *Iz istorii sufizma: istochniki i sotsial'naia praktika* [*From the history of Sufism: sources and social practice*]. Tashkent: Tashkent, 74–89.
———. 1999. "Ahmad Yasavi i ranniaia sufiyskaia traditsiia Srednei Azii," [Ahmad Yasavi and early Sufi tradition in Central Asia], in *Ozbekiston tarikhining dolzarb muammolariga yangi chizgilar* [*New directions for the history of Uzbekistan's most challenging questions*], Occasional Paper No. 2, Tashkent: Tashkent, 40–52.
———. 2000. *Yasaviia i khodjagon-naqshbandiia: istoriia real'naia i vymishlennaia.* [*Yasaviia and Khojagon-naqshbandiia: History Real and Imaginable*]. Tashkent: Tashkent.
———. 2003. *Khoja Ahror: Hayoti va faoliyati* [*Khoja Ahrar: His Life and Accomplishments*]. Tashkent: Tashkent.
Karimov, Elyor, et al. 2004. "Uzbekiston yoshlarida dunyoqarash uyg'unligining

shakllanishi muammolari" [Challenges facing the formation of a harmonious worldview for Uzbekistan's youth]. Tashkent: Tashkent.

"Manoqib-I Amir Kulol" Rukopis' IV. Manuscript, Institute of Oriental Studies, Uzbekistan Academy of Sciences, Inventory No. 8667/II.

Maqamat-i 'Abd al-Haliq Gugduwani wa 'Arif-i Riwgiri, edited with commentary by Sa'id Nafisi. 1954. Farhang-i Iran Zamin II/I.

21. Everyday Negotiations of Islam in Central Asia: Practicing Religion in the Uyghur Neighborhood of *Zarya Vostoka* in Almaty, Kazakhstan

Sean R. Roberts

DAILY RELIGIOUS PRACTICE IN CENTRAL ASIA:
MAKING SENSE OF DIVERSITY

To the person unacquainted with Central Asia, the religious life of its people appears filled with contradictions and is difficult to comprehend. Most indigenous Central Asians will proclaim that they are Muslim, but the ways in which they practice their religion are extremely varied and often seemingly contradictory. This phenomenon emerges from the post-Soviet context in which the Muslims of Central Asia are torn between multiple tendencies influencing their attitudes toward religion.

Firstly, the Muslims of the region are in the process of rediscovering their religious roots in Islam, a tendency that is also interconnected with their nationalist revival, since Islam is seen as a critical part of one's national identity for most Central Asian Muslims. In direct conflict with this tendency, decades of Soviet atheism campaigns have created a strong tradition of atheism and secularism that is difficult to reverse not only on a societal level, but on a personal level for many Central Asians as well. This tendency is also reinforced by the post-Soviet states of Central Asia, which are essentially run by former Soviet *nomenklatura* officials who fear Islam as a threat to their retention of power and therefore attempt to control Muslim religious practices and to repress public discourse on the role of Islam in social and political life. Finally, while not in direct conflict with either the tendency of religious revival or the legacy of Soviet atheism, globalization and its related phenomenon of global capitalism present a third tendency influencing the practice of Islam. The influence of globalization, however, is more amorphous and difficult to characterize uniformly, since it carries with it competing and often contradictory messages.

These competing influences have fostered a context of varied attitudes toward Islam and its practice and, consequently, make it almost impossible to easily characterize the nature of Muslim practices in any single country or among any single ethnic group of Central Asia, let alone in the region as a whole. In this chapter, I attempt to do none of the above. Rather, I provide one example of a community and its daily religious practices in order to highlight the dynamic ways in which Central Asian Muslims with varied religious points of view are able to interact in their practice of Islam. While a specific example of daily life in one community cannot be generalized across the region, it does provide a fairly accurate snapshot of the negotiations that are ongoing in the daily life of virtually all Central Asian Muslim communities. Although these negotiations are played out in daily life differently in different communities, both urban and rural, and among different ethnic groups, the issues with which Central Asians are grappling in their practice of religion are fairly common across the region.

BOURDIEU'S "THEORY OF PRACTICE" AS A MEANS OF UNDERSTANDING EVERYDAY LIFE IN CENTRAL ASIA

As other chapters have shown, the analysis of everyday life can be undertaken using a host of different theories and methodologies. In my analysis of everyday behavior, I am partial to the work of Pierre Bourdieu, who provides us with a "theory of practice" to understand community dynamics and group consciousness as they are played out in the daily practices of a community's members (Bourdieu 1977). My partiality to Bourdieu's work stems from his understanding that the foundations of collective identity are in the daily behavior of those who ascribe to that identity, thus giving concrete basis to the otherwise nebulous concept of identity.

Being highly influenced by Karl Marx's writings on class consciousness, Bourdieu examines habitual activities as the basis of other forms of group consciousness. While in Marx's interpretation of class consciousness shared daily experiences are forced on people by their respective roles in a mode of economic production, in Bourdieu's interpretation of more general group consciousness the habitual practices shared by members of a community or group are reproduced as part of each member's participation in a competitive economy of cultural production.

Bourdieu characterizes the daily rituals and customs of groups of people as being essentially habitual and socialized into children's consciousness at a young age, and then afterward reproduced almost unconsciously as an assumed order of daily life. Bourdieu calls this body of practical knowledge that is socialized in one as a child and reproduced throughout one's life *habi-*

tus. According to Bourdieu, the habitus of any given community is like a road map to life, functioning not as rules or laws do, but as a field of unconscious assumptions about how people are supposed to act on a daily basis. It includes such aspects of daily activity as rituals and ceremonies, but it also includes more mundane behavior such as etiquette concerning how one relates to others, how one eats and drinks, and how one carries out virtually every other daily activity that he or she undertakes. In effect, habitus is one model for the slippery concept of culture that has been the focus of anthropological study since the discipline's inception. Since Bourdieu's approach to this concept involves the self-production and reproduction of a community's behavior, it is a notion of culture that is fluid and changes as the community encounters new experiences and socializes new generations into its always-transforming ideals of what people are meant to do in their daily life.

At first glance, the articulation of habitus is not a very earth-shattering revelation in itself, but Bourdieu goes further to explain the motivation behind the community's reproduction of this "cultural roadmap" as emerging from the community's interpersonal dynamics. According to Bourdieu, the motivation to reproduce a community's habitus throughout one's life is related to a certain competition for symbolic capital within the community (Bourdieu 1977:171–183). Bourdieu characterizes symbolic capital as essentially a sense of honor and respect that is earned, within the community in which one lives, by demonstrating mastery of those norms that people in that community are expected to fulfill in daily life. The drive for acceptance and respect in the community, therefore, leads each individual to adopt the norms of the community, thus reinforcing and reproducing those norms for others. As Bourdieu states, "The agent who 'regularizes' his situation or puts himself in the right is simply beating the group at its own game; in abiding by the rules, falling into line with good form, he wins the group over to his side by ostentatiously honoring the values the group honors" (Bourdieu 1977:22). This is not to suggest that people go about their daily lives as "zombies" following the roadmap of habitus. To the contrary, Bourdieu notes that there is significant room for individual will within the assumptions of one's habitus, but the habitus governs our most fundamental assumptions about what one should and should not do in daily practices (Bourdieu 1977:159–171).

In this chapter, Bourdieu's theory of practice is used to analyze how the competition for symbolic capital and the assumptions of habitus interact in the daily practice of religion in one Central Asian Muslim community, the mostly Uyghur neighborhood of *Zarya Vostoka* (Russian, The Dawn of the East) in the Kazakhstan city of Almaty. On the one hand, the habitus of this community provides its residents with a common set of daily practices, many of which are essentially religious in origin if not overtly religious. On the other hand, the complexity of this community's history, including its present post-Soviet moment, provides for numerous influences that must be negotiated within the rubric of accepted practice. In order to understand the community's habitus and its complex history, therefore, the reader first needs some background on Zarya Vostoka and its inhabitants.

ZARYA VOSTOKA: FROM COLLECTIVE FARM TO LAND PORT ON A NEW SILK ROAD

While sharing much with the experiences of other communities in the region, the history of Zarya Vostoka and its inhabitants has several specificities that are important to note. The community's habitus includes a history of experiences not only in the Soviet Union but in China as well, since the majority of its inhabitants are refugees who came from China in the 1950s and early 1960s. In fact, because most of the residents of this community are refugees from China who only came to the USSR some thirty years after the Bolshevik Revolution, they have been less socialized into Soviet ideals of atheism and have had more experience with the practice of Islam than most Central Asians.

At the same time, the community is situated next to what is now the largest wholesale bazaar for consumer goods in Kazakhstan, thus bringing the inhabitants into contact with a wide range of individuals, including traders from other countries, on a daily basis. As one resident expressed to me, this bazaar has turned what was a marginal collective farm into a cosmopolitan "port" on a new "silk road" between China and Russia. One important link in this new silk road is the reunification of Uyghurs living on both sides of the border, and the interaction between Uyghurs from both sides at this bazaar is yet another critical influence on the habitus of Zarya Vostoka.

Another specific attribute of this community is that its structure is based on the traditional community formation of the settled people of Central Asia known as the *mahalla*. While it is located on the edges of one of Central Asia's most cosmopolitan and non-traditional cities (i.e., Almaty, Kazakhstan), Zarya Vostoka's mahalla structure shares much with those in rural and more traditional urban settled communities in the region.

All of these factors contribute to the formation of the community's habitus and thus to the ways in which its residents negotiate the practice of Islam on a daily basis. Due to the fact that most members of this neighborhood had been less acculturated to Soviet ideals, the community in Zarya Vostoka adapted to the post-Soviet context of religious freedom, nationalist revival, and free market capitalism more quickly than most communities in the city. Already during *perestroika* the community had established a local mosque, which quickly became a central public meeting place for the neighborhood elders as well as a location for worship. The community's proximity to Almaty's largest wholesale market also meant that the people of the neighborhood quickly took to small-time trading as a means to weather the transition from socialism to independent Kazakhstan's quasi–free-market capitalism. Furthermore, increased trading encounters with Uyghurs from China piqued the interest of the residents in the neighborhood concerning both the plight of their nation and the proper observance of Islam.

When I began my fieldwork in Zarya Vostoka in 1994, therefore, I found a vibrant community that was far less Soviet and more religious than the rest of Almaty. With the coordination of the *zhigit beshi* (or headman of the neighborhood) and the mosque's *imam*, life cycle rituals including child-naming ceremonies, circumcisions, weddings, and funerals had become community events that were explicitly religious, at least on some levels. The new mosque in the center of the neighborhood had become the brain center of the community, where elders gathered daily and made community decisions. The major religious holidays of Islam had become large and important community events and had quickly replaced the former Soviet civic holidays in the community's imagination. Within this context, however, the residents of Zarya Vostoka's Uyghur mahalla could hardly be characterized as sharing a singular ideal of Islam. While virtually all residents considered themselves Muslims, there were significant variances in what that meant to different individuals in the community dependent upon their history of experiences.

Most of the elders in the community, for example, had originally been socialized into a Muslim society while growing up in China, but they were forced to adopt Soviet values in their adult life while living in the Soviet Union. Depending upon the nature of their life and work in both the USSR and China, the degree of Soviet influence on their habitus varies. Most of the younger generation, however, was socialized into a Soviet lifestyle, albeit in a relatively traditional Muslim neighborhood with many of the religiously inspired institutions that Uyghurs had in their communities in China prior to Communist rule. Most of the men served in the Soviet army and went to Soviet schools. Yet many of them also have been influenced by their travels later in life to their homeland in China, where Islam also has experienced a revival, especially among the younger generation. Finally, several Uyghur men from China had settled in the neighborhood and now were part of the community, and most of these men were devoutly religious; this group even included one of the *alims* (religious scholars) who directed prayers at the mosque while I lived in the community.

As I will demonstrate below, all of these very different residents interact in the same community religious rituals and activities together, albeit interpreting these activities' religiosity in different ways. On the one hand, this interaction creates a common Muslim consciousness within the community. On the other hand, these interactions are pregnant with subtle negotiations concerning the meaning of Islam and the proper behavior of Muslims and are propelled by competition for symbolic capital that is won in part by exerting and justifying one's own perspective on Islam.

DAILY RELIGIOUS PRACTICE AND NEGOTIATION IN ZARYA VOSTOKA

For the remainder of this chapter, I will examine the actual mechanics of community activities through examples from everyday life, stressing the negotiation between different elements in the community for whom these daily activities bear different meanings and accenting how the shared practice of these activities among residents with different perspectives reinforces their common identity as both Muslims and Uyghurs. I have chosen three critical events in daily life to examine: the celebration of the religious holiday *Qorban Hayit (Qurbon Hayit)*, the blessing of the neighborhood's new soccer field, and a wedding. Each of these events, at which I was present and in which I participated during my residence in the neighborhood as a fieldworker in 1997, bears a different relationship to Islam.

Qorban Hayit in Zarya Vostoka

The first event I will analyze is the neighborhood celebration of Qorban Hayit. In 1997, when I was in Zarya Vostoka for Qorban, many people were still experiencing various rituals associated with this holiday for the first time. While the holiday was observed by the community during the Soviet period, it was not openly celebrated and did not benefit from the organization provided by the institution of a neighborhood mosque. Furthermore, since the neighborhood is directly next to the bazaar, the day's events involved not only residents of the neighborhood, but also Uyghurs from throughout the city and Uyghur traders from China. Given the many visitors coming from other neighborhoods, it is not surprising that everybody in Zarya Vostoka, regardless of their religiosity, tried to conduct the rituals of the holiday as accurately as possible. This was done to demonstrate that their neighborhood had a particularly good grasp on Uyghur "culture," which in virtually all of its guises, of course, includes the practice of Islam. The result was that the holiday became a truly community affair, and practically everybody in the neighborhood actively took part in the festivities.

On the morning of the holiday, at dawn, the crowd began to gather for Qorban prayer, and the mosque gradually filled up for the better part of an hour as the crowd reached close to a thousand strong, spilling into the entire courtyard. People entered in groups, coming to the mosque's gate, stopping all together to say a prayer, and then entering together. The ages represented spanned all generations as many men brought their young sons to their first Qorban prayer. A young Uyghur alim from China gave the sermon, which discussed the meaning of the holiday and its proper observation. He then led an impassioned prayer that included blessing the Uyghurs in China, asking God to help them endure the repression there by maintaining the unity of the nation. At the end, music bellowed from the mosque's loudspeakers in an attempt to mimic the large Qorban celebrations at Kashgar's *Id Kah* mosque, but nobody danced as is the custom in Kashgar—they merely filed out as they had entered.

Following the prayer, people from the neighborhood went back to their homes, many to conduct the sacrifice of livestock associated with the holiday. At my home, I watched as the eldest son of the family uncomfortably slit a sheep's throat as instructed by his father. After the sacrifice, the family all went together to the graveyard to clean the gravesites of relatives who had passed away and to pray for them, a practice undertaken by most families in the community. Later in the day, however, the real celebrations began as the elders conducted *heytlap*, a practice of visiting others during a religious holiday.

I went with the elders to virtually every home in our section of the neighborhood to briefly taste the food from different household's sacrifices. The young alim from China joined us and blessed all the meals. It was during this process that the subtle cultural negotiation began. Various households demonstrated different understandings of the ritual, and the young alim from China found himself offering advice on how to serve the food and how to hold the ceremony in many households. The wealthiest inhabitants of the neighborhood, of course, provided generous portions to show their wealth, while poorer households offered soup with scant meat that had been donated the day before by a foreign Muslim charitable organization. Those families more influenced by Soviet traditions included plates of Russian pickled salads, and those who sought to demonstrate their ties to their homeland that is now part of China included plates of roasted beans and other snacks brought back from China on trading jaunts.

Despite varied degrees of understanding in the neighborhood about why this holiday was celebrated and how, it was a unifying experience. Some elders would comment on the quality of the meal at different households, but generally there was no discussion of various people's degrees of religiosity or relative wealth. The religiously knowledgeable alim from China did not ridicule those who took part in the ritual despite never going to mosque, and all residents showed him great respect. Even in the homes of those most influenced by Soviet traditions, there was no overt drinking of vodka, at least until the elders had already left a home. The ritual was practiced in a more or less unified manner by an extremely diverse population with very different attitudes toward Islam. The negotiations between different groups in the community concerning the proper observance of Islam, however, still existed. They only remained quite subtle because, on this important religious holiday, virtually everybody agreed that the day should be one of religious practice.

Blessing of the Zarya Vostoka Soccer Field

The second example of daily life I will examine provided another unifying community event, albeit one where the event itself was only partially religious in nature. In the spring of 1997, a group of younger adult men in the neighborhood took on the task of building a new soccer field in an open area by a swamp. These young men were all children of immigrants. Some of them had been born in China, but most were born in the Soviet Union after their parents arrived from China in the late 1950s and early 1960s. They were also all businessmen, mostly petty traders, who had some access to disposable income and a desire to raise their profile in the neighborhood and amass additional symbolic capital. While they were not particularly religious and did drink alcohol fairly frequently, all had learned to pray and went to the mosque occasionally, mostly on religious holidays. In general, this particular group of young men was viewed suspiciously in the Uyghur community as a whole and by many residents in their own neighborhood. Many local Uyghurs (i.e., those whose families had been in Kazakhstan since the nineteenth century) from other neighborhoods saw them as *spekulianty*, a Soviet word with negative connotations used to describe traders. Many of the more religious Uyghurs in the neighborhood, including most of the Uyghur traders from China, viewed the men as poor Muslims who drank and rarely went to the mosque.

Despite the suspicion with which many Uyghurs viewed this group of men, when they had built the soccer field people in the neighborhood were appreciative, since it provided a healthy outlet for children after school. The group of men, however, had higher expectations, as they were getting to the age when they wished to have more respect in their neighborhood, and they decided to organize an opening celebration for the soccer field that would include a blessing as a means to this end. Furthermore, it was to be a large affair, complete with the participation of the neighborhood elders and the imam, a variant that would also inevitably maximize their accumulation of symbolic capital both as community philanthropists and as good Muslims. I, as the resident documentarian, was enlisted to videotape the event for neighborhood history.

The event was organized for the first Sunday of April, and preparations began weeks before. The preparations included finding a live Uyghur pop music band, a cook to make a large quantity of pilaf, and an amplified sound system to ensure that all speakers were audible to everybody in attendance. When the day came, they planned the opening to occur after a daytime prayer session so as to ensure that all the elders were together. Once prayers ended, the elder men began to walk toward the field. To accent their entrance, music was played and the rest of the neighborhood was gathered awaiting their arrival. The effect was impressive, to be sure, and it lent the entire event the air of ritual that its organizers had desired. Once the elders entered the field, the music stopped.

First, one of the organizers spoke, welcoming everybody to the celebration and stressing the importance the new soccer field would hold for the youth of the neighborhood. Then, the *zhigit beshi*, or neighborhood head, gave a speech noting the great accomplishment of these young men in constructing the field on their own. This was followed by an official blessing by the imam, during which all present were silent. Once the field had been blessed, the organizers began serving pilaf and tea on makeshift tablecloths spread on the ground just as if this had been a wedding or a *sunnat toi* (circumcision feast). After all had eaten, the imam once again said a prayer, and the elders left with great ceremony. During the entire time there had been no alcohol present, but once the elders had left, the organizers pulled out bottles of vodka and began to enjoy an afternoon of drinking and toasts.

In discussing the event with people present, I found that there was general consensus among everybody that it was a great success. The elders were pleased that these young men had organized such a proper blessing and had honored the elders in the process. Several Uyghur traders from China who had joined the celebration after prayers at the mosque likewise were pleased with this display of generosity and general good work for the neighborhood, viewing it from the lens of Muslim alms giving, or *zakat*. Finally, the group of organizers and their friends, most of whom had a strongly Soviet habitus, were very pleased with the whole event, including the drunken fest that followed.

In a very simple way, this small ritual event had fulfilled everybody's wishes. Consequently, it also provided its organizers with important symbolic capital in the neighborhood, as benefactors who could speak to the diverse desires of the community. The religious aspect of the event, however, had different meanings for different people in the community. For the devoutly religious, it was a sign of the growing religiosity of the community, since the event in effect was organized in order to ensure that the field was blessed by God. For the organizers, it was more an act of habitus, since it was assumed that something new in the community needed to be honored and a blessing was the way that one always honors something new. For the elders, it was a sign that the next generation showed them respect and was demonstrating responsibility and religiosity, suggesting that the next generation would be able to take care of the neighborhood. As was the case in the celebration of Qorban Hayit, the negotiation of these different attitudes was subtle, since all had reasons to sanction the blessing of the soccer field as important to their understanding of the role of Islam in the community.

A Wedding in Zarya Vostoka[1]

The summer months in Zarya Vostoka, as in all Central Asian communities, are usually filled with weddings. These are vital events in the community, and the zhigit beshi serves an important coordinating role by ensuring that weddings do not overlap, that all members of the community can be in attendance, and that necessary resources are at the disposal of those holding the weddings. The fact that so much of the zhigit beshi's work involves weddings suggests that they are among the most important events in the community and among the most contested sites in the competition for symbolic capital.

Since weddings bridge the personal and public spheres of Uyghurs' lives in Zarya Vostoka, they also constitute events where personal preference and habitus cross paths. On the one hand, the habitus in Zarya Vostoka calls for a certain structure to be adhered to in the celebration of weddings that involves three public *tois* (celebrations) of general uniformity that take place in rapid succession.[2] On the other hand, within the context of these three celebrations, there are numerous opportunities for the two families involved to demonstrate their personal understanding of what a wedding should be and to what degree it is a religious ceremony. In the context of Central Asia, one of the major decisions reflecting the religiosity of the event is the decision of whether and how alcohol is consumed.

The wedding I will describe here is one that I attended in the summer of 1997 at the home of a bride. It was the event for the older men in the neighborhood, and it reflected the intense competition for symbolic capital in the community over how Islam should be observed. This was a wedding between two moderately religious families in the community. The event began with people straggling into the courtyard of the bride's house at about 10:00 AM. As is usual practice, people are offered to wash their hands as they enter the courtyard and are seated at benches beside long tables. Also, as is usual, there is a room inside the home reserved for elders and the most honored guests. Being a foreigner, I was among the honored guests and, after saying hello to friends in the courtyard, I entered the room inside the house. Inside, I found the elders seated on soft cushions around the room, joined by the zhigit beshi, the imam, and a younger alim who was from China but had recently attained Kazakhstan citizenship by marrying a local woman. While we awaited the beginning of the ceremony, we discussed politics, community problems, and the bride and groom.

The ceremony began with two elders acting as proxies for the two families in negotiating the *kalym*, or bride-wealth. This part of the event, however, was essentially theatrical, since the zhigit beshi of the neighborhood had set the kalym price of all marriages in the neighborhood at a symbolic rate to avoid competition in displays of wealth between members of the community. Once the kalym negotiation had been accomplished with a good deal of humor and exchange, the bride and groom entered the room for the *neka*, or religious marriage ceremony. The bride, per tradition, veiled her face during this event, although few women in the former Soviet states of Central Asia wear a veil in daily life. The alim from China then addressed the couple and discussed the importance of this wedding and the responsibilities it held for the newlyweds. Among other responsibilities that the couple would have, according to the alim, was to ensure that their children would speak Uyghur and know the Uyghur culture. The imam then performed the actual neka ceremony by blessing the couple.

At the conclusion of the neka, the imam recited a prayer from the Quran, and everybody outside gathered their hands in silence until the prayer was finished, at which time they wiped their faces with their hands. After this, the people outside began talking among themselves and eating some snack food provided at the tables until the imam emerged from the house. When he came out with the other elders, the alim, and me, many of the men present stood and slightly bowed with their right hand on their chest in the direction of the imam, who in turn nodded his head to them in recognition. As he left the gate of the house's courtyard, several young men brought bottles of vodka and cognac to each of the tables.

Having already observed the neka with the elders inside the home, I decided to stay for the other festivities outside. I had been to many weddings, so I knew that I should be prepared for toasts. As I have elaborated elsewhere, toasts are an important site for cultural negotiation among the Uyghurs as well as for other Central Asians (Roberts 2004). Backhanded compliments are frequent in toasts, and a good toaster inevitably increases his symbolic capital in the neighborhood. Furthermore, given Islam's presumed prohibition on alcohol, it is a particularly contested site for the negotiation of the Muslim religion.

This particular wedding had a variety of attendees from different backgrounds who all saw themselves as important members of the larger Uyghur community, including Soviet-educated Uyghurs from other neighborhoods who worked at the academy of sciences, Uyghurs from China now living in the neighborhood, and the most prominent members of Zarya Vostoka, with the exception of the elders, the imam, and the alim. As is customary at such events, all of these men would be called upon to give toasts, and it would be expected that these toasts would sound profound and sincere, at least in the haze of vodka drinking. This amounted to an afternoon of some twenty toasts, but I will only offer a small sample here.

As the toasting part of the celebration was to begin, plates of food were brought to the tables, and the *tamada* (master of ceremonies) began setting up the first toast. The first toasts, given by members of the two families involved in the wedding, generally served the purpose of welcoming their guests to the food and drink provided and commenting on the bond they were establishing between new in-laws.

The next toast was given by a Soviet-educated scholar. He began his toast with a short Uyghur poem about love. He then followed it by saying that this indeed was a great event since it marked the union of two great Uyghur families. Furthermore, he noted that it was important that the couple continue the traditions of their families by teaching their children about Uyghur culture, including Uyghur literature, history, and language. The scholar did not make any allusions to religion, and he was very much promoting a Soviet-influenced concept of Uyghur culture, which, while not necessarily atheist in nature, was based in secular rather than religious notions of the nation.

After more food and some dancing, the next toast was given by a teacher of Arabic at the local school who had emigrated to Almaty from China. He began by noting that he would not partake in the drinking of a toast, but he would say some words. He stressed that the Uyghurs are fortunate to be Muslims, the followers of the only true religion, and he prayed that God would bless this union. He further noted that it is important that the future children of this couple continue Uyghur traditions by being knowledgeable of Uyghur culture, language, and religion. That is the future of the Uyghur people, he said, and they must all work to make sure their children see a better future. With the exception of a couple of guests who were already drunk, most present declined drinking to this toast in respect for the devout young Muslim who had given it, and many muttered *Allah Aqbar*, "God is great" in Arabic, under their breath. In contrast to the first toast, therefore, this young teacher of Arabic from China promoted an overtly religious interpretation of Uyghur culture in his toast.

The wealthiest merchant in the neighborhood, who is also a *hajj* pilgrim, gave the last toast I will describe. He began by saying that he went to Mecca last year and had not partaken in alcohol since that time, because he is now a servant of God. Nonetheless, he did want to say some words. He then stated that he was pleased to see so many important Uyghurs gathered in his neighborhood, and he welcomed them. He said that he wanted to give a toast to the neighborhood, and he continued by noting all of the improvements in the area, emphasizing his role in financing these developments at the local school, the mosque, and the new soccer field. He said that these improvements would be for the next generation of children in the neighborhood, and, God willing, for the children of the couple being married today. After the toast was finished, a man next to me muttered in my ear that this *hajji* used to drink more than anyone present. He added, with even more skepticism, that this man shouldn't even be considered a hajji since he went to Mecca to conduct business, not to make the holy pilgrimage.

Several more people, including myself, gave toasts before the celebration was closed with a prayer. While all of these comments from the toasts given at the wedding involved congratulatory remarks for the newlywed couple, they also all provided commentary on the different perceptions of religion in the community. Furthermore, the combination of alcohol and the intense competition for symbolic capital that are present at weddings brings the negotiation of these different perceptions more into the open. While the tensions latent in these negotiations rarely lead to outright conflict in the community, they serve to make weddings and other life-cycle rituals one of the most transparent communal arenas for observing the conflicting perceptions of religion in the region.

CONCLUSIONS: TOWARD AN EVERYDAY UNDERSTANDING OF
RELIGIOSITY IN CENTRAL ASIA

In conclusion, I would like to suggest that analysis of community events from daily life is perhaps the best means to shed light on complex questions concerning group characterizations of identity, such as the religiosity of a given community. In a globalizing world, where people are constantly bombarded by multiple influences from outside their cultures, generalizations about the characteristics of any group of people are inevitably oversimplified and ignore the variances within communities. By examining the negotiations of daily life, however, one is able to gain a better generalized picture from the variations that inevitably exist and their interaction through group dynamics.

As I noted at the outset, however, the generalizations arising from such analysis essentially relate only to the specific community or group that is analyzed. There are many communities in Central Asia, for example, where religion is more strictly adhered to in daily life than in Zarya Vostoka, and there are also many communities in the region where Islam is a far less pronounced part of the everyday routine. Furthermore, such analysis in today's world is inevitably frozen in an "ethnographic present," reflecting a certain point in time, and can never capture a timeless generalization. In this context, the analysis of everyday religious observance presented here is only fully applicable to the neighborhood of Zarya Vostoka in 1998–1999, when I lived there.

Nonetheless, I do believe that such observations can be broadened to make larger generalizations about similar communities throughout the region. As I have already noted, virtually all Muslim communities of Central Asia are grappling with the same tensions highlighted above: tensions between the desire to revive religious practices, the legacy of Soviet atheism, and the forces of globalization and capitalism. Furthermore, while much has changed in Central Asia in the years since the events described above took place, most Central Asian Muslims continue to grapple with these same influences of past and present. Today it is true that the Soviet past is gradually disappearing from Central Asia, but its legacy continues through socialization that is passed from generation to generation. Furthermore, while those reviving traditional Muslim practices are more knowledgeable of their religion now than in the late 1990s, the forces of globalization are also challenging this revival as Western cultural products and mores are more pronounced in the region.

Aside from these common cultural tensions that play roles in the religiosity of Central Asians, there is another general aspect of the practice of Islam in Central Asia that is demonstrated in my analysis of daily religious behavior in Zarya Vostoka. In looking at the sum of the events I have described above, the picture of religiosity that emerges is one of tolerance and moderation. And, I would argue, this is mostly accurate for all Central Asian Muslims. While there were instances of tensions over the differing degrees of religiosity in Zarya Vostoka, overall the examples examined demonstrate that differing religious values are respected as long as one fulfills the duties of habitus and partakes properly in community activities and norms. This is not to say that religiously intolerant people do not exist in this community, or in Central Asia more generally, but my research has shown that wide variations in attitudes toward religion are mostly tolerated across the region. In general, this tolerance likely emerges in part from an overall attitude toward religion, reinforced during the Soviet period, suggesting that faith is a personal rather than a public issue.

This tolerance regarding religion does not extend to community responsibilities and norms, which communities in Central Asia view as an important part of the public sphere of behavior, and for which they are more likely to pass judgment. While many community responsibilities and norms in the region are indeed religious in origin, they do not necessarily require religiosity. Before Communist rule in Central Asia, these responsibilities were often more stringently regulated by a consciously developed canon of etiquette known as *adat*, but these duties are now more the domain of an unconscious habitus into which community members are socialized.[3] This habitus governs such aspects of behavior as respect paid to elders, familial responsibilities, hospitality, and gender roles, all of which are often strictly adhered to in Central Asian communities. As long as one fulfills the duties and abides by the norms expected of community members, one's own religiosity remains more a personal issue between oneself and God. The duties themselves, whether or not they are characterized as religious and have their origins in Islam, are not necessarily indications of one's religious beliefs.

While this state of affairs has led many visitors to the region to characterize Central Asians as "culturally Muslim" as opposed to "religiously Muslim," I take issue with this understanding of religiosity in the area. The majority of Central Asians will declare themselves to be believers in Islam, and this should be respected. Variations in the ways that they observe their beliefs should not suggest that they are any less Muslim than more fundamentalist believers. Rather, for most Central Asians, religiosity is a personal issue, and a multitude of attitudes are tolerated in the social interactions between Muslims in the region, especially if these attitudes do not interfere with the community's assumed ideals of proper behavior. In a world where religious intolerance has led and continues to lead to many wars and violent acts, this attitude is in many ways a pleasant surprise.

NOTES

The research that went into this paper was funded by two grants from the International Research and Exchanges Board (IREX) that were awarded to the author for language study and dissertation research in Kazakhstan in 1994 and 1997 respectively.

1. Parts of this section have been adapted from Roberts (2004).

2. These are events to which the entire neighborhood is usually invited. Other related ceremonies involve only the families between which the marriage is being held. The first is at the home of the bride and takes place during the day, at which time a celebration for older members of the community is held, almost always organized separately, as two different events, for men and women. The second is held the following day and involves a similar celebration at the home of the groom. Finally, that same night the groom's family holds a sexually desegregated party for the neighborhood's youth, usually referred to as a *vecher*, the Russian word for both "party" and "evening."

3. *Adat* is often translated as "customary law" as opposed to the religious law of the *shariat*. For more on adat and its distinction from sharia, see Khalid (1998:55).

REFERENCES

Bennigsen, Alexandre A. and S. Enders Wimbush. *Mystics and Commissars: Sufism in the Soviet Union.* Berkeley and Los Angeles: University of California Press, 1985.

Bourdieu, Pierre. *An Outline of a Theory of Practice.* Cambridge, UK: Cambridge University Press, 1977.

Gladney, Dru C. *Muslim Chinese: Ethnic Nationalism in the People's Republic.* Cambridge, Mass.: Harvard University Press, 1991.

Jälilov Ilakhun. "Zarya Vostoka." *Uighur Avazi.* 17 January 1998.

Khalid, Adeeb. *The Politics of Muslim Cultural Reform: Jadidism in Central Asia.* Berkeley: University of California Press, 1998.

354 / *Sean R. Roberts*

Roberts, Sean R. "Locality, Islam, and National Culture in a Changing Borderlands: The Revival of the Mäshräp Ritual Among Young Uighur Men in the Ili Valley." *Central Asian Survey*. 17(4):673–700 (1998a).

———— "Toasting the Nation: Negotiating Stateless Nationalism in Transnational Ritual Space." *The Journal of Ritual Studies*. 18(2):86–105 (2004).

————. "The Uighurs of the Kazakstan Borderlands: Migration and the Nation." *Nationalities Papers*. 26(3):511–530 (1998b).

22. *Namaz,* Wishing Trees, and Vodka: The Diversity of Everyday Religious Life in Central Asia

David W. Montgomery

Two years ago, Murat began praying. This is not to suggest that two years ago he "found" religion, for he never questioned the idea that he was Muslim. For him, as with most ethnicities indigenous to Central Asia, being Kyrgyz meant being Muslim.[1] It is only that two years ago he began to seek out more about how to practice Islam. His neighbors were going to mosque on Fridays and, not wanting to be left out, Murat started attending. In reflecting back, he is quick to speak of how little he knew about Islam and exceedingly proud to overemphasize what he has learned. Now he considers himself to be among the most knowledgeable in his community. He no longer drinks. He recites verses of the Quran in Arabic, though he does not understand Arabic. And he goes to mosque at least once a day, to pray and to talk within his community of adherents.

Last year, Murat celebrated the *Orozo Hayit* (*Eid al Fitr*), a holiday that marks the end of *Ramazan* (Ramadan), by joining his friends at a mosque for morning prayers and then visiting with his friends and family in the afternoon. Bakyt also went to mosque for Orozo Hayit, but for Bakyt, *namaz* (prayer) is something he does only on holidays. He too will say that he is Muslim, though he admits to being unfamiliar with the Quran and says that he has to watch others to make sure that he gets the order of motions correct. Orozo Hayit is, after all, a celebration, one in which both Murat and Bakyt want to take part. Bakyt also spent the afternoon with his family and friends, but he did not keep the fast during Ramadan and sees all holidays as occasions to drink vodka, with religious holidays being occasions to toast Allah and Muhammad.[2] Furthermore, on the way home from mosque, he stopped at a *mazar* (sacred site) to continue his worshipful celebration, to honor his ancestors with prayer, and to make a wish by tying a piece of fabric on a tree.

While each considers the other to be Muslim, Murat calls Bakyt a "bad" Muslim, and Bakyt accepts the label by referring to Murat as a "good" Muslim. Regarding orthodoxy and orthopraxy, both approach Islam differently, but labels of "good" and "bad" oversimplify the diversity of practice in Central Asia. It is not enough to say simply that Bakyt is a bad Muslim merely because he interprets his obligations differently than Murat. Bakyt agrees that it is important to go to mosque on special days, but he also speaks of an obligation that he has toward continuing ancestral traditions; he insists that the combination of religious practices is meaningful to him and does not make him less of a Muslim than Murat.

For Murat and Bakyt, as well as most in Central Asia, religion is a component of individual and group identity. But if one wants to understand what religion means to people in any location, it is not enough merely to apply a religious designation to the population. While the Muslims of Central Asia are mostly Sunnis of the Hanafi school, such a label sheds little light on what Islam means to most people. One can read any number of books about Islam, or even about Sunni Islam, and only gain a vague understanding about the interpretation, practice, and syncretic understanding of what religion means for people.[3] There are numerous articles and books written about radical Islam in Central Asia and Islamic groups that the state has banned as threatening.[4] And while this is useful to understanding the political setting of religion, as well as the motives and goals people who join these groups may have, the reality of everyday religious life is markedly less dramatic and less sexy.

The reality of everyday religious life is, in fact, significantly more diverse than the "predominately Sunni Islam" moniker leads most to believe. It is Murat's Islam as well as Bakyt's. True, the majority of people in ex-Soviet Central Asia consider themselves Muslim, but as the above example relates, assuming a corresponding homogeneity in interpretation and practice would be wrong. It is important to make this distinction here. My concern is not about truth claims, which is often the heart of what religious intolerance (at least at the ideological level) is all about. Rather, what people claim they believe and, more empirically, what people do and how they practice may or may not appropriately coincide with their stated ideology.[5] But despite the fact that these acts are often filled with inconsistencies and contradictions, they nonetheless exist in relative harmony.

Historically, Central Asia's religious geography has been home to a diversity of faiths, including Buddhism, Zoroastrianism, Manichaeism, and Nestorian Christianity, as well as shamanism, veneration of ancestors, and the worship of nature.[6] As Islam spread, the populations of the region took on Islam at the expense of earlier religions, but not necessarily excluding them completely—many practices associated with earlier faiths, were retained as "traditional" and understood as compatible with Islam.[7] The Soviet period led to a general suppression of religion,[8] which in turn led to

Men at prayer under Lenin Statue marking *Orozo Hayit* (Ending of Ramadan Fast) in Bishkek, Kyrgyzstan.

the generalization of the region as being religiously wayward or under-developed.[9]

Despite the Soviet experience, the overall perception of Central Asia is of an Islamic region, if not in all of its practices, at least in how people culturally ascribe their religious identity.[10] Since independence from the Soviet Union there has been greater opportunity for religion to be practiced more openly. This does not mean, of course, that during the Soviet period religion—despite some restrictions placed on those who practiced their religion, for example (Communist) Party jobs being denied those who were openly religious—was not practiced.[11] Rather, there has been an increase in people expressing their religious affiliation in the public sphere. With the opening up of the public space to religiosity, albeit mark-edly controlled in some places (which meant a state version of religion that is at times state regulated and controlled), there has been an influx of missionaries, teachers, and religious adherents wanting to influence the religious practices of a population that they view as backward. Is-lamic and Christian missionaries, as well as their supporting organiza-tions, expanded the scope of their operations in the region, but more tra-

Cloth ribbons to grant prayers on a wishing tree overlooking Osh, Kyrgyzstan.

ditional religious practices such as veneration of ancestors and the cult of nature continue to be important.

As stated earlier, religion is part of people's everyday lives. As such, it is a component of their lives and *part* of what they do, but generally it is *not the essence* of what they do or who they are. Labels like "extremist" and "fundamentalist" imply an essentialist character to an individual's religious practice (not necessarily to that individual's religious understanding) and only make sense relative to the religious practices of the population to which the terms are applied. The applicability of such terms is generally more political than useful, for it does not capture the nature of what religion means to people; the terms seek to justify a given person or person's actions. And although groups labeled extremist and fundamentalist often garner the most attention, they represent a minority. Thus my focus is less on groups at the far end of the ideological spectrum, but more centered on an ethnographic discussion of the diversity of everyday religious life in Central Asia. In Osh, Kyrgyzstan, for example, the man on the corner who sells honey is Russian Orthodox; the woman who runs the laundromat is a new Christian convert; one taxi driver in the center of town is an atheist while another is a member of *Hizb ut-Tahrir,* and a third is merely a practicing Muslim who sees Lenin as a good leader and speaks vehemently against Hizb ut-Tahrir; the keeper of one mazar believes in the power of nature and listens to people's concerns while he burns cotton and prays for them; and a fortune-teller at the bazaar performs namaz five times a day. Together this allows us the opportunity to see what is represented in the diversity of religious practice and the complexity of the task of trying to understand what everyday religious life means.

IDEAS OF ISLAMIC ORTHOPRAXY AND THE PROBLEM OF PURITY

Stereotypes often speak of the fear and biases of a population. Iqbol is a young Muslim who wears a long black beard and dresses in white. He prays five times a day, teaches the Quran at a mosque, and walks around with prayer beads moving regularly between his fingers. He is from the town in which he currently resides, but after Kyrgyzstan gained independence he went to Pakistan and India to study Islam. He has returned to his home village to teach his fellow villagers about Islam, and because of his appearance and missionary work at a mosque he is respected by some and feared by others, who refer to him as an "extremist," a "Wahhabist," and a "terrorist." Ideologically, he speaks of being influenced by Sayyid Qutb[12] and Bahauddin Naqshband,[13] but when one engages him in dialogue it is clear that he is driven by his passion to educate his fellow Muslims on the "right" way to practice Islam. He has not been implicated in any wrongdoing or crimes against the state, though he knows that the police watch his every move. He spends most of his time at home or at the mosque because he knows his appearance and devotion to Islam make others uncomfortable. He does not consider himself an extremist, though his views are much more orthodox than those of most of his fellow villagers, who think that he is an Arab.[14] And whereas those who call him a terrorist have bought into the state's rhetoric of fear and the stereotype of what a terrorist looks like (long beard and white turban),[15] Iqbol's work is centered on orthopraxy and his understanding of how to live a meaningful religious life, which has the caliphate as his frame of reference.

The visions of Islam held by Murat, Bakyt, and Iqbol are different, and that difference revolves on the issue of orthopraxic pureness. Each practices Islam in a way that is meaningful for him, but challenging to the others' sensibilities of religious expression. All three will be found at mosque on a holiday, and certainly Murat and Iqbol will meet each other for *Juma namaz* (Friday prayers), when the mosque overflows with worshippers and takes on the role of a meeting hall. Friday prayers are a social event as well as a religious event. While the purpose is for the community to come together and pray on a regular basis, greetings are exchanged upon entering and exiting the mosque; and in communities where relations are well known, there are social pressures to attend.[16] This is not to discount the religious motivation for many to attend, but it should draw attention to the fact that there are other motivations in religious practice and that it is not ideology (or at least not ideology alone) that guides people's religious actions.

The issue of ideology raises two important points that return us to stereotypes. One is connected to the emphasis of public discourse on groups like the Islamic Movement of Uzbekistan (IMU), Hizb ut-Tahrir (HT), and most recently, the *Akromiya* movement, which skews the general perception of reality: most people in the world, and certainly most people in Central Asia, are not extremists (a term which is imprecise, mainly making it useful in the arena of political rhetoric).[17] This discourse around the IMU, HT, and Akromiya often involves painting an image of what a "terrorist" looks like and how he acts. Iqbol may or may not be associated with any of these organizations, but his appearance and the frequency of his religious practice give him the reputation of being in agreement with such groups. This is due largely to the rhetoric of the state, which repeatedly speaks of the threat of extremism.

The second issue, which is closely connected, is the common misunderstanding that ideological changes take place overnight—that is, that everyone wants to be an extremist, and if the borders open tonight, tomorrow the extremists will establish a caliphate. The reality is that ideological changes take time, and most people are just practicing religion and trying to make a life out of what they do, a life that usually does not involve employment in the religious sphere. This is not to downplay the significance of religion in people's lives, but rather to emphasize that the rituals of religious devotion do not always take place at a conscious level and are merely a component of being in the everyday world, not necessarily the central point of what people do. While Iqbol is an exception in that he is a missionary, he is not Murat and definitely not Bakyt. Not all people are in agreement that Islam should be practiced with a conservative interpretation,[18] even if they maintain that Islam should be practiced.

TRADITIONAL RELIGIOUS PRACTICE, SYNCRETISM, AND EVERYDAY RELIGIOUS MEANING

The issue of practice is one that centers on the idea of interpretation and what is believed to be required religiously. Bakyt, Murat, and Iqbol represent the tension between interpretations of what Islam is. While the media and government largely focus their attention on religious groups like the IMU and HT, the incorporation of traditional religious practices is part of the everyday religious experience that is often overlooked (or discounted as

Elderly woman at prayer at *mazar* (sacred site), near Talas, Kyrgyzstan.

insignificant) in discussions about Islam in Central Asia. In some areas, mazar worship is increasing rather than decreasing, and there are some who advocate the reclamation of traditional religious practices, in combination with an understood Islamic heritage, as part of an effort to construct nationalist religious identity.[19]

Mazars hold special meanings for all who go to them. They can be either natural, such as the origin of a stream or a tree in an unexpected location, or connected to the tombs of pious individuals, such as the *sahaba* who learned directly from the Prophet Muhammad or a less well known local saint. People visit mazars for a variety of reasons, which include incantations or sacrifices to attain health, communication with ancestors, or more generally connection with the spirit world. Often, people prepare to visit a mazar on Thursday nights, bringing *borsok* (traditional fried bread) and other foods believed to have a smell that attracts and appeases the spirits of the ancestors.[20]

Although this seems exceptional and distant from an understanding of orthopraxy in Islam, the syncretic reality is that all of the activities take place alongside prayers from the Quran and in submission to the power of Allah. Guardians of the mazars and individuals believed to have special powers all invoke Islam within the worship of nature and the veneration of ancestors with a conviction of compatibility that is meaningful to them.

For those who look down upon mazar worship, the claim is connected to the issue of religious authenticity, that is, whether it is correct to pray namaz and also pray to one's ancestors. This debate is one that takes place among elites, and although the discussion does touch all within the community, for most mazar worshipers it is not a concern. People do what they believe to be correct, be it because of religion or because of tradition. Sometimes they are convinced that their practices should change—for example, if someone they view as an authority says the ritual should be repeated ten times rather than just three—but if the change is radical, such as Gulmira being told by her relatives that she should no longer wear a talisman to ward off the evil eye because it is against Islam,[21] there is reluctance.

MULTIPLE MEANINGS OF SACRED SPACE: THE CASE OF SOLOMON'S MOUNTAIN

While many relegate orthodox understandings of Islam to the center, and syncretism with traditional religion to the periphery, the reality is much more pervasive and less defined. In bazaars, fortune-tellers who pray namaz five times a day use prayer beads and talismans or herbs and animal oils for healings, and speak of the value of the mosque as well as the mazar, nature, and ancestors. On the streets, people walk with burning *isirik* (herbs) or *archa* (juniper), blowing the smoke into cars or businesses to promote health and wellbeing and to rid the space of evil spirits. And everywhere the meaning of sacred spaces is shared by people with different understandings of what makes the place sacred. One of the most obvious examples of a mazar where traditional religion and Islam share space is Solomon's Mountain in the center of Osh.

Solomon's Mountain is believed to be sacred for a number of reasons, including the legend that King Solomon once prayed there, as well as Zahir al-Din Babur, who later founded India's Mughal dynasty. And despite the mountain's early history as a place for Zoroastrian worship, it is viewed as a sacred site to many Muslims, some of whom refer to it as "the second Mecca."[22] An ethnographic walk around the mountain, however, reveals the diversity and syncretism of religious practice in this part of the Ferghana Valley.

At the base of the mountain is the Rabat Abdullah Khan Mosque, one of the city's main mosques. From here the daily call to prayer is made, and on Fridays all men in the neighborhood gather to pray. After prayers many return to work and others depart together for lunch, where they discuss social and personal events within the community and at times reflect on the message given by the imam before prayers began (a message that is usually concerned with how members of the community should live a moral and meaningful life). It is here that we find Murat and Iqbol every Friday, and it is here that we find Bakyt joining them on holidays. This space is held by men since there is not a space designated for women to pray, though women beggars position themselves at the exits to collect the gifts of worshipers.

Ascending the mountain from the approach nearest the mosque, one first encounters a remnant from the region's shamanistic past: trees laden with pieces of cloth tied upon them. It is the location of the trees along the path to the mountain's summit that gives them their sacred quality.[23] The trees are seen as living extensions of sacredness; a wish is made as fabric is tied to the branches. Bakyt and Gulmira always stop here to petition the spirits and take advantage of the mountain's sacredness; Murat occasionally stops here, though he is less certain; and Iqbol at least does not admit to stopping here.

At the top of the mountain is a small building. Called *Dom Babur* (House of Babur), it is believed to mark the site where Babur once prayed. The caretaker listens to the concerns of pilgrims and dispenses advice during a brief session of Quranic recitation and prayer. With a panorama of the city and a physical structure that most closely resembles a mosque, Dom Babur is seen by casual observers as the highlight of the mountain's sacredness. It is here that everyone stops—Bakyt, Gulmira, Murat and Iqbol—and it is the most visible and straightforward location for prayer.

For many pilgrims, however, it is only one of the many sacred places on the mountain; and to Bakyt and Gulmira, it is certainly not the most sacred. Continuing along the eastern side of the mountain, one encounters more locations for practices that challenge a non-syncretic sense of Islamic orthopraxy. Immediately behind Dom Babur is a rock upon which people slide three, seven, or ten times (there is not consensus on the appropriate number of times). Allegedly, doing so will either keep your back healthy, assist you in becoming fertile, or grant you a wish.

Farther down is a hole where, tradition has it, placing one's hand horizontally in the hole four times and vertically three times, opens a path of travel without impediment or grants a wish. Near the hole is a spot where cotton is burned to reinforce the petition, and where, as with all other places at the mazar, a small amount of money can be left—a notion of exchange implying that if something is given to the keepers of the sacred (be the keepers understood as ancestors, nature, or Allah), something greater will be returned to the giver.

Still farther is a sacred cave, believed to be the site where Solomon prayed. Upon entering the small cave, one follows the legend of Solomon's routine and kneels in the place where he reportedly knelt, placing one's head on the entrance stone to the inner part of the cave. After doing so, one

Women sliding down Solomon's Mountain in Osh, Kyrgyzstan, possibly to ensure fertility or grant wishes.

applies the holy water which drips from the cave to the eyelids and proceeds to enter the small cavern. Candles illuminate the back part of the cave where one crawls to place a hand upon a rock which is in the form of a book. One makes a wish, utters a brief prayer, and moves one's hands over one's face. Tradition dictates leaving a small amount of money before departing.

Outside the cave is a small cove known as the sacred place for childless mothers, where women who cannot conceive submit their petitions. The keeper of the cave and cove recites prayers from the Quran (in Arabic, Kyrgyz, Russian, or Uzbek), much like the keeper of Dom Babur, but here it is done over burning cotton and with other accessories uncommon to most understandings of Islamic prayer. That the mountain has sites specialized for major concerns such as fertility is not surprising, for here a need is served in a way that it is not at the mosque—women can commune and pray with the spirit world here. And while there is a host of rituals associated with the mountain—combining shamanism, Zoroastrianism, the worship of nature, and ancestral veneration with Islam—those who visit the mountain are often not in agreement about the proper context of worship. But all who visit the mountain consider themselves Muslim, even though their understanding and practice of Islam can be very different.

RUSSIAN ORTHODOXY, THE NEW CHRISTIANS, AND THE CHALLENGE OF PLURALITY

Much of the conversation thus far has focused on religious diversity within Islam. For the most part Central Asia has been religiously homogeneous, and the challenge of religious plurality has not been as great as in Bosnia or Israel. The tradition of Christianity in Central Asia is generally associated with the Russian presence and Russian Orthodox Christianity.[24] Since independence, a large number of ethnic Russians have left Central Asia for Russia. Yet wherever a large concentration of Russians remains, there is an Orthodox church that is likely being reconstructed and expanded. Olga is typical of those who regularly attend the church. She is an ethnic Russian who, since the death of her husband and migration of her children to Russia, has devoted her pension years to the church. She is joined largely, though not exclusively, by other elderly women in the community.

The service itself is highly ritualized and takes place in a church that is populated with icons, laden with candles, and infused with incense. Worshippers stand for the duration of the service, which can go from one to three hours, often crossing themselves and bowing before the icons which they kiss or the Bible raised by the priest. Women wear head scarves and men do not cover their heads. Communion is part of the service, and a semi-chaotic line organizes to receive it. As the service ends, people depart, again crossing themselves and engaging in conversation and cordial greetings of wellbeing. Some will remain to pray for the recently deceased, and the priest will read names and prayers dedicated for the remembrance of the dead.

In Osh it is a small community that regularly attends the Orthodox Church. Families visit most frequently when someone dies or on holidays. While I have never seen the man who sells honey on the street corner at the Orthodox Church (though I have seen his wife), he identifies himself as a Russian Orthodox Christian even as he concedes that he is not a regular practitioner. He explains that this has a lot to do with having spent his childhood in the Soviet Union when open religious practice was unfashionable. When asked why he considers himself religious and Orthodox at all, he says it is because religion is important and because he is Russian.

In a region where there has been relative homogeneity of religious belief, there have been fairly good relations between Russian Orthodox and Islamic leaders. The relationships have largely been peaceful due to the perceived boundaries of who belongs to whom. The Muslim majority have little problem with the Russian Orthodox because they see the Orthodox as being Russian and all of the other ethnic groups of Central Asia belonging to Islam.

New non-Orthodox Christian groups, however, have proved to be a source of tension as they gain converts from Islam. The numbers of these new Christians, whose denominational affiliations include Baptists, Seventh-day Adventists, Pentecostals, and non-denominational Protestant groups, are not large relative to the broader culture of self-proclaiming Muslims, but the perception is that these Christian groups pose a threat to a cultural understanding of Islam that has not included a tradition of religious pluralism.

Elnura is a young Kyrgyz girl who became interested in Christianity through regular visits to her Christian missionary neighbors who, according to her, offered the message of a "God of forgiveness and love" rather than a "God of fear."[25] Russian Orthodoxy did not appeal to her because she was Kyrgyz and saw Orthodoxy as the faith of Russians and Islam as the faith of Kyrgyz. That the missionaries she met were Kyrgyz piqued her curiosity, and in secrecy she accepted their invitation to learn more about Christianity.

When her father learned about her visits to the neighbors, he was furious and banned her from seeing them again. He immediately sent her to a mosque to begin regular studies with the imam. The response of Elnura's father was curious only because he was not a practicing Muslim and had never been to a mosque, though the convictions he held were that his ethnicity belonged to Islam and the fear he articulated was that if his daughter became Christian, she would lose her Kyrgyz identity.

These new Christian converts challenge the conception of a mono-religious culture. They confront a population that will increasingly have to address the issue of religious pluralism, as well as the problem posed by what one defines as ethnic and what another defines as religious. If there is anything that Murat, Bakyt and Iqbol can agree on, it is that Elnura's Kyrgyz identity means she should be Muslim and that her conversion is a threat to the community. The reality is, however, that Elnura, far from being an aberration, is yet another example of religious diversity in Central Asia.

RELIGION ON THE STREETS

The argument put forth has been that religion is an important part of what people do. It is part of their everyday. A common gesture with religious connotations is the wiping of the hands over the face after saying "*omen.*" It is a practice seen as belonging to the realm of that which is Islamic and can be seen before leaving the table, when leaving on a trip, or when passing a cemetery—a gesture explained as honoring the souls of the ancestors. It marks the end of prayers, welcomes the reunion of friends, or implores blessings upon a task to be undertaken.[26] At one level it is a very common religious gesture made by Murat, Bakyt, Iqbol, Gulmira, and even Elnura (though not Olga), but all will agree that it is not always a conscious act. Sometimes it is imbued with sincerity of thanks being offered to God, but other times it is just an act of everyday living in Central Asia.

How religion impacts the daily life of anyone in Osh is difficult to express. When asked to describe themselves, most people give reference first to their occupation or ethnicity; their religious identity is often something that, while not taken for granted, is generally seen as an everyday aspect of who they are, but not their essence. The man who sells honey is a Russian honey salesman; the woman at the laundromat, while she has religious literature in her store, is a businesswoman who trades with other members of the community. The taxi drivers are equally concerned with getting passengers, and even tradesmen who are members of groups like HT are largely concerned with finding a way to provide for their families and create an environment for their children that is safe and meaningful.

Religion exists on the streets in a variety of ways, be it the "omen" before a trip; the recitations of religious praise offered by beggars to their benefactors; fortunetellers with cards and beads; women walking in the streets burning isirik, whose smoke is to keep away the evil spirits; the talisman and prayer beads hanging from rearview mirrors; or the greetings of "*asalaamaleykum*" which are passed to all. Many of these things, however, have become so common that they are part of the obligation of culture. This does not mean that they are dispossessed of their religious meaning, but it is important to note that maintaining an intensity of meaning in all of these everyday religious signs is difficult. People give money without listening to the blessings of the beggar, and hanging Islamic scripture from the rearview mirror is fashionable even to those who can only read "Allah" and "Muhammad" in Arabic.

It is thus relevant to recognize that religion is not often consumed with extreme dialogues that protest against the state (and even when it is, those protests often embrace religious language and justifications for political rather than religious reasons), but is more generally a part of what people do on a daily basis. Religion is an aspect of people's individual and collective identities in Central Asia, but it is often not something that completely consumes them and prevents them from engaging in meaningful social lives. And as individuals interpret their practice of religion traditionally and within a contemporary broader faith community, the level of syncretism and diversity of religious practice remain significant and meaningful to those who try to make sense of their place in the world.

NOTES

1. It is generally the case that Kazakhs, Tajiks, Turkmens, Uzbeks, Dungans, Uyghurs, and Turks, to name a few of the ethnic groups in Central Asia, share the feeling that they were born Muslim.

2. The image of any one region as one of pure devotion to the pillars of Islam is not entirely accurate. While the restaurants of some neighborhoods may close during the month of Ramadan, in other neighborhoods such contradictory acts can be seen as vodka toasts to Allah and Muhammad (made by some with a sense of sincerity and observed by others with a sense of sacrilege).

The issue of alcohol is problematic. The Hanafi school in Central Asia historically allows drinks such as *kumyz* (fermented mare's milk) which is slightly alcoholic. It is clear, however, in its prohibition against other alcoholic drinks. Posing the question to the population becomes complicated. I have met many Central Asians who consider only vodka to be alcohol, thus excluding beer, wine, and cognac from the list of prohibited beverages. Furthermore, I have met many drunken Central Asians of all ethnic groups who will argue, even in their intoxicated states, that they are "good" Muslims.

3. While works designed to give an understanding of Islam—for example, Fazlur Rahman, *Islam*, 2nd ed. (Chicago: University of Chicago Press, 1979); John L. Esposito, *Islam: The Straight Path*, 3rd ed. (Oxford: Oxford University Press, 1998); Seyyed Hossein Nasr, *Islam: Religion, History, and Civilization* (San Francisco: HarperSanFrancisco, 2003)—are important, they can only give a general understanding of Islam and do not account for the cultural interpretations of practice. Ira Lapidus in his 2002 *A History of Islamic Societies*, 2nd ed. (Cambridge: Cambridge University Press), gives important contextual information about Islam in certain regions, but his task is more historical, rather than an ethnographic concern with the meaning of religious practice to the individual.

4. See, for example, Ahmed Rashid, *Jihad: The Rise of Militant Islam in Central Asia* (New York: Penguin, 2002); Farideh Hayet, "Re-Islamisation in Kyrgyzstan: Gender, New Poverty and the Moral Dimension," *Central Asian Survey* 23 (3–4) 2004: 275–287; Emmanuel Karagiannis, "Political Islam and Social Movement Theory: The Case of Hizb ut-Tahrir in Kyrgyzstan," *Religion, State & Society* 33 (2) 2005: 137–150; International Crisis Group (ICG), "Radical Islam in Central Asia: Responding to Hizb ut-Tahrir," 30 June 2003, available at: www.icg.org.

5. Belief is difficult if not impossible to assess and can only be observed in the acts and rituals in which people engage.

6. For more on the history of religions in Central Asia, see for example: J. Baldick, *Animal and Shaman: Ancient Religions of Central Asia* (London: I. B. Tauris, 2000); Richard C. Foltz, *Religions of the Silk Road: Overland Trade and Cultural Exchange from Antiquity to the Fifteenth Century* (New York: St. Martin's Press, 1999).

7. For example, dancing around a fire prior to the groom entering the house of his bride is a tradition of Zoroastrian influence, even though Tajiks or Uzbeks who do this often claim it is part of a traditional Islamic wedding or at the very least is compatible with Islam. The Zoroastrian background of the ritual is generally ignored. For more on Zoroastrianism, see Mary Boyce, *Zoroastrians: Their Beliefs and Practices* (London: Routledge, 2001).

8. For more on the Soviet suppression of Islam, see Shoshana Keller, *To Moscow, Not Mecca: The Soviet Campaign against Islam in Central Asia, 1917–1941* (Westport, Conn.: Praeger, 2001). For more on the internalization of religion in response

to institutionalized suppression, see Bruce G. Privratsky, *Muslim Turkistan: Kazak Religion and Collective Memory* (Richmond, UK: Curzon Press, 2001).

9. Expressions of this sense of lacking in religious knowledge are seen in statements such as *"negramotnye"* (not literate) Muslims, or that members of a particular ethnic group "are bad Muslims."

10. For two articles on the development of a particular characteristic of Islam in Uzbekistan, see Adeeb Khalid, "A Secular Islam: Nation, State, and Religion in Uzbekistan," *International Journal of Middle East Studies* 35 (4) 2003: 573–598; and Russell Zanca, "Believing in God at Your Own Risk: Religion and Terrorisms in Uzbekistan," *Religion, State & Society* 33 (1) 2005: 71–82.

11. One former Communist Party leader in Kyrgyzstan lost his job for giving his father a Muslim burial. Shortly thereafter, the country gained independence and he became one of the leading "democrats," though his political ideology had not changed in any significant way. Another individual in Kyrgyzstan, who was kept out of government work because he was an observant Muslim praying five times a day, was given a government job post-independence in part because he *had* been a practicing Muslim during the Soviet period.

12. Qutb was the founder of the Muslim Brotherhood. For more on Qutb, see Richard P. Mitchell, *The Society of the Muslim Brothers* (Oxford: Oxford University Press, 1993); and Robert D. Lee, *Overcoming Tradition and Modernity: The Search for Islamic Authenticity* (Boulder, Colo.: Westview Press, 1997).

13. Naqshband was the fourteenth-century founder of a Sufi order near Bukhara. For more on Naqshband, see Elisabeth Özdalga, ed., *Naqshbandis in Western and Central Asia: Change and Continuity* (Istanbul: Swedish Research Institute in Istanbul, 1999); Marc Gaborieau, Alexandre Popovic, and Thierry Zarcone, eds., *Naqshbandis: Historical Developments and Present Situation of a Muslim Mystical Order* (Istanbul: l'Institut Français d'Études Anatoliennes d'Istanbul, 1990); and J. Spencer Trimingham, *The Sufi Orders in Islam* (Oxford: Oxford University Press, 1998).

14. Interestingly, in a survey of religious practice I conducted in Kyrgyzstan in 2005, Kyrgyz and Uzbeks tend to list Arabs as the most religious ethnic group, suggesting a belief that Arabs more correctly practice Islam. The foundation of this assumption involves an importation of cultural practices that are often foreign to the Central Asian context.

15. See, for example, the rhetoric of Uzbek President Islam Karimov's response to the Andijon killings on 12–13 May 2005. The problems were blamed on the Akromiyasts, who were alleged to be Islamic extremists and therefore a threat. See ICG, *Uzbekistan: The Andijon Uprising*, 25 May 2005, available at: www.icg.org. While what happened in Andijon is still largely surrounded by uncertainty, it would be an oversimplification to say that the preponderance of those protesting in the square and those killed were Islamic militants. It is worth recalling that many of those who supported Khomeini during the 1979 Iranian Revolution did so not so much in support of an Islamic state as much as in opposition to the Shah and his government.

16. In addition to social pressures to attend Friday prayers, there are increasing social pressures to keep the fast during Ramadan, a growing number of people making Haj, and more mosques being built, with the assistance of both foreign funds and those of local benefactors. There is prestige of orthopraxic purity associated with all of these.

17. What is threatening to the state is the fact that the transnational nature of religion is not always compatible with the national and nationalistic conceptions and rhetoric of the state. Groups like Hizb ut-Tahrir claim that what matters is not ethnic or national identity but rather religious identity. States, on the other hand, exist on the notion that ethnicities and state boundaries do indeed matter.

18. Anecdotally, one can see an increase in conservative dress and the veiling of women in certain regions where more conservative interpretations of Islam exist. Some women with whom I have talked take on the veil with a sense of pride and religious rightness. Others, however, see it in practical terms: their lives are made easier if they veil, i.e., they receive fewer hassles at school or in the market. Veiling is, of course, more common in villages. In cities, short skirts and form-fitting Western dress are more prevalent.

19. In Kyrgyzstan, philosopher Choiun Omuraly uulu writes of this traditional religion in his book, *Tengirchilik: Uluttuk Filosofiianyn Unggusuna Chalgyn* (Bishkek: "KRON" Firmasy, 1994) [in Kyrgyz]. Dastan Sarygulov, a member of parliament from 1995 to 2000 and current state secretary in President Kurmanbek Bakiev's administration, is an advocate for the propagation of Tengirism as a religious and moral framework for Kyrgyz that keeps the traditions of the ancestors and is compatible with Islam. See, for example, his *Kyrgyzy: Proshloe, Nastoyashchee, i Budushchee* (Kyrgyz: The Past, the Present, and the Future) (Bishkek: n.p., 2005) [in Russian].

20. For more, see Gulnara Aitpaeva, "The Phenomenon of Sacred Sites in Kyrgyzstan: Interweaving of Mythology and Reality," unpublished article, 2005; Gulnara Aitpaeva, "A Phenomenon of Mazars in Kyrgyzstan (Raising a Problem and Hypothesis)," *Academic Review*, Bishkek, 2004: 128–129 [in Russian]; Gulnara Aitpaeva, "Ancient Mazars in Talas," *Conference Collection*, Bishkek, 2005: 70–76 [in Kyrgyz].

21. Gulmira wore a talisman of black beads with white dots meant to keep the evil eye from harming her. There were places on the beads where the white dots had broken off, and she viewed that as a sign that the bracelet was working. She visited some of her relatives who told her that the evil eye was not compatible with Islam and that she should take the bracelet off, which she did. After a few days, however, she returned to wearing it, because without it, she claimed, she felt vulnerable and at risk to the threats of others.

22. I have heard some visitors say that it is only after visiting Solomon's Mountain that an individual can be prepared to go to Mecca. Others say that multiple visits to the mountain (some say three visits, others say ten) is equivalent to Haj.

23. To give a sense of proportion, the walk from the base of the mountain to the top takes about twenty minutes.

24. For more on Russian Orthodoxy, see Nathaniel Davis, *A Long Walk to Church: A Contemporary History of Russian Orthodoxy*, 2nd ed. (Boulder, Colo.: Westview Press, 2003); Kallistos Ware, *The Orthodox Way*, rev. ed. (Crestwood, N.Y.: St. Vladimir's Seminary Press, 1995).

25. There is a sense among some foreign Christian missionaries that the conversion rate among Christians has come to a plateau, which they explain as an aspect of these new Christians trying to reclaim the culture that was at times discarded during the conversion process. This cultural reclamation is seen in people claiming to be, for example, Kyrgyz and Christian and using traditional symbols in worship, such as the cross pattern common in the *shyrdak* (traditional Kyrgyz felt carpet).

For more on the conversion of Kyrgyz to Christianity, see Alyona Faletskaya, *Identity Among the Kyrgyz: Moving Tent Towards Christ or Christianity* (master's thesis, American University in Central Asia, Department of Anthropology, 2005).

26. During the special 2005 Kyrgyz Presidential elections in Osh, for example, elderly Uzbeks and Kyrgyz often did "omen" after placing their ballots in the ballot box.

23. Christians as the Main Religious Minority in Central Asia

Sebastien Peyrouse

Christians in Central Asia constitute a unique case, having been subject to Soviet state atheism and constituting a religious minority in a Muslim region. I will analyze the stakes in the post-Soviet era, when Christians face the challenge of newly independent states that recognize Islam as their main religion. Has independence resulted in changes in Christians' everyday life? Has it provoked new relations between political and religious authorities on the one hand and religious movements on the other? What is Christianity's current place in Islamic Central Asia, and how do denominations plan to develop?[1]

The five post-Soviet Muslim republics of Central Asia count many Christian minorities—Orthodox, Catholic, and Protestant, with the latter group including Lutherans, Baptists, Seventh-day Adventists, Pentecostals, Jehovah's Witnesses, Presbyterians, and members of the Charismatic churches. Unlike the religious communities of the Near and Middle East, Christians in Central Asia consist primarily of Europeans—mainly Russians, Germans, Poles, Armenians, and Greeks—who settled in the region following tsarist colonization from the eighteenth to the twentieth centuries. At present, large Russian communities exist in Kazakhstan (4,500,000), Kyrgyzstan (600,000) and Uzbekistan (at least 500,000), with tens of thousands in Tajikistan and Turkmenistan.[2] Over the last three decades their numbers have considerably decreased, as have those of other Europeans. Ukrainians number 500,000 in Kazakhstan, 100,000 in Uzbekistan, and 50,000 in Kyrgyzstan. A 1999 census recorded 47,000 Poles in Kazakhstan, which contains as well 111,000 Belarusians and 353,000 Germans. The communities exist in far smaller numbers in other republics. Other Christian groups include Koreans, numbering 160,000 in Uzbekistan and close to 100,000 in Kazakhstan in 1999; Greeks, recorded at 10,000 in Uzbekistan; and Christian Tatars, the largest group consisting of 248,000 in Kazakhstan. A small Armenian minority numbers 42,000 in Uzbekistan at present, and 40,000 in Turkmenistan in 1995. In the post-Soviet era, Christian—particularly Protestant—missionary activity among Kazakhs, Kyrgyz, Uzbeks, and others has led to an increase in the number of converted Christians in Central Asia,

THE NEW CONTEXT OF INDEPENDENCE

After independence, each new state of Central Asia ended the atheistic policies of the Soviet Union. New constitutions guaranteed freedom of conscience for all, with each person having the right to practice any, or no, religion. All religions are equal before the law and separate from the state: they are to have no governmental functions, are not to interfere in state affairs, and may not form political parties. Incitement to religious violence is strictly forbidden. At the same time, within the framework of "nation-state building," Central Asian indigenous elites have used Islam in their efforts to impose new national histories, with the faith occupying a superior place as the main religion of titular nationalities. These elites sought, among other goals, to assert the region's place on the international scene and develop relations with foreign Muslim states. Political authorities seek to balance this reassertion with a desire to rule and control religious discourse in order to avoid a politicization of Islam.

Legislation in all republics forbids any attempts to raise interethnic antagonism. Constitutions avoid any reference to "Islam," "Muslims," or the "Quran," and all religious legislation ostensibly applies equally to all faiths. Leaders of the Central Asian states have underlined, in their speeches and written declarations, their desire for the pacific cohabitation of Islam and Christianity in Central Asia and have banned any movement that challenges a secular vision of the state.

Religious freedom is far from complete, however, despite the precautions mentioned in constitutions and laws. (The law changed in 2005 in Kazakhstan.)[3] Any group conducting religious activities must register with the Ministry of Justice. This process allows political authorities significant control over religious movements and activities. Differing censorship regimes in each republic affect the ability of denominations to publish literature. Uzbekistan and Turkmenistan ban proselytism. Political authorities also seek to control religious education, though the concern here is mainly with Islamic schools, more suspected of political engagement.

CHRISTIAN MOVEMENTS' STAKES AFTER INDEPENDENCE

The collapse of the Soviet Union has brought about important changes in the Christian structures established in Central Asia. All movements have had to confront two important phenomena in the post-Soviet era: first, the extensive emigration of European populations; second, the arrival of new missionary movements. European out-migration from Central Asia began in the 1970s, when Moscow ceased to consider these republics as an industrial and strategic development region, and intensified during perestroika. Emigration reached an apogee between 1992 and 1995, as European populations, now acutely aware of their minority status, feared reduced power in the newly independent states and experienced increased economic difficulties. Half the European population, those with the means or the will, has left, though migratory fluxes have since decreased.

This emigration has posed a major challenge to Christian denominations and worshippers alike. Christians remaining in Central Asia have seen many of their religious communities evaporate. The case of Lutherans is instructive. In Kazakhstan, heavy German out-migration led to the closing of several Lutheran churches; others are now dominated by non-Germans. Likewise in Bishkek, Kyrgyzstan, long-established Lutheran communities have disappeared, weakened by competition from other Protestant denominations. Whereas some relatively dynamic communities, such as those in large cities or in northern Kazakhstan where the majority of the population is of European descent, managed to subsist, groups situated in areas mainly peopled with Central Asians have progressively died out. In the central Kazakhstani regions of Kzylorda and Zhezkazgan, Lutheran communities consist uniquely of seniors and the renewal of followers is jeopardized. This concern drives them to consider measures to stop this hemorrhage.

PROSELYTISM AND CONVERSIONS

Most Christian movements, except the Orthodox, Uniate, and Armenian churches, have decided to use new conditions of religious freedom to proselytize. Proselytism and the support of foreign missions have become crucial tools for congregations to find new followers and reach necessary levels to be allowed to register with the state. Missionary activity is aimed principally at the local Islamic majority. Missionaries, from the west or from South Korea as well as from congregations operating in the Central Asia since Soviet times, have been working in the region since perestroika and independence. They tend to view the local population, Christian and Muslim alike, as "easy targets" ready to be awakened to religion after seventy years of Soviet atheism. Christian missionaries feel that most Central Asian Muslims practice a tolerant and traditional Islam, sometimes without theological grounding; these factors, they believe, would ease these believers' transition to Christianity. This perception is especially strong in areas of Kazakhstan and Kyrgyzstan that were Islamized much later, in the eighteenth century as compared to the eighth century for the oasis areas of Central Asia. Missionary movements are also driven by the doctrine of Christian universality to target the local population, whom they see as vital to the long-term survival of Christianity in Central Asia. This view has provoked conflict with Muslim leaders, who see all non-European locals as *de facto* Muslims rather than potential Christians.

RELIGION AS THE EXPRESSION OF MINORITY FEELING IN CENTRAL ASIA

Individuals use religion as an expression of their minority feeling. As such, religion constitutes an important element of Christians' daily life. Such an expression is realized in general terms, as an individual's sense of his or her place in the world, or in specific ones, linked to a concrete national affiliation or particular religious practices. Religion at once enables an individual to identify with a body apart from the nation or state, builds group ties that are felt to be fraying, and offers answers at a time of confusion on the individual and community level. As national tension rose surrounding the Soviet collapse, many individuals considered themselves more Russian than Christian, more Uzbek than Muslim; this feeling, however, was not universal. Among many believers, across individuals and denominations, belonging to Christianity or Islam remained more important than national affiliations. Religion was seen as universal, transcending national boundaries, and therefore more important— this view was expressed in particular by Baptists or other Protestants, as well as among non-official Muslim groups.[4]

Orthodox leaders, for their part, have sought to exploit the national factor to gain support from Russians, who now must face a new status as cultural and political minorities. The Orthodox Church allows believers to feel part of a vital community on an everyday basis. The prayer house enables people to meet "compatriots," while the liturgy uses multiple specific cultural aspects, such as icons and the celebration of services in Slavonic, to allow for cultural self-assertion. The link between religion, church, and nationality grows increasingly important as the more conservative republics in Central Asia—Turkmenistan, and, to a lesser extent, Uzbekistan—have progressively excluded European cultural expressions and no longer broadcast Russian television programs. In Kazakhstan, Russians have used the church to solidify a national identity in a different manner: the Orthodox Church has supported and solidified a historic discourse that claims the northern Kazakh steppes as a Russian "home."

This rising "ethnic-religious" combination constitutes an important response to the new Central Asia, supporting minorities within a "modernity that dissolves the historic religious traditions inside a nebula of symbols and values,"[5] Emigration to "home" republics has strengthened the combination of ethnicity and religion in some cases, linking both to movement and territory, but has weakened it in others; for example, the Baptist Church has now replaced ethnic affiliations with universalism. Other Christian churches and groups have tried to blend national difference and universalism: Catholicism celebrates services in several languages, and the Baptist and Adventist churches have formed subgroups for locals (Kazakhs, Kyrgyz, Uyghurs) in order to mitigate their concerns of entering a European denomination. In Central Asia, the national criterion remains important even in Universalist churches and reveals its fundamental role in the believers' and new followers' everyday life.

ORTHODOXY VERSUS OTHER CHRISTIAN DENOMINATIONS

The new context of independence has influenced inter-religious relations among Christian denominations as well as between Christianity and Islam. Historic legacies and the contemporary political situation, rather than theological disputes, govern relations among Christian groups. A surface consensus on universalism is widely limited, as each Christian movement must take a position on Islam. The Orthodox Church seeks simultaneously to justify its predominance over other Christian movements in Central Asia and to assert its presence as equal to Islam. Church leaders argue that every Russian is inherently connected to eastern Christianity, with "Russian" and "Orthodox" as virtual synonyms. Orthodox leaders consider the entire post-Soviet space their canonical territory, which would give them right of preeminence over all other churches today.[6] This preeminence extends to non-Russians as well, who are also considered to be "automatically" Orthodox. Two exceptions exist: non-Slavs whose history and culture are bound to another religion (Islam in Central Asia and Azerbaijan, the Armenian and Georgian Christian churches for their respective populations); and those whose nationality is culturally linked to a church situated beyond the borders of the former USSR (Catholic Poles and Protestant Germans, for example). Yet Orthodoxy argues that activities of these churches should be limited, and they should not have the right to proselytize. Orthodox leaders still believe their faith has a claim on anyone who does not view religion as a national tradition but who only expresses a desire to enter in a religious community. Russians who convert to a denomination different from Orthodox Christianity are strongly criticized. Non-Orthodox Christian churches, unsurprisingly, are strongly critical of this approach, and argue in particular in Central Asia that the Orthodox Church is unable to meet the spiritual needs of all non-Muslim believers.

Orthodox leaders argue from history that the first European settlers in the region were Orthodox Russians; Protestant movements, who cite the large number of non-Russians in the tsarist empire who arrived during colonization, contest this claim. The Catholic Church placed its missions in the territory as early as the thirteenth century, with a Central Asian bishopric established the following century, and refers to the Catholic Poles and Germans that arrived during tsarist colonization.

CHRISTIAN MISSIONARY ACTIVITY AND ISLAM

Missionaries have continued their activities in Central Asia despite hostility from the Orthodox Christian and Islamic churches. Missionaries use various tactics to proselytize, knocking on doors or meeting people in the streets in republics where such activity is authorized, or through humanitarian aid or various activities including foreign language or computer lessons, sporting activities, and summer camps for underprivileged children. Christian branches have also constructed large church buildings to attract individuals who may be seeking new spiritual values.

Muslim clergy have reacted with hostility to the appearance of foreign Christian missions and conversions among "their" local population. Proselytism among traditional Muslim communities has strained the official Islamic position of respect for Christianity and the Bible. In 1994, the mufti of Tajikistan, echoing Islamic doctrine, declared that "it is intolerable that a Muslim leaves his religion."[7] A conversion to Christianity is considered treason and can cause tensions in the new convert's social and family circles. Protestant missionary reports have noted that official declarations are equaled by resistance to conversion on the ground. Hostility to proselytism crosses the region, not only in republics considered "strongly" Islamic, such as Uzbekistan and Tajikistan, but among populations who are seen to be less influenced by Islam, as in Kyrgyzstan, where missionaries are more active.[8] Kyrgyz mosques have circulated petitions demanding a halt to all missionary activity, including that of Baptists, Adventists, and other Protestant denominations.[9] Muslims adhere to a strict formula of: Local/Islam and European/Orthodox.[10] Muslims have tried to prevent Protestant movements from organizing summer camps in places in Kazakhstan where proselytizers are especially dynamic. A few violent altercations have been reported in Kyrgyzstan and in Tajikistan, where a Korean Protestant church was bombed during a service. An Orthodox church and an Adventist prayer house came under attack in Dushanbe on January 1, 2001.[11]

Popular reactions against Christianity have been most virulent in Tajikistan. Authorities in other republics have sought to restrict missionary activity in order to prevent Islamic "radicals" from becoming violent and spinning away from government control; they are also uncomfortable with widespread Christian missionary activity.[12]

THE ISLAM–ORTHODOX ALLIANCE

Orthodox leaders have supported the efforts of Muslim clergy (*ulema*) to pressure authorities to restrict missionary activity. Orthodox leaders believe that the post-Soviet framework has brought so many churches that the "devil, as well as the church, can act."[13] The Orthodox Church recognizes its ambiguous position on religious freedom, complaining that the post-Soviet states are using a Western model of freedom of religion. Orthodoxy, not regretting the Soviet period, would prefer greater continuity, citing the Belarusian example where the state recognizes the Orthodox Church as the "national church."[14] Other Christian churches contest that a unique faith would guarantee the stability of a country, contending that this is "only a myth that leads to inquisitions and monastery jails. Religious freedom is a right for anyone, for small and large denominations."[15]

The current Orthodox Church in Central Asia considers itself a victim of Christian proselytism, Russians' emigration, and people's indifference to religion. Church leaders, despite their official apolitical stance, have turned to the authorities for support. Central Asian archbishop Vladimir Ikim, supported by Patriarch Alexis II, has met Central Asian state presidents several times and confirms good relations with all. Vladimir and Islamic muftis in Central Asia have not hidden their intention to put pressure on authorities in order to restrict religious freedom.[16] In 1996, I. Nazarbekov, responsible for external affairs of the Kyrgyz Muslim office, and the Orthodox archbishop asked political authorities to require re-registration of all religious communities and declared that a native had to be Muslim and a Christian had to be Orthodox.[17] Archbishop Vladimir's virulent and denigratory attitude toward other Christian movements, echoed by high and low clergy, reflects a trend across the former USSR. Orthodox clerics in Central Asia have attacked the Catholic Church, claiming it has "always tried to seize the Orthodox Orient."[18] In 1998, Archbishop Antonii of the Uralsk and Gureev regions of Kazakhstan declared: "What can we think of a church that has systematically violated God's law? The Pope, who has declared himself God's substitute on the Earth, who is he? The Antichrist!"[19] Criticism against local missionary movements, whose discourses are considered alien to both Muslim and Christian faiths, fill the pages of local Orthodox journals.[20] A Kazakhstani journal defined Protestantism as a religion of "the aggressive bourgeois."[21] Orthodox writers attack Jehovah's Witnesses as the most dangerous movement, which, among other things, would convert people using narcotics and hypnosis.[22] Many articles explain how Orthodox Christians should confront missionaries, Jehovah's Witnesses in particular.[23] The leader of an Orthodox parish in Dushanbe condemned denominations for proselytizing with "a meal in one hand and a Bible in the other."[24]

Orthodox leaders claim other Christian movements divide the religion, threatening to provoke unrest between Christians and Muslims and destabilizing the region. Accusations seek to label rival movements, particularly those not as established as the Catholics, Lutherans, Armenians, and Old Believers, as "sects," or even "Satanist movements."[25] Astonishing comparisons have emerged from Church literature; one writer argued that Jehovah's

Witnesses "promise a terrestrial paradise, as the Bolsheviks used to. (. . .) Jehovah's witnesses lead the struggle against the Orthodox people, as the Communists used to."[26] Sharp rhetoric is aimed not only at believers, to prevent conversions, but at state leaders, to convince them of Orthodoxy's loyalty in fighting destabilizing religious movements in their country.

Orthodox and Muslim leaders have agreed to share their role and influence in Central Asia around the Orthodoxy–Islam duality. Leaders express the notion that "in Central Asia and in Russia, there is a natural distribution of the sphere of influence between the two main religions, Orthodoxy and Islam, and no one will destroy this harmony."[27] Leaders of each religion have agreed not to proselytize among nationalities traditionally belonging to the other religion and to fight all other proselytizing movements. Official inter-religious conferences and meetings between muftis and Orthodox hierarchy publicly confirm their mutual understanding as well as their will to contribute to peace and social concord and to develop a religious conscience in order to put an end to Soviet atheism.[28] Orthodox leaders claim that warm relations with the local populations and Islam date back to the nineteenth century, conveniently omitting some more embarrassing elements—especially the existence of an "anti-Muslim mission" in the Kazakh steppes that contradicted the official tsarist line forbidding proselytism in Central Asia. Orthodox leaders regularly participate in celebrations of Muslim feasts of common commemorations of local history, but rarely participate in the events of other Christian churches, such as the 2000 Jubilee organized by the Catholic Church.

Below the level of central hierarchies, tensions simmer between church officials and believers of various Christian denominations. One Catholic priest in Karaganda, Kazakhstan, complained about so-called "Satanist" movements, which were "particularly dangerous and more and more numerous in the area."[29] Lutheran pastors strongly criticize other Protestant denominations; one priest in Tashkent condemned "all the sects developing in the country."[30] Lutheran officials, expressing particular hostility to Baptist and Jehovah's witnesses groups, criticize the activity of "foreign" missions and have been suspected of pressuring political authorities to place limits on Presbyterian, Pentecostal, and Charismatic movements. Such hostility varies greatly from the ecumenism in Western Europe or North America; in Central Asia denominations at best ignore each other, but much more often label rivals as "sects," at times collaborating with the government to ban these movements.

Several aspects of the Central Asian religious context show continuity from Soviet times. Christian denominations once demonized by Soviet atheism now struggle again against official hostility as Islamic leaders pressure state authorities to limit their movements in majority Muslim lands. The Orthodox Church also continues its Soviet-era tradition of criticizing other denominations and, as in the tsarist and Soviet periods, assumes and even claims submission to political powers, identifying with the new states and ostensibly their interests. Protestant movements are now returning to their own legacy of dissidence and efforts to avoid relations with hostile political authorities.

CHRISTIANITY, THE STATE, AND EVERYDAY LIFE

Religious tensions have provoked many changes in state legislation, which has affected the everyday life of believers, especially of smaller denominations, and the activity of religious proselytizers. Uzbekistan passed a law on May 1, 1998, that constitutes a considerable shift from more liberal provisions of its 1991 law and adds several repressive measures. The law's main change raises the number of signatures that must be collected for any religious community to gain registration from 10 to 100, and states that none of these may include "foreigners." Any group not registered is considered illegal. The 1998 law bans proselytism and forbids religious organizations from claiming as an objective the propagation of their faith. Instead, recognized organizations are restricted to "the common confession of a faith, the celebrations of services and rituals henceforth." Only clergy, and not lay believers, can wear religious dress in public. A Committee for Religious Affairs now controls and checks all religious literature. Any proselytism or religious activity contravening this ban is subject to repression and several years' imprisonment.

The government of Turkmenistan has put similar restrictions in place. To this point, only Islam, Orthodoxy, and the Catholic apostolic nunciature in Ashgabat have been able to gain registration. A 1995 amendment to the religious law requires 500 signatures to gain registration. International pressure led to the abrogation of this amendment in May 2004; the situation of Christian communities in the country has in no way improved, however. Turkmenistani law demands that every religious meeting, demonstration, or publication requires the consent of authorities. Islamic and Orthodox clergy are expected in their services to revere, alongside the Bible or Quran, the *Ruhname,* the official philosophy of President S. Niyazov.

These new measures, alongside others aiming to control civil society, have had an impact on the everyday life of believers. Legislative restrictions threaten to shutter many Christian denominations, which rarely consist of more than 20 believers in villages and 50 to 70 believers in small to middle-sized cities of Uzbekistan and Turkmenistan. Laws against proselytism have endangered movements of religious officials, even those of the more established religions, who cannot tend to believers' spiritual needs. Political authorities have carried out aspects of the law quite arbitrarily; in Turkmenistan, some Protestant communities have been refused registration despite gathering 500 signatures, while Orthodox Church parishes, which rarely consist of more than 50 people, are allowed to maintain their religious activity. Any denomination suspected of proselytism—or at least too visible proselytism—is denied registration in Uzbekistan, regardless of the numbers of signatures collected.

Believers of these primarily Protestant denominations are thus forced to celebrate services at home, even though conducting religious activities in private places is forbidden. A central feature of the everyday life of believers—religious worship—therefore effectively criminalizes them. State authorities also consider the distribution of religious literature in Uzbekistan or Turkmenistan as proselytism; the Biblical Society of Uzbekistan was required to stop importing religious books written in local languages. Entering Uzbekistan with more than two copies of a book is considered to be importing, and thus subject to strong taxes; only twenty-five different religious books can be introduced on the territory by an individual. Religious literature of any kind in local languages is in fact banned for so-called "foreign" Christian denominations, severely limiting the number of religious books, which are available only in private, secure locations. Authorities do not hesitate to seize material in homes or even in registered religious buildings.

Many believers, especially Protestants, undergo unofficial pressures from political authorities in addition to this legislative enforcement. These pressures show a real continuity with Soviet anti-religious practices; they vary from subjective interpretations of the law to other repressive measures, including police raids during services, temporary illegal internments, and psychological pressure. The acuteness of these extra-legal measure differs between republics, with the situation in Turkmenistan and Uzbekistan worse than in Tajikistan, with Kazakhstan and Kyrgyzstan still presenting degrees of religious freedom. All republics, however, face pressure to crack down further on non-Orthodox Christian minorities.

Registration formalities continue to be the main form of pressure exercised by authorities upon believers and their leaders. State authorities ignore legislation in their refusal to register Christian groups and extrapolate legislative frameworks to provide justification. Special efforts to deny registration concentrate on "foreign" and mainly proselytizing movements such as Presbyterians, Charismatic churches, or Jehovah's Witnesses. Several groups have been refused registration on the basis that their leader is a foreigner. In recent years, some legally registered churches have also been suppressed. The Turkmenistan government has closed nearly all Protestant denominations in recent years, from Baptists to Pentecostals to Jehovah's Witnesses. The Seventh-day Adventist prayer house in the capital of Ashgabat was destroyed in November 1999. Several Protestant denominations regained registration in July 2004, but apart from Islam, Russian Orthodoxy, and Catholicism, all other religions are persecuted in Turkmenistan.

CONCLUSION

The Soviet legacy remains fundamental in the religious and other fields of Christians' everyday life. As in the Soviet era, the state fears the influence of religions. Secularism becomes a way to face not only "foreign" Christianity but Islam, a force that could lead to a questioning of the elite's acquired privileges and could thus destabilize political power. Leaders treat poorly known religious movements with a combination of nitpicking and arbitrary applications of the law, extra-legal measures, and everyday administrative humiliations. As in the Soviet era, the national question remains the predominant way of examining group identity. This explains the ability of the Orthodox Church to gain a status as a type of "official" religion for Russians, whom political powers want to see remain in their republics. It also explains the difficult situation of proselytizing movements, considered as "sects," which do not fit any national diagram and often try to convert the local population. The post-Soviet states have divided into two groups, with Kazakhstan, Kyrgyzstan, and, to a lesser extent, Tajikistan as more liberal than Uzbekistan and Turkmenistan, though church-state relations continue to evolve, and new projects redefine relations between the state and the multiple denominations present in its territory.

In all republics today official secularism excludes any reference to the Quran or sharia and grants to Christianity, especially to Orthodoxy, the same rights as to Islam. No numerically important Muslim group pressures nor incites violence against Christians, as long as they do not try to convert locals. Discrimination against several Protestant movements—such as Baptists, Seventh-day Adventists, and Pentecostals—as well as, at times, the Catholic Church and even non-Christian currents such as the Baha'i or Hare Krishna movements, result more from general restrictions on freedom and national considerations rather than religious ones. Christian believers in Central Asia, nowadays as in Soviet times, do not match the model of "Christians in Islamic lands" in other Muslim countries. The situation of Christians in Central Asia resembles more that in Belarus or Russia, where Orthodox believers meet no real difficulties, but repression of other Christian groups significantly affects the everyday life of believers, who are not even able to celebrate regular services. These difficulties stem primarily from the fact that these groups are considered "foreign denominations," imported from Western countries. As such, political authorities and the hierarchies of the so-called traditional religions view them as a threat to internal security and stability. In worse cases, repression and restrictions touch believers beyond the parish framework: several locals recently converted to Christianity were threatened with expulsion from university in Uzbekistan; in Turkmenistan, suspicion of Protestantism can lead to loss of one's job. Even in more liberal Kazakhstan, and despite the separation of church and state in each Central Asian constitution, the Soviet framework remains in several fields.[31] It appears through administrative structures that control—often quite strictly—religion through administrative pressures and/or repression against people, either leaders or simple believers, who refuse to remain in the religious space accorded by the state.

NOTES

1. About Christianity in Central Asia after World War II, see Sebastien Peyrouse, *Des chrétiens entre athéisme et islam. Regards sur la question religieuse en Asie centrale soviétique et post-soviétique* (Paris: Maisonneuve et Larose, 2003).
2. Considering the absence of serious religious sociological studies in Central Asia, I will not give figures on believers, nor their national distribution. I prefer to give the figures of nationalities that constitute the majority of Christian believers, even though these figures should be considered cautiously. Sources for these figures include: *Kratkie itogi perepisi naseleniia 1999 goda v respublike Kazahstan* (Almaty: Agentstvo respubliki Kazahstan po statistike, 1999); N. E. Masanov, Z. B. Abylhozhin, I. V. Erofeeva, A. N. Alekseenko, G. S. Baratova, *Istoriia Kazahstana, narody i kul'tury,* (Almaty: Dajk-press, 2001); *Etnicheskii atlas Uzbekistana* (Tashkent, Fond Sodeistviia, 2002); C. Poujol, *Dictionnaire de l'Asie centrale* (Paris: Ellipses, 2001); Pal Kolstoe, *Russians in the Former Soviet Republics* (London: Hurst & Company, 1995); Marlene Laruelle and Sebastien Peyrouse, *Les Russes du Kazakhstan. Identités nationales et nouveaux Etats dans l'espace post-soviétique* (Paris: Maisonneuve et Larose, 2004).
3. In Kazakhstan there are ongoing proceedings to tighten control on religious activities.
4. For more details on the connection between Christianity and nationality in Central Asia, see Peyrouse, "Christianity and Nationality in Soviet and Post-Soviet Central Asia: Mutual Intrusions and Instrumentalizations," *Nationalities Papers* 32, no. 3 (September 2004): 651–674.
5. D. Hervieu-Léger, *La religion pour mémoire* (Paris: Cerf, 1993), 230. On the "ethnic-religious combination," see D. Schnapper, "Le sens de l'ethnico-religieux," *Archives de sciences sociales des religions,* no. 81 (January-March 1993): 149–163.
6. G. Stricker "Die Missveständnisse häufen sich . . . ," *Glaube in der Zweiten Welt,* July/August 1995: 21; Stricker, "Fear of proselytism: the Russian Orthodox Church sets itself against Catholicism," *Religion, State and Society,* 1998, no. 2: 155–165.
7. See F. Sharifzad in "Islam—ne politiki," *Nauka i religiia,* 1994, no. 11: 32.
8. A. Alisheva, "Multiconfessional Kyrgyzstan," *Central Asian Post,* 3 July 1997.
9. These petitions were not only aiming at the new movements, such as the Unification Church of Reverend Moon, but at all Protestant denominations (Baptists, Adventists etc.); *Glaube in der Zweiten Welt,* 1992, no. 7/8: 5–6.
10. *Slovo Kyrgyzstana,* June 1996: 4–5.

11. "Sprengstoffanschläge auf Kirchen," *Glaube in der Zweiten Welt*, March 2001: 9.

12. Nevertheless, there were a few incidents as some local mullas attempted to prevent the Protestant denominations from teaching religion; Ia. F. Trofimov, *Gosudarstvenno-tserkovnye otnosheniia v sovremennom Kazahstane* (Almaty: Edilet, 1997), 93.

13. Interview with the Bishop of Uralsk and Gureev, *Vedi* 17, no. 3 (1998): 2–8.

14. "V Belorussii zapreshena deiatel'nost' obshchestva soznaniia Krishny," *Svet pravoslaviia v Kazahstane* no. 5 (1999): 16–17.

15. *Blagovestnik. Gazeta Iuzhnoi konferentsii tserkvi khristian-adventistov sed'mogo dnia*, March (1996): 3.

16. *Slovo Kyrgyzstana*, 1October 1994; Alisheva, "Multiconfessional Kyrgyzstan."

17. *Religious Liberty in the OSCE* 20, no. 9 (September 1997): 94.

18. *Vedi* 17, no. 3 (1998): 2–8.

19. Ibid: 5.

20. E. Luzanova, "Religious Renaissance or Political Game?" *Central Asian Post*, March 23, 1998: 4.

21. "Protestantizm kak religiia agressivnogo burzhua: ekskurs v istoriiu," *Svet pravoslaviia v Kazahstane*, no. 6 (1997): 12–14.

22. *Slovo zhizni*, no. 9 (120), 19 December 1995: 3.

23. See for example : "Svideteli Iegovy, i kak k nim otnosit'sia pravoslavnym khristianam," *Vedi*, non-dated and non-numbered, 26.

24. Interview with the leader of the Orthodox parish in Dushanbe, Tajikistan, October 2000.

25. *Vedi* 17, no. 3 (1998), 2–8.

26. "Svideteli Iegovy, i kak k nim otnosit'sia pravoslavnym khristianam," 26.

27. I. Botasheva and V. Lebedev, "Krestonostsy kontsa XX veka" *Kazakhstanskaia pravda*, 2 April 1996.

28. *Svet pravoslaviia v Kazahstane* 1993, no. 1: 8.

29. Author interview with a Catholic, Karaganda, Kazakhstan, 2000.

30. Author interview with a Protestant pastor, 1999.

31. Sebastien Peyrouse, ed., *Gestion de l'indépendance et legs soviétique en Asie centrale, Cahiers d'Asie centrale*, no. 13–14, (Aix-en-Provence: Edisud, 2004).

SELECTED BIBLIOGRAPHY

Abramson, David. "Engendering Citizenship in Postcommunist Uzbekistan." In *Post-Soviet Women Encountering Transition*, ed. Kathleen Kuehnast and Carol Nechemias. Baltimore: Johns Hopkins University Press, 2004: 65–84.

Allworth, Edward A., ed. *Central Asia: 130 Years of Russian Dominance, A Historical Overview.* Durham: Duke University Press, 1994.

———. *The Modern Uzbeks.* Stanford: Hoover Institution Press, 1990.

Anderson, John. *Kyrgyzstan, Central Asia's Island of Democracy?* Amsterdam: Harwood Academic Publishers, 1999.

Bacon, Elizabeth E. *Central Asians Under Russian Rule: A Study in Culture Change.* Ithaca, N.Y.: Cornell University Press, 1966.

Baldick, J. *Animal and Shaman: Ancient Religions of Central Asia.* London: I. B. Taurus, 2000.

Balzer, Marjorie Mandelstam, ed. *Shamanism: Soviet Studies of Traditional Religion in Siberia and Central Asia.* Armonk, New York: M. E. Sharpe, 1990.

Beliaev, Viktor. *Central Asian Music: Essays in the History of the Music of the Peoples of the U.S.S.R..* Middletown, Conn.: Wesleyan University Press, 1975.

Bennigsen, Alexandre, and S. Enders Wimbush. *Mystics and Commissars: Sufism in the Soviet Union.* Berkeley: University of California Press, 1985.

Berdahl, Daphne, Matti Bunzl, and Martha Lamplan, eds. *Altering States: Ethnographies of Transition in Eastern Europe and the Former Soviet Union.* Ann Arbor: University of Michigan Press, 2000.

Bradsher, Henry S. *Afghan Communism and Soviet Intervention.* Oxford: Oxford University Press, 1999.

Bregel, Yuri. *An Historical Atlas of Central Asia.* Leiden: Brill, 2003.

Brower, Daniel. *Turkestan and the Fate of the Russian Empire.* London: RoutledgeCurzon, 2003.

Buckley, Mary, ed. *Post-Soviet Women: From the Baltic to Central Asia.* Cambridge: Cambridge University Press, 1997.

Canfield, Robert, ed. *Turko-Persia in Historical Perspective.* Cambridge: Cambridge University Press, 1991.

Chadwick, Nora K. *Oral Epics of Central Asia.* London: Cambridge University Press, 1969.

Collins, Kathleen. *Clan Politics and Regime Transition in Central Asia.* Cambridge: Cambridge University Press, 2006.

Critchlow, James. *Nationalism in Uzbekistan: A Soviet Republic's Road to Sovereignty.* Boulder, Colo.: Westview Press, 1992.

Dawisha, Karen, and Bruce Parrott, eds. *Conflict, Cleavage, and Change in Central Asia and the Caucasus.* Cambridge: Cambridge University Press, 1997.

de Certeau, Michel. *The Practice of Everyday Life.* Translated by Steven F. Rendall. Berkeley: University of California Press, 1984.

d'Encausse, Helene Carrere. *Islam and the Russian Empire: Reform and Revolution in Central Asia.* Trans. Quintin Hoare. Berkeley: University of California Press, 1989.

Edgar, Adrienne Lynn. *Tribal Nation: The Making of Soviet Turkmenistan.* Princeton, N.J.: Princeton University Press, 2004.

Fierman, William K. ed. *Soviet Central Asia: The Failed Transformation.* Boulder: Westview Press, 1991.

Fitzpatrick, Sheila. *Everyday Stalinism. Ordinary Life in Extraordinary Times: Soviet Russia in the 1930s.* Oxford and New York: Oxford University Press, 1999.

Foltz, Richard C. *Religions of the Silk Road: Overland Trade and Cultural Exchange from Antiquity to the Fifteenth Century.* New York: St. Martin's Press, 1999.

Frye, Richard. *The Heritage of Central Asia: From Antiquity to the Turkish Expansion.* Princeton: Markus Wiener, 1996.

Gladney, Dru C. *Muslim Chinese: Ethnic Nationalism in the People's Republic.* Cambridge, Mass.: Harvard University Press, 1991.

Graham, Stephen. *Through Russian Central Asia.* New York: MacMillan Company, 1916.

Grousset, René. *The Empire of the Steppes: A History of Central Asia.* Trans. Naomi Walford. New Brunswick, N.J.: Rutgers University Press, 1970.

Hahn, Chris, ed. *Postsocialism: Ideals, Ideologies and Practices.* London: Routledge, 2002.

Haugen, Arne. *The Establishment of National Republics in Soviet Central Asia.* London: Palgrave-Macmillan, 2003.

Highmore, Ben. *Everyday Life and Cultural Theory: An Introduction.* London: Routledge, 2002.

Humphrey, Caroline. *The Unmaking of Soviet Life: Everyday Economies after Socialism.* Ithaca, N.Y.: Cornell University Press, 2002.

Irons, William. *The Yomut Turkmen: A Study of Social Organization among a Central Asian Turkic-Speaking Population.* Ann Arbor: University of Michigan, 1975.

Kamp, Marianne. *The New Woman in Uzbekistan: Islam, Modernity, and Unveiling under Communism*. Seattle: University of Washington Press, 2006.

Kandiyoti, Deniz, and Ruth Mandel, eds. *Market Reforms, Social Dislocations and Survival in Post-Soviet Central Asia*. (Special issue) *Central Asian Survey* 17, no. 4 (1998).

Keller, Shoshana. T*o Moscow, Not Mecca: The Soviet Campaign against Islam in Central Asia, 1917–1941*. Westport: Praeger, 2001.

Khalid, Adeeb. *The Politics of Muslim Cultural Reform: Jadidism in Central Asia*. Berkeley: University of California Press, 1998.

———. *Islam after Communism: Religion and Politics in Central Asia*. Berkeley: University of California Press, 2007.

Khazanov, A. M. *Nomads and the Outside World*. Cambridge: Cambridge University Press, 1984.

Kunanbaeva, Alma. *The Soul of Kazakhstan*. New York: Easten Press, 2001.

Laruelle, Marlene, and Sebastien Peyrouse. *Les Russes du Kazakhstan. Identités nationales et nouveaux états dans l'espace post-soviétique*. Paris: Maisonneuve et Larose, 2004.

Levi, Scott C., ed. *India and Central Asia: Commerce and Culture, 1500–1800*. Delhi: Oxford University Press, 2007.

Levin, Theodore. *The Hundred Thousand Fools of God: Musical Travels in Central Asia (and Queens, New York)*. Bloomington: Indiana University Press, 1996.

Luong, Pauline Jones. *Institutional Change and Political Continuity in Post-Soviet Central Asia: Power, Perceptions, and Pacts*. Cambridge and New York: Cambridge University Press, 2002.

———, ed. *The Transformation of Central Asia: States and Societies from Soviet Rule to Independence*. Ithaca, N.Y.: Cornell University Press, 2004.

Martin, Virginia. *Law and Custom in the Steppe: The Kazakhs of the Middle Horde and Russian Colonialism in the Nineteenth Century*. Richmond, UK: Curzon, 2000.

Massell, Gregory J. *The Surrogate Proletariat: Moslem Women and Revolutionary Strategies in Soviet Central Asia, 1919–1929*. Princeton, N.J.: Princeton University Press, 1974.

Michaels, Paula A. *Curative Powers: Medicine and Empire in Stalin's Central Asia*. Pittsburgh: University of Pittsburgh Press, 2003.

Mousavi, S. A. *The Hazaras of Afghanistan: An Historical, Cultural, Economic and Political Study*. Richmond, UK: Curzon, 1998.

Northrop, Douglas. *Veiled Empire: Gender and Power in Stalinist Central Asia*. Ithaca, N.Y.: Cornell University Press, 2004.

Olcott, Martha Brill. *The Kazakhs*. Stanford: Hoover Institution Press, 1995.

Özdalga, Elisabeth, ed. *Naqshbandis in Western and Central Asia: Change and Continuity*. Istanbul: Swedish Research Institute in Istanbul, 1999.

Peyrouse, Sebastien. *Des chrétiens entre athéisme et islam. Regards sur la ques-*

tion religieuse en Asie centrale soviétique et post-soviétique. Paris: Maison-neuve et Larose, 2003.

Poladi, Hassan. *The Hazaras.* Stockton, Calif.: Mughal, 1989.

Privratsky, Bruce G. Muslim *Turkistan: Kazak Religion and Collective Memory.* Richmond, UK: Curzon, 2001.

Rashid, Ahmed. *Jihad: The Rise of Militant Islam in Central Asia.* New Haven, Conn.: Yale University Press, 2002.

Ro'i, Yaacov. *Islam in the Soviet Union: From the Second World War to Gorbachev.* London: Hurst & Co., 1997.

———. *Muslim Eurasia: Conflicting Legacies.* Portland: Frank Cass Publications: 1995.

Roy, Olivier. *The New Central Asia: The Creation of Nations.* New York: New York University Press, 2000.

Ruffin, M. Holt, and Daniel Clarke Waugh, eds. *Civil Society in Central Asia.* Seattle: University of Washington Press, 1997.

Rumer, Boris, ed. *Soviet Central Asia: A Tragic Experiment.* Boston: Unwin and Hyman, 1989.

Sahadeo, Jeff. *Russian Colonial Society in Tashkent, 1865-1923.* Bloomington: Indiana University Press, 2007.

Schatz, Edward. *Modern Clan Politics: The Power of "Blood" in Kazakhstan and Beyond.* Seattle: University of Washington Press, 2004.

Schuyler, Eugene. *Turkistan: Notes of a Journey in Russian Turkistan, Kokand, Bukhara and Kuldja.* New York: Scribner, Armstrong and Co., 1876.

Shalinsky, Audrey. *Long Years of Exile: Central Asian Refugees in Afghanistan and Pakistan.* Lanham, MD: University Press of America, 1993.

Soucek, Svat. *A History of Inner Asia.* Cambridge: Cambridge University Press, 2000.

Strong, Anna Louise. *The Road to the Grey Pamir.* New York: Robert M. Mc-Bride & Co., 1930.

Weinthal, Erika. *State Making and Environmental Cooperation : Linking Domestic and International Politics in Central Asia.* Cambridge, Mass.: MIT Press, 2002.

Winner, Thomas. *The Oral Art and Literature of the Kazakhs of Russian Central Asia.* Durham, N.C.: Duke University Press, 1958.

CONTRIBUTORS

DAVID M. ABRAMSON holds a Ph.D. in cultural anthropology from Indiana University and works as a Central Asia analyst at the U.S. Department of State. Recent publications include the chapters "Identity Counts: The Soviet Legacy and the Census in Uzbekistan" and "Engendering Citizenship in Postcommunist Uzbekistan" in two edited volumes. Current research interests include the religious dimension of foreign policy and Islamist–secularist dynamics in Uzbekistan.

LAURA ADAMS received her Ph.D. in sociology from the University of California at Berkeley. She is currently an associate of the Davis Center for Russian and Eurasian Studies at Harvard University and teaches in Harvard's Expository Writing Program. She is completing her book, *The Spectacular State: Cultural and National Identity in Uzbekistan*, and has previously published articles in *Slavic Review, European Journal of Cultural Studies, Journal of Arts Management, Law, and Society*, and *Transitions Online*. Her new research includes collaborative projects with scholars from Central Asia on ethnic and religious tolerance.

ROBERT L. CANFIELD is Professor in the Department of Anthropology, Washington University at St. Louis. His early work was on factions and coalitions in the Hazarajat, Afghanistan. Since the early 1980s he has worked on how the Islamic idioms dominant in Central Asia have enabled people to understand their personal experience. Current work includes an analysis of how symbols inform social action. He is author of numerous books and journal articles on Central Asia and Iran. A forthcoming book is titled *A Decade of the Taliban, 1994–2004*, and he is currently editing with Gabriele Rasuly-Paleczek *New Games in Central Asia: Great and Small*.

VICTORIA CLEMENT received a Ph.D. from The Ohio State University and is currently Assistant Professor of History at Western Carolina University. She was an instructor at the International Turkmen-Turk University in

1997 and lived throughout Turkmenistan from September 12, 2001 through spring 2003. Her dissertation, "Re-writing the Turkmen Nation: Language, Learning, and Power, 1904–2004," focuses on the influences of language and educational policy in Turkmen culture.

ELIZABETH A. CONSTANTINE is Director, Grants and Research Services Office, and Adjunct Assistant Professor at the University of Iowa. She has served as Assistant Director of Policy Analysis and Dialogue for the Stanley Foundation; managed the Asia-Pacific Initiatives (API) program, addressing the prospects for the peaceful integration of the Asia-Pacific states into regional and global security structures; and served as Assistant Director of the Center for Russian, East European, and Eurasian Studies at the University of Iowa. She spent three years studying and working in China and two years in Uzbekistan. Constantine received a B.A. degree from the University of Wisconsin, an M.A. from the Monterey Institute of International Studies, and a Ph.D. in Central Eurasian Studies from Indiana University.

ADRIENNE L. EDGAR received a Ph.D. in 1999 from the University of California at Berkeley and is currently Associate Professor of History at UC–Santa Barbara. She is author of *Tribal Nation: The Making of Soviet Turkmenistan* and of several articles and book chapters. Her research interests center on questions of ethnicity, nationality, and gender in Soviet Central Asia.

PETER FINKE holds a Ph.D. in anthropology from Cologne University. Since 1991 he has conducted field research among Kazakh pastoralists in western Mongolia and (with Meltem Sancak) on the migration of the so-called Kazakh diasporas to Kazakhstan. In 2000 he joined the Max Planck Institute for Social Anthropology, where he is doing research on collective identity in Uzbekistan.

MARIANNE KAMP is Associate Professor of History at the University of Wyoming. Publications include *The New Woman in Uzbekistan: Islam, Modernity, and Unveiling under Communism* and "Between Women and the State: Mahalla Committees and Social Welfare in Uzbekistan," in *The Transformation of Central Asia: States and Societies from Soviet Rule to Independence.* Current research concerns the collectivization of agriculture in Uzbekistan in the 1930s.

DR. ELYOR E. KARIMOV is Chair of the Medieval and Ancient History Department at the Institute of History, Uzbek Academy of Sciences, and Chair of the Uzbek National Society of Young Scientists (http://nsys.freenet.uz). He specializes in the history of Islam and Sufism in Central Asia and has numerous publications related to his field of research. Dr. Karimov has conducted extensive research on sacred sites and associated Islamic schools of thought in Uzbekistan, Turkmenistan, and southern Kazakhstan. Most

recently he has researched religiosity among Uzbek youth and their relationship to radical Islam.

SHOSHANA KELLER is Associate Professor of Russian and Eurasian history
at Hamilton College. She is author of *To Moscow, Not Mecca: The Soviet Campaign Against Islam in Central Asia, 1917–1941* and "Story, Time, and Dependent Nationhood in the Uzbek History Curriculum," *Slavic Review* (Summer 2007).

SCOTT LEVI earned a Ph.D. in history at the University of Wisconsin at
Madison and is currently Assistant Professor of Central Asian and Islamic
World History at the University of Louisville. He is author of *The Indian
Diaspora in Central Asia and its Trade, 1550–1900* and is currently working
on a history of the Khanate of Kokand (1798–1876).

MORGAN Y. LIU is Assistant Professor in Near Eastern Languages and Cultures at The Ohio State University. Publications include "Post-Soviet Paternalism and Personhood: Why 'Culture' Matters to Democratization
in Central Asia," in *Prospects of Democracy in Central Asia*, Birgit Schlyter
(ed.), and journal articles on Central Asia. He is completing a book about
conceptions and practices of authority within an Uzbek community in the
Kyrgyz Republic, titled *Yearning for a Modern Khan: A Central Asian Imaginary for a Neoliberal World*. His next project concerns the link between Islamic piety and economic empowerment among the new wealthy in the
southern Kyrgyz Republic.

ERIC M. MCGLINCHEY (Ph.D., Department of Politics, Princeton), is Assis-
tant Professor, Department of Public and International Affairs at George
Mason University. He has written articles on Central Asian political
change and Islam for the *Journal of Asia-Pacific Policy Research*, Freedom
House, the Center for Strategic and International Studies, and Radio Free
Europe/Radio Liberty. He is the co-principal investigator of a new study,
"The Effect of the Internet on Society: Incorporating Central Asia into the
Global Perspective."

KELLY M. MCMANN is Assistant Professor of Political Science at Case
Western Reserve University. She is author of *Economic Autonomy and Democracy: Hybrid Regimes in Russia and Kyrgyzstan*. Her work has also appeared in the edited volume *The Transformation of Central Asia: States and
Societies from Soviet Rule to Independence*. Her research focuses on state–society relations, political activism, and capitalism and democracy.

PAULA A. MICHAELS is Associate Professor of History at the University of
Iowa. She is author of *Curative Powers: Medicine and Empire in Stalin's Central Asia*, which received the Heldt Prize from the Association of Women in

Slavic Studies and was a finalist for the PEN Center USA Literary Award. Her articles have appeared in *Feminist Studies, Russian Review, and Nationalities Papers*. She is currently at work on a transnational history of the Lamaze childbirth method, which had its origins in the USSR.

DAVID W. MONTGOMERY is a Ph.D. candidate in the Department of Religion at Boston University and a research fellow at the Institute on Culture, Religion, and World Affairs. He has worked on Central Asia since 1999 and most recently conducted field research in Kyrgyzstan and Uzbekistan as an IREX IARO Scholar. His research focuses on how the transmission of religious and cultural knowledge influences religious and cultural practice.

DOUGLAS NORTHROP is Associate Professor of History and Near Eastern Studies at the University of Michigan. Author of *Veiled Empire: Gender and Power in Stalinist Central Asia,* he is currently writing a history of natural disasters in the Russian/Soviet empire.

SEBASTIEN PEYROUSE is a Ph.D. scholar at the French Institute for Central Asia Studies. He has published books and journal articles on religion and national identity in Soviet and post-Soviet Central Asia. Most recently he has edited, with Marlène Laruelle, *Islam et politique en ex-URSS.*

MADELEINE REEVES received an M.A. from the University of Chicago and is currently a Ph.D. candidate in social anthropology at the University of Cambridge, United Kingdom. Her dissertation research focuses on citizenship, political authority, and subjectivity in border areas of the Ferghana Valley.

SEAN R. ROBERTS received an M.A. in visual anthropology and a Ph.D. in social anthropology at the University of Southern California. He has spent several years studying and researching in Central Asia, primarily in Almaty, Kazakhstan, focusing mainly on the Uyghurs of the Kazakhstan–China borderland. His documentary, *Waiting for Uighurstan,* examines cross-border trade and nationalism in this community, which also constitutes the topic of his several academic articles and of a manuscript in progress based on his dissertation research. Dr. Roberts has traveled extensively in China's Xinjiang Uyghur Autonomous Region and worked in various capacities on programs promoting human rights and the development of democracy in Central Asia. He presently is Senior Democracy Advisor for the United States Agency for International Development (USAID) mission in Central Asia, located in Almaty.

MICHAEL ROULAND (Ph.D., Georgetown University) is a Postdoctoral Fellow at the Miami University's Havighurst Center. His dissertation, "Music and the Making of the Kazak Nation, 1920–1936," considers the Soviet policy of rooting both socialist and nationalist messages in public performance culture as part of a modernization campaign to promote nationalism and a national state in Kazakhstan. His interests include filmic, literary, and musical expressions of Central Asian identity. He is currently researching a biography of Mukhtar Auezov, a folklorist who chose to work within the Soviet system.

JEFF SAHADEO is Assistant Professor at the Institute of European and Russian Studies and the Department of Political Science at Carleton University. He is author of *Russian Colonial Society in Tashkent, 1865–1923* (Indiana University Press, 2006). He has contributed articles on Central Asia to *Slavic Review, Central Eurasian Studies Review, Canadian Slavonic Papers, Canadian Review of Studies in Nationalism,* and *McGill International Review.* He is currently researching Central Asian migration to Russia.

MELTEM SANCAK studied sociology and anthropology at the Middle East Technical University, Ankara, and at Cologne University, where she received an M.A. She conducted field research on life perspectives of second-generation migrants from Turkey in Germany. Together with Peter Finke she worked among Kazakhs who had migrated from China to Kazakhstan after the latter's independence. In 2000 she joined the Max Planck Institute for Social Anthropology, where she is doing research in Uzbekistan on the relationship between economic change and social identities.

GRETA UEHLING received a doctorate in cultural anthropology from the University of Michigan in Ann Arbor. She completed a postdoctoral fellowship with the Solomon Asch Center for the Study of Ethnopolitical Conflict at the University of Pennsylvania in 2004. Her publications include *Beyond Memory: The Crimean Tatars' Deportation and Return* as well as articles in *Central Asian Survey, Journal of Refugee Studies, Ethnic and Racial Studies, Nationalities Papers,* and *New Issues in Refugee Research.*

RUSSELL ZANCA is Associate Professor of Anthropology at Northeastern Illinois University. He has carried out numerous ethnographic projects in Uzbekistan and Kyrgyzstan since 1992, including work on collective farm living, inter-ethnic conflict, sheep pastoralism, religion, oral history, and cuisine. He is currently writing a book, *Big Cotton Plantations: Uzbeks after Soviet Socialism.* Introducing students to Central Asian societies and cultures continues to provide him intellectual pleasure.

INDEX

9/11: 302; impact of, 1, 308

Abd al-Rahman Jami, 27
Abraham, 200, 211
Achmaenid dynasty, 16–17, 256
Afghanistan, 4, 10, 15, 45–65, 75, 91, 184, 301–302; British presence in, 5; Soviet invasion of, 7; mujahideen of, 302, 308; U.S. military actions in, 308
adat (customary law), 131, 269, 352
aitis (singing competitions), 219, 221, 223–225, 227
Akaev, Askar, 9, 76, 76n16
akin (bard), 218–219
Akromiya movement, 360
aksakals (elders), 219
Alay mountains, 290
al Biruni, 20, 256, 258
al-Bukhari, 258
alcohol, 128, 154, 168; Islam and, 122, 154, 346, 347, 349, 355n2; post-Soviet consumption of, 79, 155–156, 168, 174, 176. *See also* toasting; vodka
Alexander the Great, 17, 257
al Khwarezmi, Jafar Muhammad, 20
Almaty (Alma-Ata), 9, 145, 220–221, 225, 237, 303, 339–353
Amir Temur. *See* Timur
Amu Darya river, 4, 19, 37
Andijon, 97, 254, 259; 2005 killings of civilians in, 2, 9, 316, 369n15
Aq Zhol, 163–168
Arabic language, 68, 69, 310, 350, 355, 364
Arabic script, 230, 254, 267–269, 271–272, 312, 315, 327, 367
Arabs, 200; eighth century invasion by 19–20; Tajikistan and, 129. *See also* Saudi Arabia
Aral Sea, 7, 233
Asgabat, 266, 268, 276
Azerbaijan, 89, 94, 206, 375

Babur, Zahir al-Din Muhammed, 13, 27, 28, 362

Bahaism, 76
Baku, 272
Bamian province, 45–55
Baptists, 366, 371, 374–376, 378, 380. *See also* Christianity
Basmachis (*Bosmachi*), 104, 107, 111, 259
Batken, 287–289, 291–292
bazaars, 34, 97, 284, 342, 359, 362; early history of Central Asia and, 18; post-Soviet era importance of, 68–72, 185–187, 238; negative perceptions of, 75, 167; leisure and, 191–192; variety of food at, 192; international trade and, 287. *See also* business; trade
Bible, 365, 376–377, 379
Bishkek, 73, 285, 291, 357
Black Sea, 257
blood feud, 40, 43
Bolshevik Revolution of October 1917, 5, 36, 85, 96, 183, 230, 252, 259, 270–271, 342, 378
borders and borderlands, 127, 281–297. *See also* national delimitation
boundaries, 287; Central Asian, 2; international, 285
Bourdieu, Pierre, 54, 162, 286, 296, 304, 340–341
Brezhnev, Leonid, 190, 255, 281
bribes, 60, 61, 62, 176, 282, 287–288, 293–294, 297. *See also* corruption
bridewealth (bride-price or *kalym*), 34, 41–42, 48, 50, 52, 112, 118–119, 161, 348–349
Buddhism, 18, 28, 356
Bukhara, 311, 320; oasis of, 160–161, 168–176; emirate of, 5, 29, 38, 118; Samanid capital of, 20, 22, 24; Timurids and, 27, 28; women secluded in, 118; as center of Uzbek cuisine, 179; performers from, 208; Jadid educators in, 251–252; Soviet secular education in 254; as center of Naqshband Sufism 324, 329–330
business, 69, 71, 80, 171–172, 320–321; nega-